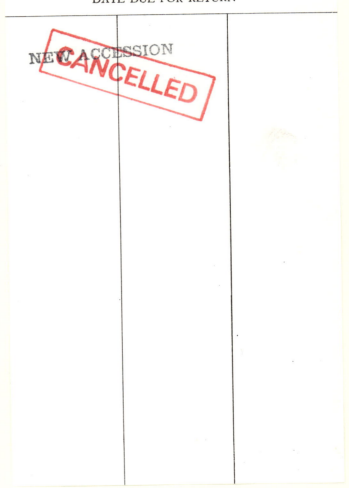

DATE DUE FOR RETURN

BENCH AND BUREAUCRACY

Ætat Svo 57

BENCH AND BUREAUCRACY

*The Public Career
of Sir Julius Caesar,
1580-1636*

L. M. HILL

James Clarke & Co.
Cambridge

Published with the assistance of the Committee on Research
and Travel of the School of Humanities, the Dean of
Humanities, and the Academic Committee on Research,
University of California, Irvine

Frontispiece: From E. Lodge, *The Life of Sir Julius Caesar, Knt.*
(London, 1827)

James Clarke & Co.
P.O. Box 60
Cambridge CB1 2NT

British Library Cataloguing in Publication Data available

ISBN 0-227-67906-7

First published in the UK 1988 by James Clarke & Co.

Printed in the United States of America

For Ellen

Acknowledgments

SINCE I FIRST BEGAN to work on Sir Julius Caesar as a graduate student in London, I have been given unstinting assistance by more scholars than I can possibly acknowledge. I cannot fail to thank all of those whose names are not mentioned here. A few, however, must be singled out for their efforts.

The late Professor Joel Hurstfield introduced me to Sir Julius Caesar many years ago and shared with me the delights of uncovering this redoubtable judge and minister. Professor G. E. Aylmer, my external examiner, provided a wealth of valuable detailed suggestions. Professors Sir Geoffrey Elton and Conrad Russell have patiently listened to me talk about Caesar for years and have contributed more than they may realize to my understanding of the complexities of his career. Dr. D. E. C. Yale was a wealth of advice on technicalities of the Admiralty, as was a colleague in graduate school, Dr. David Fischer. On more occasions than I can count, Professor T. G. Barnes provided answers to intractable legal questions. Professors Elizabeth Foster, W. J. Jones, and Linda Levy Peck were also unfailingly generous with their advice.

The University of California, Irvine; the American Philosophical Society; and the National Endowment for the Humanities have awarded research grants, grants-in-aid, and a Fellowship for Younger Humanists, respectively.

I am most grateful to His Grace, the Duke of Northumberland, K.G., and to the Most Honourable, the Marquis of Salisbury, K.G., for having allowed me access to microfilmed copies of their respective manuscript collections held by the British Library. Likewise, I am grateful to Lord Sackville for allowing me to make copies of several folios of the Sackville manuscripts then in the temporary custody of the Royal Commission on Historical Manuscripts. My thanks also to the Guildhall Library, London; the Bodleian Library, Oxford; the Henry E. Huntington Library, San Marino, California; and to the Kenneth Spencer Research Library, University of Kansas, Lawrence, for providing access to their manuscript collections. In addition, the cooperation of the production staffs and officers of the Department of Manuscripts of the British Library and of the Public Record Office have made this task both possible and enjoyable.

I owe a special debt of thanks to an ad hoc Tudor-Stuart Seminar made up of students and colleagues who listened to me read versions of several chapters and were rigorous critics. It has been my good fortune to have had such keen and aggressive intellects among my graduate students as Professor David Heifetz, Dr. Michael Weiss, Dr. Nancy Bjorklund, and Ms. Roseanne Desilets. More than they might possibly know, they have made important contributions to me and to this work. And I am especially grateful to Ms. Desilets for her invaluable assistance in preparing the Index. I am indebted to the University Library at U.C. Irvine, and especially to Ms. Ellen Broidy and Ms. Sarah Eichorn, for developing and maintaining an important microform collection that has made possible a remarkable degree of detailed research at home.

And finally, I wish to recognize the marvelous cooperation of Stanford University Press. Mr. Norris Pope was good enough to solicit the manuscript and patient enough to await its completion. I have had the very good fortune to have a remarkable copy editor, Ms. Ellen Setteducati, assigned to my work. It has been a pleasure to respond to her sensitive and intelligent reading of the text.

Needless to say, with all of this assistance and material support, the errors and omissions are entirely my own responsibility.

My wife has borne with heroic patience the burden of my finishing this book. I dedicate it to her, knowing that it is a pale reflection of my affection and gratitude.

Irvine, California   L.M.H.
Hilarytide, 1987

Contents

Introduction

WHEN I FIRST ENCOUNTERED Sir Julius Caesar, I was interested
in the professional behavior of the second level of public officials who
actually made government work but who had little to do with policy
making. With hundreds of volumes of correspondence extant spanning a career of more than a half-century's duration, Caesar was the
perfect subject for such a study. But when I turned to the literature for
information on the offices that Caesar occupied, I found that there
was relatively little to rely on. As a result, I found myself developing
material on the Court of Requests, the High Court of Admiralty, the
Exchequer, and the complex universe of Chancery. Taken together
with Caesar's papers, this material led me to work in areas I had not
foreseen, such as the interaction among agencies, the dynamics of
multiple office holding, the evolution of the institutionalized prerogative, and the exceptional convolutions of patron-client relations. Thus
a study of an individual became, at the same time, a study of the
mechanisms of central government from the middle of the reign of the
first Elizabeth to the middle of the reign of the first Charles. The clear
lines that I once imagined would separate the world of the judge and
lawyer from the world of the early bureaucrat simply were not to be
found; indeed, they proved to be intertwined. The title, *Bench and
Bureaucracy*, reflects this reality while also indicating the complemen-
tary paths that must be followed to understand Caesar, his ethos, and
his various offices.

The term "bench" requires no particular comment, being a common
synonym for the judiciary in the sixteenth century, but the term "bureaucracy" is always problematic in the context of that era; indeed, it

smacks of anachronism. After all, if there is a bureaucrat instead of a crown servant, there must be current an abstract notion of "state" in contemporary political thinking to replace or to supersede the personal government of the monarch. G. E. Aylmer argues that the servant of the "state" in the sixteenth century (or, for that matter, until the Republic was declared in the mid-seventeenth century) was the king's servant, and from the perspective of constitutional development, he is precisely right.[1] Yet it would be no exaggeration to think of such servants as bureaucrats when they evidence both operational and existential independence of the crown.

Caesar, for example, received his several commissions in the name of Queen Elizabeth, and invoked her name to validate his own authority, yet he was less obligated to her than he was to his patrons for the advantages he enjoyed. These patrons were essentially surrogates who exercised the queen's dispensing and commissioning authority and were therefore the effective source of power. The queen herself had neither selected Caesar nor shown him particular favor, but she did select and favor his patrons; thus, power and authority lay in their hands. Elizabeth distanced herself from the political process to such a degree that she governed almost exclusively through the circle of courtier-ministers who surrounded her. For all practical purposes they were the state, and Caesar, among others, was a state servant.

Analyzing Caesar's career is complicated by the difference in his functions as a judge and as a bureaucrat. By the sixteenth century, English judges were becoming increasingly independent of the crown, yet they were still functionaries. As a judge, Caesar exercised an increasing measure of independence, but he could not forget that he was a crown officer expected to be responsive to direction. Like the bureaucrat, the judge was appointed by the crown; unlike the bureaucrat, the judge was known to the crown and endured much closer scrutiny. The appointments in both cases were theoretically contingent on the crown's pleasure and the incumbent's good behavior. In practice, however, bureaucratic incumbents developed a property in their offices; the judges did not.

As the common law had evolved, the crown was held subject to the law rather than superior to it. As the embodiment of the law, the judge was, in this theoretical sense, superior to the crown. For practical purposes, however, when Caesar served in the High Court of Admiralty or as Master of Requests, he was rarely able to exercise judicial independence. At this stage of his career, he stood with one foot in the arena of law and justice, the other in the arena of policy and politics. In the latter part of his career, when he served as Master of the Rolls, his judicial functions were more unambiguously independent, as were his bureaucratic responsibilities.

The question of limitations becomes all the more interesting when we consider that Caesar was not a common-law but a civil-law judge. As a leading member of the diminishing civilian community, he represented an alien, mistrusted, minority legal system within the house of the common law. During his long judicial career, he was under the stress of conflicting roles as obedient servant and independent jurist. Added to this was the struggle to maintain the integrity of civil law while attempting to achieve a modus vivendi with hostile common lawyers.

Caesar's penchant for developing extensive arguments about the proper relations between civilians and common lawyers adds further depth and interest to our study. He argued that the good order of the commonwealth depended on the harmonious relationship between the two legal systems, but that achieving such a relationship would require a fundamental reorientation of common-law thinking. From a civilian's perspective, he was prepared to assign great power to the monarch while insisting that the monarch was merely the vessel in which the plenitude of sovereign power was contained. The authority of the monarch-as-vessel was significantly limited because effective power was vested in the crown's vicars: ministers, judges, councillors, and servants. These assertions were at odds with the traditional English view that the king was the principal baron of the realm and involved with every aspect of government. A judge or a minister was as a bailiff or a steward: the baron's agent in the manor whose service was subject to the whim of the baron's interference. Caesar was convinced that the crown only undermined its authority by relying on this feudal identity. Through a civilian's eyes, he saw the future of the monarchy differently. Carefully chosen officers of the crown, vicariously exercising the royal prerogative and free from the crown's intervention—this was his model of powerful and stable monarchy. In it we can discern a prefiguration of the modern state, presided over by an increasingly symbolic prince. In Caesar's day, sovereignty as an abstract concept was replacing sovereignty as the aggregated personal power of the reigning monarch. As the concept developed, the concrete reality of the governor-king was transformed into a higher-order abstraction: the state.

Caesar's arguments and his career illuminate and exemplify this transitional process. But it would be a serious error for us to think of Caesar as a theoretician, regardless of his interest in abstract theory. He was neither a scholar nor an ideologue, although he was a dedicated antiquarian. Instead, he worked carefully to preserve a place in the judicial hierarchy for a civilian, and occasionally this effort was expressed in theoretical terms. His goals were to advance himself, to establish his family, and then to advance his sons. His plans were as practical and his pursuit of profit as calculated as the commercial strategies of a City merchant.

As we shall see, Caesar advanced his career by carefully cultivating connections in high places. He had defined for himself a career path that would lead through the lower civilian courts and eventually into Chancery. From there his career goals were fixed near the top of the Chancery hierarchy in the Mastership of the Rolls. Achieving his goals would require help from his patrons, but his dependence on them forced him to acquiesce in their wishes when other plans were made for him. Such was the case in 1606 when Caesar became Chancellor of the Exchequer. His judicial career was interrupted at the behest of his patrons, and for the next eight years he was at the center of the bureaucratic world of public finance.

From entry into university until late in his career, patrons were Caesar's stock-in-trade. Historians of the period frequently write of the value and importance of patronage and connection, but they rarely anatomize the process of developing and employing patronal assistance. Caesar gives us a chance to undertake that task. He can be analyzed in detail, in different settings, and over a prolonged period. His abundant papers and memoranda describe and assess methods and tactics and also bear witness to his learning the arts of compromise and accommodation. During his early years, Caesar seemed determined to reach the highest rungs of the ladder of hierarchy, perhaps with a peerage and a firm place at Court and a seat in the country. But by the time of Elizabeth's death, he had settled into the establishment, on the brink of being a senior and prominent servant of the crown. Caesar went on to develop his fortune, to marry a second and then a third wife, and to watch his surviving children grow into adulthood.

However, he turned from a predictable attempt to scale the heights and instead rooted himself in a senior position in the seventeenth-century equivalent of the permanent civil service. Although such a career pattern was probably not uncommon, virtually nothing about it is known.

The apex, but hardly the end, of Caesar's political career was marked by the Great Contract, Salisbury's unsuccessful attempt to reform public finance in 1610. Its failure, and Salisbury's death in 1612, required Caesar to remain in the Exchequer longer than he would have preferred. Serving on the Treasury Commission, Caesar was the government's ranking expert on crown finance, and only in 1614 did he return to Chancery and the career he had pursued since his youth. For the next twenty years, Caesar was seated just below the Lord Chancellor, serving as the Master of the Rolls, effectively the executive officer of Chancery. He enjoyed valuable patronage, which he used to advance himself and his family. Even though he had to defend his interests from predatory subordinates and courtiers, his was a rich and comfortable place. At the same time, he had become the senior member of Privy Council and was engaged in a broad spectrum of their business, from the Treasury Commissions to the government of Virginia.

In both its judicial and its bureaucratic aspects, Caesar's public career reveals much about the mentality and behavior of an important second-level official. Flourishing during the important transitional period in English history spanning the reigns of Elizabeth I, James I, and Charles I, Caesar and his public career are representative of a period and a type. From the vantage point of Sir Julius Caesar, the history of the period has a distinct and instructive bias.

All dates in this study are given in Old Style, except that the year changes on 1 January rather than 25 March. The original spelling has been retained in quoted material, but contractions have been expanded and punctuation modernized.

BENCH AND BUREAUCRACY

I

In Steade of Your Father

IT HAS OFTEN BEEN SAID that the generation that rose to power
and influence in early Tudor politics was a generation of "new men,"
and that their heirs became the eminent figures of Elizabethan
England—the Cecils, Dudley, Walsingham, the Russells, and the
rest. This summary observation embodies no more than a half-
truth, for the heirs of the "new men" often married into families of
ancient lineage, as the Howards, De Veres, and Willoughbys merged
their quarterings with those of recent accession to private wealth
and public office. Nor were old branches—of the Howard family,
for example—completely cut off. Yet the later sixteenth century was
a time in which, to borrow a later French expression, career was
open to all men of talent. This process is no better exemplified than
by the public career of Sir Julius Caesar.

Among the "new men" of the sixteenth century, few could be
newer than the son of an alien. His upward passage on the professional and social ladder was steeper than that of "new" Englishmen.
Born in 1558, Julio Cesare Adelmare, known throughout his life as
Julius Caesar, was the first child of Dr. Caesar Adelmare, an émigré
Italian physician who came to England in about 1550, and Margery
(or Margaret) Perient.[1] Dr. Adelmare, or Dr. Caesar as he was popu-
larly known, was admitted a fellow of the Royal College of Physi-
cians in 1554, whereupon he began to attend upon the person of
Queen Mary. While Dr. Caesar and his children never formally
changed their family name, they were known as Caesar in colloquial
usage; only in formal documents would they write "Adelmare alias
Caesar." By 1557 Dr. Caesar was naturalized with immunity from the

taxation laid upon aliens. It was a mark of his success that his son's godparents at St. Dunstan's Church on 10 February 1558 were William Paulet, marquis of Winchester; Henry Fitzalan, earl of Arundel; and the queen herself in the person of Lady Montague.

Dr. Caesar and his wife became parents to at least six more children. Following Julius came William; then Thomas, who would become a Cursitor Baron of the Exchequer; Henry, who would become Dean of Ely; Margaret, who would marry Nicholas Wright; and Anne, who would marry Damian Peck; both Wright and Peck were men of Grey's Inn. Their last child was Elizabeth, who would marry John Hunt, a brother civilian of Julius Caesar's and a member of Doctors' Commons.[2] Although most of Caesar's brothers and sisters reappear throughout his life, William is encountered only occasionally. William was apprenticed in 1581 to Alderman Richard Martin, Julius's future father-in-law, and he appeared in Cairo in 1586.[3] His name appeared on a list of merchants trading with the Mediterranean between 1588 and 1591.[4] In 1591 he shipped on the *Toby* of London, bound for Constantinople, as purser and part-owner. He told an inquirer that he felt no danger in traveling on the *Toby*, for fifty or sixty persons would not perish together; yet two voyages later the *Toby* was wrecked and William Caesar was never heard of again.[5]

Dr. Caesar's professional reputation had carried him from Mary's court to Elizabeth's, where he attended both the queen and her principal ministers. He and his family lived in a substantial house with an attached garden in the close of Great St. Helen's, Bishopsgate, at the eastern edge of the City.[6] In addition, they enjoyed a house in suburban Tottenham, where Caesar was born, as well as several leases granted by the queen.

His success spawned networks of connections and friendships that assisted him during his own life and would later assist his son Julius. In 1556 Winchester used his influence in the physician's behalf when Dr. Caesar and his wife were arrested for showing kindness to the countess of Lennox and her followers.[7] Winchester had written to William Cecil on that occasion to arrange for the Caesars' release as he had written to Cecil nine years earlier asking for the Keeper's place at Mortlake Park for his Italian friend and his family.[8] In reply to such kindness, Dr. Caesar was wont to send his cures to his friends and patients. A cure for lumbago that he sent to Cecil in 1563 was more severe than the ailment. The address on the letter by which he transmitted the cure indicates Dr. Caesar's relationship to William Cecil, his *illustris dominus et patronus.*[9]

Dr. Caesar died in 1568. Julius, who was ten at the time, found himself the eldest male in the family, an adult role for a boy still a child. His godparents were an important part of his father's legacy, and they did what they could to assist young Caesar. Winchester wrote to the warden and schoolmaster of Winchester College soliciting a place for young Julius, "a well rulid child, geven to learneng"; but the place was not provided.[10] Lady Montague remained in contact with Caesar throughout her long life, although she was most often seeking favor for one or another petitioner whom Caesar could assist. Henry Fitzalan, earl of Arundel, was deeply involved in the plots of his son-in-law, the duke of Norfolk, when Dr. Caesar died and thus could provide no immediate assistance because he was in custody. Yet Arundel had extensive Surrey connections and was intimate with the Howards; many years later, he strengthened Caesar's connection with Charles, Lord Howard of Effingham (hereafter called Charles Howard), by then his patron and superior in the Admiralty.

A year following Dr. Caesar's death, Margery Caesar remarried. Her new alliance led to powerful linkages throughout the Puritan community. The intimate relationships Caesar would come to enjoy with Walsingham, with the Bacon family, and with the Cecils arose from his mother's second marriage. Caesar's stepfather was Michael Locke, a London mercer and an irrepressible merchant-traveler who had ventured his wealth early on in the Cathay and Levant companies. The Lockes were notable Protestants with close connections among the Marian exiles. Yet the most notable of their number was a Locke by marriage. Michael Locke's uncle, Henry, had married Anne Vaughan, the daughter of Stephen Vaughan, once Henry VIII's principal financial agent in the Low Countries. An intimate of John Knox, Anne Locke had left her husband to follow the Scot into exile in Geneva in 1557. She returned to her husband's home in 1559, where she remained, a mainstay of the London "godly," until Henry's death in 1571. Anne was an attractive woman, and, as Henry Locke's heir and executrix, she was also a wealthy widow. After a brief widowhood she married Edward Dering, London's most prominent Puritan preacher. The intermediary who had assured Anne of Dering's affection during their courtship was a Mistress Martin, the wife of

Alderman Richard Martin, who was apprentice-master to William Caesar and eventually father-in-law to Julius Caesar.[11]

In the early part of his career Caesar was particularly sympathetic to Puritanism, and the Lockes were the origin of this sentiment. Among the Lockes there was, for instance, a vigorous tradition of religious pamphleteering, which Caesar followed in 1582. He had just finished his legal studies and had barely begun a career in the law when he undertook a translation of Theodore de Beze's *Chrestiennes Meditations* entitled "Christian meditations uppon eight psalmes of the prophete David."[12] Caesar dedicated the translation to his new wife, Dorcas, although in the margin he had crossed out the name of an earlier candidate, one Elizabeth Jebson. Signing the dedication "J.D." (for Julius Dalmare or Dalmarius, two frequent variations of Adelmare), Caesar told Dorcas that the "Meditations" indicated "the true and everlasting blessednes which the children of God are assured to enjoy through the death and passion of Jesus Christ." Its readers would share the same blessings "which they take that give themselves to the hearing, reading and practisinge of the Holy Scriptures." The work revealed the "people of God from theire bottomles miseries" crying out to God who relieves them. Some will be blessed "to whome God doth not impute theire transgressions." Thereafter followed Caesar's plea to Dorcas to accept his work, "being the first worke that [he] ever committed to print" and coming as it did from a man who loved her religious zeal and her great knowledge.[13] These same sentiments had once been directed to Anne Locke by John Knox and Edward Dering.

Caesar's translation would never immortalize Dorcas because it never went to press. The queen's printer, Christopher Barker, was licensed on 14 June 1582 to print another translation of de Beze's *Meditations*, the work of the irascible John Stubbs.[14] De Beze had dedicated the original French edition to Lady Anne Bacon, the widow of the late Lord Keeper Nicholas Bacon. Stubbs, in turn, dedicated his translation to Lady Anne Bacon the younger. Both the English and the French editions were published under the sponsorship of the Bacons, and the manuscript of de Beze's work was in the possession of Anthony Bacon.[15] Although Caesar's manuscript was read and approved for publication by Robert Crowley, the noted pamphletwriter and "prebend of St. Paules," when Caesar tried to register his manuscript with the Stationers Company, he discovered that Stubbs had beaten him to the mark by only a few days. It is unfortunate that nothing more could be done with the translation because Caesar prepared a more accurate, if less polemical, version than did Stubbs.

We know very little of Caesar's early education, but one clue is found in a letter that he wrote to William Cecil, Lord Burghley, in 1588. He recounted a conversation in St. James Park in 1578, just prior to his departure for France and advanced studies in the law. Caesar recalled telling Burghley how much he regretted leaving his service to go out into the world to pursue more education and a professional career.[16] We do not know in what capacity Caesar had served Burghley, but it was possible that he had been educated by Burghley in the academy that he kept in Cecil House, his London residence. There is no record of the purchase or award of Caesar's wardship following his father's death, yet his father had held property in knight's service.[17] The absence of a record suggests that Burghley took up the wardship himself, since it was his practice to make no record of those wardships that he, the Master of the Wards, took for his own benefit.[18] As Burghley's ward, Caesar would have been educated in his household.

Eventually Caesar proceeded to Magdelan Hall, Oxford, a house reputed by contemporaries to be the most puritanical in the university. He took the B.A. in May 1575 and was advanced to the M.A. in February 1578.[19] Among his friends at Oxford, there were a few with whom he corresponded after coming down. One in particular, William Hatton, wrote frequently to Caesar, relaying gossip and godly admonitions. Hatton and Caesar's other Oxford friends wrote letters in formal Latin or in French. On the rare occasions when they wrote in English they apologized with profusion, claiming haste as an excuse. The pompous latinity of the Magdelan "old boys" was an undergraduate conceit that flourished for a time after they left the university.[20]

On his return to London, a place awaited Caesar in Clement's Inn, a chancery inn whose students prepared for places in the Inner Temple. Entering at eighteen or nineteen, young men in the chancery inns read and "commonplaced" the legal greats, thereby learning the fundamentals of the law. The students kept commonplace books, which started out as blank, bound volumes, in which were entered pithy quotations and paraphrases derived from legal, religious, philosophical, literary, and historical readings. Caesar began his commonplace book in 1577, at the age of nineteen, with a prayer he attributed to Aquinas seeking God's blessing in the pursuit of upright and faithful study.[21] Caesar's diet of reading was rich in the Bible, Calvin, St. Augustine, the classical orators, and Richard Mulcaster. The exercise in commonplacing formed the practical training in writing legal briefs that every lawyer had to master. The discovery and restatement of the central argument in an ancient text trained the mind to discover and restate the central argument in complex litigation. Most young law students on finishing their studies put their commonplace books away; they might use them for future reference, but they no longer made entries in them. Caesar, however, continued to add entries throughout his life, making his last entry in 1636. Because his commonplace book is extant and because he wrote in it for nearly sixty years, it is a singular document preserving a lifetime of readings, thoughts, and observations.

Sometime before Caesar completed his studies in Clement's Inn, he began an association with the first of a number of patrons (in addition to Burghley) who were surrogate fathers to him. Dr. David Lewes was the Judge of the High Court of Admiralty and had been the founding principal of Jesus College, Oxford. An elderly bachelor, Lewes effectively adopted Caesar as his professional protégé and heir. He intended to bring his young friend into the Doctors' Commons, the professional society of civil lawyers, and from there to the bench of the admiralty court. Both of these were prizes of great value to a young man just starting out. Membership in the Doctors' Commons was as necessary to a civilian as was membership in an Inn of Court to a common lawyer.[22] Furthermore, the High Court of Admiralty was the premier civilian bench in the kingdom, and Lewes presented Caesar with an inside track to preferment. He held out encouragement, affection, advice, and sponsorship: in every respect Lewes was bringing a son into the family business. He stood behind his protégé's decision to study canon and civil law in France from 1578 until 1581, and their exchange of letters tells us much about Caesar's studies and Lewes's expectations.

In one letter Lewes learned of Caesar's safe arrival in Paris and that he was studying foreign tongues. Proficiency in foreign languages was essential, Lewes noted in his reply, for it gave an advantage to an admiralty judge when pleadings and other court documents were in the native language of foreign litigants. Fluency provided a means "wherebye ye may conne over the texte before ye enter into the laberinthe of the lectors or interpreters."[23] Lewes was also pleased to learn that Caesar was studying the philosophers, a necessary part of a jurist's training. However, the judge admonished Caesar not to dissipate his energies on anything that would distract him from becoming a Doctor of Laws. This was especially important for Lewes because he was determined, "ere I parte out of this life, to se[e] you placed here as one of our companye wherof I shall be glad and therebye receve greate comforte."[24]

In 1580 Caesar interrupted his studies to return to London to be admitted to the Inner Temple. Other civilians were members of one or another of the Inns, but they were generally the beneficiaries of a special admission. Caesar's, however, was an ordinary admission, and in future years he would play an active role in the government of the Inner Temple. With his place in the Temple secured, he returned to Paris, where, in April 1581, he was awarded an LL.B., a licentiate in both laws, and an LL.D.

Just prior to his return from France in 1581, Caesar was singled out for a peculiar honor: on 10 May he was admitted as an advocate in the *parlement* of Paris.[25] Advocacies were infrequently awarded to aliens, but when they were given, it was with much fanfare to distinguished visiting jurists, resident ambassadors, and, occasionally, princes. Since Caesar fit none of these categories, the award indicates just how well connected the French thought him to be. In the politically balmy spring of 1581, France and England were busily negotiating a marriage alliance between the Duc d'Anjou (until recently the Duc d'Alençon) and Queen Elizabeth. The expectant bridegroom waited in Paris while the French commissioners labored in England wooing the coy and wily queen. Burghley and Walsingham were among the English courtiers who provided entertainments for the commissioners, none more lavish than the dinner hosted by Burghley at Theobalds on 30 April. Because the French believed that Caesar was well connected at Court, they also believed that they would flatter and show their appreciation to the English statesmen by honoring their young friend who was preparing to leave Paris. Indeed, Caesar would later report to Burghley that the French had

offered more than an advocate's place. He was "offered largely to
have stayed there," and after his return to England the French had
asked him to become one of their king's English pensioners.[26]

The formal study of the civil law behind him, Caesar returned to
London to exploit in earnest whichever connections would launch
his personal career. There were his father's and Anne Locke's friends
at Court as well as congeries of merchants, Puritan leaders, and City
connections associated with the Locke family. Furthermore, the
elderly judge of the High Court of Admiralty was prepared to spon-
sor him. Armed with a number of entrées, Caesar pursued several
positions: in the City, in the Admiralty Court at a low level, and in
the service of the bishop of London. He also married into the
wealthy City family headed by Alderman Martin. Within four years,
a short time in a competitive environment, Caesar was an experienced and competent civil lawyer on the brink of a major place in
the High Court of Admiralty.

The pursuit of a career was an expensive undertaking under the
best of circumstances, especially because so much significance was
placed on appearance, an indicator of a man's personal honor. In
the rank-conscious society of Elizabethan England, a Doctor of
Laws stood just above a Doctor of Divinity and just below a knight
in social precedence. This social standing carried with it the burden
of dressing in suitable finery, of maintaining an appropriate retinue,
and of disdaining concern for the attendant costs. Thus Caesar kept
rooms in the City near St. Paul's and in the Doctor's Commons and
employed two secretaries, one for Italian and one for French. In addition, he would have been expected to employ a small retinue of
body servants and messengers. All of this would have been unremarkable had he not been unemployed. When he told Sir Francis
Walsingham of his staffing arrangements, the Principal Secretary
asked after his annual income and expenses. Caesar replied that he
spent £100 annually, while his income, derived from his father's estate, amounted to £30. Walsingham's answer characterized the
generational differences that divided them. "Merily it is a mad proportion," he said, but he added, "Be not discouraged for I will be
unto you in steade of your father."[27]

The older Elizabethan generation to which Walsingham belonged
was both more conservative in financial matters and more sober in
behavior than was the younger generation. The political uncertain-

ties of the mid-century and the moral burden of Calvinism were elementary components of Walsingham's worldview. For Caesar, on the other hand, the money would tend to itself, and he certainly felt no moral obligation to be modest. In fact, Walsingham's offer to be "in steade of your father" was for Caesar rather like being handed a blank check. With Walsingham as a surrogate father, what could stand in his way?

Walsingham shared his fatherly interest with David Lewes, who gave Caesar his first professional opportunity in 1581, naming him a commissioner for piracy causes.[28] Civil-law procedure had been applied to the trial of piracy for centuries, but it was a clumsy process in criminal prosecution. The act of 18 Henry VIII, cap. 15, gave the trial of piracy to commissioners of oyer and terminer who used the more speedy criminal procedure of the common law. The commissioners remained responsible to the High Court of Admiralty, but because they resembled commissioners of the peace, they were frequently (although incorrectly) called justices of the peace for piracy causes.[29]

Less than a week after Lewes placed Caesar on the piracy commission, he made him a second gift of office: the commissary of the Master of the Royal Hospital of St. Katherine next to the Tower.[30] The hospital, of which Lewes was Master, was an ancient royal peculiar answerable only to the crown. A small riverfront community to the east of the City, the peculiar consisted of a chapel, a hospital, and several score houses, shops, wharves, and warehouses all surrounded by a wall. Within the wall the Master exercised civil authority over the inhabitants. The Master and Brethren governed St. Katharine's, but the day-to-day affairs of the community were the commissary's responsibility. St. Katharine's was situated downstream from the City, separated from it only by the Tower, and thus was a haven for foreign merchants who wished to trade next to London while avoiding its encroaching and exclusionary jurisdiction. As the commissary, Caesar kept order and dispensed the Master's justice to residents and alien merchants alike. When Caesar later petitioned the City for an office, his close association with St. Katharine's was a mark against him.

As important as Burghley and Walsingham were to Caesar in political terms, David Lewes had special professional significance. He had no independent political base of any consequence, but he was perfectly placed to dispense professional patronage. Of even greater significance, he took the trouble to be a father to the young civilian. Caesar accounted one of Lewes's greatest favors to have been his insisting that Caesar supplicate a D.C.L. from Oxford. He had sponsored Caesar's candidacy, and on 3 March 1584, a few weeks before Lewes died, the degree was awarded. Caesar would later write that the judge had been the "cause of my proceeding doctor."[31]

Lewes provided Caesar a fine start, but repeated victories were necessary to sustain the momentum of success. In Elizabeth's England, successful social and professional careers were manifested by attaining higher rank and more offices. Each was unimpeachable evidence of a public career of consequence. The growing number of contenders for a fixed number of places became a problem before the 1580's ended; in the beginning, however, there seemed to have been no limits to professional advancement. The advancement that Caesar sought was more than a mark of success; it was a necessity. He had married Dorcas Lusher on 26 February 1583. The widowed daughter of Alderman Richard Martin, Caesar's new wife brought to him additional financial responsibilities. She had been married to Richard Lusher of the Middle Temple, but we have no record of the value of her marriage portion when she married Caesar.[32] His annual expenses, earlier reported to Walsingham to be £100, probably increased by half again upon his marriage. With £30 per annum from his father and a few pounds more from the commissaryship (the piracy commission only reimbursed expenses at a fixed rate), Caesar needed a regular and steady income. He later alleged that he had been forced after his marriage to rely on his father-in-law, another of his many surrogate fathers, to make ends meet.

When he turned his attention to securing a place of profit, Caesar demonstrated several characteristics that would reappear in future years in other circumstances. He sought a place for which he was not seen to be fully qualified, he tried to turn out an incumbent, he employed the good offices of powerful patrons, and he willingly ventured a great deal of money in his attempt. Because he wanted a prestigious office, one that would bespeak honor and power, and because he required a steady source of revenue, Caesar petitioned the City of London to make him their Common Serjeant. By custom, the Common Serjeant was a common lawyer, not a civilian, who served as the Corporation's barrister and as the guardian of the estates of the orphaned children of London freemen.[33] Besides his being a civilian, three obstacles stood between Caesar and the Common Serjeantcy: the incumbent, Bernard Randolph; the owners of the reversions to the office; and the Corporation of the City of London. Caesar hoped to settle with Randolph by paying him £100 per annum for life after he vacated the office. The first reversion, owned by one Thomas Kirton, was to be bought out for £300 within twenty days of Caesar's assuming the office. Inferior reversioners were to be bought out or ignored on a case-by-case basis. Yet there was one inferior reversioner, the Remembrancer of the City, Thomas Norton, who was to be paid £300 because of his important political standing in the Corporation.[34] Furthermore, the Corporation itself promised to be a particularly difficult obstacle. With all of his connections, Caesar remained an outsider in a City that jealously guarded its internal independence of action.

Dr. Lewes began Caesar's suit with a letter to Walsingham on New Year's Eve, 1582. He worried about "the olde and feble man in London who hath there the office of their Common Serjeant." His great age and failing health no longer permitted him to supervise the legal affairs of the City freemen and to be a "prolocutor and orator for the cytizens amongst them self and to other whatsoever." Lewes then directed Walsingham's attention to the provisions in the City's charter requiring the annual election of the Common Serjeant. Randolph had held the office for a number of years without reelection. "For the honor and common weale [of London] it is not mete and right that suche officer be continued further," wrote Lewes, but the City could restore its good name by appointing as Common Serjeant "Mr. Dr. Caesar, a man . . . not unknowen to your honor, learned in the cyvill lawes, of good parentage, and well alyed [allied] havinge matched in mariage with Mr. Alderman Martyns daughter, havinge the knoledge of the Latyne, Greeke, Italyan and French tongue, fytt to be orator of so honerable a cytie, and as fytt for his knoledge in the cyvill lawe for testamentary causes and all dependance thereof."[35]

Following Lewes's lead, Walsingham wrote to the City, and then the queen herself wrote on Caesar's behalf, reviewing the status of his suit and expressing her personal solicitude for the City's good government. The Lord Mayor should persuade Randolph to "take his rest, as his age and infirmities doe nowe require, and [to] retaine some reasonable portion of the profitte of that office during his life; the rest to be allotted to Caesar for occupying the place." If Caesar performed his duties well, Elizabeth wanted him to be assured election as Randolph's successor. The queen's letter closed with ominous references to alleged violations of the Corporation's charter and of the acts of the Common Council.[36] The threat of a review of a corporate charter, with its attendant costs, was a favorite means of bending independent burghal jurisdictions to the queen's will. Yet the City was the queen's principal banker, and she was not likely to alienate her banker over the appointment of a fledgling lawyer. Her heavy-handed threats were of little consequence; the City was in no hurry to replace its Common Serjeant.

Still, the queen could not be rudely ignored. The Lord Mayor asked Walsingham to indicate to Elizabeth that the City had good reason not to appoint Caesar, his inexperience in the common law being sufficient cause. Walsingham, in turn, offered a compromise. Although the suit was dragging on, he had managed to keep Caesar from raising the delay with the queen. But the young civilian was both ambitious and impatient. Perhaps the entire affair could be settled if the Corporation would give Caesar the freedom of the City, award him a place as its counsel for civil-law matters, and grant a small pension.[37] On 11 June 1583 the Court of Aldermen agreed to keep Caesar quiet by making the award, but care was taken to indicate that the appointment was extraordinary and that no precedent was being set by their having made it.[38] Caesar would also receive an annual pension of 40 marks and the right to keep whatever fees he collected. At the same time, Caesar was enfranchised without fee and admitted to his father-in-law's company, the Worshipful Company of Goldsmiths.[39] In the middle of June, Walsingham expressed his thanks to the Corporation for their actions and renewed his promise that "what cawses soever of your Cities [which] shall be hereafter committed to Mr. Caesar to bee sollicited here shall succeade the better even by the industry and credit of the Sollictor."[40]

This first attempt of Caesar's to secure public office is an instructive reflection on the tactics of an ambitious young man as well as on the limits of the power of patronage. Caesar risked much at such an early point in his career: he mustered impressive support for a position he had no assurance of winning, and he was willing to venture a great deal of money for the honor of a place that could not repay the investment. Indeed, one of his memoranda indicated that he was willing to forego the Common Serjeant's annual stipend in order to secure the appointment.[41] Winning the office was worth at least as much as its monetary rewards, for, having gathered powerful support, including the queen's, Caesar could not afford to be rejected. The City, for its part, was put in an awkward position. Caesar's not being a common lawyer should have disqualified him, yet his patrons were too powerful to be intimidated or ignored. Furthermore, there was the question of whether Caesar could be trusted to be their second-ranking lawyer when he was also the principal lawyer and judge for the Hospital of St. Katharine, a perennial challenger to London's control of commerce in the *banlieue*. A pragmatic and successful solution to these problems was found in the creation of the extraordinary office plus the attendant honor of enfranchisement. Although Caesar's patrons had not been able to secure for him what he wanted, they were still satisfied that the City had been appropriately forthcoming. Everyone saved face, an equally important consideration: Caesar won preferment, the City was able to fend off a direct intervention in its internal affairs while making a gift of their own creation, and the patrons were content in knowing that their patronage had been effective. As for the conflict of interest, the City limited Caesar to civil-law issues and required him to disqualify himself in the event of a conflict. His honor had been preserved by the City's compromise, but his purse had hardly been fattened.

Later in 1583 Walsingham displayed his fatherly concern for Caesar yet again when he helped him to secure an appointment in the ecclesiastical courts. The brother-in-law of John Aylmer, the bishop of London, resigned his place as commissary to the diocesan in order to take up a living. Caesar had some experience practicing in the ecclesiastical courts whose judge the commissary was. Thus, in October Walsingham wrote to Aylmer nominating his client for the recently vacated position.[42] The bishop was amenable to the nomination, but Walsingham had to write again to ask that the commission be made to run for Caesar's life rather than at the bishop's pleasure, to protect Caesar from the whim of a successor bishop should Aylmer be translated.[43] He then wrote to the Dean and Chapter of St. Paul's asking them to confirm the commission, thus doubly assuring Caesar's tenure.[44] Toward the end of December, Caesar was

commissioned for life as the bishop's commissary for Essex, Hertfordshire, and Middlesex.

The commissary's jurisdiction ranged over the broad spectrum of
human shortcomings: matters of morality, clerical impropriety, and
tithe-failing all came before his court. But the most important business of the commissary, especially in the crowded and volatile environs
of the metropolis, was the enforcement of the religious settlement.
While Caesar was sympathetic to Puritans who appeared before
him, he was not unreasonably harsh in his treatment of Catholics.
He was, in short, no fanatic, and his patrons, Walsingham and
Howard, accommodated religious dissent among their clients.

Caesar's scrupulous and careful treatment of recusants was evidenced in his questioning of a group of suspected Catholic priests
and laymen. Confining his inquiries to matters of politics, Caesar
avoided dealing directly with their faith because, he said, a political
confession was easier to secure. He was successful; the defendants
denied their loyalty to the queen, alleging that they would assist an
invasion from overseas if it were mounted by their coreligionists.
Caesar reported to the Council that he found the accused treason-
ous in heart but not in deed.[45] His zealous aversion to recusancy
had only appeared in 1582, when Caesar believed that he might jeopardize his own advancement were he to allow his recusant brother,
Henry, newly home from France, to enter his house. A nigh-official
sanction from Walsingham assuring Caesar that he was in no danger was required before Henry Caesar was allowed to cross his eldest
brother's threshold. But, as we shall see, Caesar had little to worry
about: Henry was probably in Walsingham's service as a spy.[46]

When Puritans appeared before the court, Caesar gave them whatever assistance he could. His disposition of an alleged conventicle in
Aythorp Roding, Essex, illustrated his sympathies. The vicar of
Aythorp Roding, having been suspended from his living because of
his Puritanism, had joined a number of his former parishioners for
dinner. Neighbors had reported the gathering, which had lasted late
into the evening. The participants were subsequently charged both
with seditious assembly and with engaging in an unlawful religious
exercise, otherwise known as a conventicle. After carefully examining the participants and witnesses, Caesar dismissed the charges.
When his decision reached the Privy Council, he was asked to explain himself. Caesar noted that the group had supped together and

that, following their meal, some had listened to a reading from the
Acts and Monuments of John Foxe while others had gathered round
the hearth to listen to the suspended vicar read from the authorized
catechism. In his final draft of the letter, Caesar crossed out the reference to reading the catechism and reported instead that those who
did not listen to the reading from Foxe were engaged in some
"honest talke." Finally, they all sang a psalm and said a prayer before
departing at ten o'clock. "I dismissed them from the Court as men
whose example was rather to bee followed then their weldoing to
bee reproved or themselves therein discouraged."[47] At a time when
Archbishop Whitgift had launched his campaign against Protestant
dissidents, Caesar had displayed courage, bending the letter of the
law for the alleged conventiclers and holding up their behavior for
the Council's approval. But his honor was at stake as well, since he
had initially found in their favor.

During his first few years as a civil lawyer, Caesar had used his patrons effectively. A piracy commissioner, the commissary to the
Master of St. Katharine, counsel to the City, commissary to the
bishop of London — Caesar had toeholds in the several institutions
in which a civilian could make a career. He was fully occupied, particularly in the church courts, and soon he began to make a place
for himself on the bench of the High Court of Admiralty. The opportunity to occupy the admiralty bench presented itself suddenly
and sorrowfully with the death of Caesar's old friend and patron
David Lewes. The Lord Admiral, the earl of Lincoln, asked Caesar
to fill the office of the judge temporarily because it was owned in
reversion and the reversioner was out of the country. Lincoln and
Walsingham told Lord Chancellor Bromley that Caesar had been
chosen because he was well qualified and because he was "a man
heretofore accustomed thereunto by D[r] Lewys."[48] In addition to
his experience in the admiralty both as a piracy commissioner and
as an advocate, Caesar had often sat in the court for Lewes when he
was absent. During his last years, Lewes's ill health, great age, and
devotion to his native Wales frequently caused him to be away, thus
giving Caesar valuable experience as his deputy. On one occasion,
following a meeting with Mendoza, the Spanish ambassador, Caesar had reported to Walsingham explaining that it was he who "Mr.
D[r] Lewes left as his deputie in his absence."[49]

The appointment to the admiralty bench was *durante absentia* the owner of the reversion, John Herbert, a civil lawyer and diplomat who was in Poland on the queen's service.[50] On the first day that Caesar presided, the Register, William Harewood, noted in the Act Book that he was the deputy judge sitting in Herbert's place.[51] But Caesar was determined to secure the judgeship for himself, although he had no idea how long and costly a process it would be and how much antagonism it would generate.

Caesar's first objective was to distinguish himself as a hardworking and conscientious judge. To this end, he reported to Burghley that he had given up all of his other duties, at a cost of more than £100 per annum in lost earnings, but that only by such a sacrifice could he "followe and in a better conscience exercise the high office of a judge committed unto mee."[52] Burning his bridges in this fashion was rash, but Caesar was ambitious and Lincoln apparently favored him; however, the Lord Admiral's death in January 1585 suddenly and radically altered Caesar's plans for seizing the judgeship. He would have to begin again, currying favor with a new and as yet unnamed Lord Admiral.

Queen Elizabeth moved quickly to stabilize the Admiralty. She left the responsibility for the fleet in the hands of Sir John Hawkins, Treasurer of the Navy, whereas the coastal defenses remained under the command of the incumbent vice admirals. The judgeship of the High Court of Admiralty, traditionally considered to be in the Lord Admiral's gift, was another matter because the queen wanted to resume direct control over as many appointments as possible. She was assured by her counsel that the judge was appointed "not by any authorite that the Lord Admirall had soe to doe in his owne person, but by the right derived from the Kings letters patent, soe that he is Judge of the Admiralltie, bee there an Admirall or no Admirall so long as there is a Courte of Admiralltie, which must not die; and he is Judge by the Crown, though not imedeatlie."[53] Acting on this advice, the queen named Caesar and Dr. Valentine Dale, another civilian, joint commissioners general for admiralty causes, when the court reconvened on 4 February 1585, Dale had joined Caesar on the bench.[54] Caesar's previous service in the court did not go unrecognized: the joint commission awarded Caesar two-thirds of the fees and profits that would normally be allowed to the judge.[55] Although the commission awarded unto Caesar what was Caesar's and unto Dale what was left, the ultimate disposition of the judgeship would be made according to the desires of the queen and the new Lord Admiral, her cousin Charles, Lord Howard of Effingham.

Howard was nearing fifty when he was commissioned in July 1585.[56] His public career had begun early in service with his father, the Lord Admiral to Mary Tudor. In 1559 he had represented Elizabeth in France upon the accession of Francis II. During the Rising in the North, Howard had been general of the horse under Warwick's command, and in the following year, he had commanded the English escort fleet, which convoyed a Spanish flotilla through the Narrow Seas as it carried their young queen home from Flanders. Succeeding to the barony of Effingham in 1573, he was created Knight of the Garter in the spring of 1574. As a gesture of respect and affection, Elizabeth made Howard Lord Chamberlain in 1583, the post he held until his appointment as Lord High Admiral. He was at home in the highest circles at Court, and his wife, Catherine Carey, was among the queen's closest friends.[57]

Although Charles Howard differed greatly in terms of social origins from Caesar's principal patrons, Burghley and Walsingham, he shared important values with them. While all three men were ambitious, they were not as obviously driven in their aspirations as were Caesar and his contemporaries. The young civilian's soaring ambition and his impatience for advancement presented a problem for all of them. Burghley and Walsingham, however, knew Caesar well and showed affection for him. Howard, on the other hand, did not know the judge, who was merely John Herbert's locum tenens. If Caesar wanted to secure the judgeship for himself, he would have to win the Lord Admiral's confidence without having any assurance that Howard was disposed to like him. Great skill and patience were required. Neither Caesar nor Dale had any assurance of tenure; Howard could have dismissed either of them at will on the unimpeachable grounds that the judgeship belonged to another man who was away from England in the crown's service. Their dismissal, under such circumstances, would have enjoyed Elizabeth's support. In any event, two years would pass before Howard granted Caesar the bench in his own right, two years during which the judge was on trial.

Caesar lost no time making himself known to his new master. Shortly after he became the Lord Admiral, Howard received a letter from him explaining that Caesar's service in the admiralty was ruining him financially and that he was seriously threatened by John Herbert's impending return to England. Furthermore, Caesar claimed that Howard had promised to rid the Admiralty Court of Herbert when he returned from Poland. Howard was shocked by the tone of the letter, and his reply was peevish and evasive. If Herbert could not be satisfied with some other place of honor and profit, Howard would be sorry; but, he reminded the judge, he had never promised to remove Herbert for Caesar's benefit. While Howard would be pleased to have Caesar remain in office, he added that "I ever tolde you I coulde not take away the offys from him [i.e., Herbert] but with his good wyll, being my kynsman and in her Majesties sarvys."[58]

A month later, Caesar asked Burghley to help him to preserve "possession of an office, whereof I have the right by lawe, and wherein I have spent and lost to the valewe of 2100 libri." Preserving the office meant keeping John Herbert at bay while procuring for him a place as a Master of Requests. As much as Caesar wished to approach the queen in the matter, he dared not do so. If, however, he turned to anyone other than Burghley, his patron, he would be dividing his loyalties. The apparent quandary was purely rhetorical; throughout his career, Caesar maintained multiple alliances without disadvantage. The letter to Burghley ended with a plea to expedite the suit that he was making in Herbert's behalf, "so much the soner for my sake."[59] Although Burghley eventually supplied the Mastership of Requests, Caesar had also to compound with Herbert for the reversion of the judgeship, paying him a lump sum in compensation for long-term loss of income. He told Howard, in 1592, that the composition had cost £1,300 in principal and interest over a seven-year period.[60]

From the start, Caesar's and Howard's relationship was complicated by their divergent perceptions of the function of the Admiralty Court and the role of its judge. Howard believed that the court belonged to his office in the same way that a manorial court might belong to one of his estates. When he gave instructions, he expected them to be carried out without delay. Caesar, on the other hand, was an ambitious careerist and a professional lawyer trained in the civil law. As a civilian he looked upon the court as an element of the broader system of English justice, not as a separate and alien tribunal inferior in status to the common-law courts. As a careerist with bountiful ambition, he did not wish to be seen as the Lord Admiral's lackey. Honor demanded that he be accorded the respect due to an independent judge of an independent court. If he were to expect such respect from the world at large, he would have first to establish the respect of his own superior. But Caesar's expectations did not accord well with Howard's own style and dignity. Furthermore, Caesar's expectations failed to account for the profound differences between the admiralty judge and a common-law judge. Whereas the latter was the crown's agent, with responsibility for adjudicating in the monarch's name, the former was an administrative dependent of a minister, the Lord Admiral. Regardless of Caesar's civilian theories, the judge of the Admiralty Court was a subordinate servant to Charles Howard, not an independent jurist.

We must not forget that, whatever differences divided them, Caesar needed Howard to win the bench for him, and Howard needed Caesar to make his own task easier. As simple as it would have been for the Lord Admiral to confirm Herbert as judge, such a course of action would have presented its own difficulties. Because Herbert owned a claim to the bench, he would have regarded his appointment as the confirmation of an office that was already his. Caesar, however, because he was ambitious and because he enjoyed no claim of right, would owe his appointment to Howard. In the long run, his dependence on the Lord Admiral suggested that he would be more compliant to his master's will. For his part, Caesar recognized that he had to educate the Lord Admiral to the advantages that would follow from the appointment of a competent and quite independent-minded judge.

Howard's keen interest in a subservient magistrate was more than an expression of aristocratic arrogance; the judge was the essential figure in the effective exploitation of the perquisities of the Lord Admiral's office. He supervised the receipt of the fines, fees, penalties, and confiscations arising in the High Court of Admiralty. Furthermore, beyond personal financial considerations, the Lord Admiral was the minister of the crown responsible for the smooth and effective operation of the Admiralty Court. Complaints about the court and its decisions caused the queen and his fellow councillors to look to him for remedies. In the prebureaucratic milieu of sixteenth-century England, subjective profit motives and objective ministerial functions were thoroughly intertwined and frequently in conflict.

Caesar believed that the conflict reduced his power as judge, causing him to enjoy less esteem than was accorded to the jurists presiding in King's Bench, Common Pleas, and Chancery.

It appeared to the judge that the Lord Admiral was bent on undermining and frustrating his own court because of his frequent interventions in its process. A stream of letters, some merely a few scratched lines, flowed from Charles regarding the disposition of specific cases. His words were courteous and he admonished the judge not to do anything contrary to the law. Yet he was a Privy Councillor and the Lord Admiral; he left no doubt as to the desired outcome of his correspondence. The civil law was at least as resistant as the common law to interference by a layman wielding political power but knowing no law. This resistance was fortified in the mind of a doctrinaire civil lawyer such as Caesar because of the admiralty court's exceptional symbolic value: it was the last English court of any consequence still governed by the civil law. But Caesar's resistance and his criticism of the Lord Admiral suggest that he believed that his honor and prestige were threatened by Howard's behavior, leading him to utter harsh and somewhat naive criticism. Howard was, de jure, the admiralty judge, although the magistracy had long since been delegated to a professional lawyer. Still, petitioners addressed themselves to the Lord Admiral, and much of the correspondence between Howard and Caesar amounted to little more than cover memoranda accompanying redirected petitions. In short, Caesar had much less to fear than his words would suggest.

There was, of course, cause for concern that the foreign litigants who had recourse to the court and their English counterparts would lose respect for the Admiralty Court if they were obstructed by unpredictable political considerations. Consider the contemporary appraisal of the value of an independent court to the welfare of the state made by Antonio in *The Merchant of Venice*:

> The duke cannot deny the course of law,
> For the commodity that strangers have
> With us in Venice: if it be denied,
> 'Twill much impeach the justice of the state;
> Since that the trade and profit of the city
> Consisteth of all nations.[61]

Neither the queen nor Howard nor the Privy Council could deny the course of law, for the same reasons. But a close examination of several instances of Howard's dealing with the Admiralty Court reveals that, in most instances, the Lord Admiral was performing his ministerial duties responsibly, often hastening the course of law, and that it was Caesar who would not, or could not, appreciate the rationale underlying his master's behavior. We have noted the presence of many foreign litigants in the court; if they were displeased, their only recourse to higher authority was to the queen and Privy Council. The Lord Admiral was the principal link between Council and the court. Thus, because it was important for diplomatic and commercial reasons for Council to have immediate and reliable access to the judge, we frequently find Howard addressing Mr. Dr. Caesar.

In 1585, for example, the need for rapid communication between Council and the court led to a series of actions that sidestepped the court's cumbersome procedure but were well within the law. Dispute arose over the ownership of a French vessel brought into London as a prize. Acting for the master and owners, the French ambassador had intervened with Howard, who gave Caesar two days to interview the master and mariners and to report his findings. Within a week a preliminary determination was made, the goods sorted out, and the ship arrested by the Queen's Coroner. Although their ship was in custody and the trial had not yet started, the French appeared to be satisfied that admiralty process was working effectively.[62] The Lord Admiral's role in this matter was consonant with the proper function of his office.

On another occasion, Caesar and Howard disagreed sharply, and more seriously, over which of them properly exercised judicial authority. A cargo of corn had been confiscated by the crown in order to relieve a shortage of grain in 1586. The price of cereal grain was high that year, the supply low; under these circumstances, the confiscation was especially painful to the merchants who owned the corn.[63] Howard ordered Caesar to dispose of the cargo, but the judge ignored the order. Jasper Swift, the marshal of the court and the Lord Admiral's eyes and ears, wrote to Howard complaining that his efforts to obey Howard's instructions had come to nothing because Caesar would not issue the necessary enabling orders. Upon hearing of this insubordination, Howard angrily wrote to Caesar asking him whether he put his own interpretation of justice ahead of the instructions of his master.[64] Caesar had intended to restore the grain to the merchants who owned it even though the owners of the ship that had carried the grain were demanding their rightful freight charges. But the law was clear: the confiscation had been made to meet a pressing public need, and compensation was set at an unfavorable rate that afforded little profit. If the merchants took their corn from Caesar, reloaded it on another vessel, and left London, the owners and mariners of the first ship would lose their freight. Caesar had decided that the seizure was illegal, and he was prepared to allow the merchants to have their cargo regardless of the rightful freight claims.

Howard absolutely refused to concur in Caesar's disposition of the suit. Following a short delay to permit the parties to consult their principals, the corn was to be sold and the several contending parties were to be given their shares.[65] The Lord Admiral's actions demonstrated concern for the well-being of the mariners whose shares he was protecting, and they accorded with the law. At this point, Caesar did as he was instructed, selling the corn and paying the mariners' wages. He then wrote to the Lord Admiral to tell him that he would consider Howard's order to sell the corn to be his acquittance from any responsibility. The Lord Admiral could hardly have been more angry if Caesar had continued to refuse him outright. He reminded the judge that law and tradition sanctioned the confiscation of foodstuff in an emergency. Furthermore, the Lord Treasurer had concurred in Howard's action; Caesar had presumed too much by doubting the legality of the order. But Charles Howard was as hurt as he was angry: he told Caesar that he was never to doubt that he enjoyed the full support of his master in the execution of his orders, nor was he to doubt that the orders were legitimate. "I wyll [not] wryght unto you any thynge that you shall dowte it shalbe both honorable and lafull."[66] The Lord Admiral's sense of justice had been impugned. "I pray, Mr. Caesar, when did I ether wryght or speke to you to dow otherwyse then ryght justes? I protest it before the fase of Almyghty God, I never in my lyfe thowght to dow it and I besyche God I like not to dow it. Therefor . . . wryght unto me in what thynge I ever moved you ether by worde or deede or wrytyng to hynder procedynge of justes. Truly I lok to be satysfyd in it."[67] With these words, Caesar was put squarely on the defensive, with few doubts as to the Lord Admiral's attitude.

There were, of course, more instances of the Lord Admiral's active involvement in the court. He ordered a prisoner to remain confined even though Caesar had acquitted him.[68] In another instance, he caused Caesar to pay particular attention to the complaint of Sir Walter Leveson, "a man that I dearly love and an espetial friend of youres." Caesar was to bend every effort in his behalf to prevent any trouble for him.[69] The judge who was, after all, Howard's deputy— could not expect to be free to make his own decisions if the Lord Admiral chose to involve himself or if the Council saw fit to indicate to him the direction in which their favor lay.

However much Caesar wanted to act on his own, he knew that direct disregard of Howard's orders was foolish. He tempered impatient ambition and outraged honor with caution and patience. He was not prepared to sacrifice his career prematurely for the sake of injured pride and imagined principle. The judge sought means to direct grievances to the Lord Admiral without making himself odious to his master, for he risked either the loss of his position or isolation from the lucrative business of the court. Caesar thus contained his ambition until November 1587 when he was awarded a commission for life as the sole judge of the High Court of Admiralty. Having won Howard's confidence, and with John Herbert's challenge to the judgeship behind him, Caesar turned his attention to introducing a number of fundamental changes in the court, which will be discussed in the next chapter.

Although Caesar possessed a patent for life in the queen's service, this did not necessarily mean that he would be compensated from the queen's revenue. In fact, compensation was most frequently tied to the fees and profits of the office. Without a fixed salary, the judge of the High Court of Admiralty depended on the income generated by fees paid by the litigants at each step in the judicial process, according to an established schedule. He also received gifts from the litigants, which were identified on the tallies of costs as being *pro sportulagiis*. Defined as a dole or small gift, this was a gratuity tendered to the judge, especially when extraordinary services were performed, such as providing extra court days out of term time. The size of the gift was consistently 17s. 8d., suggesting that, its name notwithstanding, it was regarded as a fee. In the light of the hun-

dreds of extraordinary sessions that Caesar convened each year during his long career in the admiralty, these gifts would have made him
a wealthy man.

Caesar was also entitled to a share of the droits (or revenues of
right) that were the Lord Admiral's compensation for the office he
occupied. The actual collection was undertaken by various local officials in the Lord Admiral's name. Indeed, Caesar, in his capacity as
Vice Admiral of the Thames, collected the droits arising within his
vice admiralty. Otherwise, very little of the Lord Admiral's money
passed directly through Caesar's hands, although much was collected by the court and the judge was responsible for the process. In
October 1589 Charles Howard granted his judge, "for and in consid-
eracon of the true loiall and faithfull service . . . heretofore done,"
one-twentieth of his tenth part of the value of all prizes, one-tenth of
all money paid in for passports issued to Flemish merchants, one-
quarter of all goods confiscated because they had avoided customs
or had been exported without a license, and one-quarter of all "casual profits and advantages whatsoever." This latter was a catchall
that included fines, penalties, amercements, and forfeitures.[70]

Howard's award to Caesar upset the established procedure for
collecting and paying out the droits because accounts would now
have to be kept of payments to Caesar as well as to the Lord Admiral. This complication made it difficult for Caesar to collect his
share, for he had to rely on warrants from Howard authorizing local
officials to pay his stipulated share of the droits from the revenues
they held.[71] Having to depend on repeated warrants was a source of
continuing irritation. As late as 1602, after nearly fifteen years of
their sharing the droits, if the Lord Admiral's warrants were im-
properly dated, the collector of the tenths in the West Country, William Hardie, could be relied on to refuse to honor them. Howard,
on one occasion, wrote to Hardie ordering him to pay Caesar the
proper share of the value of a captured prize.[72] The collector explained to Caesar that the prize in question had been taken before
the date on the Lord Admiral's warrant, and he was insistent that he
would not honor it. Yet he left Caesar with the hope that a solution
might be found.[73]

When Caesar tried to collect his share from Howard's brother-in-
law, Sir George Carey, a privateer and the Vice Admiral of Hampshire and the Isle of Wight, Carey refused to remit directly to the

judge. Howard assured him that while Carey would publicly refuse to pay the judge's portion, he would pay Howard, who would, in turn, give Caesar his share. Carey's pride was at stake, and he wanted to save face by dealing only with the Lord Admiral. As Howard put it, he would "leave them [the money] to him for his credits sake, as he termeth it, and he will pay me."[74] Faced with these delays, Caesar adopted an alternate and more direct means of collecting his share of the droits. As various sums were received in the High Court of Admiralty to the Lord Admiral's account, Caesar appropriated them to his own use, up to the amount of his twentieth of Howard's tenth. Howard never objected.

The value of his fees and his share of the Lord Admiral's profits were important parts of Caesar's growing wealth, and, fortunately, he kept a record of his receipts for six years after the award was made. During the first two years that he shared in the profits, the judge received £238 15s. 9d.; the second two years yielded £105 9s. 6d.; but during the last two years of his record (November 1593 through November 1595), his receipts rose sharply to £1,220 9s. 9d.[75] It is small wonder that Howard, in a letter written in 1596 to a widow who was interested in marrying Caesar after his first wife had died, estimated Caesar's wealth at £2,000 per annum and compared it to the wealth of most of the barons of England.[76] As we shall see, this was not a fanciful estimate.

At the peak of the judge's productive period in the High Court of Admiralty, and just after having been sworn an ordinary Master of Requests, Caesar, in 1596, finally received from the queen a favor that he had sought virtually from the day he entered the crown's service. Elizabeth granted him a pension of £100 per annum during her pleasure.[77] Although the pension represented only a fraction of his income, it had great symbolic value. After more than fifteen years in her service, Caesar was being paid directly by the queen.

II

To Rule and Governe
as an Admirall in Deede

DR. JULIUS CAESAR had achieved his first major career goal in November 1587; he was the judge of the High Court of Admiralty with a patent for life. For nearly two decades, until 1606, he would preside over a court that was propelled into the epicenter of politics and diplomacy by the force of events. A complicated privateering war with Spain, the assertive competition of the common-law courts, the de facto independence of many of the provincial ports—together these elements brought the Admiralty Court into prominence and shaped its institutional character. But the judge's personality was also a significant factor. Caesar was imaginative, aggressive, competitive; and he thrived on further advancement. Although he became judge in the midst of conflict with his superior, Charles Howard, they eventually became amicable colleagues making common cause against those who opposed their court. However, their individual styles were quite distinct. Howard chose to champion his court quietly in the private council of the queen and among his brothers of Privy Council. His private efforts were nicely complemented by Caesar's aggressive public defense of the High Court of Admiralty.

In the following pages we shall examine some of Caesar's many attempts to make fundamental changes in the High Court of Admiralty and, at the same time, to improve his own personal fortunes. He strove to strengthen admiralty procedure, to elevate the professional stature of the civil lawyer and of the court, and to enhance the majesty of the judge. Moreover, he tried to blunt the attack of rival courts that tried to control the admiralty bench. As we develop the context in which these changes were to be made, we must ask ourselves whether the time was right to undertake them. Because a complex "private" naval war was being waged between England and Spain, the government needed an Admiralty Court that concentrated its attention on its juridical duties rather than a court diverted by institutional rivalry and procedural change. Yet these very circumstances militated in Caesar's favor. In more quiet times the High Court of Admiralty attracted little official notice; in the turmoil of the late sixteenth century it became an essential agent of English policy. Taking advantage of this new significance, Caesar insisted that his court was unable to serve the queen's and the nation's interests without a number of fundamental changes. That he would share personally in the benefits of these changes was an unremarkable piece of good fortune. As we shall see in the next chapter, the times could not have been better for an ambitious man, possessed of the drive and the stamina for the long struggle, to capitalize on the circumstances at hand.

Caesar's primary motive was to enhance his own position as a civilian judge in a prerogative court. Facing him were the judges of the common law, insisting on their judicial supremacy. Caesar's civilian training had instilled in him a commitment to the prerogative, unlimited in theory but circumscribed in practice. In order to preserve the prerogative, it had to be institutionalized and depersonalized, for its gravest weakness was its subjective and idiosyncratic application. Although he never argued the logical conclusion of his position, Caesar was moving toward a structure of institutionalized prerogative, that is to say, toward the structure of the secular sovereign state.

Institutionalizing the prerogative—a process that necessarily preceded the emergence of the modern "civil servant"—had already begun in the Chancery, Exchequer, King's Bench, and Common Pleas. These agencies owed their origin to the crown and its plenary prerogative powers, but, as they assumed institutional identities, they became seised of the prerogative, leaving the crown less able to interfere with their processes. The well-documented establishment of chamber government in the late fifteenth and early sixteenth centuries is an example of the crown's inability to bend the old institutions to the king's will.[1] The prerogative courts, however, had not undergone a similar transformation. In this distinction we have a measure of both Caesar's challenge and his accomplishment.

Caesar's many proposals for effecting significant change in the High

Court of Admiralty were made throughout his tenure as judge. He expressed himself in the tradition of the advice books for princes and magistrates, which had become, by the end of the sixteenth century, firmly rooted in European political literature. While advice books were most frequently addressed to a prince or a king, Caesar's memoranda to Charles Howard belong to the same genre. A "Means to further the execution of Justice in England touching Admirall causes," dated February 1588, is an early expression of Caesar's ideas. Closely written on both sides of two long foolscap sheets, the document discusses government and law in the context of the High Court of Admiralty. After beginning with a description of the admiralty court's organization, Caesar advanced proposals for change and explained why they were necessary. They focused on the Lord Admiral, his authority, and the relationship of that authority to the operations of the court.

Although the Lord Admiral served at the crown's pleasure, exercising the queen's delegated authority, he needed a sound bureaucracy if he was to perform his duties effectively. If he staffed his court well and gave it his overt support, Caesar argued, his reward would be the fear and the respect of all men who fell under his jurisdiction. Earlier Lord Admirals had employed their judges as their lieutenants, entrusting their honor to them without untoward interference. But this arrangement no longer obtained, Caesar contended, because Howard would not support the judge as his predecessors had done. However, if the Lord Admiral would place the weight of his dignity behind his judge, especially as the court was under pressure from rival jurisdictions, the judge could meet any challenge without fear of intimidation. Under such circumstances, Caesar could help his master to "rule and governe as an Admirall in deede."[2]

As we have already noted, Caesar derived his concept of the prerogative from his study of the Roman law. Good government, whether political or judicial, was conducted by officials who governed vicariously, deriving their authority from a greater power rather than exercising their own authority. Translated into the terms of the High Court of Admiralty, this meant that the judge was the Lord Admiral's vicar, and that the judge alone could wield the sword of office granted to him until it was withdrawn. Once granted, the sword was not "to be taken from him or used by the Lord Admirall till the judge be discharged of his office."[3] Thus Howard's intervention in the business of the court violated Caesar's understanding of the Lord Admiral's

appropriate role. He believed that Howard had, by his conduct, cast
a long shadow over the dignity of the High Court of Admiralty.

Caesar urged Howard to exercise his prerogative with responsibility lest it be weakened and made ineffective. The Lord Admiral should
not interfere with the judge of his court any more than the queen
should interfere with the judges of her central common-law courts.
Caesar was quick to point out that both the honor and the profit of
the Lord Admiral depended on the respect, the reverence, and the obedience accorded to the writs and warrants of the High Court of Admiralty. Thus, when Howard issued ad hoc letters of reprisal without
using the established procedures of his own court, he gravely undermined his own authority. If admiralty warrants were "crossed or cleane
displaced by private [i.e., Howard's] warrants or letters, things in truth
not warranted by the lawe," then they become "so blunted and dis-
graced in the opinion of the people, that they, being freed from the
sharp warrant of the lawe, doe become careles of the Judge and of the
Lord Admirall, whose place he representeth." Caesar feared that when
"the Lord Admirall hath blunted his lawfull sword so that it can noe
more cutt, his unwarranted warrant maie safely be disobeied."[4]

For all of his complaining, Caesar was not pessimistic. He had a
number of ideas for giving the court the full authority that, presently,
it only partially exercised. Clearly, some of his suggestions would have
improved Caesar's own lot; many others would have benefitted the
court. For himself, Caesar had wanted a life patent for his office and
one-quarter of the Lord Admiral's profits from the fees and perquisites
of the court. The patent he had achieved; the profits, estimated at a
value of £400 per annum, were still to come. This amount, he believed, would be sufficient to provide for his family in the event of his
demise.

As for the court, Caesar proposed that, from that day forward, all
admiralty trials should be conducted according to admiralty law and
admiralty procedure rather than in Privy Council or at the personal
whim of the Lord Admiral. Although extraordinary means of disposing of admiralty business seemed, perhaps, to be expedient, the expediency was an illusion. More time was spent coping with extraordinary procedures than with the ordinary course of the law, largely because of the masses of petitions and appeals that followed in their
wake. The crowd of foreign litigants, confronted with unpredictable
ad hoc practices, was growing insolent and turning to such alternatives

as the anarchy of self-help. Caesar insisted that the Lord Admiral, if he had the will, could quiet the mounting disorder that obtained in large parts of the admiralty jurisdiction. Among his proposals was a scheme for an admiralty circuit along the south and west coasts of England. He wanted to be commissioned to ride the circuit to try cases on the spot, to investigate local conditions, and to extend the effective authority of the court to the many provincial seaports that claimed maritime jurisdictions independent of the Lord Admiral. The circuit was attempted in 1591, but with little success.[5]

Both of these proposals, to divide the Lord Admiral's profits and to ride an admiralty circuit, exemplify the pursuit of private advantage as well as of public good. These were not casual suggestions; they required detailed planning and costly execution. Caesar suggested that Howard could be assured of an honest division by his appointment of a special treasurer whom Caesar would pay £100 per annum. The treasurer would receive all of the profits, keep an account of their receipt and division, and periodically remit the appropriate shares to their recipients. As for the circuit, Caesar imagined that its success would strengthen the admiralty's authority and breed new respect for the civil law. This was particularly important, he said, because the Lord Admiral was the last remaining patron of consequence for the civilians of England. Caesar put his case somewhat grandly: the "civill lawe, whereof his Lordship is the only patron in England, and the professors thereof shall encrease and florish, and . . . the common wealth [shall be] furnished with hable and sufficient men for publicke and forraine services."[6] But this was no mere flattery; Caesar believed that the Lord Admiral was uniquely placed to patronize and advance the civil law.

The changes that Caesar presented in the "Means" were thoughtful and necessary, but they frequently were not feasible. Two significant obstacles lay in the way: one, which we have discussed, was Charles Howard; the other was the privateering war with Spain and her allies, which, after 1585, overwhelmed the court and its judge at the cost of their other concerns.[7]

From the moment of her accession in 1558, Elizabeth was faced with the problem of her brother-in-law, Philip II of Spain. He wanted to marry her, to make permanent the establishment of Anglo-Spanish unity, and to preserve the restoration of the old religion. But these were not items on Elizabeth's own agenda. Politely but firmly she put Philip off until she had better control of her domestic inheritance. Soon both monarchs became thoroughly engaged in national politics, and, during the next twenty years, relations between Spain and England worsened. At first, this was because the queen would not commit herself to Philip; later, because England was supporting the rebellion of Philip's Protestant subjects in the Netherlands. However, the deepest division between them stemmed from Philip's belief in his divine commission to pull down Elizabeth's heretical regime.

Determined though he was, even Philip had to await the proper moment to strike. His subordinates were less careful; they possessed their master's zeal but not his discretion. Two of Philip's ambassadors were expelled from England, in 1572 and in 1584, for their outrageous plotting against the queen. Even his ally, the pope, was determined to force Philip's hand. In 1570, Rome published throughout Europe a bull of excommunication against Elizabeth without first consulting Philip. Although the pope could excommunicate without taking secular advice, prudence suggested consultation with Spain because the pope expected Philip to enforce the bull with Spanish arms. In terms of Spanish interests, the time was not right for Philip to commit himself to such an enterprise.

The principal restraint on Spain was France, a traditional adversary. Philip strove to insinuate Spanish interests into the domestic and foreign policy of the French, and he realized success by 1585, when he made an alliance with one of the factions in the protracted French religious wars. The Guise faction, politically and religiously compatible with Philip, joined in an association known as the Holy League, French in membership but Spanish in inspiration and finance.[8] By 1585, therefore, with the Holy League in place and with the leader of the rebellion in the Netherlands dead by an assassin's hand, Philip made his move against Elizabeth. In May, he ordered all English ships in Spanish ports seized and their crews imprisoned. Elizabeth responded to this seizure by permitting Englishmen to make private reprisals against the ships of Spain, the Catholic Netherlands, and the Holy League. Thus began the privateering war against Spain and her allies, which continued until James I made peace following his accession in 1603.

At the center of England's prosecution (and resolution) of the undeclared war was the Admiralty Court and its new judge, Dr. Julius

Caesar. Their task was to regulate and supervise an irregular naval action as if it were a matter of private reprisal. The principal responsibility for setting the policy governing the war belonged to the Privy Council. The war was a complex and fluid imbroglio, demanding constant conciliar supervision. Day-to-day administration was the province of the High Court of Admiralty.

The privateers sailed under letters of reprisal that were, quite simply, authorizations to conduct private warfare under the protection of the crown.[9] Under normal circumstances, a letter of reprisal permitted an injured English party to enforce a claim against a foreign party by authorizing the seizure of the goods of the foreigner, or of his countrymen, up to the value of the claim. The procedure for alleging damages, for specifying means of redress, and for receiving authorization to seize reprisal or "prize" ships had been established for generations. Before 1585 this procedure had been carefully directed toward the recovery of specific prizes; in the years after 1585 the process became a means of waging war. Public policy was implemented by private means and for personal gain.[10]

Because of the political delicacy of undeclared war, diplomacy played a crucial role in the Anglo-Spanish conflict. Diplomatic postures frequently shifted, requiring the Admiralty Court to be sensitive to each change.[11] The hundreds of copies of treaties, the memoranda of interviews with ambassadors and foreign commercial agents, and the briefs containing the historical background to England's relations with foreign powers that crowd Caesar's papers bear witness to the intimate relationship between diplomacy and admiralty procedure. With these papers for reference, and with the Council's directives in hand, Caesar attempted to conform the actions of his court to the queen's fluid foreign policy. Rapid and uncluttered lines of communication were crucial between the queen and the Council, on the one hand, and between the queen and the High Court of Admiralty, on the other.

The withering array of diplomatic difficulties occasioned by the privateering war are well exemplified by England's relations with France. Although England was not at war with France, she was hostile to any ally of Spain, and although France was not a Spanish ally, significant numbers of her aristocracy were allied with the Holy League and thus with Spain.[12] From the English point of view, the French posed problems because there were so many varieties of them.

Leaguers, Valois loyalists, Huguenots — all were French, but only the Leaguers were fair game. On the high seas, in the heat of boarding and seizing a prize ship, the many types of French were impossible to tell apart. As a result, charges and countercharges were hurled back and forth at the diplomatic and mercantile level. The crowded calendar of the High Court of Admiralty bore the burden. Extraordinary commissions, charged with expediting the ever-mounting backlog of complaints from French mariners and merchants, provided occasional respites in the commotion, releasing some of the pressures by summarily settling as many French complaints as possible. But the commissions were a palliative rather than a solution to the problem. Since the commissioners did not have terminal authority, their decisions were never binding and rarely satisfactory. Dissatisfied litigants would take their causes from the commissioners to the Privy Council, to King's Bench, or to Chancery. Although extraordinary commissions did have some diplomatic and cosmetic value, they were a judicial nuisance.

The failure of the extraordinary commissions, and of the admiralty court itself, to settle the issues raised by foreign litigants was a part of a much more serious problem. In the midst of the complexities of the privateering war, the High Court of Admiralty and its judge faced seriously damaging attacks from other English courts. The High Court of Admiralty considered itself an equal member of the pantheon of central courts, but the other courts did not agree.

The legal chauvinism that was developing toward the end of the sixteenth century caused the common lawyers to disparage the High Court of Admiralty because it practiced an alien law, the law merchant, with its roots in the Mediterranean basin rather than in England. The law merchant had emerged from local customs in various ports of the Levant and eventually was incorporated into the Roman law. Centuries after the demise of the empire, essentially the same law was being used in towns along the Atlantic and North Sea coasts. Gerard de Malynes (who, as late as the early seventeenth century, was the first to codify the English sea law) said that the Law of Oleron, the mercantile law that was recognized among most Europeans, had first been brought under the authority of the English crown by Edward III, who had "caused, with the advice of diverse men of knowledge and experience, diverse Articles to be set downe, and these inrolled and obeyed for the government of the Admirall court."[13]

When Edward III assumed control over admiralty jurisdiction, he seriously upset traditional structures that had been in place for centuries. Merchants and mariners had, for good reason, become accustomed to settling their own disagreements rather than to committing them to a professional law court. As men of the sea, their lives were controlled by the elements. Their movements were governed by fair or foul weather, falling or rising tides, fresh and steady winds or gale-force storms. If the weather was right to sail, they were ill-disposed to postpone their departures to await court days, whether they were parties to litigation or witnesses. Thus, they had settled their difficulties among themselves, using summary and equitable procedures on beaches and quaysides wherever the disputants might be. In time, the towns where they traded assumed jurisdiction over the merchants and mariners, but they remained active participants in the courts. The coastal towns of France and the empire were not much bothered by what passed for central territorial government and could, throughout most of the medieval period, continue to manage their own mercantile affairs. But in England, even at an early date, the crown had sufficient power to aspire to the control of local jurisdictions. Yet the contest between town and crown was long and slow; indeed, it was still unsettled when Caesar occupied the admiralty bench.

We see, then, a form of law flourishing in England with foreign rather than domestic origins: sufficient reason for the xenophobic common lawyers to go on the attack. Moreover, they disliked the Admiralty Court because continental mercantile law was closely related to Roman law. For centuries, the only English tribunals experienced in the procedure of the Roman civil law had been the courts christian, and it was natural that the emerging Admiralty Court had been associated, albeit indirectly, with the law of the church. In the years prior to the Reformation, this association resulted in the High Court of Admiralty being regarded as one of the great rivals of the common law, along with the church courts. Holdsworth has observed that, whereas civil law had influenced the technical development of the law merchant, canon law had influenced its structure and machinery.[14]

The common lawyers had good reason to feel that the Admiralty Court was a rival of some consequence because the Lord Admirals had been encroaching on their jurisdiction for several centuries. The passage of the act of 13 Richard II, st. 1, cap. 5, barring the Lord Admiral and his lieutenants from meddling in causes arising within the realm rather than at sea, marked the beginning of the common-law resistance to the Lord Admiral's authority.[15] In the following year, 1391, another piece of legislation restricted the Admiralty Court even further when it declared that in "all manner of contracts, pleas, and quarrels rising within the Bodies of the Counties, as well by land as by water, and also by Wreck of the Sea, the Admiral's court shall have no matter of cognizance, Power nor jurisdiction."[16] By the early fifteenth century, additional legislation provided the statutory basis for the common lawyers to regulate effectively the High Court of Admiralty. After 1401, any person who felt that he had suffered damages simply as a consequence of an action being brought against him in the Admiralty Court, rather than at law, was to "have his action by writ grounded upon the case against him that doth so pursue in the Admiral's court and so recover his double damages against the pursuant," who was also to be fined £10 for his misconduct. It is important to remember that the common law had not as yet reached the point where prohibitions were directed against the Admiralty Court; for the moment, the restrictions and penalties were directed against individual litigants.

Caesar was well versed in the statutory provisions circumscribing the Lord Admiral's authority, but he doubted that such legislation could limit the royal prerogative, and it was the prerogative on which his authority rested. Parliament had, after all, not spoken with a consistent voice. In one act the jurisdiction of the Admiralty Court had been limited; in another that same jurisdiction had been expanded, giving to the High Court of Admiralty powers that exceeded its original mandate.[17] In rebuttal, the common lawyers noted that legislative expansion of the admiralty's jurisdiction simply emphasized their conviction that the court's authority was dependent on legislation. According to this line of reasoning, the court was subject to Parliament and not to the prerogative. This point of fundamental disagreement would eventuate in a bitter struggle between Caesar and his colleagues and their rivals. This struggle, and the demands of the privateering war, constituted the principal business during Caesar's years in office. A detailed examination of the issues dividing the common lawyers from the judges of the prerogative courts will clarify for us the problems that Caesar faced.

Serious questions regarding the province of the prerogative and of the prerogative courts were complicated by equally serious questions of judicial competence raised by the civilians about their common-law colleagues. The common lawyers, for all of their asserted supremacy, could not replace the admiralty because they lacked expertise in mercantile affairs and because of certain important limitations that the common law placed on its own authority. The common-law venue requirements, when applied to admiralty causes that arose outside the "Bodies of the Counties of England," made it impossible for the common-law courts to try such disputes. Not until the sixteenth century had there been sufficient evolution in common-law procedure to facilitate incursions into the admiralty jurisdiction and to permit the common lawyers to present a fully developed alternative to the Lord Admiral's authority. The alternative was realized through the use of a patent legal fiction.

In an overseas mercantile case where the locus of a cause of action was, in fact, foreign, common-law writs asserted that the locus was, in law, domestic, being situated "in the parish of St. Mary le Bow, in the Ward of Cheap."[18] This legal fiction was an extension of the theory underlying the writ of trespass. Originally, an action in trespass could be brought only in the county where the property on which the trespass had been committed was located. As the doctrine of trespass was expanded to include trespass on the person as a means to recover damages suffered for bodily injury—for tort, in other words—a distinction between "local" and "transitory" actions was made. Trespass on property was local in nature, while trespass on the person was transitory. The courts came to favor the transitory plea unless the nature of the action clearly mandated the local plea to assure proper litigation. Because goods were not fixed in one location, trespass on goods became a transitory action. Thus, it made no difference whether the port of Cádiz was in Spain or in the ward of Cheap because the defendant could not traverse the plea (i.e., deny an allegation of fact, thus invalidating the pleading) merely on the grounds that the venue was improper. The action was transitory by definition, dealing with the goods themselves and not their location. It was necessary to allege the fiction in order to get the action into a common-law court in the first place. When a defendant objected to the venue, the plaintiff answered that it made no difference because the action was transitory, and proceeded with the case.

For the common-law courts to assert jurisdiction in overseas causes was one thing; for them to enforce their subsequent judgments was quite another. Here the courts were greatly assisted by the two new actions, assumpsit and trover, which supplemented the fiction. Assumpsit was an actionable agreement, made valid not by a writing but by the acceptance of some valuable consideration. Trover was a means by which the value of illegally converted personal property could be recovered, although the property itself could not be seized.[19] Prior to the writ of assumpsit, the common law had no means of enforcing foreign contracts, the mainstay of the merchants who dealt in charter parties (i.e., ocean transport contracts and agreements to perform services or obligations in foreign ports). Assumpsit did away with the necessity of a written contract, made and performed in England, for it permitted enforcement upon the allegation of valuable consideration given. Because of this new action, merchant contracts began to appear before the benches of the common-law courts, to the detriment of the High Court of Admiralty. The other new action, trover, allowed the common law to enforce title to goods, even if they were not physically present, and to seize the defendant wherever he might be. By suing a writ of trover, the plaintiff alleged that the possessor of certain property had illegally converted it to his own use and was liable for its value. Because the Admiralty Court had traditionally assumed jurisdiction over the goods of merchants engaged in overseas trade, the introduction of trover was another serious challenge. By the last quarter of the sixteenth century, the common-law courts, armed with the fiction and the new writs, effectively penetrated the hitherto exclusive domain of the High Court of Admiralty.

Important though questions of historical origins were to the contending benches, an immediate and more pressing strain on the relations between the High Court of Admiralty and the common lawyers lay in their divergent perceptions of the correct process for taking appeals from the admiralty bench. A fundamental question of authority informed this divergence because the concept of judicial appeal acknowledges a hierarchical ordering between the court of first instance and the appellate court. In most rational-legal systems, litigants wishing to lodge appeals may expect that the process will move along accustomed and predictable lines. Indeed, such predictability is the essence of due process. As we shall see, however, this was not the case when appeals were taken from the Admiralty Court to the King's Bench.

There was a formal appellate structure that applied to the High Court of Admiralty and another that applied to the common-law courts. The Admiralty Court could be appealed to the Lord Chancellor, who in turn would empower the Court of Delegates. Appeals from the common-law courts were directed to the King's Bench. But the system broke down because King's Bench also exercised a supervisorial jurisdiction over the sizable array of liberties, peculiars, and special courts responsible for limited jurisdictions (such as the Piepowder Courts). From the point of view of King's Bench, the High Court of Admiralty was another special jurisdiction and, thus, subject to supervision. Needless to say, the Admiralty Court strenuously disagreed. The result of their divergent perceptions was that King's Bench gladly received appeals from the admiralty without that court's consent and, in many instances, before judgment was delivered.

Before the Reformation, the two principal civilian courts, the ecclesiastical courts and the High Court of Admiralty, had their own separate procedures for the dispatch of appeals. The church courts sent appeals up through the church hierarchy, whereas the judgments of the admiralty court were appealed directly to the crown, after which appropriate commissions were appointed to hear the cause. Following the Reformation, it became necessary to establish a domestic appeals procedure for the courts christian because their hierarchy now terminated in the monarch rather than in Rome. The procedure the admiralty had been using for some time was made to apply to the church courts as well. In the Act for the Submission of the Clergy (1534), Parliament declared that ecclesiastical appeals were to be submitted to the crown in Chancery. Thereafter, commissions would be constituted of "such persons as shall be named by the King's highness . . . like as in the cases of appeal from the Admiral court to hear and definitively determine such appeals and causes concerning the same."[20] Thus, the church courts and the Admiralty Court came to share a common appeals tribunal known as the High Court of Delegates. Its principal drawback was that it had no permanent personnel. It only had life when the Lord Chancellor, after receiving an appeal, determined a list of commissioners, issued the commissions, convened the court, and submitted the appeal for their consideration. This was a slow process, and it is not surprising to discover that the appellants, dissatisfied with this way of doing business, sought different and faster avenues of appeal.

King's Bench, with its supervisorial authority, was able to intervene quickly in the affairs of other courts that it deemed inferior; thus, it was to the King's Bench that litigants turned for redress. When King's Bench was asked by a party to take cognizance of a case, it would issue a writ of prohibition ordering the recipient court to stop all further action and to transfer all documents in the case to King's Bench, where the case would continue under the procedures of the common law.

Caesar was well aware of the problems presented by the prohibitions, and, after studying the law, he realized that there were simply too many avenues of appeal open to a disgruntled or obstructionist party. As a case in the Admiralty Court neared its conclusion, either party could remove it to the King's Bench without giving notice to the admiralty judge. Even when he did learn of the appeal, the judge lacked the power to stop these attempts to change jurisdiction; until that time, the case languished in limbo, since no final decree could be made until the appeal was heard. But the grounds for removing an action were rarely appeals to a judgment because a judgment had yet to be made. Instead, these were appeals challenging the sufficiency of the jurisdiction of the Admiralty Court. More than a decade before, Caesar's predecessor, David Lewes, had been faced with a similar problem, but in 1575 he had reached an agreement with the Lord Chief Justice of the King's Bench and his colleagues allowing the admiralty to get on with its business with less interruption.[21]

Their agreement stipulated that the common-law courts would no longer interfere with an admiralty cause after the Court of Delegates had reached a decision on appeal and a grace period of two law terms was provided for an appeal to be lodged. After that time had lapsed, if there were no appeals, then the prohibition could proceed as usual. Furthermore, contrary to its long-standing policy, the King's Bench allowed the High Court of Admiralty to appear at prohibition hearings to raise objections and to defend its jurisdiction. Lewes had extracted this concession in order to restrain prohibitions based purely on surmise and hearsay, as well as to reduce the mounting instances of litigious harassment. The common lawyers also agreed that the High Court of Admiralty had sole authority over contracts made on and beyond the seas, and over charter parties (i.e., agreements to carry goods) undertaken for overseas voyages, even though the instrument itself was negotiated on English terra firma, the most fundamental test of common-law jurisdiction. In these matters, no stay or prohibition of any kind was to be permitted. In order to restore the King's Bench

and the High Court of Admiralty to an acceptable status quo, the Lord
Chief Justice promised to return to the Lord Admiral's custody those
prisoners who had been summoned to the King's Bench by a writ of
corpus cum causa.[22] The *corpus cum causa* required that the prisoner
and his action be brought into the King's Bench, as opposed to the *habeas corpus*, which was concerned with the person of the prisoner.[23]
The Lord Chief Justice did not return the cause to the High Court of
Admiralty, for he intended to keep the matter for trial, but he did permit the prisoner to be returned to the Marshalsea, thus preserving the
integrity of the Lord Admiral's power of arrest and quieting the frequent complaint that a prisoner in the custody of the Admiralty Court
could be enlarged on virtually any pretext.

For a time, in 1575, the courts had momentarily agreed to cooperate, but their basic differences had not been settled. The central courts
did not seriously object to the singularity of admiralty jurisdiction in
matters of waterborne disputes and offences. Their quarrel was over
the particular question of the competence of the High Court of Admiralty to adjudicate contractual causes and charter parties, both
those made in England and those made beyond the seas. While the
Lord Chief Justice had suffered the Admiralty Court to continue to exercise jurisdiction in those matters, he had not recognized any clearly
defined, unimpeachable right. Appeals were still to be taken to the
central common-law courts, although with certain limitations that
could be withdrawn at the Lord Chief Justice's pleasure. By the time
that Caesar sat on the admiralty bench, Lewes's agreement with the
Lord Chief Justice was a dead letter.

Although the most potent weapon of the King's Bench was the prohibition, it could, nonetheless, be challenged. If the prohibited litigant
in the inferior court could demonstrate that the court was, in fact,
competent to try the matter at hand, a prohibition could be rebutted.
In the event that a court could show that it was competent to try a case
or that its jurisdiction extended to the subject matter of the case, the
writ of prohibition would be vacated by another writ from Chancery,
known as a consultation. The consultation confirmed the original
jurisdiction, using the important phrase *prohibitione nostra non obstante*. Because the High Court of Admiralty had, in 1575, secured the
right to challenge prohibitions in the King's Bench, a successful appearance in that court would lead, eventually, to the issuing of a consultation.

In the dusty disorder of the High Court of Admiralty Miscellany, in the Public Record Office, lies a box containing two bundles of documents that constitute the extant prohibitions and consultations of the court.[24] The bundles purport to span the years from the reign of Henry VIII through the reign of Charles I, but it is evident from the prohibitions commented on in the *Acts of Privy Council* alone that the contents of the bundles in the Admiralty Miscellany hardly scratch the surface. Nevertheless, these bundles indicate a favorable ratio of consultations to prohibitions, of successes to failures, in the admiralty's attempt to foil the denial of its lawful jurisdiction by King's Bench. Among the documents are nineteen that relate to Caesar's years as judge, but, of the nineteen items, only four are prohibitions. The remaining fifteen are consultations. Thus, there were three successful consultations for every prohibition that was allowed to stand. The ratio must, of course, be severely qualified in the light of the patchy evidence on which it is based; but if this ratio could be extrapolated to all prohibitions that the Admiralty received during Caesar's years, it would seem that, although the judge and the Lord Admiral were kept busy defending the court, the defense was successful. We must remember that every consultation began as a prohibition that was received in the admiralty, contested in the King's Bench, and vacated in Chancery.

Even though the King's Bench seemed to have plenary authority to prohibit actions in the High Court of Admiralty, it could not act unless one of the litigants from the admiralty came to the court seeking relief. After Coke came to the Common Pleas as Lord Chief Justice in 1606, the King's Bench had to share the prohibiting power; after 1610, Coke managed to secure for Common Pleas the exclusive authority to prohibit, on its own initiative, without the necessity of a litigant bringing the action. Common Pleas could, and did, intervene whenever it chose to do so.[25] By that time, however, Caesar had left the Admiralty Court, although he continued to be interested in its problems.

To conclude this discussion of intercourt hostility over the question of superior jurisdiction, several specific instances will illustrate not only the dimensions of the problem but also the manipulation of uncertain procedures by clever litigants. In the first instance, arising in 1584, Lord Admiral Lincoln begged the queen to restrain the Lord Chief Justice of the King's Bench and his colleagues from interfering with the Admiralty Court. One Percy of Norfolk, who had been sued in the admiralty by a "certain Portingall" merchant, had procured a prohibition against the complainant on the ground that the Admiralty Court had no authority to hear the case. After taking legal advice, Walsingham wrote to the King's Bench that, because "this cause is said to be determined properly by the cyvill law and in the Admiraltie, her Majestys pleasure is and so hath her highness willed me to signify unto you that your Lordship and the rest of your associate judges of the said court have a special care not only in this matter of Percie and the Portingall, but in all other like matters concerning the Admiraltie, that the same being triable by mere civill lawe be not admitted to triall before you at the common law, which of these marine and forraine causes is thought not soe properly and aptly [for you] to take knowledge." But Walsingham's directive was easily ignored because in the very next sentence he indicated that the justices' discretion would ultimately determine whether they heard a case or not. Admiralty jurisdiction was to be respected "unless the matter shall appeare soe manifestly to be triable by the common lawe as that you may and will so warrant it."[26] And in the Percy case, as Caesar forlornly reported, King's Bench was not returning the trial to the admiralty.[27]

Lincoln, an old man in 1584, wrote to his brothers of Privy Council that, "if speedie order not be taken [in Percy's case], all other causes in that court, being of the same nature with this [i.e., a contract made and performed overseas] will be carried away with the like prohibitions contrary to expresse lawe, and to her majesties prerogative in such causes." If Council would stand with the Admiralty Court, Lincoln indicated that it would "greatly comfort me in myne old yeres, who ame desirous to mainteine the reputation and credit of that Court during my life."[28]

Several years later, the problem was no closer to a solution, although Lincoln was no longer alive to be disturbed by it. Several Welshmen had committed piracy on some French ships, and the stolen goods had found their way, mala fide, into the possession of one Tobie French of Cardiff. When he was served a warrant demanding the surrender of the goods, under bond, into the custody of the Admiralty Court, French refused to obey. He continued his defiance from prison, saying that he would rather remain in custody than pay the fine for his disobedience. This was not a remarkable situation; many a man cooled off in prison before purging himself of contempt. But French procured a writ of *habeas corpus* returnable in

King's Bench. Caesar would not honor the writ because French was an accessory to a maritime felony punishable only by the Lord Admiral. The judge reported this to Burghley and advised him that the only authorities having jurisdiction in the case were himself and the Commissioners for French Causes.[29] Nonetheless, the *habeas corpus* was enforced, and Tobie French soon was enlarged.

Occasionally, the processes of the common law were employed not to appeal the jurisdiction of the Admiralty Court but to stop it dead in its tracks by attacking its personnel. There could be no more unequivocal statement of the asserted superiority of King's Bench than a lawsuit directed against an officer of the admiralty for performing his duties. A striking instance of this behavior is found in the matter of an admiralty constable who was sued for trespass by a certain Linier of Ipswich because the constable had executed an admiralty process on him. When he learned of the suit, Caesar was furious. He had Linier arrested, and he intended to keep him in prison until he dismissed the action against the constable. If stern countermeasures were not taken, no command or order could be given by the admiralty because no officer would place himself in jeopardy.[30] Unfortunately, we do not know the outcome of this particular action, but Linier might have followed in the tradition of Tobie French by suing a writ of *habeas corpus*. Such a move would have been in perfect accord with the tactics used by litigants who took advantage of the wars between the courts.

Caesar was himself sued in the King's Bench for his zealous protection of the rights of his court. He had initiated a suit in the Admiralty Court against an official of the Lord Mayor of London, Simon Nicholas, "for measuring [weighing and sealing] coals at Wiggins Key, in the parish of St. Dunstan in the East."[31] Caesar considered coal measuring on a tidal river to be an admiralty prerogative, but the City claimed a traditional right to weigh and seal coal on the Thames, and it submitted extracts from ancient charters to prove its point. The Admiralty Court based its jurisdiction on the location of Wiggins Quay: below the first bridge on the river and within the limits of the high water at flood tide. There was an additional grievance: the City had established a public office of coal measurer. For coal to be sold within the City, it had to bear the seal of the new City official. Caesar and the Lord Admiral considered this to be extortion.

Serjeant Fleetwood, appearing for the Corporation, prayed that a prohibition be awarded by King's Bench to stop any further action on Caesar's suit in the High Court of Admiralty. The writ was awarded, thus bringing Caesar into King's Bench as a defendant in the City's action. Two grounds were advanced for awarding the prohibition: that Wiggins Quay lay within the common-law definition of the "Body of the County" and that the judges did not want to allow Caesar to lay a bill *ex officio judicis* before himself. Wray, J., wrote that Caesar should not "be both plaint[iff and] the judge, and that his jurisdiction should [not] be tried before himself. Mr. Solicitor Egerton, appearing for Caesar and the Admiralty Court, tried to soften the justices' opinion, saying that the Lord Admiral believed the Lord Mayor was guilty of extortion. If Egerton thought that this would appease the court, he misjudged them. Wray and Goodwin, J.J., held that there was no remedy for extortion in the Admiralty Court, such a remedy being available only at common law. Gawdy, J., added that any redress should be sought in a quo warranto proceeding. Although there was a question of the propriety of Caesar's actions, the Admiralty Court was struggling to maintain its own jurisdiction and privileges. The common lawyers were equally determined to stop them.

The war between the courts was subject, ultimately, to the good offices of the Privy Council, which could not allow an internal dispute to disrupt the delicate diplomacy surrounding the privateering war. When an agent of the rebellious United Provinces, Mr. Ortell, sought Council's permission for several of his countrymen to circumvent Caesar's court, where their cause had been stalled for more than a year, he was refused.[32] Had Council decided for the Dutch, they would have provided the common lawyers with even more evidence that the High Court of Admiralty was incompetent and unable to manage its own affairs. On another occasion, the Council was petitioned by some English merchants who wanted Caesar to satisfy their several claims against a Spaniard doing business in London. Caesar had given judgment in their favor, but, because the case was under prohibition from the King's Bench, the judge was not able to enforce his decree without assistance from Council. In this instance, a conciliar letter was sent to the Lord Chief Justice and his associates requiring them to allow Caesar to satisfy the claims against the Spaniard.[33] Caesar was thus forced to depend on the Privy Council to enforce his own sentences.

As we noted earlier, the real beneficiaries in the conflict of jurisdictions were the litigants who were clever enough to play one court off against another, raising a smokescreen to cover their own actions while confusing their opponents with their maneuvers. William Holliday of London, a promoter of privateering ventures, was a brilliant practitioner of these masterfully executed delaying techniques.[34] Holliday had spoiled a number of Dutch ships and sold their goods in Barbary. The United Provinces complained of Holliday's attacks on their merchants' ships, and their agent, Michael Leeman, was granted a commission by the High Court of Admiralty to recover the losses. When Leeman executed the commission, Holliday sued him in the King's Bench for an action in trover for £6,000. Leeman was being held liable for carrying out the mandate of the High Court of Admiralty, as the constable in the Linier case had been. Yet in the following year, 1597, when Privy Council discovered what Holliday had done, they notified the King's Bench of his duplicity, and his arrest and imprisonment for contempt and perjury followed. Holliday agreed to a negotiated settlement, with Caesar and the Lord Chief Justice serving as arbitrators. He also agreed to stay his action against Leeman.[35] Holliday, who appeared to be repentent, was released from prison on the condition that he perform certain obligations as part of the settlement. Once released, however, Holliday failed to abide by the settlement, and he was returned to custody, adamant in his renewed contempt.[36] A fortnight later, Caesar, the Attorney General, and the Solicitor were commisioned to examine Holliday once more because he had made another offer to comply with the order. The commissioners were to determine whether Holliday had the means to pay and whether he was, in fact, stalling or prepared to obey.[37] The whole prolonged controversy had been permitted to involve the time and the energies of the principal legal officers of the kingdom simply because Holliday had had available an alternative to the process of the High Court of Admiralty that he had used skillfully to confound his opponents.

In the last decades of the sixteenth century, the High Court of Admiralty was not the only court that found itself fending off the intrusions of prohibitions. The Court of Requests, with which Caesar was also associated after 1591, faced a similar attack and was more vulnerable than the admiralty. Nonetheless, it was the admiralty that attracted the most attention, not only from Caesar but also from William Lambarde, the legal scholar, and Francis Clerke, an attorney in the court, who rose to the defense of the Lord Admiral's jurisdiction in the face of the assertive common lawyers.

When the common lawyers analyzed the propriety of any court that they regarded as a rival, they employed a threefold test of legitimacy. Sir Charles Ogilvie has written that "the Common Lawyers had evolved a theory that to be legal a Court of Law must have been established by Ancient Commission, or ordinance; or by statute; or have existed from time immemorial."[38] Ironically, Caesar and his colleagues, civilians rather than common lawyers, defended their courts precisely in these terms: by uncovering their immemorial antiquity, displaying the royal patents by which they were institutionalized, and citing the statutory authority they had from time to time received. Although, as we have already noted, the High Court of Admiralty had its origins both in the *lex mercatoria* and in the reserved powers of the crown's prerogative, the common lawyers were unimpressed by this recitation of classical origins because they were not English. Thus, attempts to defend the court had to adduce its domestic antiquity and assert the crown's unassailable prerogative.

Francis Clerke observed that "the jurisdiction of the sea and overflowen [i.e., tidal] places are manifestlie and undoubtedlie knowne to be fixed to the imperiall crowne of this realme" because all power and dignity of justice emanated from the prince into the "two severall governments [of justice] as they are separate in nature and place."[39] To Clerke's observation should be added Lambarde's paraphrase of John Britton, Edward I's legal genius. Lambarde recalled that Britton had clearly indicated that those areas of the law over which no specific court had jurisdiction remained in the "soverainge jurisdiccion of all causes in the kinge, so that whatsoever the kinge hath not particularly delivered out to others his justices, Commissioners and delegates, that still remayned in himself, and was exercised either by himself in person, or by his Chauncellor, Councellors of estate and justices of lawe that contynually attended on him for that service."[40] The civilians were certain that the jurisdiction of the Admiralty Court was as old as the monarch's inherent powers to dispense justice. While the common lawyers would have agreed that the king had these powers, they were unwilling to accept his right to delegate them outside of their own courts.

There was no doubt that all justice in the kingdom was royal in origin. As Clerke noted, the prince had entrusted elements of his omnicompetent authority to be "exercised by several officers applying themselves to minister justice in ther severall courts."[41] This statement was axiomatic among civilians and common lawyers; the difficult problem arose when the civilians tried to ascertain the date of the prince's transfer of his authority to the Lord Admiral. If this transfer, or grant, of authority could be unequivocally established, then another of the three tests of jurisdictional legitimacy would be satisfied. William Lambarde held that "the decision of marine causes was not put out of the kings house and committed over to the chardge of the Admirall until the tyme of Edward 3."[42] Lambarde fixed the date in Edward III's reign because of the reference in 13 Richard II, st. 1, cap. 5, to the restoration of the Lord Admiral's authority to its status during the reign of Richard II's grandfather, Edward III. Caesar was not satisfied with Lambarde's dating because it was too modern; he wanted to discover the greatest possible antiquity for his court. Lambarde, who was "verie learned otherwise, was mistaken in his opinion of the Lord Admiralls beginning."[43] Historically interesting though Caesar's observation was, all that he produced in his attempt to correct Lambarde was a list of earlier incumbents in the Lord Admiral's place. No new light was shed on the origin of admiralty jurisdiction or on the antiquity of the prince's investment of his prerogative powers in his lieutenant.

Holdsworth has stated that there was no specific date for the foundation of the court, although the legal powers granted in the patents of various Lord Admirals help to trace the development of its jurisdiction. We cannot make a strong case for an Admiralty Court of ancient origin, nor can we discover precisely when it was that the crown placed its marine authority in the hands of the court; the statutory evidence is not conclusive. Although one of the three criteria advanced by Ogilvie can be convincingly satisfied, Caesar contended that the jurisdiction of the High Court of Admiralty could trace its origin to the royal prerogative, and thus could not be contravened by the common law.

Caesar's characteristic reply to the flood of prohibitions from the King's Bench was another extensive memorandum, a "briefe note," as he described it, spelling out the reasons why the King's Bench should be prevented from interfering with the High Court of Admiralty any further. The note was written in 1592 with the assistance of two other civilians, but there is no indication that it was ever circulated. Nevertheless, the memorandum was Caesar's brief when he defended his court.[44]

The "briefe note" argued that the use of prohibitions to stay admiralty causes was an unwarranted and dangerous innovation and a perversion of their original purpose. Before the English Reformation, as we have noted, when the courts christian were extensions of a foreign jurisdiction, it had been necessary to stop proceedings in the church courts and to remove them to the king's jurisdiction. But it was a dangerous innovation when one domestic bench employed the prohibition against another domestic bench, both of them royal courts. That the High Court of Admiralty was a royal court was clearly stated in the Lord Admiral's letters patent; common-law assertions to the contrary could not alter this basic fact. Indeed, there had been various statutes limiting the authority of the Admiralty Court, but Caesar relegated them to secondary importance because no statute could limit the queen's prerogative to extend the jurisdiction of her courts as she saw fit. The queen was always "seized without impeachment of any law, in the right of her imperiall crowne of this realme, of all jurisdiction as well by sea as by land."[45] In this right she could commission the Lord Admiral in any fashion she chose with whatever authority she wished to vest in him. The court of England had always been vested with the crown's authority to dispense justice according to their particular competence (e.g., King's Bench, Common Pleas, Chancery, Admiralty), but the High Court of Admiralty had enjoyed an additional peculiar distinction. Caesar likened the autonomous authority of duchies, principalities, and counties palatine to the authority of the Admiralty Court. In these provinces, as in the provinces of the Roman empire, there were plenipotentiaries who exercised viceregal powers delegated to them by the central authority. Caesar believed that the High Court of Admiralty's jurisdiction over the sea was a provincial jurisdiction, and that the Lord Admiral was the plenipotentiary.

Caesar's assertions of absolute prerogative authority were tempered by his belief that there were reciprocal responsibilities between those who exercised the prerogative and the queen who delegated it. The queen could delegate this authority as she chose, and she was entitled to expect a high level of competence from her delegates—in this instance, the Lord Admiral and his court. Absent those qualities, the prerogative would be abused. In order to assure this competence and expertise, Caesar emphasized the importance of employing civil lawyers in the court. While he wrote at length about the prerogative courts and the civilians, his view was myopic. Star Chamber, the Court of Wards, and the Duchy Court were never mentioned in his writings because, although they were "prerogative" courts, they were not courts in which civilians played any part. It was, after all, the beleagured civilian and his quest for place and profit that occupied the judge's mind.

The civilians in the Admiralty Court possessed experience and expertise to perform functions that exceeded the abilities of the common lawyers. Although the common lawyers were well trained and experienced in the trial of causes arising within the counties of England, "where the eye of the jurors may give them the intelligence to enquire and give verdict of truth in fact of all controversies," at sea and in foreign lands, the civil law possessed unique advantages. The procedural rules of the civilians were common to most of Europe, and they were well suited to the circumstances of causes arising where no English juror's eye could assist in determining the facts. "The civill lawes imperiall were best suited for the sea: which for that by long continuance in the most flurishing commonwealth of Rome, they have been many ages since, the most perfect and equal lawes of the world and are generally received throughout al nations about us." Consequently, the civil law was esteemed "not onely the most fittest for our traffick and other dealing with straungers, but also (for such causes as concerne the sea) are most necessary to bee practised amongst our selves."[46]

Having made his case for the superior qualifications of civilians in admiralty causes, Caesar turned to another concern, quite political in nature. If the several courts were allowed to proceed as they wished, intervening in the business of other courts, no bench would be safe even though its jurisdiction was stipulated. The queen's letters patent to the Lord Admiral expressly delineated the limits of his court's authority; hence, "it cannot seeme to bee laweful for magistrates of the land to prohibit the course of the said commission within those limits without greate impeachment of her highness prerogative and power and unjust injury of theire equall."[47] The common lawyers might advance statutes as their justification for their actions, but, as Caesar had asserted time and again, no statute could impeach the queen's prerogative. The queen was the governor and regulator, keeping the courts and other agencies of government from internal warfare; the power that allowed her to function in this capacity was her prerogative. It followed, then, that the prerogative had to remain beyond the reach of any component of government, including Parliament. When the queen's powers and statute law were in conflict, she always had at her disposal the authority and the means to enforce her will by invoking "a clause *non obstante*."[48]

The *non obstante* ("notwithstanding") clause was an omnibus exception of the prerogative from the force of statute law that could be invoked only by the queen. We encounter the *non obstante* in the letters patent of 8 July 1585 that vested in Charles Howard full jurisdiction, power, and authority to hear and determine all civil and maritime causes among merchants, ships' owners, and sailors wherever and whenever they might arise. His authority extended both to those causes arising *in partibus ultramarinis* and to any allied causes, be they at home or overseas. Provision was made for the Lord Admiral's jurisdiction over contracts, debts, spoils, and the droits of the crown. In executing the office, the Lord Admiral exercised the full powers of the crown, including the power to inhibit anyone who might encroach on his authority. The entire tone of the grant of authority was set in the opening words, *concessiones facte*, and in the phrase that appeared near the end of the document, *non obstante statuto*.[49] Both phrases explicitly asserted the queen's untrammeled prerogative.

In *The Fourth Institutes*, Sir Edward Coke, the nemesis of the civilians, took the *non obstante* clause and its relationship to the Admiralty Court as his text when he addressed the far larger question of the relationship between the crown's prerogative and the common law. Coke wrote on the *non obstante* following Elizabeth's death, when he began to oppose the crown. Yet his writings reflect a position that had been forming throughout the queen's long reign. Although the *non obstante* was employed in Howard's patent of office to give him the same freedom from statutory restrictions that the queen herself enjoyed, Coke ignored that issue, declaring simply that no statute could be dispensed with by the words *non obstante statuto*. He believed that any question of the validity of this expression of the prerogative was "therefore not worthy of an answer."[50] Coke reflected the common lawyers' conviction that the Admiralty Court was not a court of record and, thus, could have no standing in the law of the land. Furthermore, he was firm in rejecting any suggestion that the monarch had the power either to alter or to set aside the statute law.

By 1592 Caesar was finding the common lawyers' premises increasingly untenable. He cited such continental authorities as Zarius, who held that the prince's power to set aside the statute "is grounded uppon that most certaine observation that every prince imperially raigning is at free libertie for all lawes possitive to annihilate the same."[51] Caesar added that this sovereign power did not extend to the impeachment "of the lawe of nations and nature." Nonetheless, if common lawyers wanted to defend their prohibitions and attack the Admiralty Court, using the supremacy of statute as their sword and buckler, then Caesar was prepared to turn the evidence around and use statutory authority against the attackers.

Earlier in this chapter, we discussed the pre-Reformation origin of the writ of prohibition. The statutes that introduced the writ made no mention of the High Court of Admiralty. Thus, since there was nothing of an ecclesiastical nature involved in the substance of admiralty causes, the lay magistrates of the common law had "no warrant to countermaund the jurisdiction of their equall by anie such courses in the exercise of the marine authoritie graunted them by commission." If litigants believed that the Lord Admiral had overstepped his authority or that they had been injured by him, there was a suitable procedure for seeking redress. The High Court of Delegates, convened at the order of the Lord Chancellor, was the proper authority, established by statute, for settling grievances against the Lord Admiral and his court. Caesar readily pointed out that this was a statutory provision, first enacted in the Act for the Submission of the Clergy and later confirmed by the act of 8 Elizabeth I, cap. 5. The common lawyers made several unsuccessful attempts, in the last quarter of the sixteenth century, to have the Court of Delegates abolished and to assume its authority. The civilians, for their part, discussed the establishment of an appellate division of the Admiralty Court. Neither the abolition of the Court of Delegates nor the establishment of an appellate division came to anything; and, as Caesar pointed out, the decision of the Delegates had to be "taken as finall in all civill and marine causes, and no further appeale or complaint to anie other court was allowed."[52]

Caesar brought his "briefe note" to a conclusion by restating the queen's pleasure that the Lord Admiral should enjoin all of her subjects to obey the terms of the letters patent by which she perpetuated the court, "uppon pain of contempte and perill ensueng." Howard would employ only legal means to secure the integrity of his court, and, as Caesar almost ironically alleged, he "shall avoyde all such impeachments of the landcourt, offered nowe commonly at every common mans sute upon bare untrue suggestions to the damage of her highnes imperiall crowne of this realme, and to the overthrowe of that settled government which hath alwaies remained in the same, to the great encrease of traffick and navigation." As if to assure himself of the ancient order of the "settled government," Caesar added the following phrase: *"ordinatis fuit tempore E. 1 an. reg. 2*, that all marine causes shoulde be tried before the Lord Admirall."[53]

The protracted struggle between the Admiralty Court and the common lawyers was an early skirmish in the conflict over jurisdiction (and profits) that characterized the early seventeenth century. At this early stage, Privy Council had perhaps the best opportunity available to any agency to moderate the assertions of the common lawyers, but even the Council was not assured of its ability to curb the behavior of the central courts.

It was apparent that piecemeal attempts to quiet the struggle were getting nowhere; the Admiralty Court continued to complain bitterly of the conduct of the prohibiting central courts. Eight years later, on 4 February 1600, the Council commissioned the Attorney General, the Solicitor General, Mr. Serjeant Yelverton, and Mr. Francis Bacon to determine among themselves how the common law might accord the High Court of Admiralty the dignity and respect that were due to it in the light of the queen's expressed favor and of its long history as a principal central court. The queen's subjects had been complaining to her of long delays in the Admiralty Court that were occasioned by writs of prohibition. In some cases, these delays were leading to court costs that exceeded the value of the goods to be recovered in the action. The commissioners were reminded that the court had an especial responsibility for dealing with foreign powers in the queen's name and, thus, should be enabled to dispense justice quickly. Caesar was to meet with the commissioners, who, in turn, were to meet with the judges of the King's Bench and the Common Pleas.[54] The results of this commission were lukewarm admonitions that provided no alleviation of the pressure on the admiralty's jurisdiction.

The contest with the common-law courts had been a significant drain on Caesar's energies during his tenure on the admiralty bench.

But when Caesar also became a Master of Requests in 1591, he encountered in that arena even more acrimonious and destructive competition with the common law. Such was the lot of a civilian at a time when the law that he practiced and professed was perceived to be a statement of an unpopular, and eventually untenable, political position. Turning to Caesar's parallel career as a Master of Requests, we shall examine how he procured the office, how he continued his struggle with the common lawyers once he had arrived, and how he used the Admiralty Court and the Court of Requests in tandem.

III

The Last but Not the Least

WHEN CAESAR BECAME the permanent judge of the High Court of Admiralty, he was not yet thirty. His progress from occasional piracy commissioner to judge had been phenomenal. His early successes were a testimony to his abilities, to be sure, but they owed at least as much to his unusually rich corps of patrons who gave him their assistance. But as the eighties drew to a close, there were fewer places available, both because a larger population created more aspirants and because the costs of war imposed extraordinary economies on the queen's treasure. A dangerous bottleneck in the upward flow of advancement was developing, costs were escalating rapidly, and, to make matters all the more difficult, an aging queen was growing ever meaner in distributing wealth and favor. In these altered circumstances, the younger Elizabethans found that fewer and fewer opportunities for advancement were being chased by more and more candidates.

Caesar met the new circumstances with dogged persistence, calling even more frequently on Burghley, Walsingham, and Howard. Their efforts in his behalf had been so often successful that providing for Caesar's well-being appeared a natural extension of their own high offices. Yet Caesar dared not relax his pursuit of advancement, for a client could easily be forgotten by his patrons if he did not continually promote his cause. Caesar's flood of letters to his many patrons assured that his interests could not easily be overlooked. Exaggeration was a commonplace in his letters: witness an early instance in a note to Walsingham written a few months after Caesar assumed the admiralty bench. The young judge suggested that he ought "in discretion

[to] seeke rest rather than further travell" because his duties occupied so much of his time.[1]

A careful reading of Caesar's massive correspondence with his patrons shows that, while he appeared to reach for any and all opportunities for promotion, he had a specific career goal at or near the top of the Chancery establishment. Throughout his professional life, Caesar was most frequently associated with Chancery, the court in which a civilian had unique opportunities to prosper. Although a civilian could be appointed Lord Chancellor, in practice the highest public office open to a civil lawyer was that of the Master of the Rolls, who was effectively the deputy Lord Chancellor. In time, Caesar would occupy that place, but in the interim, he progressed through lesser Chancery offices. He began his upward climb as a Master in Chancery at about the same time that he was seeking a permanent commission in the High Court of Admiralty. After he was secure in these offices, he turned his attention to a Mastership of Requests. Taken together, offices in Chancery, Admiralty Court, and the Requests would provide practical experience and exposure, all the better to prepare him to become Master of the Rolls. But this observation carries us far ahead of the story.

His contemporaries in 1588, especially among the civilians, would have counted Caesar a success. He held important offices, and his prestige was ascendant. But Caesar was not satisfied; he wanted to take his place among the queen's advisors at Court. In his capacity as judge and Master in Chancery, Caesar was a senior member of the permanent establishment of crown officers. He was an executor and administrator of crown policy, including law, but he was not a policy maker, and he only occasionally gave political advice. The transition from the upper reaches of the executive and administrative echelon to the arena of policy advising and policy making had to be accomplished in stages: he could not expect to be advanced from judge to Councillor or advisor in one move. Hence, Caesar's next short-term objective was a place as a Master of Requests. The transition from the Admiralty Court to a place in Elizabeth's personal service as a Master of Requests was achieved following a course of parallel advancement in admiralty (from surrogate to permanent judge) and in Chancery (from extraordinary to ordinary Master). Only after these places were secure did Caesar launch a sustained effort to enter the Requests.

Armed with powerful patrons and multiple offices, Caesar pursued his goal. Yet it was uncommon for one so young who had achieved so much to aspire to even more. Caesar's letters teem with comparative references to the awards made to his predecessor, David Lewes, and to a seated Master of Requests, John Herbert. Not yet thirty himself, Caesar was trying to match the offices that had been acquired slowly over long years of service by men who were his seniors. For them these positions represented reward for faithful service; for Caesar they were stepping stones to further advancement. Although he may not have realized it, Caesar appears to have upset a value system based on reward for service, and his behavior may well have threatened and offended those who had worked long years to achieve what he wanted at the start.

Thus, it was something of a surprise for Caesar to find that the generally unimpeded advancement that he had experienced in the admiralty and in Chancery was abruptly halted when he reached for a place in the Requests. His career was meeting resistance, a sort of surface tension that required extraordinary effort to penetrate before he could rise any further. Caesar struggled with the obstacles in his path, eventually overcoming them to emerge with the office he sought, along with the scars of a rough-and-tumble political education. As we reconstruct Caesar's efforts in detail and analyze the nature of the resistance that he faced, we shall examine his frustrations, the consequences of the queen's dilatory procedures, and the bottleneck in advancement that promised eventual political destabilization among the legions of aspirants for office in later Elizabethan England. Finally, we shall be able to assess the effects of plural office holding on a busy public officer.

Caesar's first step beyond the judgeship in the admiralty had been easily realized; it was a prelude to further advancement, but it did not signal continued success. Shortly after the old judge of the admiralty, David Lewes, died, the Lord Admiral, the earl of Lincoln, joined Walsingham in asking the Lord Chancellor to make Caesar an extraordinary Master, "as Mr. Lewys was while he lived."[2] Their petition led quickly to the swearing of the surrogate judge as an extraordinary Master in Chancery.[3]

The Chancery was served by a small number of ordinary Masters and a very much larger number of extraordinary Masters.[4] Among the extraordinary Masters were a few young Chancery careerists who were learning on the job. Their work experience would eventually prepare them to move up to be ordinary Masters when a position became vacant. But the majority of the extraordinary Masters had no aspirations within the Chancery; they were officials from other institutions who were sworn Masters in Chancery for honorific reasons, or for the convenience of their courts and agencies. As extraordinary Masters, they could administer oaths and record certain obligations without having to come into Chancery.[5]

The ordinary Master in Chancery, on the other hand, was not part of a dispersed corps of adjunct officials; he was one of eleven men who provided the administrative and quasi-judicial backbone of the equity side of Chancery. There was, technically, a twelfth ordinary Master in Chancery, the Master of the Rolls, but his position as "deputy Lord Chancellor" set him far above the rest. The ordinary Masters prepared documents, administered oaths, and presided over the complex process of taking evidence. Aided by two or three assistants who were authorized to write in his name, no Master was heavily burdened or heavily compensated. The Masters were on duty in rotation and could, therefore, satisfy their requirements of attendance upon the Lord Chancellor and still have time to serve elsewhere in public office. Thus, we find ordinary Masters in the Court of Requests, in the church courts, in the High Court of Admiralty, and in the queen's service as ambassadors or as technical advisors to the Council on civil and canon law matters.[6] In short, for the "ordinary civilian careerists . . . the [ordinary] masterships in Chancery were the highest positions to which they usually aspired."[7]

Caesar must be counted among that smaller number of extraordinary Masters who sought to secure an ordinary place. In November 1584 Walsingham and Lincoln again approached the Lord Chancellor, this time to request the award to Caesar of the next vacant ordinary Mastership.[8] Yet, regardless of their intervention on his behalf, Caesar was not sworn until the autumn of 1588, by which time there had been a vacancy for nearly a year.[9] Having attained both the ordinary Mastership and a life tenure as judge of the High Court of Admiralty, Caesar had achieved the highest positions ordinarily open to a civilian, with the sole exception of the Master of the Rolls. He was also learning that powerful patrons were not necessarily able to secure immediate results, but it would take some years for that lesson to sink in. In the meantime, he was prepared to climb another rung to a Mastership of Requests.

A Master of Requests derived his importance from his position at a particularly sensitive point in the organization of the queen's Court. A Master received incoming petitions and requests for grace and favor addressed to the queen, and he saw to their proper routing. When asked, a Master would advise the queen or make recommendations in specific cases. A Master also sat as a magistrate in the Court of Requests, an extension of the crown's prerogative responsibility to provide a tribunal for equitable remedies—in this instance, to paupers and members of the Household. An ambitious and resourceful Master of Requests could use his office as a springboard to a variety of high ministerial and judicial positions. Caesar was both resourceful and ambitious.

Caesar's strategy was to couch his suit for place in terms of both personal necessity and the advantages that a Mastership would present to the High Court of Admiralty. He asserted that his family was suffering because he worked so hard for so little compensation. The Requests would compensate by providing a supplementary income. Furthermore, Caesar insisted that there were cases peculiar to the jurisdiction of the High Court of Admiralty requiring the attention of the queen and her councillors. By Caesar's reckoning, the Admiralty Court should not have needed to involve the queen in its cases, but the fact remained that the court operated in a gray area between judicial independence and the demands of the queen's diplomacy. As a Master of Requests, Caesar would have ready access to them and could, thus, expedite the business of his own court. By implication, a mere judge was disabled by his distance from the Court. More to the point was Caesar's argument that his appointment as a Master of Requests would demonstrate to such rival courts as the King's Bench that the Admiralty Court was well favored, notwithstanding the aggressive rivalry of the common lawyers.

While frequent access to the queen would have been important for the judge, Caesar probably overstated his case. The tone and substance of his correspondence with the queen and his patrons suggest that there was no significant obstacle to Caesar's approaching the Court without being a Master of Requests. On the contrary, he did so frequently. The problem did not lie in access as such but in the expenses occasioned by journeys to Greenwich, Whitehall, St. James, and Nonesuch. These trips were undertaken without reimbursement, and it was becoming burdensome for him to pay his own costs and those of his servants—costs that multiplied with each day's postponement and delay. It made little difference whether Caesar went to see the queen's ministers (or the queen herself) at his own initiative or, more often the case, in obedience to a summons to appear; no provision was made for his room and board, nor was he given an allowance. A Mastership, however, would give Caesar a place in the queen's household and an allowance for his expenses at Court. The High Court of Admiralty would benefit because its judge would be at Court anyway and could deal with admiralty business at the same time.

The frequent summonses to Court were expensive, and the time they consumed compounded the complaints of dilatory procedure that were frequently the cause of the summonses. Most of the complaints to the queen about the High Court of Admiralty came from distressed litigants who were upset about the excessive length of time it took to settle an action: for instance, goods sequestered pending judgment might spoil or lose their value. Ships were ordered impounded but could not be found, and the failure was blamed on the court's procedures. Whatever the circumstances, when Caesar was summoned to explain to the queen or the Privy Council, he had to drop everything and obey. In the meantime, the High Court of Admiralty was left in the care of deputies recruited from Doctors' Commons who served as surrogate judges during his absence. Because the surrogates were unfamiliar with the daily routine of the court and with the details of the pending actions, they further slowed down a court that was already under scrutiny because it did not proceed more quickly. So it was that Caesar arrived at Court only to sit in various anterooms awaiting an audience. Since he could afford neither the time nor the money for a protracted stay, he often begged leave to return to London, leaving his business at Court unfinished. Another day would be lost in the future when he would have to return to Court to finish up what had been left over. Returning to London, Caesar would find that the crowded calendar of the Admiralty Court had fallen even further behind. More complaints were made, more summonses followed, more delays in the Admiralty Court eventuated; the process went full circle. Hence, Caesar found it perfectly logical that he should be given a place at Court if he were to continue to answer complaints about the Admiralty Court and to take delicate admiralty business to the Council for advice.

There were financial problems as well. It was not at all unusual for Caesar to receive a directive in the queen's name instructing him to show uncommon favor to a particular litigant. Such interference aggravated his sense of propriety; that these orders frequently cost him money from his own purse was much more painful. At the heart of the matter was the queen's desire to expedite a settlement for diplomatic reasons; it made little difference that it was often impossible to bring the parties to a settlement as quickly as the queen wished. The judge was frequently left to pay claims himself knowing that the queen would probably not reimburse him. An instance of this practice grew out of Elizabeth's solicitousness for the Scots and their interests in the wake of the execution of their queen. She wished to extend every courtesy to them, a policy that cost Caesar about £200 per annum.[10] He settled grievances for the Scots, loaned them money, and sent their ambassador's messengers on the road north with sufficient funds for the journey.[11] James VI himself wrote many letters to Caesar to express his thanks, and to borrow more money.[12] In the long run, the loans and courtesies to James and the Scots were an investment in Caesar's own future; in the short run, they were ruinously expensive.

Both Caesar's long-term goals and the immediate problems of making ends meet provided sufficient reasons for his ambition to become a Master of Requests. But the queen's reluctance to pay her servants was legend. By understaffing her services and underpaying her servants, she encouraged an extraordinarily high level of self-help among her subjects. She preferred not to make actual cash payments to her officials; instead, she awarded inherently self-supporting places in her service or the gift of the use of some portion of her wealth or her prerogative. The recipient was expected to make his money from fees (in the case of an office), from entry fines (in the case of leases of crown land), or from the fruits of the enforcement of monopolies of trade and production. While these practices seemed less costly than the payment of money, they were terribly expensive because they permitted the recipient, in the queen's name, to help himself to whatever wealth he could find, and to do so effectively beyond the queen's control. Because these practices were as widespread as they were, Caesar was understandably angered that he had been overlooked. During his years of service in the High Court of Admiralty, more than seven before he was sworn a Master of Requests, he had not received even token compensation from Elizabeth even though he was considered a principal judge. By comparison, David Lewes had received a gift or reward about every three years. The queen had awarded Caesar two-thirds of the fees from a joint commission with Valentine Dale, but the award had been made at Dale's expense, not Elizabeth's. Caesar had good cause to press any advantage in pursuit of compensation.

Although Caesar had once told Walsingham of his reluctance to continue his career because he was overworked, he had changed his mind by 1587 when he asked Essex to assist him to advance in the queen's service. Caesar was still under thirty when he asked Essex, who was just twenty-one, for his assistance. As young as they were, they had known one another for several years. Essex had been a ward of Burghley's and had received a part of his education in Cecil House; Caesar may well have been a part of the Cecil House establishment at the same time. Essex was frequently at odds with many of Caesar's prominent patrons, but he was closely allied with Francis Bacon, one of Caesar's closest friends throughout his adult life.

When he wrote to Essex, Caesar reported that his seven years' service in the Admiralty Court, dated from the first piracy commission, had been excessively costly. He alleged that, during those years, he had spent £2,100 more on his office than he had received from it, and that his father's lands, as well as the value of his wife's marriage portion, had gone to make up the deficit. In one category alone, "horsehier and my servants bourdwages at Court in attending her Majesties service," he declared that he had spent £200 annually. Furthermore, the quieting of foreign claims and foreign suitors at the queen's direction had put her in his debt for more than £190. Caesar believed that if Essex would intercede for him, he would procure a Mastership of Requests and that the Mastership would relieve him of the burden of his losses.[13] But Essex was prudent; he asked Burghley's advice. Knowing both Essex and Caesar, Burghley could tell the earl whether he approved the suit, and Essex indicated that, with Burghley's blessing, he would do what he could at Court.[14] There is no record of Burghley's reply, but an exchange of letters between Essex and Caesar indicates that they remained friends for several more years, continuing to do favors for one another.

That Caesar, a client of Burghley's, chose Essex as a patron says much about the nature of patron-client relationships in the late sixteenth century. Whereas the traditional interpretation of patronage holds that there were competing networks answering to such key patrons as Burghley, Leicester, Walsingham, or Essex, the evidence in Caesar's case suggests that there was more fluidity in the system than one would expect, and there is nothing to suggest that Caesar's circumstances were unusual.[15] In this instance, both the earl and the judge were Burghley's clients, and Caesar was also a client of Essex. Multiple lines of patronage were not unusual, and access to them was governed by the common sense and discretion of the participants: one did not offend one patron in order to seek help from another. A century earlier, exclusive bonds of allegiance obtained between clients and patrons, as the express obligations of the written indentures indicate.[16] By the end of the sixteenth century, however, exclusive personal allegiance had given way to a patronal free market in all but the most remote parts of the kingdom. A client sought the most effective patron to achieve his goals, and if the queen, the Cecils, and a handful of allied noblemen controlled the flow of patronage from the top, the freedom of the marketplace at inferior levels was tolerated. Professor Mac-Caffrey's assessment of Burghley's motives as the linchpin in the patronage system bears on this observation: "Although he did not escape the stigma of partisanship or faction, he used his immense resources, at least until the 1590's, not to build up a Cecilian party but to secure the loyalty of the great English families for the Elizabethan establishment."[17] And there was no better way to realize this goal than by allowing them to be both successful clients in their own rights and successful patrons for their own suitors. If, however, a patron stepped outside the acceptable limits of the marketplace, the results were disastrous. When Essex began to exercise his own patronage with respect to Puritans and in conferring knighthoods, and when he undertook the conduct of his own foreign policy, he exceeded the limits of the free market and began a process that would end in 1601 on the executioner's block.

After he had dealt with Essex, Caesar turned next to Burghley, his oldest patron. He told him of accounted losses of £2,700, a sum greater than he reported to Essex, and he indicated that his attention to duty had prevented his seeking private employment to supplement his income.[18] A month later, Caesar told Walsingham that his deficit had risen another £300 to a total of £3,000. He reminded Walsingham that Lewes had received gifts from the queen exceeding £300 in value.[19]

Caesar wanted to secure from the queen either a gift of equal value or an appointment as Master of Requests. While there is no reason to believe Caesar's figures, they were the basis of his pursuit of greater income. His method was clearly outlined in a postscript to his letter that is a monument in the literature of importunity.

Below his signature the judge wrote "a note of certain sutes to her majestie on behalf of Doctor Caesar." The first asked for a number of leases in reversion without fine for as much land as would be required to yield a clear annual value of 100 marks. Although this sum appears ridiculously small in the light of Caesar's alleged deficits, a recent study of reversions on crown lands has shown that these reversions were generally used to reward minor royal servants. The benefit to the recipient arose not from the annual rents but from the negotiations with the seated tenant for a new entry fine when the reversion matured: "The majority of leases in reversion were granted without any fine being charged and were given to people who had no connexion with the land which was being leased. This is because the leases in reversion were, in many cases, a delegation to the so-called reversioners of the Crown's right to levy entry fines."[20] The negotiations for new leases could produce a rich return.

If the gift of the reversions was not acceptable to the queen, Caesar told Walsingham, he would accept the first vacant deanery in the dioceses of York, Durham, Winchester, or Bath and Wells. Failing in this request, Caesar would ask for the next vacant Mastership from among three hospital establishments: St. Katharine's by the Tower, St. Cross's near Winchester, or Sherborne in County Durham. Should this supplication, likewise, not have been acceptable to the queen, Caesar wanted the Provostship of Eton College when it next fell vacant. These four alternatives were followed by a modest fifth choice that ended the list: "that it maie please her Majestie to make him one of her Masters of Requests in extraordinary and to cause him presentlie to be sworen into the place."[21]

Such a list of preferments may seem to be the product of remarkably naive expectations, yet Caesar was no innocent. It is doubtful that he entertained any serious expectation that the queen would honor his grandiose requests. Nonetheless, he chose well. As he told Walsingham, "Of the several [positions] specified in the note hereinclosed, of all which [in] myne opinion, the last is the least."[22] It may have been the least, but it was also the most likely. Caesar constructed his list to suggest to Elizabeth that the place as a Master of Requests was what he really wanted. When compared to the other preferments, it was both the most modest and the one that could easily calm the commotion that Caesar was raising in his own behalf.

Caesar's note is of particular interest, quite apart from its skillful importuning, because we rarely encounter evidence of the private calculations of a sixteenth-century Englishman. While Caesar was trying to extract a position of value from Elizabeth, he was also displaying a remarkable degree of candor about his view of the avenues of advancement open to an aspiring civilian careerist. Each of Caesar's suggestions, save for the Mastership of Requests, involved land. The first was for reversions to leases that Caesar could exploit. The remaining three—Dean, Master of Hospital, and Provost of Eton College—involved the exploitation of extensive corporate real property holdings. The management of such holdings promised to be a lucrative personal enterprise quite apart from any remuneration accompanying the position. With lands spread throughout England, the opportunities to profit from their management and to exercise extensive patronage were impressive. Yet the immediate objective of Caesar's quest was not the exploitation of land but a place as a Master of Requests. The remainder of the list had been a part of his ploy.

By April 1588, Caesar's machinations were apparently bearing fruit. Burghley had advised the queen of the judge's "pains and charges in her service," and she knew of the judge's present decrepit means. The joint efforts of Burghley, Walsingham, Essex, and perhaps Howard bore fruit. Elizabeth announced at Court in 1588 that it was her intention to swear Dr. Caesar as an extraordinary Master of Requests.[23] After so long a chase, Caesar was wary of apparent success. In a letter to Walsingham he remarked that "Isocrates taught me long sithence, that albeit every deliberacon should be long, yet the dispatch of the thing determined should be spedie." But speed had been conspicuously absent, and Caesar mused, "The better I ame both thought and spoken of by her Majestie (being fully resolved to make mee one of hir Masters of Requests) the further I ame from my admission to that place."[24] He would, perhaps, have been less disturbed had the queen been less public in making known her intentions.

Caesar was still supplicating the Lord Chancellor for an ordinary Mastership in Chancery, and he did not want the queen's promise to hurt his chances there. He placed his future in the Chancellor's hands.

An ordinary Master in Chancery, a Mr. Harris, had died, and Caesar wrote that same morning to ask after the vacancy: "I referre my selfe to your Lordships accustomed and assured favour, whether that you will bestowe Mr. Harris his place upon me according to your honorable promise, or hasten me to be sworen Master of Requests." And why was he in such a hurry? He had the queen's promise, "which I must hold as done because it was the word of a princesse," but he was concerned that the Chancellor might find that "my negligence in myne owne cause [in Chancery] might preiudice me hereafter"—hence Caesar's rush to be made either a Master in Chancery or a Master of Requests "before Mr. Harris his place be bestowed on anie other, least in expectation of one I lose both."[25]

As it turned out, Caesar had good reason to doubt the queen's intentions: Walsingham advised him that she was in no hurry to make good on her promise. "Touching your particular suite, I knowe by the answere I received from her Majestie, at my last motioning thereof, that it wilbe very offensively taken if I should importune hir in it with such expedition as you desire." The Secretary advised patience; if he were to pursue the matter presently, it would "do . . . more hurt than good" because of the queen's particular "humor."[26] Walsingham's politic advice frustrated Caesar, who thought that the time was right to apply pressure. One Master, John Herbert, was ill, and another, Ralph Rookesby, was lame; the Court of Requests needed a vigorous and healthy new Master.

Caesar advanced his cause, telling Burghley of the sorry state of the Court of Requests and insisting that he only wished to contribute to the better administration of justice.[27] But when Burghley advised him to bide his time patiently, Caesar knew that he had to comply. In a remarkable display of self-control, Caesar settled back from April until June awaiting a cue from one of his patrons. He comforted himself with the observation that "the common wealth is upheld by reward and punishment, [as] policy teacheth."[28] But such nostrums did not prevent his alleged deficit from growing to £4,000; nor, by his account, did they help him retain his wife's marriage portion or his own inheritance.[29]

If Caesar's claims of personal financial loss are to be believed, we might ask why he would risk so much with no certainty of compensation. Yet we must ask in reply what alternatives he had had since he had decided to seek high office in the queen's service. Certainly the quality of Caesar's patrons, and the initial successes that he had enjoyed, made the venture of his personal wealth in pursuit of advancement appear a prudent risk. Furthermore, as a civilian, he had quite limited paths of advancement. Thus, we find Caesar taking a reasonable risk, investing in his own future—and, at the same time, having few alternate paths to follow. Caesar had invested too much in his career to abandon it for another, and there was at that moment no office as promising for him as a place in the Court of Requests. He had simply to await the outcome of events over which he had no control.

The waiting eventually caused Caesar to step up the pace of his letter-writing campaign. To Essex he complained of his hard work that had "welnere cost mee my life," while to Walsingham he bemoaned "the daily iniuries offered mee in my place" because of the queen's persistent delays.[30] What was perhaps the most abject of Caesar's many groveling supplications accompanied a request for a small reward of land or money, as much "as will provide me an honest burial when I die, and keepe my poore wief and children from open beggery."[31]

His advancement also was impeded because there were some who thought of Caesar as an alien. Although he was half Italian by parentage, he was entirely English by birth and preference. Yet the fact that Caesar's father had dropped their surname, Adelmare, in favor of the more familiar and less patently foreign Caesar, indicates that being an alien presented problems. It would seem that most Englishmen could accept Caesar without a second thought, whereas Adelmare attracted attention and raised doubts. In addition, because he was young and in relatively high office, some of Caesar's contemporaries thought he was corrupt, although there is little evidence of corrupt behavior. If age and success advanced together, then his older contemporaries could explain Caesar's early success by alleging that he had corrupted others and was corrupt himself. Such allegations often accompany public office, but they especially troubled Caesar because he was told that the queen believed them.

In order to set the record straight, Caesar asked the Dowager Countess of Warwick, another patron, to intervene with Elizabeth: "It hath bene told me that her Majesty hath thought me unfitt [to be a Master of Request] bycause I ame Judge of the Admiralty, bycause my father was an Italian, and bycause I ame yong." These were allegations that he believed the countess could overcome, aided by some documents that he was sending along with his letter. "It hath bene likewise told her Majesty that I gott this place which now I have, by corruption: but my Lord Tresorer, my Lord Admirall, and Mr. Secretary Walsingham do knowe and will testifie the contrary." Indeed, Caesar asked that the queen put his qualifications and his motivations to the test of the Privy Council's opinion. But, he told the countess, he did not question the queen's judgment. Elizabeth was being given malicious advice by "some one about her person who hindereth the Course of her Sacred disposition and gracious nature."[32] This was no mere formality; a distinct pattern of obstruction had emerged. The queen's hesitation and prevarication had begun after she had promised him a Mastership. Malicious gossip at Court stood in his way, and he was certain that he knew its origin.

Dr. John Herbert enjoyed a Mastership of Requests because Caesar had slipped into the judgeship of the High Court of Admiralty a few years before, when Herbert had been in Poland on diplomatic business. Herbert, a mature and experienced civil lawyer, had gone abroad owning the first reversion in the admiralty bench. He had waited a long time to get this high judicial position, nevertheless, on his return to England, after Lewes had died, Herbert found that the temporary judge who had filled in for him, a young upstart civilian, the son of an alien physician, had pushed him aside. Caesar had insinuated himself into the favor of the old judge before he died, thus snatching from Herbert his rightful place. Although Herbert was a distant cousin of the Lord Admiral, and regardless of his reversionary interest, he had little choice but to sell his reversion for a high price and accept another position. Caesar not only paid him handsomely for the reversion but also used his access to Burghley to procure a Mastership of Requests for Herbert. There was no gratitude for this business transaction, but there was much resentment, all the more because Caesar had been able to play his patronal cards so well.

Caesar had begun to hear of the things Herbert was saying about him, and he was desperate. After Elizabeth had announced her promise to swear him, he wrote to Essex: "I am desirous to knowe whether that Mr. Harbartes speeches have wrought in her Majestie any purpose to alter her former determination, which I dare not once suspect, least the thought thereof should kill me, to wit, that a promise made by a most wise and learned and gracious Princesse, of a thing determined after long deliberation and recommended to her Majestie by her noble Counsell . . . be countermaunded or suspended uppon the words of Mr. Harbarte bringing my yong age and [the] uniting of both offices [i.e., Requests and Admiralty] nowe in question, which your Lordship and her Counsell have already aunswered." A "great Ladie mine honorible frend" had told Caesar that Herbert's arguments on these points "have wrought some impression in her highnes alreadye."³³ A month later, in a mood of hurt and anger, Caesar once more wrote to Essex that he had withdrawn "his senses" from the Court to the country, "where my grosse capacity shall be lesse acquainted with courtlie crosses." His anger was explained by his realization that "Mr. Harbarts credite should stoppe that favoure, which your Lordships travell in six monethes have wonne by [the queen's] promise."³⁴

Quite apart from the impediments of imagined disqualifications or personal animosities, Caesar's tortured progress toward a place in the Court of Requests was complicated by the struggle between the civilians and the common lawyers. We have already discussed the competitive pressure suffered by the High Court of Admiralty in the face of rival courts of the common law. Caesar believed that if the judge of the Admiralty were promoted, his court would share in the honor, and he was, generally speaking, correct: the respect shown to the Admiralty Court was directly related to the personal respect shown to its judge. Since Lewes before him had been sworn a Master of Requests, Caesar reckoned that if he were not treated similarly, the common-law judges would assume that he was in disfavor. Without this sign of the queen's favor, Caesar imagined that it would become all the more difficult for him and his court to resist the prohibitions. There is certainly no evidence to suggest that the queen's favor would have affected the judges, yet there was a prejudice against civilians, as a letter that Cecil's aunt wrote to him about a Mastership for a Mr. Dale reflected. "If you will get yourself credit," she told her nephew, "do your best to place Mr. Dale for a temporal [i.e., common] lawyer, a Master of Requests; for want whereof there is exceeding want and complaint by the subjects, poor suitors." She continued her letter with a reference to how much this man was favored by the Lord Chief Baron of the Exchequer and the rest of the chief judges, all of them common lawyers. Her letter ended with a bitter admonition: "And let not Dr. Caesar, a civilian, deprive him of the fee, due by patent to a temporal lawyer and not to a civilian, who besides, hath enough already, if these days could acknowledge what is enough."³⁵

When Sir Francis Walsingham died in 1590, his protégé had not as yet been sworn a Master of Requests. Caesar permitted the question of his long-awaited appointment to rest for several months until, on 1 October 1590, he wrote once again to Burghley and to Essex. With Walsingham's death still fresh in their minds, Caesar wanted to bring up his suit while major changes were being considered at Court and while he was still remembered as Walsingham's client. Then, quite without warning, Caesar was summoned to appear before the Council board at Richmond on 10 January 1591, where he was sworn an extraordinary Master of Requests. In the Council record it was noted that after Caesar was sworn he was "greatly commended for his diligence, and great discretion used in executing the office of Judge of the Admiralty."[36] Nothing in Caesar's papers explains the sudden volteface, but we can imagine some plausible explanations. Illness and death had deprived the queen of several of her Masters, and she needed to appoint replacements. Furthermore, her anger with Burghley and his adherents over Mary Stuart's execution had abated. The various intermediaries who had sponsored Caesar's suit could not be kept waiting much longer because Elizabeth had an interest in preserving their credibility. If they were not seen to be credible patrons, her own credibility was affected. Whatever the reason may have been, Caesar had now added to his dignities his hardest-won office and had assumed a place at Court.

During most of the sixteenth century, two ordinary Masters of Requests were in daily attendance upon the monarch's person, while two extraordinary Masters remained at Westminster to receive petitions and to hold sessions of the Court of Requests. During Mary's reign, the number of Masters had dwindled to two, one civil lawyer and one common lawyer. In the 1570's Elizabeth began to restore the complement to four, and later in her reign she upset the balance between civilians and common lawyers. In 1596 the queen replaced a common lawyer who had been an ordinary Master with Caesar, a civilian, and she named another civilian to Caesar's former extraordinary place. Elizabeth persisted in favoring civil lawyers, a policy that continued until James I decided to limit his appointments to common lawyers, who by the end of his reign were once again in control.[37] Elizabeth, as her reign grew longer, had found the civilians more in tune with her own sympathies regarding the prerogative than she had the common lawyers; James I, whose notions of kingship were consonant with his predecessor's, appointed common lawyers as a sop to hostile political and legal opinion.

When Caesar was admitted to Requests, he joined Ralph Rookesby, the other extraordinary Master (who served throughout his career with no compensation), and John Herbert, the only ordinary Master. Ten days later, William Aubrey was admitted to the second ordinary Mastership. However, by mid-1596, both Rookesby and Aubrey were dead. For two years Herbert and Caesar, both of them ordinary Masters, served alone until Christopher Parkins and Daniel Dun were sworn extraordinary Masters in 1598. Herbert was appointed Second Secretary to the queen in 1600, and Caesar thus became the senior Master. Roger Wilbraham, a common lawyer, was soon added to the court. This was an important appointment, since the court was much occupied with complex property litigation and a common lawyer's advice was needed.[38]

The court met during the law terms at the Palace of Whitehall in Westminster. Its Masters were served by a small number of minor officials and assisted by a larger number of commissioners and lawyers who were not actually in the service of the court.[39] The Register (more commonly called the clerk) was one of the Clerks of the Privy Seal, an important connection for the court because the processes of the Requests were authenticated under the Privy Seal. The clerk was paid a yearly stipend of £5 by the Privy Seal Office but he received no additional compensation from the Requests. Yet the fees in the court and his share of the profits of the Privy Seal Office made the clerk's place profitable.

Next after the clerk in the hierarchy of the Court of Requests was the Examiner, who took depositions, performing an analogous task to a Master in Chancery. However, the large number of depositions that were taken out of court by commissions of *dedimus potestatem* somewhat reduced the value and importance of the Examiner's place. In the same way that a Clerk of the Privy Seal was the clerk of court, one of the five Messengers of the Chamber was the messenger (or Poursuivant) of the court. He served the processes issuing from the Requests, recovering his expenses and collecting his fees from the litigants and witnesses.

The parties to litigation were expected to appear in person at every stage of the hearings and to wait in attendance upon the court until they were dismissed. In fact, the parties were represented by attorneys who appeared for them. There had traditionally been three attorneys when Caesar tried to have his brother-in-law, Damian Peck, installed as a fourth attorney. The other three were unhappy about this unwarranted addition to their number, and John Herbert, while sitting alone in 1599, ordered that Peck not be admitted to practice until his appointment had been discussed in the Privy Council. The result was that Herbert, never a friend of Caesar's nor of Caesar's clients, kept Peck at bay until a seated attorney had died and there was a vacancy to fill. The attorneys were able to accommodate the heavy caseload in the court (even though there were only three of them) by using auxiliaries, akin to modern solicitors, who fashioned profitable careers for themselves as the attorneys' deputies.

Throughout the kingdom there were ordinary subjects who, though not employed by the Requests, made it possible for the court to serve a national jurisdiction with a small professional staff. They served on the many commissions that took evidence or that were empowered to hear and determine particular causes. Counsel was retained by the litigant unless the party had been admitted *in forma pauperis*, in which case the court would assign counsel. An extensive list of lawyers drawn from the Inns of Court and Doctors' Commons were available for assignment, among them Caesar's brother, Thomas. Yet, even with counsel available, many litigants chose to represent themselves.

Little more is known of the Court of Requests and its Masters because they have been in a historiographic backwater since the sixteenth century. The only sustained study of this important court was written more than forty years ago and remains an unpublished M.A. thesis. Its limitations were that it dealt only with the Elizabethan period and that, while it was a pioneering piece of legal-administrative history, its techniques were descriptive rather than analytical.[40] That the Court of Requests has not been thoroughly examined is unfortunate because of the wealth of social, legal, and political data its records contain. But of even greater importance was the link that the court provided between a nation of individual subjects and the central government at a time when the power of regional magnates was weakening but was not yet defunct. The Court of Requests was an alternative to the traditional absolutism of the local magnate or the lord of the manor. It contributed to the evolving identification of the individual with the increasingly more powerful state.

The most complete record of cases from the court, in a volume published by the Selden Society, was limited by the editor's decision to stop in the middle of Elizabeth's reign.[41] The introductory material is, nonetheless, significant. Sir William Holdsworth, of course, touched on the Court of Requests in his volume on jurisdictions, as did Coke, three centuries earlier, in *The Fourth Institutes*.[42] G. R. Elton devoted a part of his discussion of conciliar courts to the Court of Requests, and he has written on the origins of the Privy Council, a subject which illuminates the origins of the Requests as a separate institution.[43] Sir Charles Ogilvie analyzed the court as an agency of the kings' government as distinct from the agencies of the common law, a discussion that explained the intense conflicts the court encountered throughout the later sixteenth century. He drew a sharp distinction between the court's right to exist as an extension of government and the (alleged) ideological determination of the common lawyers to see it destroyed.[44]

The first author to devote an entire study to the Court of Requests was Dr. Julius Caesar. In 1597 he published *The Ancient State, Authoritie, and Proceedings of the Court of Requests*.[45] The most recent study of the court is my own edition of *The Ancient State*.[46] Because Caesar's work is not easily understood in its original form and because he continued to add to it in manuscript for the next thirty-five years, a critical edition was necessary; my introduction to *The Ancient State* analyzes the court from its origins to the end of the sixteenth century. Much more work needs to be done, for the records of the court present extensive evidence of the frustrations and, occasionally, the triumphs of sixteenth- and seventeenth-century English peasants, villagers, and townspeople who were often unable to speak for themselves. While Star Chamber heard criminal complaints against the mighty, the Requests entertained civil process against the same class of Englishmen.

Caesar had hardly oriented himself to his new duties as a Master of Requests when an action, brought in the Common Pleas, visited an old, familiar problem on his new court. The long struggle with the common lawyers over their use of prohibitions continued in the High Court of Admiralty, and in 1591 the conflict was taken up in the Court of Requests. Caesar's past experience had taught him to prepare for a long engagement with the lawyers. He sent his clerks into the archives to find precedents useful in the defense of the court.[47]

The case that first brought a prohibition against the Court of Requests, *Locke v. Parsons*, was sent to Privy Council by the Common Pleas for final determination. Council found that the Court of Requests had acted properly, and the prohibition was dismissed. More prohibitions followed, so many, in fact, that an anonymous commentator fashioned a "melancholy list" of prohibitions from 1591 until about 1600. Privy Council, with more important business to attend to, was clearly irritated when it had to take time to mediate these jurisdictional quarrels, but it had no choice if public order and respect for authority were to be preserved.

While prohibitions were clearly a nuisance, they had not attacked the legitimacy of the court; at most they had asserted the supervisorial superiority of the common-law courts. All of this changed in 1598 when the Common Pleas, in the case of *Stepneth v. Flood*, refused to enforce a bond taken by the Sheriff of Carmarthen upon the execution of a writ of attachment issuing from the Court of Requests. The judges agreed that a defendent ordinarily would be liable for satisfying the bond, yet in this instance the judges held that the bond was unenforceable. The writ of attachment was held to be invalid because the Court of Requests was *coram non judice*: its process had no force at law. In *obiter dictum*, the Common Pleas clearly divided Requests from the other prerogative courts, such as the Court of Wards and the Duchy Court, because they enjoyed statutory sanction and Requests did not. Unlike the case of the constable sued by Linier of Ipswich for serving an admiralty process, this decision attacked the sufficiency of the court to act in any capacity, and Caesar lacked the power that he had possessed as an admiralty judge to imprison the contumacious litigant.[48]

The notes that Caesar and his clerks had been gathering since 1591, together with a topical index, appeared in print in 1597 before the *Stepneth v. Flood* decision was published. Caesar had probably heard that the Court of Common Pleas was considering an allegation of *coram non judice*, and he brought his closet scholarship out into the open. The premise that informed the argument in Caesar's little book, *The Ancient State, Authoritie, and Proceedings of the Court of Requests*, held that the court was, and always had been, a part of the King's Council. Thus, if the Common Pleas attacked the legitimacy of the Court of Requests, it was simultaneously attacking the Privy Council and the queen's prerogative.

Caesar's premise was grounded in historical research. The Court of Requests had grown out of the undifferentiated King's Council (the collective name for a large cadre of personal advisors) toward the end of the fifteenth century. In order to attend to the civil pleas of the poor and members of the Household, ad hoc committees of the King's Council, together with a Clerk of Council, would assemble from time to time. This arrangement became so popular that a second Clerk of Council was assigned to join them in 1483 to receive and dispatch the petitions of the poor. The members of the King's Council who assessed these petitions adopted the informal name of the "Court of Requests" (as well as the "Court of White Hall"), but they were not an established court. Then, in 1493, a series of order and decree books began to be kept routinely as the record of the court. Because these books eventually became the record of the autonomous Court of Requests, Caesar chose 1493 as the foundation year of the court. Although the Requests may have been a committee of the Council from at least as early as the accession of Henry VII, there were those who thought of the committee as an independent court. In Henry VII's first Parliament a bill was sent to the king for the permanent suppression of the Court of Requests. Henry chose not to sign the bill; several years later, in 1493, he quietly revived the court. The start of the order and decree books coincided with that revival.

G. R. Elton has demonstrated that the order and decree books were one of two series of records kept for the specialized functions of the King's Council.[49] Regardless of the separate records, Council remained an undivided body possessing separate committees to perform its tasks in the name of the whole and of the king. The division of the King's Council into specialized entities was accomplished under the aegis of Cardinal Wolsey in the 1520's. He established the Court of Requests with its own record and, at the same time, created an institutionally autonomous privy council. It appears from Caesar's copy of a no-longer-extant record of the Court of Requests that on 14 July, 13 Henry VIII, this notation first appeared: "the Kings honorable Counsell sitting in his Court of Requests."[50]

The relationship of the Requests to Council was further evidenced by its reliance on the privy seal to authorize its processes. Caesar contended that only the monarch and the Privy Council could use the Privy Seal and thus demonstrated that the court was an extension of the Privy Council and the queen's prerogative. Also, the Lord Privy

Seal was, de jure, the president of the Court of Requests, although he took no part in its proceedings. Caesar found the relationship of the Requests to the Privy Council so essential to his argument that he continued to add relevant notes to his interleaved personal copy of *The Ancient State* as late as 1630. One note, dating from 1623, was headed "for civility in sittings either in Cappell or elsewhere in the court." It consisted of elaborate rules of protocol limiting approach to the royal person to individuals of the noble rank of baron or above and to Privy Councillors. But the Masters of Requests could still approach the king, and this privilege gave Caesar the opportunity to restate their association with the Council. In 1630 he included a document requiring the members of Council to attend meetings regularly, to come to these meetings with impressive dignity, and to pass through public rooms at Court rather than move along secluded back passages. The "Orders for Council" appeared just before the *Book of Orders* was published in 1631; the King in Council, without the impediment of Parliament, had asserted political dominion over the kingdom. This was perhaps Caesar's idea, at seventy, of the realization of a proper political order reminiscent of Elizabethan governance. The inclusion of these documents many years after he had left the Court of Requests suggests that his motivation was ideological and that his sentiments were deeply felt. The Crown in Council was the locus of legitimate authority, and, by implication, the common lawyers erred in trenching on its jurisdiction as well as on that of the adjunct, the Court of Requests.[51]

The common-law courts and the prerogative courts were, therefore, at odds throughout most of Caesar's career. In the particular instance of the relationship between the Court of Requests and the law courts, the hostility was animated by hardening ideological positions and exacerbated by the absence of a moderating equity from the rigorous procedures of the law. Those litigants who wanted to pursue an allegation of injustice could find their remedy either in the expensive procedures of the Chancery or in a petition to the queen. Because the crown was the *fons et origine* of all English justice, the queen was expected to receive the petitions of her subjects; indeed, the appointment of the Masters of Requests institutionalized her obligation.

As rigid as was the common law, we must keep in mind that changes had been evolving in its procedure for more than a century and a half, but these changes were evolving more slowly than the cir-

cumstances that demanded them. Furthermore, change is not necessarily reform, and thoroughgoing reform was needed. By way of illus-
tration, we might observe that the development of legal fictions and
the extension of old writs to fit new circumstances through the process of analogous reasoning were manipulations of the existing structure rather than fundamental reforms of the common-law process.
Common-law courts were, for example, quite competent to deal with
ordinary freehold and leasehold, but the notion of transitory possession of property held in trust was beyond their ken. Likewise,
manorial tenants, by custom or copy, were technically unfree before
the king's law; their recourse was to the court of the lord of the manor.
But in the sixteenth century, groups of unfree tenants wanted to sue
their lords in order to enforce their customary rights, only to find that
the common lawyers were ill-prepared to represent them. Turning to
a third and final example, we note that, when the lawyers tried to
marry the requirements of contemporary litigation with the limitations of traditional forms of pleading, the result was a peculiar hybrid.
For instance, there was no provision in common-law pleadings for alleging tortious damages even though the circumstances of tort were
evident in abundance. The answer was to apply the principles of simple trespass on the person to allegations of tort and, thus, to extend
jurisdiction. Ironically, the strength of the common law—its reliance
on objective, impersonal precedent rather than subjective, personal
prejudice—was also its weakness. Where no precedent governed (or
could be made to govern), there was no case law. Thus, litigants who
were frustrated by the limitations of the law turned to courts less
bound by precedent. Such a court was the Court of Requests, where
equity rather than law obtained.

The Court of Requests (along with its sister conciliar courts and the
Admiralty Court) did not depend on precedent but derived its
authority from the undelegated royal prerogative. Chancery and the
Requests were the principal repositories of equitable relief in England.
As important as this function was, the Court of Requests fell victim
in the late sixteenth century to early constitutional skirmishes that
would grow to pitched battles in the seventeenth century. If Coke's observations can be taken as more than his peculiar prejudices, the common law was associated with constitutional propriety, whereas civilians and equity were associated with capricious assertions of the
prerogative. More to the point, however, the incrementally more com-

plex structure of English society in the sixteenth century demanded equitable remedies. The growth of courts of equity was less a matter of the assertion of the prerogative than of the fact that there was a vacuum that had to be filled.

Had the Court of Requests limited itself to its traditional jurisdiction, paupers and the Household, there would have perhaps been less difficulty with other courts. As it was, the common lawyers, and particularly the Court of Common Pleas, were not inclined to challenge the Requests' authority to hear the pleas of members of the Household, their servants, and persons otherwise engaged in the queen's service. There were hundreds, perhaps thousands, of persons serving the queen whose civil disputes had to be settled within the Household because, as the queen's personal servants, they shared her immunities. Furthermore, the queen could not afford their absence during a trial in an ordinary court.

The common lawyers were also not averse, in principle, to the Court of Requests' fulfilling its other major function as the Court of Poor Men's Causes. It was commonly recognized that the queen was obligated to provide to each of her subjects a means to redress alleged wrongs. In most instances her obligation was satisfied in the law courts, but the high costs associated with a trial at law prevented the poor from instituting their actions even if they were free at law to do so. Thus, a genuine pauper or an unfree man was welcome to take his petition to the Court of Requests, since, in an action that might otherwise not have been initiated, he was not depriving the common lawyers of their fees. But by the end of the sixteenth century, the lawyers reckoned that there were too many false paupers whose poverty was fraudulently attested to by local authorities in order to open the door to the Requests for them. A cursory perusal of the gentry and aristocratic titles of the litigants in the later Elizabethan Requests bears out the common lawyers' complaints. The Requests was taking on the appearance of a fully developed alternative to the ordinary course of the law, a Chancery on a reduced scale. It was becoming a de facto court of appeals from common-law judgments and an additional forum for purposes of litigious harassment. Here the lawyers drew the line between tolerating the Court of Requests and attacking it.

In the conflict between the jurisdictions, it would be folly to imagine that the common lawyers were selfless purists. In a marketplace of possible tribunals, they were competitors aspiring to become

monopolists. They believed that the prerogative courts enjoyed a competitive advantage over them, and they were determined to put an end
not only to the advantage but also to the competition itself. It was the
Court of Requests' great misfortune that it was one of the several
courts in the "governmental heart of England" that, W. J. Jones tells
us, were not classifiable either as Chancery or as common law. They
used procedures lying outside the mainstream of English legal tradition, and the local authorities frequently did not consider these courts
strong enough to enforce their own writs. The High Court of Admiralty, the Court of Requests, and some of the ecclesiastical courts
were "central but specialized in jurisdiction, recognized and yet dis-
tinctive, and they lived increasingly in the no-man's-land between
metropolitan advantage and near provincial disregard. Prohibitions
and other processes were to make most of the courts feel threatened.[52]
Small judicial fragments were being crushed by the monolithic national judicial systems.

The common-law courts were not the only ones against which the
Court of Requests had to maintain its vigilance. The Duchy Court,
with jurisdiction over causes arising in lands of the Duchy of Lancaster, was essentially a very large manorial court, but because the
monarch was the hereditary duke of Lancaster, it was regarded as a
prerogative court. An instance of the potential problems between the
Duchy Court and Requests arose when one Nicholson sued a certain
Reddick in the Court of Requests. Reddick tried to move the issue to
the Duchy Court, alleging that the lands involved were subject to the
Duchy of Lancaster. Caesar rejected this allegation on the grounds
that the Court of Requests, as a prerogative Court, possessed the
authority to hear all cases assigned to it by the queen: *quia de plenit-
udine potentiae Reginae non desirendum est*. This uncompromising
assertion of the prerogative was congruent with the facts of the case.
The queen was Chancellor of the Duchy, pro tempore, and was also
the duke of Lancaster. As Chancellor, she had assigned, for the time
being, all equity cases arising in the Duchy's jurisdiction to the Court
of Requests. Her prerogative fiat assured that there was no alternative
court in which to plead. Although the queen's assignment was a sufficient defense of the court, Caesar was in no mood to leave any loose
ends. He argued that, without regard for the queen's assignment of
Duchy causes to the Requests, this particular issue belonged in his
court because the land in question was not Duchy land and was not

subject to Duchy jurisdiction. In a holographic margin note, he added that the question of jurisdiction in this case had been decided "in the Court of Equity" and jurisdiction had been continued in the Requests.[53] The doctrine expressed in these notes could only have confirmed the darker suspicions of the common lawyers: the power of the Court of Requests was limited only by the queen's restraint in her exercise of the prerogative. The common lawyers were not suggesting that there was no prerogative, but simply that it was limited and constrained by tradition and statute. The civilians, to the contrary, insisted that the monarch had "the power both to regulate the jurisdiction and proceedings of his courts and to authorize [them] to exceed their statutory authority." The prerogative was beyond the limitations of custom or statute. Nonetheless, the civil law surrounded the monarch with limitations that would prevent the onset of tyranny.[54]

Whether the charges of the illegitimacy of the Court of Requests that were raised in *Stepneth v. Flood* were well founded or not, and whether or not the earlier prohibitions were properly directed, in both cases they obstructed the Masters and the litigants. Thus, Caesar, in mounting his defense, had to remember that vigorous claims of superiority were only words if his court did not take steps to improve its procedure and make it less vulnerable to attack. Since the Requests had its origins in an ad hoc committee of Council, its procedure had emerged in response to the circumstances of the individual cases and was not highly formalized. Hence, there was some confusion regarding the proper function of the Masters, in both their judicial and their secretarial roles. As early as 6 Edward VI, a permanent commission was given the responsibility for receiving from the Masters of Requests petitions addressed to the queen for her grace and favor. After examining the petitions, the commissioners were to determine the most suitable court or official to dispose of the matter. In some instances, a fixed procedure was laid down: the disbursal of royal land or treasure was subject to the detailed scrutiny of the Lord Treasurer, the Chancellor of the Exchequer, and the Privy Council. In most instances, however, the disposition of the petitions was left to the discretion of the Masters.[55]

When Caesar came to the Requests, a half-century following the promulgation of the Edwardian regulations, the commission had fallen into disuse. The Masters, who were again under attack, were not well served with guidance and supervision. As a result, they were

vulnerable to the barbs of their critics. In order to strengthen their procedure, Caesar was instructed to prepare an internal memorandum for
his brother Masters to follow as they set their house in order. His
memorandum was inspired by the Edwardian regulations, but there
was a major difference. Whereas a commission had overseen the work
of the Masters in the earlier order, Caesar made the Masters themselves responsible for their own work. Virtually every sort of petition
was identified in a long outline, together with the name of the officer
or agency to be consulted in each instance. He divided the suits and
petitions into two general categories: requests for justice and requests
for grace. Requests for justice included, for the most part, requests for
the redress of grievances arising in another court. This was accomplished with a privy seal warrant requiring the recipient to transfer his
case to the Court of Requests. Requests for grace, a far more extensive category, included every imaginable type of petition: leases and
pensions; charters and free denizations; letters of favor; pardons and
protections. Caesar was careful to indicate precisely which officers
were to be contacted about which issues. In order to reduce resistance
to the court, he wanted to omit no civility or point of protocol. In this
way, he could assure himself, and others, that the court would not in-
advertently usurp another's authority or jurisdiction. This policy was
further emphasized by the requirement that no further protections or
pardons would be issued without the countersignatures of the Lord
Keeper and at least one other Privy Councillor. Gunners' rooms, a
primitive form of veterans' pension, and almsrooms required proper
certification of the petitioner's eligibility and need. But the most significant governor on the engine of supplication was the requirement
that no grant of any kind could be made without the signature of the
Lord Treasurer, Burghley.[56] The effect of these regulations was to mit-
igate the frequent complaints about the Masters' allegedly arbitrary
conduct by giving the power to satisfy petitions to the relevant ministers. But these regulations also made order out of the secretarial side
of the Requests, giving the Masters more time to attend to their important work in the equity court.

According to his own rhetoric, Caesar had joined the Mastership of
Requests to his judgeship in the High Court of Admiralty in order to
become a more effective judge. Since a Master of Requests routinely
enjoyed access to the queen and her advisors, the simultaneous trans-

action of admiralty business would naturally follow. The coincidence of both offices in one officer was intended to have a synergistic effect, yet we must consider how the two positions actually fit together. How did Caesar use his time and his new opportunities after 1591? Was synergy a consequence of the combination, or did one of his functions flourish at the expense of the other?

A sense of spatial relationships in Elizabethan London aids in answering these questions. The High Court of Admiralty met in its courtroom in a former church in Southwark near the southern end of London Bridge and in Doctors' Commons in Great Knight Rider Street. The Court of Requests met in permanent session in the Palace of Whitehall in Westminster. Caesar's residences in London were in Paternoster Row in the shadow of St. Paul's, in chambers in Doctors' Commons, and, eventually, in the Inner Temple to the west of the City and in St. Katharine's Hospital to the east of the Tower. With a bit of luck, the tides rising or falling in the direction he wished to travel by barge on the Thames, Caesar could possibly spend a part of his working day in Southwark and a part in Westminster attending to his duties in his two courts. But although he could have maintained such a schedule, it is unlikely that he did so over any appreciable period of time, for the strain would have been too great. In general, Caesar worked either in the Admiralty Court or in the Requests on a given day, not in both.

During term time, on scheduled court days, Caesar, the Register, and a small entourage gathered in the courtroom in Southwark in the presence of the silver oar mace of the High Court of Admiralty. Out of term and between court days, the Recorder, William Harewood, noted that the judge or a deputy, along with other officers of the court and the parties to the actions, met in Caesar's house in Paternoster Row, *in aedibus suis*, or in Doctors' Commons. Occasionally they met in one of Caesar's other chambers, but the most frequent location was Caesar's residence. When there were four Masters in service, an ordinary Master was attendant upon the queen, wherever she might be, and at least one extraordinary Master was on duty at Westminster. Usually, no single Master was overworked. Yet from Hilary Term 1596 until Trinity Term 1600, there were only two Masters of Requests, Caesar and Herbert, and their duties did become more burdensome. One of them had constantly to be with the queen, and the other had constantly to be on duty in the Court of Requests. This increase in

Caesar's duties at Court was reflected in his reduced presence in the High Court of Admiralty.

Although we are discussing the Court of Requests and Caesar's tenure in that court, we must return to the Admiralty Court in order to assess the allocation of Caesar's time. His quest for a place in the Requests had been couched in terms of its making him a more effective judge of the admiralty. It is in that context that his tenure in the Requests should be examined. Fortunately, Caesar kept a careful record of his activities during his first eighteen months in the Admiralty Court, thus providing a basis for comparison in later years. This record, kept in quarto-size volumes from July 1584 through December 1585, was matched by no similar account at any other time.[57] It does, however, provide the basis for assessing Caesar's twenty-two years in the admiralty, a part of which was also spent in the Requests.

Because his personal record stopped in December 1585, we have to reconstruct similar time periods from the records of the Admiralty Court, for comparison's sake. From the Act Books we can determine the volume of business in the court and who dealt with it.[58] From the files of libels we can establish patterns of attendance in court.[59] In the three sample periods under consideration, the judicial entries (regardless of their nature) have been tallied on a monthly basis to create composite totals for each period. The purpose of this survey is to assess the overall volume of work accomplished. No attempt has been made to break down the figures into such components as new cases, continuations, swearing of witnesses, and so forth. The data indicate that, throughout the period, Caesar came to depend more and more on the assistance of his brother civilians in the Doctors' Commons to get through his work load. These deputies made it possible for him to function in his two offices. Indeed, toward the end of his career in the High Court of Admiralty, Caesar was more the chairman of a committee of deputies than he was the principal judge of the court.

During his early years in the admiralty, Caesar acted alone, the significant exception having been when Caesar and Valentine Dale were joined as commissioners general of admiralty affairs from February 1585 through July 1586. While Caesar shared the bench, he was known in the Act Books as Her Majesty's principal officer and commissioner general in the Admiralty Court; but after Dale left the commission, Caesar was to be known for the rest of his service as Judge of the High Court of Admiralty and the Lord Admiral's principal lieutenant.

Caesar was thereafter more likely to act alone or to leave the bench to his deputies. He rarely sat in joint sessions. Among his colleagues in Doctors' Commons who assisted the admiralty judge were John Howe, John Hunt (his brother-in-law), William Ferrand, and Thomas Creke (who had the longest tenure). John Amye, John Pope, and Thomas Crompton joined the court later on. When the time came, in 1606, to replace Caesar, Thomas Crompton was chosen from among the civilian deputies.[60]

War with Spain made the Admiralty Court adapt to the increased amount and intensity of English privateering. The increase is reflected in a comparison of the sample periods in the table on page 84; however, we must remember that the High Court of Admiralty was continuously available to litigants throughout the year, regardless of regular court days. Thus, for each sample period, there were 549 days during which an entry might have been made reflecting activity in the court. In the 1584–85 period, the court met on 199 days, but by 1594–95 the number of days had risen to 252, only to fall off slightly to 243 in 1604–5. During the 1584–85 period, the impact of privateering could hardly be measured; its full impact was apparent in the later periods.

A calculation of the number of days spent in admiralty court sessions is only a partial measure of the way in which the court did business. Consider how Caesar attended to the court's affairs. In 1594–95 the number of days the court met increased by 26.6 percent over the 1584–85 period. In both of these sample periods, Caesar sat alone for 82 percent of the court days recorded, although the number of days, in absolute terms, had risen from 164 to 206. In 1604–5, however, the number of days on which he handled court business by himself dropped to 88 (36 percent of the total for the period). The proportion of court days when Caesar sat with his deputies in the three simple periods fluctuated from 12 percent to 5 percent and back to 15 percent. But the most interesting tabulations concern the deputies' acting alone. They had acted on their own in 1584–85 and in 1594–95, 5 and 13 percent of the days that the court met; in 1604–5 they were attending to 49 percent of the court's sessions.

Simple tabulation of recorded court days does not, however, indicate the pattern of appearance before the court or changes in the level of productivity. To capture that information we turn to a measure of the number of items recorded in the Act Books for each sample period and the average number of items recorded for each day. The volume

Activities of the High Court of Admiralty,
Selected Periods, 1584–1605

Category	July 1584– Dec. 1585	July 1594– Dec. 1595	July 1604– Dec. 1605[a]
Total possible days	549	549	549
Days recorded in Act Books as court days	199 (36%)	252 (46%)	243 (44%)
Recorded court days attended by:			
Caesar alone	164 (83%)	206 (82%)	88 (36%)
Caesar and deputies	23 (12%)	14 (5%)	36 (15%)
Deputies alone	9 (5%)	32 (13%)	119 (49%)
Items recorded in Act Books	1,064	1,449	1,913
Items per court day	5.35	5.75	7.87
Items disposed by:			
Caesar alone	793 (75%)	1,309 (90%)	1,271 (67%)
Caesar and deputies	214 (20%)	52 (4%)	406 (21%)
Deputies alone	55 (5%)	88 (6%)	236 (12%)

SOURCE: Public Record Office, HCA 3/19, 22, 23, 25, 26; HCA 24/52, 53, 61, 62, 70, 71.
[a]The month of September 1604 is missing from the Act Books.

of business in the court as measured by the number of recorded items in the Act Books had increased even more dramatically than had the number of days devoted to admiralty business. Part of this increased volume of work was attributable to the circumstances of the war with Spain: more litigants than ever before crowded into the court. But another important factor was the extent to which cases were continued from term to term. Each continuation called for an appearance in the court; when prohibitions were involved, delays could cause a suit to drag on inconclusively for years. Regardless of the reason, the court's calendar was increasingly more crowded. The average number of items per working day rose from 5.35 to 5.75 from 1584–85 to 1594–95, nearly a 7.5 percent increase. From 1594–95 to 1604–5 the increase from 5.75 items per day to 7.87 items per day accounted for a 36.9 percent change. Thus, from the first to the last sample period, we encounter an overall increase of 47 percent in the average number of items per working day, but there was only a 22 percent increase in the number of days that were noted in the Act Books. As the volume of work grew greater, Caesar depended more heavily on his deputies. At the same time, he was busy as a Master of Requests.

In the first sample period, the newly appointed judge was able to dispose of 75 percent of the items entered in the Act Books by himself, and by 1594–95, he was able to deal with 90 percent of the items alone. However, in the last sample period, Caesar dealt with only 67 percent of this business by himself. On the other hand, Caesar and his deputies were dealing with the same proportion of items in 1584–85 and 1604–5, about 20 percent, yet in absolute terms the number of items had virtually doubled from the first sample period to the last. The proportional increase in the court's business explains the relatively heavy involvement of the deputies acting on their own by the end of the years that we are sampling. In the first two sample periods, the deputies handled 5 percent and 6 percent of the court's business, an increase from 55 to 88 items. In 1604–5, however, the deputies alone were responsible for dealing with 236 items, or 12 percent of the items entered in the Act Books. If we consider the increase in each category from the first through the last sample period, we find that Caesar dealt with 60 percent more cases and Caesar and his deputies with 90 percent more, but the deputies alone with 329 percent more!

These simple tabulations indicate that Caesar was initially able to combine the offices of judge and Master. In the 1594–95 sample period, the first after he held both offices, he was dealing with 90 percent of the items in his court without assistance. This suggests that Caesar's initial assessment of the effect of combining the two offices was correct. He was able to accomplish a very large volume of work in the Admiralty Court, and the reason may well have been because he was a Master of Requests who could expedite the business of his bench even though it had grown from 1,064 items in 1584–85 to 1,449 items in 1594–95, a 36 percent increase. But this does not account for the drop in the number of items he handled alone in 1604–5. By then, he was only dealing with 67 percent of the items, which were nearly as numerous as in 1594–95. Caesar was less able to do both jobs well as time went on, and his service in the Court of Requests was the reason why.

After 1595 Caesar became an ordinary Master of Requests, meaning that he had to travel with the queen. This was not, by itself, a sufficient explanation of the reduced ability of the judge in the admiralty to conduct his affairs by himself. Ralph Rookesby died in 1595, as did William Aubrey in the weeks before Hilary Term 1596. Consequently, all of the work in the Court of Requests was handled by Caesar and

Herbert until 1600, when Herbert was made the Second Secretary and was replaced by a common lawyer. When Herbert and Caesar served in the Requests together, Herbert had no other responsibilities; the same was not true for Caesar, who continued on his own until 1603.

So we find that Caesar was more involved with the Requests because there were fewer Masters to share the load. He was barely able to appear for half of the court days in the High Court of Admiralty by 1604–5. His deputies stepped in to act in his behalf, and by delegating his authority, Caesar was able to manage. Even though he was a pluralist, Caesar saw to it that his duties were performed in his absence. In addition to the increased work in the Court of Requests and in the High Court of Admiralty, Caesar came to occupy places on sensitive commissions, he sat in Parliament, and his advice was sought on matters of foreign law and mercantile policy. He was fully occupied.

Unfortunately we do not have the same quality of evidence for the Court of Requests that we have for the admiralty. Thus, to compare Caesar's work in the admiralty with the Requests will require that we take a one-year period, close to one of the sample periods used in analyzing the High Court of Admiralty, and study Caesar's work in the Requests for that year.[61] Our comparison will be further limited by our use of the days of term time rather than all of the available days of the calendar year. When we examine the number of days that Caesar sat in the Court of Requests, we have to bear in mind that by 1596 Caesar and Herbert were the only Masters in the Requests. Caesar was more heavily involved than was his colleague, even though Caesar was also responsible for the Admiralty Court. A possible explanation for this division of labor was the fact that Caesar remained in London to attend to the Court of Requests and the Admiralty Court, while Herbert moved about within the queen's entourage.

In Hilary Term 1595, Caesar sat alone in the Admiralty Court for each of the thirteen days that the court met. During Hilary Term 1596, he sat alone for 44 percent of the Court of Requests meetings, a total of seven days. In Easter Term 1595, he sat for seventeen days out of eighteen in the admiralty, but in the Requests, in Easter Term 1596, he sat alone for thirteen of the twenty-two days that it met (59 percent). In absolute numbers, he had nearly doubled his number of court days in the Requests from one term to the next. By Trinity Term 1595, Caesar was assuming sole responsibility on fourteen of the sixteen days that the Admiralty Court met (88 percent). However, in the

Requests, the number of sessions in which he sat alone returned to six (38 percent). The last term of the year 1595, Michaelmas Term, found Caesar presiding over 79 percent of the court days in the admiralty, or 27 out of 34 days. In the Requests he presided over seventeen sessions (43 percent). John Herbert, on the other hand, sat alone once during Hilary Term 1596, three times in Easter Term, once during Trinity Term, and five times in Michaelmas Term.

The two Masters did accomplish a significant amount of their business together in the Court of Requests in 1596. Out of the 86 days when the court was in session during the year, they sat together for 33 of them (38 percent). It is interesting to note that in 1597 Herbert and Caesar sat together on 45 of the 90 days that the court conducted business. Caesar alone sat on 36 occasions (40 percent), and Herbert sat alone on nine occasions (10 percent). The proportions did not change materially from Easter Term 1599 through Hilary Term 1600, the last period for which we have good data for these years. Although we do not have sufficiently complete data to analyze the volume of work on court days, the Requests data does suggest that Caesar was trying to hold on to both courts for as long as he could. It is also apparent that until the number of Masters fell to two, Caesar was able to deal with large burdens of work in the Admiralty Court while sharing the burdens of the Requests. After the reduction in numbers, Caesar's involvement in the Requests grew greater as the deputies assisted him in the admiralty. By 1604–5, when Caesar allowed 50 percent of the business in the admiralty to be handled by his deputies, it was clear that it was in the Requests that he would be spending his time. This was where his career goals directed him.

IV

The Eldest Judge,
the Youngest and the Poorest

THE YEARS BETWEEN 1584 and 1606, between Caesar's first service
in the High Court of Admiralty and his appointment as Chancellor of
the Exchequer and Privy Councillor, were the years of his transition
from obscurity to significance. We have already examined the ways
that Caesar manipulated his several patrons in order to capture and
improve on a number of positions: the judgeship of the admiralty, a
Mastership in Chancery, and a Mastership of Requests. But we have
also learned that Caesar complained of financial difficulty at every
turn — overworked, underpaid, expending his wealth in the queen's
service, losing an inheritance (so he said) for want of compensation.
In the following pages we shall see an entirely different side of Caesar's
life, the private and the personal. His frequent allegations of poverty,
encountered in earlier chapters, reflected the conventional expectations of wealth and reward in public office, as well as his costly investment in higher office. But for the private man — husband, father, older
brother, stepson, investor, creditor, bencher of his Inn — his wealth was
his own business, to be revealed or secreted as best suited him. In his
public life Caesar sought parity of reward and advancement with his
peers; in his private life he sought respect, recognition, and wealth. Although his two lives often crossed one another, Caesar appears to have
regarded them quite separately; he could compartmentalize them
without any apparent sense of deceit or dissimulation. When we turn
to Caesar's private pursuits, we encounter many of his familiar public characteristics: manipulation, kindness, and a canny sense of tim-
ing. Indeed, his extensive private life was the background against
which his public career unfolded. By 1606 Caesar was a substantial

Londoner with suburban connections. He was an experienced, dependable, and successful public figure with a background in Parliament. In 1584 he was Mr. Dr. Caesar of Paternoster Row in London; in 1606 he was Sir Julius Caesar of Mitcham, Surrey. This chapter is a study of this transition.

Caesar's families, both conjugal and fraternal, the bedrock on which he built the edifice of his public career, provide an excellent approach to a study of his private life. We begin with his conjugal family. As he proceeded from his first to his second marriage, making cool assessments of an advantageous and profitable union, we are reminded of his progression from one public office to another in his judicial career.

Dorcas Lusher, his first wife, was delivered of their first child, a daughter who was named for her mother, in 1584, the year of their marriage.[1] Two years later, Dorcas bore their first son, Charles, but he lived only for a few months. Their second son, Caesar's namesake, was born in 1588, and their third son, the second Charles, was born in 1590.[2] Dorcas did not survive the birth of their fourth son, Richard, who in turn died six weeks later.

Caesar provided a lavish funeral for his late wife. He spent £439 11s. 3d. to bury her, an expense that may have encouraged him to think seriously, although briefly, of remaining unmarried.[3] "Nowe, God willing," he wrote, "I will marry myselfe in all faithfull diligence to the service of my place."[4] A year later, however, he had decided to marry himself to his second wife, Alice, the widow of Alderman John Dent, late of the Salters' Company. Having married the daughter of one alderman and the widow of another, it would appear that Caesar moved comfortably in the society of the London oligarchy. John Dent provided legacies for his nieces and nephews and for his surviving brothers. He left the remainder of his estate to his wife and two daughters, Mary and Elizabeth.[5]

Alice bore Caesar three more sons: John, in 1597; Thomas, in 1600; and Robert, in 1602. In addition, Alice's daughters were Caesar's wards. He had purchased their wardships from the Master of the Wards, Burghley, and it had been a relatively speedy transaction because Alice, within a month of John Dent's death, had extracted from Burghley a promise to grant her the wardship of the bodies and the lands of her daughters. The grant would cost her £1,000, to be paid to Sir Thomas Wilkes, the diplomat, upon the queen's command. Alice was to make bond to satisfy Wilke, and she was also to undertake to "find the Office" at her own expense, meaning that she was to find and display in the Court of Wards the documentation regarding the lands in question.[6] The competition for female wards was keen because the profits from their guardianship were greater than those of males. There was no expensive education for a female, and the control over the selection of her spouse was a source of profit for the guardian. The fact that Alice was able to secure a commitment from Burghley suggests the strength of her connections and that, perhaps, Caesar, knowing of her plight before their marriage, had intervened for her. Her haste in procuring the promise from the Master of the Wards was motivated by her private knowledge that her late husband's kinsmen would soon be fighting vigorously for the guardianship of her daughters and to break Dent's will.

John Dent appears to have been a crafty man. He possessed great wealth in property, and it seems that he used his brothers to increase his holdings while, at the same time, he cut them out of his inheritance. When Dent died, his brothers and their sons found that they had been tricked by him. For instance, the Dent brothers had acquired title to the manor of Halloughton, Leicestershire. The indenture stated that all of the brothers were entitled to a portion of the manor, but only following the death of John Dent. Furthermore, John Dent was entitled to make changes in the inheritance by his own conveyance; the other brothers were not. Should John make any changes, the original indenture was to be held null and void and the new indenture would govern. Several years later, John Dent drew up a conveyance to use—to avoid wardship—in favor of his brother Edward and Edward's son, Francis. Dent enrolled the deed before a Master in Chancery, but he kept the document secret from everyone, especially Edward and Francis. Not until six months after John's death did they learn of it.[7] On the surface, it would appear that John had favored Edward, but, in fact, he had defeated him. By making the conveyance and having it enrolled, John had activated the condition in the original indenture by which it could be nullified: he had changed the succession by conveyance to Edward. The other brothers lost their claims to the manor, but because the conveyance had been kept secret from Edward, he was unable to enforce it. It was essential that a conveyance to use be shown to be a true bargain or it would not be enforced. Because

Edward had no knowledge of the conveyance, there could be no allegation that a true bargain had been made. The conveyance was treated as
an attempt to avoid wardship and, thus, was not enforceable. Dent had
neatly and secretly defeated all of his brothers and their male heirs. Another property had been conveyed to Dent's brother-in-law Thomas
Cater, who admitted under questioning that there had never been an
intent to make a true bargain.[8] He too lost a claim to Dent's estate.

Dent also outsmarted his brothers and their sons in his will. On 15
April 1595 he had drawn a will leaving to his brothers, brothers-in-law,
nieces, and nephews substantial portions of his estate. His wife was
barely mentioned in the will, and his daughters were given only a life-
interest in the manor of Mitcham, Surrey. A month later, Dent added
a codicil to the will declaring null and void an earlier agreement of
surrender with Alice in which she had given up any claim to his estate.
He now conveyed a one-third interest in all of his lands to his wife and
to his daughters as her successors. Furthermore, he expressly forbade
any challenges to his will by his brothers and their assigns.[9] With all
of these advance preparations to defeat the claims of his kinsmen, it
is likely that Dent told his wife what he was doing. She, in turn, moved
quickly to secure the wardships before the challengers appeared.

Caesar married Alice Dent just in time to become a party to the
legal wrangling that started as soon as Dent's will was read. Caesar
had an uncanny ability, in both his private and his public life, to step
into a situation just when the burning fuse had reached the powder
keg. However, it is likely that he saw his marriage to Alice Dent as an
investment: she needed legal advice and £1,000 to purchase her
daughters' wardships. Her brothers-in-law were claiming Mitcham,
and her nephew Francis was in hot pursuit of the manor in Leicestershire as soon as the secret conveyance was found. In addition to money
and a lawyer, Alice needed a protector who was well-connected at
Court, especially with Burghley, for the controversy would probably
become a struggle of patrons and intermediaries. From Caesar's point
of view, Alice Dent was a landed widow with two marriageable
daughters. The investment of time and money that he would make in
their behalf appeared sound. Whatever affection there may have been
between Julius and Alice, the fact was that they needed each other.
Their marriage may have been made in heaven; it was also made on
the threshold of the Court of Wards.

The business affairs of his new wife and his stepdaughters cost

Caesar dearly. The process of searching the wardship, paying fees, buying dinners, paying gratuities, and making gifts would cost him £1,739 6s. 10d. He had to negotiate a loan in order to keep abreast of these expenses; by 1605 the interest alone had cost him £649 5s. 2d.[10] In addition to securing the wardships, Caesar helped Alice protect her dower interest in her late husband's lands. Her one-third interest in his estates had been assured by the codicil to John Dent's will, but his nephew Francis and his brother Leonard challenged it. The agreement resulting from this contest caused Leonard to pay Alice £6 13s. 4d. annually in two installments. He also had to deliver a flitch of bacon to her each Easter.[11] From William Dent, Alice received, under the terms of a similar agreement, £3 6s. 8d. annually in two installments. For his part, Caesar had to pay out one-third of an annual estate of £200 to a number of beneficiaries specified in Dent's will.[12] In the following year, Francis Dent encroached on woodlots belonging to the Dent daughters' lands. He alleged a right to take wood, but the Court of Wards found that this was inconsistent with Caesar's rights in wardship, and Francis was ejected.[13]

Protecting the several properties belonging to Alice and her daughters required Caesar's vigilance, but he profited from his guardianship. His vigilance was exemplified in the matter of several tenements in London with leases secured by good sureties when the wardships had been established. Over time, many of the sureties had died and others had lost their value. As a prudent guardian, Caesar had to secure new sureties. He asked the Lord Mayor and aldermen for help, but they refused him. Thus, Caesar had to turn to his Court connections to accomplish his goal.[14] There were, however, important profits at stake. The daughters and their mother received £399 per annum from their rents, and the manor of Mitcham, where they lived, was valued at £100 per annum. By the end of June 1605, Caesar had spent £2,385 12s. on the wardships, but he had received sufficient funds to educate, clothe, and provide personal necessities for Mary and Elizabeth. This left a balance of £1,109 8s., thus reducing Caesar's deficit to £1,276 3s. 2d. When Mary Dent married Sir Henry Savile in 1607, the wardships for both daughters ended. By then, Caesar had probably reduced his deficit to about £500, and he had been living at Mitcham for ten years at no rent, which was worth about £1,000.

An interesting aspect of the wardship was Caesar's and Alice's attempt to marry young Julius and Charles Caesar to the Dent daughters. The process was peculiar: both girls were minors, and, as their guardian, Caesar could have forced a marriage upon them. Instead, he assembled witnesses and formally asked each girl whether she wished to marry a son of his. Her refusal was then noted in writing and witnessed. The only reason for this behavior seems to be that Caesar was developing a case to show that he had not exploited his wards; he had witnessed evidence to prove it.[15]

A Londoner born and reared, Caesar had little personal knowledge of country living and country manners, but his marriage to Alice Dent brought with it the manor of Mitcham, Surrey, and his residence there introduced him to the society of the suburban Home Counties. From his new country seat, Caesar dispatched letters to Court inviting the queen to visit Mitcham. Such a visit would have been a certain mark of his high standing as judge and courtier. The manor was familiar to Elizabeth, since it lay near the principal route from Greenwich to Nonesuch. She had visited Mitcham on several occasions as the guest of earlier occupants. After Elizabeth had accepted Caesar's invitation, she kept postponing her actual arrival. On five different occasions, she said that she was coming to Mitcham, only to cancel at the last moment. These cancellations were terribly expensive because Caesar had to be prepared on each occasion in case the queen actually did arrive. However, on the sixth occasion, 12 September 1598, the queen and her entourage turned into the gates of Mitcham. As John Chamberlain reported to Dudley Carleton, "The Queen is gone towards Nonesuch, taking Dr. Caesar's in her way."[16] There were hundreds of people to feed, and it required all of Caesar's craft and cunning to have all necessary provisions on hand.

Upon her arrival, the queen listened to her host's supplication, full of double meanings and ambiguities. Caesar spoke of his being "the eldest judge, the youngest and the poorest," referring to his ancient name, his relative youth, and the paucity of his reward.[17] After the supplication was presented, and after Caesar had made his welcoming speech, he gave Elizabeth the first of three gifts she would receive during her stay: "a taffetta hat white with several flowers and a jewel of gold set therein with rubies and diamonds." On the way to dinner that evening, Elizabeth was given the second gift: "a black network mantle with pure gold."[18]

The central event of any royal visit was the entertainment, whether a fully staged play, a dramatic recitation, a masque, or a musical performance. On this occasion, Caesar had commissioned John Lyly to write a verse entertainment. The author's title for the verse has been lost, but L. Hotson, a modern literary scholar, has entitled it "Poet, Painter, and Musician."[19] It was presented on the second day of the queen's visit following a meal that was probably served *al fresco.* First, after the meal had ended, a song was presented with a lute accompaniment. The verse, written in Greek, Latin, and English, was entitled "The Wounded Cupid" or "Cupid and the Bee."[20] Following the verse, three young men stepped forward to present "Poet, Painter, and Musician."

The verse, written in dialogue form, told of a dispute between Poet and Painter over who could prove a claim of artistic superiority. Painter made a more convincing argument than did Poet, while Musician was the object of the mocking humor of his fellow artists. Yet Musician was able to insert humorous rebuttals of his own. Before bringing the entertainment to its expected conclusion, the presentation of the host's principal gift, Painter made a telling observation about the growing middle class that was causing his art to go stale: "For where in elder ages, none were colored but memorable for their virtues to paynt out imitation to posterity, nowe every Citizens wife that weares a tafetta kirtle and a velvett hatt, and every gentlewoman that boord a pair of borders must have her picture in the parlour."[21] Gold and pictures and beautiful lines of poetry, the artists said, were all but passing vanities compared to virtue, and, since they could never produce a work befitting the queen, they begged her to accept instead Caesar's ultimate gift of a "gowne of cloth of silver, richly embroidered."[22]

When the festivities had ended, the queen and her party departed for Nonesuch. Caesar had been highly honored by the visit, but the honor had cost him dearly. He claimed to have spent £700 on the gifts, the entertainment, and the goods he had to purchase to make his home fit for the royal presence.[23] In addition to the money, he had nearly exhausted his own provisions while drawing heavily on the stores of his friends and his new neighbors at Mitcham. In earlier chapters, when we encountered Caesar's complaints of great poverty in his public office, it appeared that he was near to ruin. But that was the public man; the private man was in different circumstances. The money that he spent to purchase the wardships of his stepdaughters and to entertain the queen at Mitcham indicates either that he was a wealthy man or, more likely, that he was creditworthy and could raise large sums of money when he needed them.

Caesar's brothers, sisters, and stepfather were as dependent on him as were his wife and children. In the years following their father's death in 1569, Caesar's siblings had looked up to him, and when he became an adult, they turned to him for patronage. Their stepfather, Michael Locke, was of little assistance to them, and, as time passed, he too depended on Caesar for advice, assistance, and money.

Michael Locke (or Lok) enjoyed a reputation as one of the most extensively traveled men of his day. But he was frequently in debt. To support himself, he mortgaged properties in Tottenham, Middlesex, and in the City.[24] To make matters worse, Locke had believed in the late 1580's that he had settled his debts only to discover that the acquittance proving that his obligation had been paid was a forgery. While abroad, he had given some money to a third party to settle up for him in England, but all that he had to show for it was a worthless piece of paper.[25] In 1593 Locke, already in his sixties, left London with a commission to serve as the queen's consul to the English "nation" in Aleppo. The commission obliged him to remit to the English Ambassador in Constantinople the sum of £1,000 per annum from the consular receipts. When these receipts proved insufficient both to support the consul and to remit the stipulated amount to the ambassador, Locke received permission to levy a tax on the English merchants to make up the difference. One of these merchants, George Dorrington, steadfastly refused to pay the tax, and Locke subsequently seized goods belonging to him, which he sold on the open market.[26] There followed a succession of events leading to Locke's suing Dorrington in Venice, a violation of English sovereignty and of the Levant Company's charter.[27] Locke's only reliable contacts in England were his natural son, Zacharius, who petitioned Cecil on his father's behalf, and his stepson Caesar, who served his interests as an intermediary and as a commissioner to inquire into Locke's affairs.[28] In 1598, as Locke waited in Dublin beyond the reach of his English creditors and the court bailiffs, the Levant Company finally agreed to pay him £300 in return for his surrender of a £4,000 claim against Dorrington.[29] When he finally returned to England, Locke settled into a quiet life, eventually translating Peter Martyr's *Historie of the West Indies*.[30]

With their stepfather overseas and in financial troubles, the younger

siblings turned to Caesar for aid and assistance. The most important
service that he could perform for his sisters was to settle them into
suitable marriages. Margaret was married to Nicholas Wright of
Grey's Inn in 1582; later that same year, Anne married Damian Peck
of the same Inn.[31] On his wedding day, Wright gave a bond to Caesar
in the amount of £100 to guarantee that he would never become so
indebted that his estate could not provide an unencumbered landed
inheritance of £100 annual value for his widow. Margaret would have
a marriage portion to ease her widowhood, and Caesar would not
have to pay for it. In 1586 Caesar's third sister, Elizabeth, married a fellow civilian, Dr. John Hunt, of St. Bennet, Paul's Wharf.[32]

Margaret, Anne, and Elizabeth were provided for without difficulty,
but Caesar's brother Henry, four years his junior, presented severe
problems. Although Henry Caesar may have been a recusant who
decided to become a Catholic priest but later renounced his orders and
returned to England, it is more likely that he was a spy in Walsingham's service who accepted Holy Orders in the Catholic Church in
order to infiltrate exile English Catholic communities. A. L. Rowse has
called him "one of the first Anglo-Catholics"; L. Hicks has identified
him as one of Walsingham's agents in the Catholic camp.[33] Henry's behavior suggests that this latter identity might be accurate. Walsingham
appears to have "turned" a recusant, making of him a spy. According
to Rowse, Henry Caesar was an obstreperous young Anglican priest
occupying a living in Lostwithiel, Cornwall, in the early 1580's. As an
undergraduate at Cambridge, he had been a recusant, but he had
recanted before taking Anglican orders. He was, nonetheless, under
suspicion because of his former religious beliefs. On the other hand,
Henry was making no friends by accusing no less a figure than Sir
Walter Mildmay of secret Catholicism. Following a hearing occasioned by his accusations, Henry was deprived of his living and dis-
appeared overseas.[34] In 1582 he returned for a short while, but Caesar
was afraid to receive him until Walsingham had given his express permission.[35]

On 13 January 1590, Henry Caesar, now a Roman Catholic priest,
appeared at Dieppe saying that he was a brother of Dr. Julius Caesar
and that Walsingham had promised him a ready welcome in England.[36] On 22 January, Caesar, again afraid for his own reputation
and not knowing whether to believe his brother, wrote to Walsingham
that "my brother Henry Caesar is come this daie to my howse (as I

hear, for I have not seene him, neyther will I without leave) whom I have disposed this bearer to bring before your honor to be disposed of according to your direction." After he finished his letter, but before he sent it, Caesar and his brother did see one another, and, according to Caesar's account, they fought. But, because Henry said that he had come at Walsingham's behest, Caesar told the Principal Secretary that he had sent his brother on without delay.[37] On the following day, Henry Caesar, in the presence of Serjeant Fleetwood, the Recorder of London, renounced the Catholic orders that he had taken in Paris, and signed the Oath of Supremacy.[38] For a time, Henry was held in the Marshalsea, but he was eventually released into the custody of Alderman Martin, who was ordered to lodge him in the Mint and to see that Henry was provided Anglican religious instruction.[39] It is not certain what part Julius Caesar took in these arrangements. He had not been anxious to receive his newly returned brother, but Alderman Martin, Henry's keeper, was Caesar's father-in-law. On the other hand, Martin was a notable Puritan and a former Lord Mayor. Six months later, with Henry's religious instruction completed, Caesar became his younger brother's protector. Henry was released from Martin's custody and "sett at liberty to be at the disposition of his brother," who planned to send him up to Oxford for "furtherance in learnynge."[40]

The congratulatory letters that Caesar received in the summer of 1593 attested to Henry's fine progress in the University. John Holland, the Regius Professor of Theology, reported an exceptional Bachelor of Divinity declamation from Henry and asked that he be encouraged to preach.[41] George Holland, the professor's cousin, reported Henry's outstanding examination and the signal honor accorded him by Congregation. He had been accorded "first grace," the equivalent of the highest place on the First Class Honors list.[42] The president of St. John's College lost no time in offering Henry a place in college for him to pursue a higher degree in theology.[43] We next hear of Henry Caesar in the autumn of 1595 when Julius Caesar procured from the archbishop of Canterbury the advowson to the rectory of Somersham, Huntingdonshire, to be given to his brother at its next vacancy.[44] A few weeks later, Henry proceeded Doctor of Divinity and took up a City rectory in the queen's gift, St. Christopher-le-Stocks, where he remained until Somersham was vacant in 1597. His reputation for preaching was commented on by the bishop of Lincoln on his visit to

Somersham in 1600.[45] In 1609 Henry Caesar became prebend of Westminster. Finally, in 1614, he was installed as dean of Ely, one of the richest benefices in England, where he remained until his death in 1636. Julius Caesar appeared to have brought an errant young brother within the arena of respectability, but only with Walsingham's consent. It does not seem that Caesar was privy to Walsingham's and Henry's arrangements. By assisting Henry to enter a career in the church, Caesar felt that he had spared himself the embarrassment of an articulate recusant brother standing in the way of his own career. He had felt this embarrassment particularly keenly in 1582 and again in 1590, both occasions when he did not wish to see his brother. Yet he would come to take pride in Henry's successes, which also gave Julius an entrée into ecclesiastical circles he would otherwise not have possessed.

Thomas Caesar, unlike Henry, presented no problems for his elder brother. He was only a year younger than Julius and was always in his shadow. Thomas left the Merchant Taylor's School in 1578 and was admitted to the Inner Temple in 1590.[46] He practiced law quietly in chambers and was a counsel in the Court of Requests. He married three times, his first two wives being widows who left him childless. Mrs. Susanna Longe married him in January 1589 and died in June 1590.[47] Anne Beeston soon became his second wife, but she too lived for only a short time.[48] Finally, in 1593, Thomas Caesar married Susan Ryder, second daughter and coheir to William Ryder.[49] In their seventeen years of marriage, Susan and Thomas were the parents of three sons and five daughters. He was active in enterprises other than the law. Along with Robert Webb, a London clothier, and Thomas Hayes, a draper, Thomas Caesar owned a one-half share in the lease of the alnage and the farm of the subsidy of the new draperies. This extensive tax-collecting enterprise, based on new luxury textiles from the Continent that were being made in England, demanded administrative abilities of a high order. Thomas was probably counsel to the partnership in addition to being a partner himself. In 1600 he was involved in procuring a license to export unfinished cloth in excess of the amount allowed to the Merchant Adventurers. Although Julius Caesar helped his brother when he could, George Clifford, third earl of Cumberland, was of the greatest assistance to him in this enterprise. Thomas had been associated with Clifford on previous occasions, and when Thomas went up to Westminster in 1601 to sit in his only Parliament, he was the Member for Appleby, a Clifford seat. Like Julius, Thomas knew the value of a well-connected patron.

Caesar used his brother's knowledge of the law of property—which was more extensive than his own—particularly when there were matters in the Requests requiring technical advice.[50] At Caesar's nomination, in 1595, Thomas had been admitted to chambers in the Inner Temple, having been called to the bar in 1591.[51] He was elevated to the bench of the Inner Temple in 1607. But Julius Caesar was not always able to cooperate with his brother: on at least one occasion he found against a party in the Requests for whom Thomas Caesar appeared as counsel.[52]

In the early years of James I's reign, Julius Caesar's prominence and his connections were useful to Thomas, who was recommended to the Lord Treasurer by Barons Clarke and Savile for the next vacant place as an Exchequer Baron.[53] Sir John Savile was the brother of Sir Henry Savile, who had married Mary Dent. Although the king agreed to make the appointment in 1605, Thomas was not installed as a Baron until 1610.[54] In the meantime, Thomas was named to the honorific office of Clock Keeper to Prince Henry, and in 1608 he was awarded the discovery of crown debts arising before 30 Elizabeth, a grant arranged by his elder brother, by then Chancellor of the Exchequer. Finally, in 1610, Thomas was admitted to the place of Cursitor Baron of the Exchequer and was knighted shortly afterwards. Before the year was out, having reached the heights that he had sought for so many years, Sir Thomas Caesar died intestate. He possessed a few small parcels of land and little else.

The Caesar brothers are a study in contrasts. All were ambitious, yet it seems that Thomas's ambition was to a large degree motivated by Julius. Henry Caesar, on the other hand, was as ambitious as his eldest brother. Although Julius believed he had reason to fear Henry's religious commitments early on, once he felt that it was safe to associate with his brother, he sent him to Oxford and aided his advancement to better livings until he was elected dean of Ely. Julius used Thomas for expert legal advice and, briefly, as his man in the Exchequer Court. Thomas was his brother's "Number Two," always nearby, always ready to help. Caesar assisted both of his brothers, but he also took from them as the occasion required.

As an investor and a creditor, Caesar was astute, although he encountered his share of failures. He had money to invest, but he had to spend lavishly in order to maintain his position. Charles Howard noted his reputation for wealth shortly following Dorcas's death. Howard had been asked by a prospective bride to assess Caesar's worth. The Lord Admiral praised his character and added that "his estate of living I dare make it good to be at the least twenty hundred libri a yere: his estate otherwise in purse and goods as well as most Barons I knowe in this land."[55] His memberships in his Inn and his liveried company were important indexes of his social and economic standing. In the aggregate, Caesar appeared to be prosperous, although, regardless of Charles Howard's estimate of his "estate of living," he may have been more dependent on credit than on amassed capital. Presenting appropriate gifts and participating in the government of such institutions as the Inner Temple, along with these other indicators of wealth, were as tiles in a mosaic portrait of a successful member of the bench who was upwardly mobile and determined to succeed at even higher levels as a senior bureaucrat and jurist. He required a style of living that would show him off in the best light. He had to be seen with the proper people spending money according to expectations of his station.

A mark of material success (and a burden of high office) was the presentation of New Year's gifts to one's superiors. As early as 1589, Caesar was making stunning gifts. He apologetically sent to the Lord Chancellor "a pore mite" because his "habilitie, imparied by public service, was unhable to yealde much." Belying this beggardly description was a gift of fine workmanship: "this matter cristall, stripped with ivory, and garnished with silver gilt."[56] At least one other gift of similar quality was sent to Burghley at the same time. Seven years later, Caesar asked Lady Scudamore to draw the queen's attention to his gift to Elizabeth of two gold bracelets valued at £85.[57] His gifts were lavish, establishing publically how he wished to be regarded in the social hierarchy.

Caesar's social standing was also associated with the organizations to which he belonged. Within the City of London, he was a freeman and a member of the Worshipful Company of Goldsmiths.[58] But adjacent to the City's western walls was another society, the Inner Temple, of which he was a prominent member. Although Caesar never intended a career as a common lawyer, he was admitted to the Inn in 1580 to finish his legal education. During the eighties, Caesar was not conspicuously active in the affairs of the Inn. However, on 24 January 1591, a fortnight after he had been sworn a Master of Requests, Caesar was called to the bench of the Inn and was sworn to the oath of obedience.[59] A month later, he was admitted to the chamber of Robert Waterhouse and was promised the next vacant bencher's chamber as his own.[60] Before the year was out, Caesar had been called to the outer bar of the Inn, a reversal in the usual order of progression from bar to bench.[61] For the next several years, he was an active and generous bencher and an officer of his society.

The business of the Inner Temple was conducted by its benchers assembled in its parliament. The presiding officer of the parliament (and thus of the Inn) was usually the Treasurer. From January 1592 until November 1593, Caesar and his fellow bencher, Edward Coke, presided over the parliaments, although neither had yet been elected Treasurer. Then, in November 1593, Caesar was elected Treasurer; he was succeeded by Coke in 1595.[62] Caesar regularly attended parliaments and carried out the duties of the Treasurer with sufficient care that he was elected to more than one annual term of office.

Yet it was not the term as Treasurer that marked the apogee of Caesar's career in the Inner Temple. He enjoyed his proudest moment when, in 1596, his fellow benchers praised him for making a gift to the Inn of £300 toward erecting a block of chambers later known, until well into the eighteenth century, as Caesar's Buildings. In recognition of his contribution, Caesar was granted a life-chamber in the Inn and the right of appointment, during his lifetime, both to admission to the Inn and to a chamber for his sons, sons-in-law, kinsmen, or fellow benchers. The only restriction was that there could be no more than six of his appointees in the Inn at any one time. These privileges were confirmed over Edward Coke's signature when he was Treasurer of the Inner Temple.[63] Unfortunately, the Bench Order Books (the books of account) of the Inner Temple, from before 1596 until after Caesar's death in 1636, are in such an advanced state of decay that they cannot be inspected. In these records we would find the evidence of how Caesar used his right of appointment. Space in the Inns of Court was in short supply, and a chamber was a virtual necessity if one wished to practice law. Hence, the ability to command six chambers was the equivalent of controlling the livelihoods of up to six practicing barristers.

Caesar had an extraordinary patronage asset, but we have no way of knowing how he used it other than to benefit members of his own family.

If the Inn was an index of Caesar's standing in the metropolitan society of London and Westminster, and if the gifts that he made were a mark of that standing, then his loans and investments were the source of the wealth that permitted him to live up to the expectations of a lawyer of his distinction and ambition. He received fees and pensions from the queen after he became an ordinary Master of Requests, but these were the source of his maintenance, as was the income from the Dent estate. The surplus that could make him wealthy came from his private investments and from loans that he made.

In 1586 Caesar began his entrepreneurial career by joining with one Bevys Bulmer to petition the queen for a patent to erect lighthouses at the mouths of a number of English harbors. They proposed collecting 1d. the ton from all ships entering or leaving a harbor under the safety of their beacons.[64] It appears that their proposal was never given serious consideration. In 1583, through the good offices of his father-in law, Alderman Martin, Caesar received the transfer of one-quarter of one share in the Mineral and Battery Company from John Harrison.[65] The Company enjoyed a monopoly of the founding of ordnance in England and of the mining and smelting of the component metals. Because of the exceptionally high quality of English cannon in the sixteenth century, there was a profitable, if not always legal, export market for the Company's products. Martin, along with his sons, owned nine and one-half of the thirty-six shares in the Company, which explains Caesar's heavy involvement in the Company's affairs from the moment that his fractional share was transferred to him. By 1594 he was sworn one of the two Governors of the Company, along with his father-in-law, and in 1596 he and Robert Beale were engaged in prosecuting the Company's claims against difficult patentees.[66] The legal affairs of the Company were a source of income, and Caesar's terms as Governor, together with his long association with the Mineral and Battery Company, resulted in his occupying a prominent place in its new charter, issued in 1604 by James I. William Herbert, Earl of Pembroke, and Sir Robert Cecil, viscount Cranborne, were the first two names on the new charter; Caesar's was the third.[67]

Caesar's intimate knowledge of maritime affairs and his connections in the City encouraged him to make investments in overseas adventures. He was a member of both the Northwest Passage Company and the French Company, and he also backed Penton, Cavendish, and, on his second voyage, Frobisher.[68] The Cavendish investment provides an interesting view of the dynamics and the perils of venturing. In the summer of 1586, Caesar had invested £50 with Thomas Cavendish as he set out to explore unknown parts and, eventually, to circumnavigate the globe. As a venturer, Caesar expected a share in any profits of the voyage in proportion to his investment. When Cavendish returned to England in September 1588 with the rump of his fleet, Caesar wrote to him expressing unrestrained joy. His prayers for the explorer's safe return had been answered, and the voyage had been "profittable to yourself and contrey in respect of the riches which you bring, and the traffick which you should open to our posteritie." Caesar also assured himself "that those whom Cavendish had vouchsafed to be venturers with him shall think them selves happie in some measure." In the meantime, any assistance that Caesar could offer the adventurer would be provided "to the uttermost" of his power.[69] Such a promise from an admiralty judge had great potential value for maritime adventurers, but in less than a fortnight Caesar was engaged in a dispute over his share. First, Bevys Bulmer, his former colleague in the lighthouse proposal, insisted that the judge had bargained half of his share to him in return for £25 cash that Caesar had needed at the time. An irate letter to Bulmer told him that no such bargain had been made, since Bulmer had never produced the £25.[70] Nothing more was heard from Bulmer, but Cavendish proved more difficult to deal with.

Cavendish advised Caesar at Christmas that he intended to postpone the repayment of an investment as small as £50. When Caesar wrote to him in February about the money that was due him, he indicated that he did not mind waiting to be paid as long as the other venturers were waiting for their shares. However, it seemed that the others had been paid and that Cavendish was set against paying Caesar. In the light of this refusal, Caesar informed him that the obligation had to be paid, then and there.[71] The amount owed to Caesar had now grown to £150, by his reckoning, since it included his share of the profits. Cavendish, who thought of the sum not as a debt but as a £50 free gift, wished to ignore it. Caesar told the explorer exactly when and where and in whose presence the original investment had been negotiated. Without immediate satisfaction, Caesar intended to take the entire matter to law.[72] After the lawsuit was started, Caesar wrote his last letter to Cavendish. There had obviously been some negotiation between the parties before he wrote: mention was made of a plan in which Cavendish would repay the original £50 and keep the remaining £100 as an investment in his next voyage. Caesar remained the captain's "assured good friend," and good relations seem to have been restored.[73] But Caesar never saw the return of his second, albeit reluctant investment: Cavendish and his fleet perished during the voyage. While it is not surprising that a man of Caesar's means would venture money in an expedition, it is significant that he was the judge of the court in which any disputes over the goods brought home by the fleet would be tried. In that event, he would have been hard pressed to isolate his interest in the profits of the venture from the law he was sworn to administer.

Although Caesar's papers are an abundant source of information about nearly every aspect of his career, they have surprisingly little to tell us about his loans and other personal financial dealings. Thus, the one well-documented case of a loan and its outcome that does survive becomes all the more important. The story is long, but from it we learn of Caesar's tactics and gain an insight into the disturbing social pressures attendant upon the rapidly changing society in which he flourished. The case concerned a protracted and occasionally embarrassing loan made to Sir Walter Leveson of Lineshall, Shropshire, the Vice Admiral of Wales.

Leveson first came to Caesar's attention in the course of admiralty business. He rarely came up to London, preferring the deep country where he could avoid his creditors who awaited him in the City. As they became better acquainted, the judge loaned money to Leveson, money Leveson never seemed able to repay.[74] At the same time that he was Leveson's creditor, Caesar was acting as go-between in behalf of Richard Leveson, Sir Walter's son. Sir Walter wanted to arrange a marriage between Richard and Charles Howard's daughter, Margaret. Howard, who liked Leveson well enough, was not sure whether the marriage was socially suitable. So it was that Caesar, at Leveson's request, did his best to overcome this resistance.[75] When the couple was married in December 1587, Caesar had done a favor for a provincial friend and had even more closely allied himself with the Howard family. But this happy state would soon dissolve.

While Leveson and Howard (and Caesar) had been discussing marriage, a ship owned by Leveson had been harassing Danish vessels in Norwegian ports, and the king of Denmark was furious. He wrote to Elizabeth demanding rapid satisfaction for his subjects, the ships' owners, who were heading for England to receive redress. Privy Council ordered Caesar to arrest Leveson and to hold him until he paid, or made surety to pay, a fine of £2,300.[76] The embarrassment for Caesar and Howard must have been acute. Caesar had promoted the marriage of Richard Leveson to Margaret Howard by overcoming Charles Howard's doubts. Howard, the Lord Admiral, found himself closely related by marriage to an accused pirate. Many of Howard's aristocratic friends were little better than pirates themselves, but they were of his rank, and some shared their gains with him. Leveson was an upstart and Howard had no interests in his ventures. It is not surprising that within a few weeks Howard had arranged for Leveson's release on the improbable grounds that he had not acted in a disorderly manner.[77]

There was a lesson in this for Caesar. Leveson was a pirate, but he had been exonerated; he was in debt, yet he never paid up and seemed to be in no hurry to do so. Helplessly, Caesar decided to allow Leveson's loan to remain uncollected rather than to press for a settlement. In that way, there was still something left to make a claim against when the time was right and when Caesar could join his interests with those of others. The right time first arrived two years later. The money that Caesar had first advanced to Leveson had been the surety to secure a bond for a debt owed to Sir Rowland Hayward. In 1590 Caesar proceeded to sue Hayward, who was Lord Mayor of London at the time, both at law and in Chancery, to force a settlement of the Leveson debt, which would free Leveson to pay Caesar or, better still, force Hayward to surrender to Caesar property that he was holding as security.[78] Although this suit was not successful, by July Leveson's creditors, including Caesar, began closing in. He was to be held in custody in the Counter in Wood Street, and only Hayward, Caesar, and one of the Barons of the Exchequer were to have access to him.[79] It is not entirely clear what happened in the Wood Street Counter, but it would appear that Leveson made some sort of promise in order to free himself. Once at liberty, he did not honor his agreement. In February of that year, Leveson had asked Caesar to help him get a royal protection so that he and his servants could move about freely while he settled his debts.[80] In November the protection was granted for four months.[81] The Danes were still suing him, and his creditors were hot on his heels.[82]

Now, there is little question that Leveson could have paid toward his debts had he elected to do so, although it is not at all certain that he could have settled them all. He sent £38 to Daniel Rogers, Clerk of Council, for disposing of his Danish problems for him, but he sent nothing to Caesar.[83] It will become clear that Leveson was deranged; but, for the moment, Caesar addressed him as a moral wretch who might still be saved. He told Leveson that he had resolved never to speak to him again because of the way he had abused Caesar's friendship. However, after making that promise to himself, Caesar heard that Leveson had changed his behavior, and, thus, Caesar was resolved to be once more his friend. The seeds of God's grace were not entirely distinguished within him, for "they beginne nowe to appere and bring fourth good fruits of repentance and amendment of lief which you make manifest to the world by using continuall prayer in your howse and by an earnest desire to satisfie all your creditors with all convenient speed." Caesar appended a catalogue of good behavior for Leveson's moral enlightenment: frequent prayers, the Golden Rule, and the cultivation of a reputation for personal honesty ranked next to an admonition to "abandon all manner of whores, and those felthie servants and compagnions which have drawen you there unto" and a warning to avoid all ill-advised schemes that would exacerbate a "breach between my Lord Howard and you." The breach referred to a property transaction dating from the time of Richard's marriage to Margaret. Leveson had agreed to convey a manor to his son and daughter-in-law, but he was now trying to renege on the promise even though the conveyance had been made. This was a particularly offensive gesture to Howard, whose son-in-law was at sea in command of one of the queen's squadrons while his daughter was resident in the manor and subject to Leveson's harassment. The letter to Leveson ended with a reminder that the shortest way to God's mercy (and to Caesar's heart) would be the immediate settlement of his debts. Leveson could pay part of the debt or, at the least, the interest on the money that he owed to him.[84] He replied with a promise to pay his debt to the judge, but nothing came of the commitment.[85]

The next year found Leveson in deeper and deeper trouble over the seizure of other ships.[86] In despair, Caesar decided to cut his losses by proceeding against some of Leveson's land in partial payment. He wrote to remind him of the many favors that he had done for him and of the £800 debt still outstanding.[87] By July 1595 Leveson had made over to Caesar the manor of Trentham, Staffordshire, that Richard Leveson had received from Charles Howard at the time of the marriage negotiations. According to the indenture, Sir Walter had the right to alienate the manor, which he did. Caesar was to have a 99-year lease at no entry fine, and he was to pay an annual rental to Richard Leveson. The entry fine on the manor was £400.[88] Two years later, Richard Leveson made an indenture to Caesar agreeing to abide by his father's indenture and not lay claim to the manor.[89] In addition, Richard had to pay some of the annual charges against the manor himself.[90]

Leveson's creditors finally caught up with him in 1598, sending him to the Fleet. But there was more than debt involved in his arrest; he was suspected of conspiring to poison his daughter-in-law and his son. He wrote to Cecil begging him to confront Leveson with his accuser, but without any luck.[91] In the meantime, Caesar and Herbert were trying to get some money from the queen for Leveson so that he could pay off his creditors.[92] Their only plausible grounds for asking for this grant was in compensation for his charges as Vice Admiral. In the years that Leveson had been avoiding his creditors, his son, now Sir Richard Leveson, had risen to the rank of Admiral and had distinguished himself at sea. John Chamberlain, in a letter to Dudley Carleton, reported that Sir Richard had "detained 17 sail of Easterlings and Hollanders in the Narrow Seas bound for Spain. His father is in the Fleet, having fallen into the hands of his old creditors, who caught him at Lambeth."[93] The suspicion of conspiracy regarding the elder Leveson was not mentioned and had probably been kept secret.

An examination of Leveson's solicitor, conducted while Sir Walter was in the Fleet, revealed that Leveson had been claiming magical powers and that both he and the solicitor were adept in the use of exotic poisons. The solicitor, Robert Weyland, told his examiners that Leveson had attempted to poison his daughter-in-law, Margaret, at his home at Lineshall, Shropshire during dinner one evening. Weyland had "heard Sir Walter say that if his daughter-in-law Leveson were dead, he could free all his lands, notwithstanding the books of conveyances, and that they would all come back to him, as by her death his son would lose all of his honorable friends." After administering the poison, Leveson refused to treat or comfort his sick daughter-in-law, but she eventually recovered her health; the adept poisoners had given her enough to make her ill but too little to kill her. Weyland reported that Leveson had, upon Margaret's recovery, decided to leave her alone and to concentrate instead on taking the life of his son. "He swore great oaths, and wished that his sone were either hanged or at the bottom of the sea, because he had given one of the best lordships he had to him and wished that the bundle of venomous powders he had provided, which he thought enough to kill twenty men, were in his son's belly."[94] A month later, Sir Walter wrote to Cecil to tell him that he had effected a reconciliation when his son had visited him in prison, and he begged forgiveness for his previous rash behavior.[95]

Sir Richard was posted to Irish waters. From his station, he wrote to Cecil, in December 1601, that "the miserable wreck of my father's torn estate are [sic] well known. His want of care and my want of credit with him to take up losse ends before they ravelled into extremities are the cause that my lands, long since extended, are now by forfeitures brought into the hands of strangers, who may work upon my weakness." Caesar would certainly have fit Sir Richard's description, having taken his land to satisfy his father's debts and having forced him to concur in the transaction. Leveson begged the queen to give him a gift of money that would allow him "to shore up my crazed estate" and, thus, continue in the queen's service.[96] A year later, Sir Walter was dead in the Fleet and Sir Richard was left with a frightful mess to straighten out.[97]

In this long account there are two important points to consider. One is the violent generational (and societal) conflict between the elderly provincial renegade and his son whom he married into the aristocracy of the kingdom. While Sir Walter relished the aristocratic connections occasioned by the marriage, he resented their consequences. Sir Richard had become an aristocrat, but his father simply did not understand the governing mores of his son's new station and position. He blamed his own chronic indebtedness on the marriage he had engineered for his son and on the friends whom his son had made as a naval officer and member-by-marriage of the Howard family. Sir Walter had been left out of his son's life, and the ravages of inflation and indebtedness were ruining his estate.

Closer to our primary concern is the prolonged account of Caesar's manipulation of the debt Leveson owed him. He was able to continue the debt (for which he was also paying interest, since he had borrowed in order to lend) for more than a decade. He tried to settle with Sir Rowland Hayward in 1590 by offering to pay Leveson's debts to Hayward in return for two manors that were held as security.[98] Although his bargain was not concluded, Caesar did eventually obtain the manor of Trentham, Staffordshire, although he was required to pay £20 12s. 2d. per annum to Sir Richard. Nonetheless, Caesar had entered into the long lease that he enjoyed without paying the £400 entry fine. Thus, we find Caesar turning an otherwise insecure debt into a valuable property. He may have entered into similar transactions, but the Leveson loan is the best case we have illustrating his patience and cunning.

The property received from Leveson was an important part of a growing portfolio that was the foundation of Caesar's wealth. He was assembling the elements of a diversified estate that would be used to advance both his own and his children's fortunes. In Chapter 10 we shall see how successful Caesar was in this pursuit. His accumulation of a family fortune is an important indicator of his long-range career and investment strategies. In the light of this wealth, it is useful to recall Caesar's constant complaints of economic disaster occasioned by his underpaid public service. He did not consider his personal wealth to be compensation for his service to the queen, and if he spent more on an office than he received from it, he complained bitterly to his patrons, suggesting that he was on the brink of bankruptcy. His principal goal was the careful development of a fortune for the benefit of his family, the primary beneficiaries of his exhausting efforts.

Our examination of the private life and personal wealth of Julius Caesar must consider his service as a Member of Parliament. While membership in the House of Commons was a public office, it was also as much a mark of Caesar's personal status as were his country seat at Mitcham, his memberships in various trading companies, and his treasurership of the Inner Temple. Caesar owed his career in Parliament, as well as his career in the admiralty, to Charles Howard. In 1589 he sat for Reigate, a borough owned by Howard, and in 1593 for Bletchingley, where Howard's influence was determining. In the Parliaments of 1597 and 1601 he was the Member for New Windsor, where Charles Howard was High Steward.[99] By the time that Caesar was standing for election to the Jacobean Parliaments, he used Court patronage and high office to secure a seat.

There is no record of Caesar's joining in debate during the Elizabethan Parliaments, nor can we suppose that he was considered to be a sufficiently senior officer of government to sway votes or to mute criticism by his presence. However, the extant accounts of the Elizabethan Commons do give a full record of Caesar's committee service. From it we can assemble a composite picture of Caesar's areas of personal expertise and interest. Although in his first Parliament, in 1589, he had no committee assignments, the Parliaments of 1593, 1597, and 1601 provide a good index of his early legislative career.

Understandably, Caesar was called to sit in committees discussing legislation concerned with admiralty affairs and mercantile law. In 1597 "four bills of no great moment" were read, "of which the last being for the retaining, well ordering and governing of merchants and seamen." After its second reading, the bill was committed to Caesar and a number of burgesses whose boroughs would be the beneficiaries of its provisions. The bill was given to Caesar to convene the committee; this suggests that he may have introduced it at its first reading.[100] Caesar was also "holding the bill" in the same Parliament for a measure explaining and extending the act of 5 Elizabeth, cap. 5, for the mainenance of the navy.[101] In the 1601 Parliament, Caesar joined with Sir Walter Raleigh and Sir Francis Bacon in a committee to consider a bill regulating the insurance policies used among merchants, another area of Caesar's professional expertise.[102]

As a civilian and a Master of Requests, Caesar sat in such committees concerned with criminal law, prohibitions against civil courts, and recusancy. In 1593 he sat in a large committee to discuss the Recusancy Bill, and in 1597 he joined with four other Doctors of Law in a larger committee considering a private bill for the award of costs in a prohibition.[103] In the 1601 Parliament, the committee to investigate the strengthening of the penal laws included Caesar. Another committee of the same Parliament included him because he was a Master of Requests. Its charge was to consider a bill for the confirmation of letters patent made to Sir Edward Seymour by Edward VI.[104] When a private bill from the House of Lords "for the uniting of Eye and Dunsden to the manor of Sunning" was read in the Commons in 1601, a great furor arose because of the prerogative implications of uniting lordships by legislation. It is not surprising, in the light of the matter under dispute, that Caesar was made a member of the committee.[105]

Some of his committee memberships reflected Caesar's personal interests. A bill in 1601 to confirm the jurisdiction of the City of London over a part of the precincts of the Royal Hospital of St. Katharine was committed to Caesar, who was the Master of the Hospital, and to the Members for the City.[106] Several weeks later, the amended measure was "dashed" at its third reading with a margin of 43 votes.[107] Caesar had been able to protect his interests and the independence of the Hospital. Likewise, Caesar was probably a member of the committees discussing the 1601 Ordnance Act because his association with the Mineral and Battery Company gave him more than an ordinary interest in its outcome.

Finally, we note that in 1593 Caesar took part in the committee work on the subsidy bill, a subject that would occupy his attention fully when he became Chancellor of the Exchequer. He was named to the committee to examine the government's subsidy requests and to establish an amount to be voted on by the House.[108] He was also a member of the committee for drafting the articles and the preamble for the subsidy act.[109] In the final stages of the enactment of the subsidy bill, Caesar was appointed to a joint committee with the House of Lords to reconcile the different legislation emerging from the two Houses.[110]

During the remaining sessions of the Elizabethan Parliaments, we do not find Caesar involved with subsidies. His work load in the Court of Requests and in the Admiralty Court piled higher, a possible reason for his begging off such assignments. But his fellow Members or the government may not have found him a particularly effective member of finance committees. In any case, the Elizabethan Parliaments provided Caesar with important experience for when the early Jacobean Parliaments came to resemble cockpits more than legislatures.

Upon James I's arrival in London after his accession progress from Scotland in 1603, Caesar was among the legion who received knighthoods from their new monarch. Along with Roger Wilbraham, William Waad, Thomas Smith, Thomas Edmondes, and Thomas Lake, he was knighted on 20 May 1603.[111] After the drought years of Elizabeth's reluctance to confer honors on her subjects, James I released a torrent of rewards to assuage the demand. In conferring a knighthood on Caesar, the king acknowledged his professional stature while also confirming his social position. Sir Julius Caesar, at forty-five was a seasoned judge and experienced administrator, Member of Parliament, and minor court officer. He resided in the country and also kept chambers at several places in and near the City. He was ripe for career advancement, and three years later, in 1606, the time was right for his appointment as Chancellor of the Exchequer.

V

Awaiting a Chasteminded Joseph

HISTORICAL ERAS BELONG more to the historian than to history; they are problematic, but they are conceptually useful, even if many historians tend to link the ends of eras with the deaths of notables. When, for instance, did the Elizabethan era come to an end? Was it with the death of the queen, with the death of Burghley before her, or with the death of Salisbury in 1612? Save for the queen's own demise, it is not certain that her contemporaries would have recognized epochal change in anyone's death, even the Cecils'. Yet Burghley's death ended a long-standing association, even a friendship, with the queen, and hindsight suggests that his death perhaps ended an era. For forty years Elizabeth and Burghley had worked together, each taking the other's measure, each becoming predictable to the other. Even though Burghley had become extremely irascible of late, leading Elizabeth to call him "a forward old fool" in 1596, their relationship had endured so long and had become so intimate that it was unlikely that the old queen would allow any future minister to succeed to his unique place.[1] Burghley had provided for the eventuality of his dying before his mistress. Knowing that the queen had always been uncomfortable with new faces, he had prepared his second son, Sir Robert Cecil, to assume his responsibilities. This was a twice-blessed policy: Elizabeth would be served by a familiar successor who would also preserve and advance the Cecilian fortunes. The transition from older to younger Cecil had begun in 1590 with Walsingham's death. Against the contrary efforts of the emerging Essex faction, Burghley strove to see Robert Cecil named Secretary, but it was another year before he realized his goal. Soon thereafter, Robert was sworn to Council, and father and son worked together to secure a family continuum.[2] As Burghley's health became more problematic, Robert Cecil spoke and acted for him, although the father was forever worrying the son with memoranda and reminders.[3] Just a year before his death, Burghley saw Robert made Chancellor of the Duchy of Lancaster, thus placing all revenue agencies in family hands.[4] But on the elder Cecil's death, any hope of continuing the consolidation of the offices of father and son seemed to have vanished.

The queen, for her part, had anticipated the Lord Treasurer's death, and consequently did not take it "over heavily," for she had been making her own provisions. It was known at Court that she intended Sir Thomas Sackville, Lord Buckhurst, to become Lord Treasurer, while the earl of Essex was to become the Master of the Wards. Cecil was already well placed as Principal Secretary. On 12 August 1598, Buckhurst and the incumbent Chancellor of the Exchequer, Sir John Fortescue, were appointed to issue the queen's treasure on the authority of her warrants, thus making Buckhurst's permanent appointment seem all the more certain.[5] But others at Court had different plans.

Rumors circulated to the effect that Cecil was working hard to secure the Lord Treasurer's place for himself and that Essex was in too much difficulty with the queen to be favored with the Mastership of the Wards.[6] Elizabeth encouraged no one: she allowed suitors for place to make their representations to her while she remained above the fray. By autumn yet another rumor circulated, holding that the Chancellor of the Exchequer was to become the Lord Treasurer, but a rebuttal was soon abroad: "Now they say Lord Buckhurst." As for Essex, he had not as yet been appointed to the Court of Wards, and one line of speculation even suggested that the Wards was to be dissolved.[7] In November, Buckhurst was reported to be in league with Essex, Cecil's archrival. Cecil seemed destined to lose.[8] The uncertainties surrounding the succession to Burghley's offices appeared to be resolved in December when it was reported that Buckhurst would become Lord Treasurer and Cecil would receive the Court of Wards. But the rumors were still not quieted; the contest was not yet over. Essex was reported ready to strike a new bargain. If he were to receive either £6,000 per annum or a single payment of £20,000, and if the daily administration of the Wards was to be entrusted to some "mean man," Essex would pay him a pension and not prosecute any further his supplication for the place.[9] By May 1599 the queen had made her decision public: Buckhurst to the Treasury, Cecil to the Wards.[10] Contemporaries noted that Cecil was offended by this result. "Strangnes continewes between" Cecil and Buckhurst, wrote one correspondent as late as November.[11]

The protracted maneuvering following Burghley's death reflected the political reality of Elizabeth's court in the waning years of her reign. The queen had long surrounded herself with a few advisors whom she thought worthy of her confidence, but she never extended her trust without reservation. Burghley had come as close as anyone would to enjoying her unqualified confidence, but even he had been out of favor for a time following the execution of Mary Stuart. While Buckhurst possibly was not the best candidate to succeed Burghley, he had the advantage of being a survivor from the early days of Elizabeth's reign who had demonstrated steadfast loyalty and could be trusted. Secretary Cecil, for all of his apparent talents and abilities, was pushy, aggressive, and more openly factious than Burghley had been; he was not the heir to his father's place in the queen's world. But he did not come away empty-handed: the Principal Secretary, who was a powerful voice in Privy Council and at Court, assumed the Mastership of the Wards and the great wealth that accompanied that office. Still, Cecil felt aggrieved and dishonored because he had failed to get what he wanted.

Burghley had performed extraordinary service as Elizabeth's Lord Treasurer. Faced with steadily reduced public funds, particularly after the Armada year, he had to deal as well as he could with mounting extraordinary expenses. The twin burdens of inflation and warfare made it impossible for the queen to conduct her affairs within the limits of her ordinary revenue.[12] The result was incrementally more precarious financial instability. They had only Parliament and the money market for relief, and each was fraught with difficulties. Before 1598 had passed, and with subsidies still being collected from a previous Parliament, the queen was in need of money. In addition, privy seals were abroad for the collection of forced loans and benevolences, and a £20,000 loan had just been concluded with the City. Nonetheless, the queen expected the City to lend her an additional £150,000, for which she was willing to mortgage £5,000 in rents and the customs revenues from the port of London. The aldermen of the City, for their part, were unable to produce the two- and three-thousand-pound increments needed to meet the total. When Chamberlain related this news to Dudley Carleton, he observed that the money was "hardly to be had, the City being so impoverished through decay of trade." He thought it curious that Elizabeth needed so much money, since her only remaining extraordinary expenses of consequence were related to the war in Ireland.[13] This observation confirms just how little Chamberlain and his connections knew of the real costs of the Irish war. It is likely that they knew little more of Elizabeth's and Burghley's large-scale dependence on loans since the early 1590's.

The government had for years been making do with a complex series of loans predicated on future revenue (or future loans) and necessitated by soaring extraordinary expenses.[14] Elizabeth, who could manage Parliament with remarkable skill, was reluctant to turn to Parliament when other courses were available. Adept at using the sessions for their own ends, the queen and the Treasurer considered the concessions associated with parliamentary taxes expensive and unnecessary nuisances. Their fiscal independence forced them to develop the greatest possible return on the fruits of the prerogative in order to preserve the crown's credit. Under Burghley's management, the Court of Wards had produced high yields for himself and the queen. The Church had been a virtual quarry of wealth for the queen's use; the City had been her banker. But none of these courses had been worth as much to Elizabeth as had been her penury. At every turn, she moderated the costs of government chargeable to her by passing them on to the governed in the form of fees for her official services. We have already encountered this practice in Caesar's early career: although official fees were usually his, the queen was loath to augment them with a pension or a grant of land. Taken together, borrowing, exploiting the prerogative, and restraining spending allowed the queen and her Lord Treasurer to keep the level of spending (and thus of taxation) artificially low. By the end of her reign, the Exchequer was anchored in a deficit position, although the magnitude of the debt was not generally known. But the state of this debt would shortly become a painful reality to the new English king, James VI of Scotland.

James's accession in 1603 brought an outsider to the throne whose experience had prepared him well for ruling but not for English politics.[15] Although he had been remarkably successful as Scotland's king, James was the product of a political environment characterized by factions, conspiracies, religious turmoil, and clan violence. James's success in Scotland was in part the result of his own considerable skills and in part the result of the qualities of the first among his ministers, Chancellor Maitland. Following Maitland's death in 1595, James had tried to govern without a powerful advisor, but he soon found that the poverty of his estate demanded the advice and counsel of a financially and politically sophisticated minister such as he found in George Home, the earl of Dunbar, his Lord Treasurer and alter ego after 1601.

As James awaited his English inheritance, there was no single English voice on whom he could rely for advice. Cecil exchanged letters with him, but he represented a faction. Other courtiers wrote to him from Westminster, and he was in continuous correspondence with his ambassador. All of these sources resulted in conflicting data, and there was no English Dunbar to interpret for him. Thus, when it came time for James to travel to London, he took Dunbar with him. Although James did not load the English government with Scottish ministers, he had to find suitable places for a few such as Dunbar. Unfortunately, there were no senior ministerial places conveniently available to the Scottish Lord Treasurer. Although all commissions and patents had lapsed on the queen's death, James would have created unnecessary hostility had he refused to recommission a senior English incumbent in favor of his Scottish advisor. However, Sir John Fortescue, who was not greatly liked by the king, was not a problem to deprive because there was a suitable bone to throw him by way of compensation. So it was that Dunbar was sworn to Privy Council, created Lord Berwick, and made Master of the Wardrobe and Chancellor of the Exchequer.[16] Fortescue, whose offices these had been, was made Chancellor of the Duchy of Lancaster.

Dunbar's place in Exchequer was not appropriate to his station, nor did it suit his disposition. The Chancellor, as the senior clerk in Exchequer, was subordinate to the English Lord Treasurer. But before this arrangement could present serious problems, James discovered that he required Dunbar's considerable political ability on the Borders and in Scotland. In 1605 he left Westminster for more important service in the north. Once more James was without a trusted advisor close at hand, although he was coming to depend more extensively on Cecil. Nonetheless, his want of competent and trusted counsel contributed to his seriously misreading English politics.

Among the blind spots in the new king's political vision was his failure to comprehend the constraints that had surrounded his predecessor throughout her reign. For example, it had appeared to James, from Edinburgh, that Elizabeth had only to ask her subjects for support and it was hers. "Unaware of the cussedness of Elizabeth's later parliaments, of the growth of faction and corruption in government, accustomed to a subservient Scottish parliament where the gentry were of no account, he expected little opposition to his will."[17] He did not understand her compromises and the limitations on the monarch in English politics. Furthermore, "years of penury in an economically backward country left him ill-equipped to face either the complexities of England's financial affairs or the harsh fact that the Crown's wealth was not prodigious. James, therefore, gave and spent magnificently, making less effort than before to assess the problems of his situation and to calculate the best possible remedies."[18]

James tried to translate his Scottish political experience into English practice, but the two were not compatible. For example, James had brought the Scottish parliament under control by dominating the Lords of the Covenant, a parliamentary committee through which all legislation had to pass prior to debate. He assumed the Privy Council could serve the same purpose in England. James did not seem to understand that Council had no corporate standing in Parliament. He was likewise unaware of the consequences of his elevating the leading Elizabethan councillors to the peerage. James would discover, to his regret, that he had canceled their personal legislative influence in the House of Commons when he sent them up to the Lords. No longer would they be able to manage the crown's business in the Lower House from their places on the flanks of the Speaker's throne.[19]

Under these circumstances, and in the light of the political pressures of the moment, good advice and attention to political detail were needed in Westminster, all the more so if the king and his government were to arrest the continuing deterioration of crown revenue. The Principal Secretary gave advice, but the more important arbiter of fiscal administration and policy was the Lord Treasurer, recently elevated to the earldom of Dorset. With Dunbar fully absorbed in the north and in Scotland, and to get the most from both Dorset and Cecil, who would soon become the earl of Salisbury, it became necessary to appoint a new Chancellor of the Exchequer to attend to the daily routine of the huge Exchequer establishment. Not only would the new Chancellor have to be trusted by the Lord Treasurer; he would also have to enjoy Salisbury's confidence. Caesar fit these specifications. Salisbury was prepared to advance his nomination, perhaps to pave the way for his own eventual appointment as Lord Treasurer. Dorset, for his part, had known Caesar for more than twenty years and welcomed the assistance that he would provide. So it was, in 1606, that James commissioned Sir Julius Caesar Chancellor of the Exchequer.[20] But it appears that Caesar was not prepared for the appointment that diverted him from his aspirations in the Chancery.

We have, by now, become accustomed to the pattern and pace of Caesar's methodical climb through the ranks of office open to a civilian. Self-confident, occasionally cocky, often wheedling, his tactics become commonplace and his goals predictable. Thus, it is somewhat surprising to find Caesar confronted with an unfamiliar office. His first weeks and months as Chancellor, together with the unusual secrecy surrounding his appointment, demonstrate just how little he knew of his new duties, how suddenly they came upon him, and how cautiously he went about his transition from judge to finance minister. He researched the precedents of the Chancellor's place, of the incumbent's responsibilities, and of the fees to which he would be entitled. His passage from judge to minister would be not easy, and he needed a strong superior to give him guidance and direction. For his part, Dorset, who had served as de facto Chancellor since Dunbar's departure, was happy to unload those responsibilities on Caesar. At the same time, he provided sound, practical advice born of a lifetime's experience in the crown's service.

At this stage in his career, Caesar was no longer the upwardly mobile office seeker devoted to establishing himself and his fortune. He was, instead, a successful careerist, well into middle age, who was running fast just to keep up with a job that was nearly too demanding for him. A failure at this point could have lost him the advantages he had earned during his years on the make and could have jeopardized his carefully developed strategy of advancing his family's interests. Cautious and established, the watchful and conservative paterfamilias, Caesar, as Chancellor of the Exchequer, would merit the briefest of considerations but for the early Stuart revenue crises and Salisbury's proposed solution, the Great Contract of 1610. Not only did Caesar figure conspicuously in the politics of the Contract; its failure has been attributed to him as well.

Since the 1590's Caesar had served as judge, gained place at Court, and become a leading figure in the civilian establishment. Earlier

chapters have centered on Caesar and the patterns of his career. Now
the focus changes, as the study encompasses a larger assessment of
national politics and policy, and Caesar's career will, perforce, be
dwarfed by the scale of the political world in which we find him
after 1606.

When Caesar replaced Dunbar in the Exchequer, he was the senior
ordinary Master of Requests, an office that brought him into frequent
contact with the king. Even before James's accession, Caesar had been
drawn into the councils of the inner circle of senior officials as a legal
expert. The Essex rebellion and its subsequent trials brought Caesar
face-to-face with the most sensitive issues in domestic politics as a
commissioner to examine and try the rebels. Later, the examination
of the conspirators in the Gunpowder Plot occasioned his serving in
a similar capacity. A senior jurist and commissioner in extraordinary
causes, Caesar, who was nearly fifty, had become a sage advisor and
counselor, although he had accumulated no additional offices since
becoming a Master of Requests. However, James I had knighted him
in 1603 when the royal entourage arrived in London. Then, in 1606,
Caesar's world changed dramatically with his appointment to the
Exchequer.

His appointment was made under unusual circumstances recounted
in a memorandum that Caesar presented to Dorset and Salisbury at
a meeting in Dorset House in the following year. The memorandum
reflects his own mixed feelings and sense of confusion in the spring of
1606, and it also tells us whose patronage had been responsible for
having advanced him to the new office. "In the beginning of April
1606, I was persuaded to this place by your Lordships. The patents
were then sealed, with promise of 1,000 libri from the king and this
place would bee (as my Lord Treasurer tolde mee) wourth unto mee
200 libri a yere. All which, with what els was then promised and what
since perfourmed, god sees, your Lordships knowe, and my selfe feele."
But Caesar's appointment amounted to more than a promise of reward and a sealed patent; there was also a curious element of secrecy.
He continued his account: "From thence [early April] until the 3 of
July, I doubted how I shoulde bee disposed of wither to the Court, or
to the Chancery, or to the exchequeur; the last I wisshed least and
therefor and for secrecy sake, which was enioyned mee, I endeavoured
not to fit my selfe for it." Caesar obviously sought advancement,

whether in Chancery, the goal of his ambitions from his younger days, or to another place at Court. But he had been told to keep quiet and await the outcome of the decisions about his fate. Finally, however, his appointment was public. "The third of July, being sworne into the place, and then leaving all other hopes, I held it to my lot appointed me and therefor presently resolved myself to omit no labour or means for mine enhabling to discharge the duties of the place. Especially, I endeavoured to know the true state of the kings revenue, and the issue of the same, [because] to the true survey and well ordering wherof, I ame particularly tied by mine othe."[21]

On the day that Caesar was sworn Chancellor, Salisbury's secretary, Michael Hickes, received a letter from Sir John Benet asking for his help in procuring the Mastership of Requests that Caesar would vacate in order to accept his new position. The letter suggests that the secret of Caesar's appointment was out long before he was sworn. Benet observed that for a long time after hearing of Caesar's appointment, he "could hardly believe" the news. How long a time could it have been if Caesar was sworn on the same day that Benet wrote?[22]

Caesar was unprepared for his appointment and completely lost regarding his duties, but he was anxious to make up for lost time as soon as he was sworn. He began to make inquiries, to compile lists, to draft memoranda and statements. The product of all of this activity was his textbook of data designed to instruct him about the Chancellor's office and the responsibilities associated with it. If we are to understand what he sought, as well as what he found, we should step back for a moment to learn along with him and to survey the organization of the Exchequer.[23]

The most striking characteristics of the Exchequer were its antiquity and its daunting complexity. Over several centuries, layer upon layer of traditional practice had gathered in sedimentary bands, resulting in a fossilized agency heavily encumbered with redundant officers. While there had been efforts since the fifteenth century to improve upon Exchequer practice, the agency did not significantly change, the result being that it was hard put to meet the crown's ever-growing demands for financial resources. The problem was not novel, and remedies had been sought as early as Edward IV's reign by transferring some of the accountability for revenue from the Exchequer to the Household. Henry VII and Henry VIII had gone a step further by establishing new sources of revenue in the Household that had never known Exchequer procedure. By the end of Henry VIII's reign, this experiment in Household government reached its apogee: five agencies plus Exchequer were responsible for accounting for royal revenues. Such proliferation presented its own difficulties. Inevitably, a new cycle of reform and reorganization followed, leading to the incorporation of most of the courts into Exchequer by the start of Elizabeth's reign.

In operational terms, Exchequer was divided into a receipt department or chamber (the "lower" chamber) and an audit department (the "upper" chamber). The lower chamber had traditionally been considered superior to the upper because it was in the lower chamber that the money was paid in and the royal treasure stored. The custody of treasure brought with it access to power, but there was no power associated with the audits of the upper chamber. Traditionally, the relative status of the two chambers was reflected in the relative status of their chief officers. The Undertreasurer, who presided below, was considered superior to the Chancellor of the Exchequer, a senior clerk of the audit, who presided above. The Chancellor's customary duties were, indeed, unimpressive. He named the Controller of the Pipe (a form of chief auditor), kept the seal of the Exchequer in his possession, and provided legal counsel to the Exchequer Court. Yet by the time that Caesar became Chancellor, the ancient superiority of the Undertreasurer was a dead letter, his duties having been folded into those of the Chancellor of the Exchequer, becoming secondary attributes as the two offices were joined. This reversal is quite important, for it marked a change in one of the major sources of power in government. Whereas the physical custody of treasure had once conferred power, by the turn of the seventeenth century, power was derived from access to information and from participation in policy making. This marked a transitional process in the centralizing and rationalizing of crown authority.

The transitional process reached beyond simple organizational changes. Of far greater importance were structural changes in governmental practice, epitomized by an accounting procedure that had first been developed in the new revenue courts and was later introduced into the Exchequer during the mergers. To replace a cumbersome, repetitive, inaccurate, and expensive accounting system used in the Exchequer known as the "ancient course," the new courts developed more supple and responsive techniques. Institutional inertia had made serious reform of the "ancient course" a virtual impossibility, and redundant clerical offices had often passed, as if by inheritance, from father to son. This was an unlikely climate for serious change.[24]

In the newer revenue courts, receipts were collected and disbursed with marked efficiency.[25] This was especially noticeable in the procedures developed in those courts for advancing funds on account to persons about the kingdom who were performing crown service. That the Exchequer had no such procedure was a disadvantage to the crown. In the Court of Augmentations, where the new procedure had its origin, a local collector, on the authority of a writing, paid money that he was holding to a designated recipient who was responsible for answering to periodic accountings to assure that the money was being properly spent. These advanced funds were known as prests (or imprests), and the accompanying method of accounting was called "declared accounting." Unlike the "ancient course," by which revenues were submitted to the Exchequer once a year (thus depriving the crown of their use until they were paid in), declared accounting permitted all collections to be used at any time. After the merger of the Augmentations with the Exchequer in the early 1550's, the declared accounts were taken by the newly appointed Clerks of the Prests. These accounts avoided the more complex audits prepared according to the "ancient course." Timely and readable ledgers made it possible to determine the cost of an enterprise in progress rather than at the end of the year. All of these accounts were the responsibility of the Chancellor of the Exchequer, and his access to relatively sound information eclipsed the mere custody and distribution of money associated with the Undertreasurer.

At the same time that the Chancellor of the Exchequer subsumed the Undertreasurer's office and came to dominate the Exchequer, the Lord Treasurer, during Burghley's long tenure of office, became the Lord High Treasurer. The title signified the Treasurer's elevation to the status of the most senior of the crown's ministers. The Chancellor, as the Lord High Treasurer's principal assistant, rapidly approached ministerial status as the crown's second financial officer.

Because of Caesar's propensity for attempting to effect change in the offices he occupied, it is important to keep in mind the motives behind the extensive inquiries he made as he was entering the Chancellor's office. He was on most unfamiliar ground and feared making mistakes. He also knew that the consequence of exceeding one's authority was personal liability; thus, any ambiguities in his commissions had to be settled before he would risk the exposure attendant upon unauthorized behavior. But, of greatest importance, Caesar wanted to serve the interests of his patron lest his patron not serve his interests when the proper moment came. In short, although Caesar engaged in highly technical inquiries, suggested changes in practice and procedure, and frequently employed the rhetoric of the theoretician, he cannot be taken as a serious theoretician or reformer.

Caesar queried the seated revenue officers to learn about his new office. Their answers to his questions regarding his responsibilities and authority were extensive but not sufficient. After reading them, Caesar prepared even more questions and directed them this time to Sir John Fortescue. He mined the former Chancellor's experience for all of the information he could get. Caesar's questions indicate that he was as worried about the rewards of his new office as he was about his duties. But there was another problem to be worked out: he doubted the sufficiency of his commission as Undertreasurer to issue the king's treasure.

By what authority, he asked, had Fortescue issued money from the treasury? The former Chancellor answered that he had been authorized to join with the Lord Treasurer in assigning revenue held by any of the four Tellers of the Receipt. Similarly, he had joined with the Lord Treasurer to issue money under the crown's warrant. As to the form of address used in these warrants, a question of particular interest to Caesar, Fortescue advised that the terms "treasurer, chamberlains, and the undertreasurer [are] understood under the word 'treasurer.'" Caesar remained unconvinced. With characteristic obsessive attention to form, he asked whether "a warrant directed to the Lord Treasurer and the 2 Chamberlains bee a sufficient warrant to the undertreasurer to ioyne in warrant with the Lord Treasurer for issuing the king's money." Even though Fortescue told him that custom and common law, as contained in the Black Book of the Exchequer, vested such authority in the Undertreasurer, Caesar was not satisfied. He did not intend to exceed his warrant and become liable for the consequences.[26]

Since there were no satisfactory answers to his queries, the Chancellor asked the king for a new patent expressly authorizing him to join with the Lord Treasurer to issue money without regard for the style employed in any particular warrant. He enclosed with his petition a draft privy seal spelling out the clarification that he sought.[27] A search of the privy seals for 1606 and 1607 does not reveal that the petition was granted, but, by February 1607, some warrants were addressed to the Treasurer and Undertreasurer, and, by April, to the Lord Treasurer and Chancellor. Whatever style was used, Caesar was authorized to countersign with the Lord Treasurer. It is easy to make too much of this matter of style: each year hundreds of warrants, copied from ancient formularies, were written by the Clerks of the Privy Seal. Clerical obedience to habit makes it difficult to read motive or intent into the use of one style of address rather than another. Nonetheless, Caesar worried about overstepping his commission and, thus, pursued the changes he thought were necessary to protect himself.

His meeting with Fortescue gave Caesar the information he required, particularly concerning the rewards of his office. An annual pension of £200 was the only stipend that he would receive from the crown.[28] Any other revenues associated with the office would derive from fees, gifts, and other considerations. His rooms and chambers at Court consisted in "all the Starchamber, the Tresory chamber and a chamber in the Exchequeur and Vincents howse."[29] The Lord Treasurer's Remembrancer and the King's Remembrancer were to remit sealing fees to the Chancellor. Likewise, the Clerk of the Pipe remitted fees, although many documents passed under his seal for which no fee was assessed. Each lease, patent, and exemplification earned a profit for the Chancellor, and there were other considerations for greater or lesser leases in his gift.[30] After apprising him of the value of the fees of his new office, Fortescue advised Caesar that custom held that any appointment sealed by the Chancellor for another officer was to pass without fee. Caesar's other informants, the officers of the Exchequer, also provided him with lists of duties and responsibilities, lists that were probably far more extensive than he might have imagined. He would later discover that the permanent officers jealously protected their rights to perform their several functions in the Chancellor's name and that their efforts greatly reduced the time that he had to devote to daily detail. But there were two functions he could not delegate. Together with the Lord Treasurer, he exercised the power to imprison the king's debtors and was responsible for the smooth functioning of the Customs House.[31]

The first Lord Treasurer whom Caesar served, the elderly earl of

Dorset, a royal cousin, was an imposing relic who had survived the entire reign of Elizabeth. When he was appointed to succeed Burghley
in 1599, he was just seventy. In all seasons he was swathed in furs suspected by many to carry the pox. Dorset was frequently ill but always
attentive to his office. The status of his bowels, abused by bombard-
ments of the physic, was a common subject of his own careful speculation and analysis.[32] During his long career, Dorset had amassed one
of England's great landed fortunes: his properties alone brought him,
in 1602, an annual gross rental in excess of £5,500, making him one
of the four wealthiest landowners in England after the queen.[33] We
have already noted that Dorset and Cecil had been competitors for the
Lord Treasurer's place; however, they joined in common cause with
Nottingham against the Essex faction. It has been suggested that Dorset's appointment had been a part of Cecil's housecleaning at Court
in the face of the Essex rivalry, or that he was part of a post-Essex tri-
umvirate, including Cecil and Nottingham, constellated at the center
of Court politics. In either case, Dorset was Cecil's firm ally, if not his
dependent.[34] Allies they certainly were, but Dorset showed himself to
be an independent Lord Treasurer whose policies were frequently at
odds with those of his younger colleague.

Dorset's wealth was not an accident of birth. His avarice was legend, and the greed of his daughter, Lady Anne Glemham, dwarfed
even her father's. Suitors and supplicants, in an age when "sweeteners"
were commonplace, went out of their way to please him. But Dorset
possessed a keen political instinct, characteristic of a survivor, sharp-
ened by more than a half-century in the crown's service. For instance,
in 1601, sensing the mood of the moment, he wrote to Cecil advising
that the monopolies on trade, which were causing great ill will, be examined and that many be revoked. There were entirely too many of
them, he wrote, and they were "so unfitt and so odious, neither profitable to her Majestie nor good for the Commonwealth." He wanted
the queen to scrutinize all of them, revoking those that served no public interest. Furthermore, since Parliament was about to be summoned, Dorset suggested that there would be great political advantage
if "we make a public notification [regarding the monopolies] . . . and
. . . call in as many as be thought fit before the Parliament [meets]."
A balance was necessary, though, "for to revoke too many were as
dangerous [as to revoke too few] and hurtful to her Majesties prerogative." He concluded that "we must walk in a medium and moderation

and then shall we do her Majesty as notable good service, and the sooner we begin the better."[35] Not only was this advice to emerge as a kernel of Elizabeth's "Golden Mean," but it also characterized Dorset's public policy. Greedy but not destructive in his greed, cautious but not wavering, determined to offend as few as possible but possessed of a clear and defensible policy: these were the marks of Lord Treasurer Dorset.

Surely the nadir of Dorset's career as Lord Treasurer was the moment, during the last days of Elizabeth's life, when he reportedly had gone with Fortescue to advise the dying monarch that her coffers were empty. Her rage was said to have been stunning, perhaps contributing to her death shortly thereafter.[36] By contrast, his efforts to increase James's revenues were gratifying to the old man, for they seemed to meet with success. But the increases proved chimerical. Although the deficit had been reduced temporarily by the reduction of forces at Berwick and by James's declaration of peace with Spain, the king's increased personal expenses devoured whatever savings had been made. The shortages had to be met, and the most common resort was to the ruinous practice of making one loan to repay another, as the Elizabethans had done.

By the time Caesar had joined Dorset, the rapid increase in royal expenses preoccupied the Exchequer: the coffers were bare, the debt immense. Yet, for all of their concern, they had no long-term fiscal plan to guide them out of their difficulty. Indeed, such planning would have been nearly impossible. Forward planning requires a quality of information that they could not provide even though information was becoming relatively more reliable. The methods used in accounting, both "ancient course" and declared accounts, concentrated on static "views" and "states" of receipts and issues, not on forward projections. Furthermore, a parliamentary discussion of public finance dealt with mixed categories of revenue due and payable at certain intervals. It was unremarkable that this categorical and compartmentalized expression of the necessities of public finance was reflected in the rhetoric used by the crown and its officers in Parliament. Specific taxes were justified in terms of specific needs. The Irish war, the war with Spain, threats to the defense of the kingdom or to Englishmen overseas each merited parliamentary support. But the first years of James's reign, marked by his irenic policies toward England's former enemies, seemed to militate against the need for taxation. Yet for the king to resort to intensified exploitation of his prerogative revenue sources would have cut into the very property interests that were represented in Parliament. As G. L. Harriss has noted, this quandary was not to become an issue until 1610. The initial response to James's request for revenue was positive; he met them "as heir to a remarkable sense of unity between the monarchy and its subjects which bore fruit in the first grant of the reign, of three subsidies and six fifteenths in 1606." Lavish though these grants were, they were approved by the slimmest possible majorities—a harbinger of future problems.[37]

In order to comprehend parliamentary taxation and fiscal politics in the early seventeenth century, we first must understand the fundamental division between ordinary and extraordinary expenses. The ordinary were predictable and covered most governmental functions, including many of the costs of maintaining the monarchy. They were expected to be paid from the crown's own revenues—the sale of lands, fines, rents, and the like—as well as from customs revenue voted to each monarch for life at the start of his reign. Extraordinary expenses, on the other hand, dealt with then unpredictable costs of war, defense, repairs, and improvements and the crown's gifts of pensions and rewards. These were the most frequent subjects of parliamentary taxation.

In the light of these categorical distinctions, Dorset's approach to Parliament in 1606 is especially important. Rather than appeal for funds to meet specific, extraordinary circumstances, he candidly spread out the details of the entire deficit before the Members. The discussion, thus, was elevated from the king's financial discomfort to the consolidated fiscal health of the national government. The Lord Treasurer was less interested in the traditional distinctions than in the necessary and reasonable tax demands that he was making in the king's name. In this respect, Dorset in 1606 prefigures Salisbury in 1610.

Dorset divided his comments into three parts: "the necessities wherewith the Crown is pressed," an explanation of these necessities, and an answer to the current rumor in Parliament that the king had more money than he needed. He told them that the total debt amounted to £772,000, although one-half had been inherited from Elizabeth. Even though James had been neither "privie nor partie" to the debts of his predecessor, he would honor them as his own. By 1606, fiscal management had become all the more difficult because there was a current arrearage of £117,558 in the subsidy of 1601. Additionally, although James's policy was irenic, he still had to bear the cost of forces in Ireland and the Low Countries. All of these considerations paled, however, beside the cost of maintaining a large royal family. Dorset displayed more than a little courage in reciting these expenses, for the queen had already gained a reputation as an uncommon profligate who was also singularly insensitive. Steadfastly, he recited the needs of the five members of the royal family and reminded the Members of the inability of the Exchequer to pay their bills without Parliament's assistance.[38]

The Lord Treasurer was determined to deflect any invidious comparison of Elizabeth to James. Lest any Member think that the deficit was related to the personality or policy of the present monarch, Dorset emphasized the long history of the current insufficiency. Their late sovereign "was a verie wise, warie, and reserved quene bothe in her guifts and ordinarie expenses, yet was shee forced to spend in the warrs, of treasure found in the Receipt, 300,000 libri, besides 14 subsidies, 28 fifteenths, 3 lones, [and] the sale of landes . . . and yet [she] dyed in debt 400,000 libri."[39] While the relative proportion of the categories of expense may have changed from one reign to another, the debt was a growing burden that had to be paid, and Parliament was the only means to this end.

No issue that Dorset put before Parliament in 1606 was more sensitive than the king's generosity to his favorites. After only three years in England, James was thought to be too willing to reward his intimates. Combining frankness to the Members with loyalty to his master, the Lord Treasurer advanced the notion that gifts and pensions should not be treated together as extraordinary expenses but separately under two headings that had nothing to do with the old categories. One heading included those pensions and gifts that justice demanded be made; the other included compensation to the recipient for valued service to the crown. Yet other gifts remained that were not justifiable under either heading. As he spoke, Dorset shifted the onus of the responsibility for the king's generosity with these gifts from the donor to the beneficiaries. James, a generous, decent monarch with benign instincts, was taxed unbearably by the importuning of his courtiers, but he was changing his policy. "I protest before God," Dorset replied, "he begins to have a feeling understanding of the lack of his owne means and a naturall sence, so I verify [affirm] theis incessant or importunat suitors will soon vanish awaie for they will no longer prevaile, I do assure myself."[40]

Princes, in general, he told them, "at their first entrance have alwaies extended their guifts much more amplie than afterwards they do." But a sobered king, now familiar with the limitations surrounding his new throne, having brought peace to the realm, surely merited the subsidy that Dorset required of them. Driving the point home, and linking a generalized sense of obligation to parliamentary self-interest, the Lord Treasurer reminded the Members that the loans made to the king by the City were soon payable at Easter next coming. The first priority for the use of the subsidy was to be their repayment. "The first frutes [of] whatever [subsidy] it shal bee wholie and presentlie returned unto your selves againe to satisfie the loan which hath bene made to you."[41] Dorset's candor carried the day. On numerous occasions Caesar bemoaned the excessive caution of his superior and his reluctance to play the dramatic role, yet if Dorset's performance in 1606 was an example of his political skill, Caesar never took the measure of his abilities — indicating, perhaps, his own political naïveté.

After years spent as a large fish in a small pond, Caesar had to learn the methods and techniques of a massive agency. He could not do everything himself; indeed, he could succeed only if he skillfully managed his subordinates. Dorset advised him to exploit the power of the permanent staff: "It is [in] the labour and trust of the auditors where upon I do rest and so must you."[42] The Lord Treasurer's warning had been prompted by a complaint from Caesar regarding the number of suitors who threw themselves on his mercy each day. They were owed money by the king, but they could not collect; in the meantime, they were facing ruin. Caesar disliked the "lamentaccon of the clamers and sutes made to [him] for money, and how grevous it [was] unto [him]." He was personalizing excessively the Chancellor's responsibilities. Caesar was not reluctant to dilate on his discomfort to his superior, but his ill-advised grousing earned him a dressing-down from Dorset. As Chancellor, he had the authority to satisfy the king's creditors when they pressed him for payment, but he was admonished to ask himself "how can the kings majesty pay that which he owes when that which is owing to him is unpaied."[43] By implication, he should also have asked himself what difference it made to him. Uncomfortable decisions accompanied his job, and when he found that the burdens and frustrations of his new office weighed too heavily on him after a few months, Caesar remembered the number of years that Dorset had devoted to bringing order to the diminished receipt. As consolation, the Chancellor was told "to let this be your last and chiefest comfort, that we serve a most roiall, rare, and most generous king, for whom we can never speke to[o] much nor do sufficient, no[t] though we expend our leases, lands and goods and al that ever we have in this servis." Dorset said that he had bound himself "in all my indevor to bring in monies which also must have this due time for sodenly you may not expect it."[44] As old as he was, Dorset spoke of his duty with the passion of a man younger by half than his Chancellor.

For his part, Caesar believed that he had good cause to doubt his superior's ability. When he met with Dorset and Salisbury a year after he was commissioned, he spoke of the great frustration occasioned by the Lord Treasurer's methods and of his alleged forgetfulness. He told them that during his first summer as Chancellor, after learning what he could of the details of the state of the receipts and issues, he had visited Dorset. "I attended about the end of August on my Lord Treasurer and acquainted him with my desire that the king should bee certified with expedition of the ill state, as I tooke it, of his receite, and the inconveniences thereof, if present remedy were not given there unto." The old man's reply had aggravated Caesar. "It pleased my Lord then to shewe mee divers laborious and exact tables of his own device and writing, more timely and far more perfectly representing that [which] I wisshed to be knowen, then my selfe had or could expresse, which he promised that he would acquaint the king with very shortly and voutsafe [sic] mee to bee present at the same. Whereof since, having heard nothing, and yet finding the estate of the kings receite (without present foresight to prevent it) like to growe worse and worse." In short, Caesar feared that Dorset's and his silence "might doe the king great prejudice and bring [them] in question hereafter for the same." Parliament, for instance, was already becoming too much involved in the business of the king's revenue "into which harvest some have already thrust their sickles." Finally, Caesar had asked for the meeting with Salisbury and Dorset to solicit Salisbury's aid in improving the king's finance. Dorset, by implication, could not reach this goal on his own.[45]

The list of solutions to the problem that Caesar advanced was nearly identical to the course of action that Salisbury followed nearly a year later when he became Lord Treasurer. Furthermore, they were exactly the type of projects for increasing the revenue that Dorset had advised against when he had suggested to Elizabeth in 1601 that the monopolies were more political trouble than they were worth. They were the last pressings of the fruits of the prerogative. It is not at all surprising that Dorset became testy with his Chancellor as they worked together, for he could not count on him to take his proper secondary, supporting place. On the contrary, Caesar invoked Salisbury's intervention. Dorset's tactics were very different: he quietly pursued the greatest returns of revenue from sources the least likely to create large-scale disaffection. An example of his tactics is to be found in his attempt to increase the king's revenue from the sale of tin.

Dorset's schemes to sell the crown's prerogative right to control the market for tin by preempting it at source and to establish the Great Farm of the Customs were among the most important of his attempts to raise extraparliamentary revenue. All Cornish and Devon tin was subject to preemption, and the export trade could be served only by tin purchased from the crown. In 1607, however, the Lord Treasurer suspended the existing contract to farm the preemption because the farmers had not held up their end of the bargain. He took this action even though the crown desperately needed the revenue that the farm produced. Had Dorset had his own way, he would have established a free market, but that option was not available to him. The suspension of the farm cost the crown £2,000 per annum, and the tin miners were made less productive because the farmers had made it a practice to provide a line of credit for them to purchase their equipment.[46]

That the suspended farmers were also members of the Levant Company further complicated the tin controversy. The Company opposed the preemption strenuously, claiming that it was harmful to their trade. To demonstrate their objection to the preemption, they had refused to purchase the crown's tin for export, thus choking off the overseas market. No one else could step in to replace them because their charter gave them exclusive trading rights to the Eastern Mediterranean, where the largest tin market was to be found. To frustrate the Company and to turn a profit for themselves, the former farmers engaged illegally in a spot market to supply their Turkish customers. From another quarter the principal domestic consumers of tin, the Pewterers' Company, complained that the price had been too high at home because the high prices fetched in the export market had shortened the domestic supply, thus driving up home prices. All in all, confusion prevailed. Large stores of tin went unsold in Cornwall and London, the crown was losing revenue, and the Lord Treasurer was shopping for an alternate market.[47]

Ironically, the best solution appeared to be to renegotiate the farm with the original farmers. Dorset was anxious to conclude the matter quickly because, by July, £23,000 was due "to be paied to the Cittie," but the bargain took longer than was anticipated.[48] For a man as old and as ill as Dorset, his energy and cunning were remarkable. He encouraged some Italian merchants in London to make a tentative agreement, which he then took to a group of English merchants, including the original farmers. Playing on their patriotism and self-interest, he extracted from them a contract, along with £60,000 for immediate payment to the City. But, once more, the deal began to unravel at the last minute, and Dorset, under great pressure, accepted reduced terms. Thus, "his majestie shall have 2,000 libri of revenue added to the Crown, the pore tinners maintained [i.e., provided short-term loans], and the roial commodity of the realm upheld in price as it is now advanced."[49] Several more letters followed to tie down all the details, among them being the letter in which Dorset upbraided the Chancellor for his impatience. Considering the amount of time that the Lord Treasurer had invested in resolving the preemption, his irritation was understandable.[50]

When patience and caution failed to yield results, Dorset could be a daring and imaginative minister. The fact that the customs had long been subject to piecemeal administration troubled him. Some ports had collectors appointed directly by the crown; others had private farmers who collected the customs under license. The terms of the farms differed from port to port, and the collectors were frequently slovenly. The profits of the private farmers provided a disincentive to the crown's collectors to work harder and with greater energy. After having tried for years to bring the various customers together under one common administration, Dorset had resorted to negotiating one universal contract: the Great Farm of Customs. This allowed him to rationalize the administration, to predict revenue with greater certainty, and to extract greater profit for the crown from one large plum than from many smaller fruits. F. C. Dietz regards the Great Farm with admiration. It was "something daring, [this] conception of lumping the customs in all England together, so far as was possible in view of existing leases, advancing their value by a new book of rates, and leasing them to a single company at £112,400 per annum."[51] Daring, imagination, and a keen political sense characterized Dorset's treasurership.

The Lord Treasurer met frequently with the principal officers of the Exchequer at Dorset House, a practice that anticipated the Treasury Commissions impaneled after 1612. The officers met to transact business, to take direction from the Lord Treasurer, and to supply him with detailed information. These meetings were of particular importance when Dunbar was Chancellor of the Exchequer, since the Lord Treasurer had to perform the Chancellor's functions because of Dunbar's frequent absences. The meetings allowed the entire corps of senior Exchequer officers, in consultation with the Lord Treasurer, to fill the void in the Chancellor's place. The notes of their meetings after Caesar joined them indicate that they reorganized their responsibilities after a Chancellor was appointed. The Exchequer officials devoted most of their attention to the sheriffs' accounts. The supervision of shrieval accounting required both great patience and great technical expertise because the sheriffs had become adept, creative accountants who juggled balances, concealed receipts, and developed a battery of techniques designed to minimize their personal exposure for shortfalls in their collections.

The notes from these meetings indicate that the officers were trying to make better use of their time together. Rather than take up every issue in every meeting, they divided their meetings into a number of special emphases. For instance, on the last Thursday of each term they would peruse and consider "of the bundells of old and ancient dettes as well within the office of every auditeur and the Receiver and Thresorers Remembrancer, to the end that consideration may be had of such dets as ar sperate or [are] doutful and this to be reserved to the process and audit of the Court for the spedy hearing thereof. And the rest that shal aper hopeles and desperate dets may be put into a Bundell of Oblivion and the subject . . . no more to be vexed and trobled as heretofore."[52] Under a different heading the Lord Treasurer and the Chancellor were to attend in person to improve the accuracy of the "opposal" or challenge to the accountants.[53]

The overriding concern of the Exchequer officers was the mounting debt, which was exacerbated by the king's refusal to accept any suggestions for significant reduction in his expenses. Since direct requests were not successful, the officers tried a less direct approach involving internal management practices. They developed their own lists of lands, estates, and valuable rewards that they considered suitable for the crown's free gifts. A second list spelled out those gifts that might be made only at the risk of of grave financial prejudice. The first list preserved the ancient estates of the crown but was generous with the award of newer acquisitions. In the second the elements of extraordinary revenue were equally well preserved. Monopolies, leases in reversions, leases of prohibited goods, gifts of wood and timber—all of these were to be preserved against alienation. On the other hand, the lands and goods of attainted traitors; offices of honor and profit; the custody of houses, parks, chases, and forests were thought appropriate gifts of the king's bounty that James could afford to lose. In most respects, these categories restated working distinctions made earlier by Elizabeth and Burghley. But the restatement was necessary because James, unlike his predecessor, caviled at any limitations whatsoever. The officers could use their lists when asked for advice, and, of greater importance, they were to be employed when their discretion was called for in making a grant in the king's name.[54]

By the time Dorset died, on 19 April 1608, Caesar had made a place for himself in the Exchequer, and he was prepared, indeed impatient, to join the new Lord Treasurer, Robert Cecil, the earl of Salisbury, as a partner in financial policy making and fiscal management.[55] Throughout their few years together, Dorset's vigorous schemes to improve the receipt had surprised his younger colleague. But Caesar was still not greatly impressed. Salisbury would not do much more than Dorset during his tenure of office—indeed, he could not—but Caesar considered his principal patron a brilliant politician. The least of his actions was wise and imaginative; the greatest of Dorset's was plodding and ineffectual. A few months after he had become Chancellor, in 1606, Caesar had penned a note to himself at the foot of a column of figures showing that the current deficit amounted to £52,315 15s. 1d. His woebegone words reflected exactly what he thought of Dorset and what he expected of Salisbury. "This [deficit] cannot last, but will bring a dearth, nowe therefore let our most wise, sacred, and religious Pharaoh provide for a man of understanding and wisdom, some religiously wise, irreprochably honest, uncorrupt, stout, and chasteminded Joseph, etc."[56]

Salisbury, the Joseph apparent, would bring vigor and enthusiasm to the place so long associated with his father, Lord Burghley. He was also Caesar's most important patron. In 1606 (and earlier), patronal loyalty and dissatisfaction with the incumbent had motivated Caesar. By 1610, in the midst of political turmoil, and having observed Salisbury in the breach, the Chancellor remained loyal to him, even when he despaired of his solution to England's chronic financial crisis.

VI

Dayly Labourers in the Publick Service

BY THE TIME that Lord Treasurer Dorset died, in the early spring of 1608, Caesar had gained sufficient experience to join with the new Lord Treasurer, Robert Cecil, in the forceful direction of the Exchequer. During the brief vacancy in the Treasurer's place, Caesar was put in charge of the Exchequer and made responsible for the administration of the receipt and issue of the king's treasure. In this task, he was assisted by several Privy Councillors pending the installation of a successor.[1]

There was little doubt that Salisbury would succeed Dorset, and Caesar went immediately to work preparing for the transition. His first task was to ready a view of the receipt for the new Lord Treasurer to present to the king.[2] On 4 May 1608 the king announced his intention to appoint Salisbury, and on Ascension Day, 5 May, the formal grant was made and the White Staff conferred.[3] On 6 May, after Salisbury had discussed proper protocol with the officers of the Exchequer, he was escorted in a great procession to Westminster Palace to be sworn by the Lord Chancellor. Before leaving the Palace, the new Lord Treasurer settled out of hand a long-standing legacy suit that was being argued that day before the Exchequer Bench. He then escorted the king, the Court, and the senior officers of the Exchequer to Salisbury House for a banquet and entertainment.[4] We know of these details because Caesar kept

a journall of the Lord High Treasurers proceedings within my knowledge (beesides all other his forreine or home dispatches, in matters of estate belonging to either of his offices as Secretary of Estate or Master of the Wardes, which are best knowen to himself) from Wednesday 4 May inclusive till this present 24th of July 1608 by a true frend and servant. J.[ulius] C.[aesar][5]

So complete was his account that he found it necessary to append a summary of the Exchequer business that Salisbury had attended to lest it become obscured among the details. The journal tells us that in July 1608, before the Court left London on progress, the Exchequer shifted into a more active and purposeful pursuit of the means to rectify the chronic imbalance in the receipt, and for that reason we shall examine the diary in some detail.

But first, we must ask why Caesar prepared the diary. Spedding believed that it was "drawn up for the express purpose of magnifying to the King the merits of his new Lord Treasurer."[6] This is an unlikely interpretation because there is no reason either to think that James ever saw it or to believe that he needed any testimonials to Salisbury's worth. Moreover, the only extant copy of the journal is found in Caesar's papers, although it is endorsed on the front and back in Salisbury's hand. It seems that Caesar first gave the journal to the Lord Treasurer and then managed to get it back again for his own archives, perhaps following Salisbury's death.

Fortunately, Caesar tells us in his own words why he prepared the journal; it was an expression of his gratitude to the new Lord Treasurer for his forceful leadership. Although there had not been enough time, in July 1608, to allow Caesar to evaluate Salisbury's performance, he did come to the task with a prejudice. After all, he had once likened Salisbury to a wise Joseph. And now he wrote that

the last yeres experience of the Exchequeur and the greate wantes of the Receipt, together with the continuall remembrance of the two pinching greate sommes due to the farmours and to the citizens and strangers of London (which ringed like a knolling bell in mine eares continually both day and night and made mee watch when others slept) and the litle meanes which I sawe to satisfie the same, did so much to dismay mee, as that I was weary of my life, and from my late Lord Treasurer, when I often mentioned the state of things unto him, I received causes rather of dispaire then otherwise and found him more dismayed then my self. . . . [Thus, when Dorset died] God had presently raised up another in his place, the most likely man of this kingdome to raise up the ruines of a decayeng estate, I rejoyced as the hart which being enclosed findeth the rivers of water, for that my painting [panting] sowle had nowe received hopes of future refreshments.[7]

According to Caesar, the Lord Treasurer had done more in two months than any of his predecessors in two years.[8]

The first weeks of Salisbury's incumbency showed that his bustling purposefulness was his most impressive quality. In his summary Caesar reported that Salisbury had "directed and signed 2884 letters and gotten the king in money 37,445 libri in yerely revenue 71,000 libri" in less than three months.[9] On 14 June, for instance, Salisbury "sat with other Lords [of the Council] uppon the commission of depopulation and got for the King that day, 720 libri."[10] Four days later, "hee sat with the Chancelor of the Exchequeur at Salisbury House about leasing of Kings landes for 21 yeres or 3 lives, where he did set downe divers notable observations for the avoyding of deceits heretofore too frequently offered by such as procured leases from his Majesty or the late Queene."[11] Such entries as these reflected Salisbury's determination to succeed. Caesar was impressed, and well he might have been, for Salisbury was undertaking a prodigious task. As Professor Dietz has written, "It was Salisbury's ambition not merely to wipe out the deficit, but also to pay off the debts once and for all. The collection of old debts, the arrangements of compositions for defective title and assart lands, and fines for alienations without licenses, depopulations, and new buildings, were vigorously pushed by the new commissions."[12]

Salisbury quickly set in motion the machinery for extracting every available farthing from the crown's prerogative. By August he was writing to Caesar in haste to order the immediate shipment of money to Ireland to pay the army. He told the Chancellor that, whether or not the army's pay was the cause of a possible military defeat, the two of them would bear the full blame for not providing the money when it was needed. Caesar was to summon the Customs Farmers, to whom the king already stood massively in debt, and "let them know the occasion whereof I [Salisbury] assure my self now, for such a shrewd instant perill, they will be ready to add so much more burden to them self seeing that they are alredy so farr in." The money was to be sent to Ireland immediately, for regardless of adverse tides and winds, if the money were "not in Ireland before Bartholomewtyde, they write plainly . . . that the Army must breake."[13]

Caesar acted with dispatch, and less than a week later Salisbury commended his efficiency: "I cannot forbeare to take notyce [to say] unto you how gladd I am that Ireland is soe well provided for. Wherein I doe acknowledge that the Farmors have shewed themselfes men of

understanding and most worthye of all favour and proteccon." He added that it would not do justice to the king if he did not convey to Caesar James's pleasure in the Chancellor's work and his awareness "of the
paynes you take."[14]

During their first year together, Caesar clearly enjoyed working with
Salisbury. This was particularly apparent in the fulsomeness of his dispatches to the Lord Treasurer over the course of the summer. A number of letters had been sent to various noblemen concerning debts they
owed to the crown. As their replies came in, Caesar reported to Salisbury: "The noblemens letters return daily, but without money, desir-
ing further time to consider and examine whether the debtes de-
maunded have bene already satisfied or noe. Whereby your Lordship
may coniecture howe greate your resolution must have been in theise
unpleasant and harsh encounters. In which my selfe ame resolved not
to run from you but rather to die at your foote, if neede bee."[15]

Later on in August, Salisbury advised Caesar that there was great
value in such praise and adulation in the right places. Caesar had sent
the Lord Treasurer an account of how the Lord Chancellor had dealt
with some troubles in the City. Salisbury mentioned that the letter
"gave an honorable testimony of his Lordship [Ellesmere], and therefore I lett his Majesty see it. For, Sir, when we do our selfs right (that
are but a few amongst many talkers) when his Majesty knowes who
are dayly labourers in his publick service, where neyther glory nor
gain are included."[16]

At the same time that Caesar began his service under Salisbury with
hopes for a brighter future for the receipt, Salisbury appears to have
found that he had a reliable and loyal lieutenant to whom he could
confidently leave the management of the Exchequer. Thus, one doubts
the accuracy of an observation contained in a letter of Chamberlain's
in which he commented that Salisbury's grand manner would lead him
to relieve Caesar of his place, if he could, and administer the Exchequer himself.[17]

It was clear to Salisbury that before anything could be done about
the inadequacy of the revenue, the internal procedures of the Exchequer had to be put in order. As we have already noted, the Exchequer
employed antiquated accounting techniques of limited value. But
Salisbury believed that there were better procedures. Following a meeting with Caesar in September 1608, the Lord Treasurer left an order
for the better ordering of the audits and views made in the Exchequer.

A true statement of the king's debts was to be followed by a reckoning of the ordinary receipts and issues. Then the great debts to the City and to the Customs Farmers, as well as the assignments of subsidies, tenths, and fifteenths, were to be listed separately from the rest of the debt. By placing these debts on a separate paper, Salisbury believed that "the other debts unprovided for will more orderlie appeare and less confound other reckonings." A third schedule was to contain customs, impositions, and leases, together with a notation of their accounting days in the Exchequer. In this way there would be a ready reference to expected revenue and an index of accountants.

Salisbury also intended to bring crown revenue into the Exchequer that was presently held from three months to a year by the collectors and receivers who made only paper declarations on the quarterly accounting days rather than cash deposits. They were to be listed, together with all other sources of Household revenue arising outside of the Exchequer, to avoid, for example, having money enter the Wardrobe when it was expected in the receipt. Salisbury considered this a problem because "much that hath been assigned [of the revenue] hath been otherwise disposed soe as it is but a betraying of our owne reckoninge to cast debtes uppon receipts which we know will fall short."[18] Evidence that Salisbury's system was used is found in various views, statements, and letters such as the one Caesar sent to the Lord Treasurer telling him that the accompanying statement of receipt and issue was made "according to your Lordships method."[19]

During the summer of 1608, Salisbury had been away from London. Caesar, in the meantime, attended to the implementation of the Lord Treasurer's program for increasing the revenue. Salisbury had met with the senior Exchequer officers of the receipt and the audit in May to establish rules and procedures for the better ordering of their affairs. In July they met again to inquire into the state of their various departments and to solicit their suggestions for increasing the king's revenue.[20] Written answers to their queries were submitted to Caesar, who gathered them into a comprehensive survey of the king's estate. On the dorse of each of these documents, he inscribed a letter of the alphabet; the series runs at least through the letter Q, although not all of these lettered documents survive.

The alphabet documents showed that the king's annual ordinary and certain receipts were £317,168 and that the ordinary and certain

receipts were £408,174.[21] At this rate, the annual deficit was £91,006. In addition, there were unexpected and extraordinary issues; in the year from Micheaelmas 1607 until Michaelmas 1608, they amounted to £573,157. Some of these expenses were for the repair of the works, others for parks and chases. But the largest class of issue was for the Irish War. There were also installments on the late queen's debt to be considered, amounting as they did to £1,752 3d. In addition, James was dispensing jewels at the New Year, but we do not know whether they were newly purchased or taken from the Jewel House. Sir Edward Grevill received an extraordinarily large free gift of more than £2,000, but the one issue that was nearly as large as the Irish defense money was £7,080 17s. 2d. for the king's robes.[22]

As he reviewed the state of the Exchequer, Caesar noted that the debt had increased by £113,460 in the year since Michaelmas 1607; the entire debt stood at £537,996. The revenue, on the other hand, fell short of the debt by £334,113. These figures differed from those that Caesar presented to Salisbury in May.[23] The only parliamentary revenue that the crown could rely on was the subsidy, and two of the three subsidies voted in 1606 had been collected or assigned. A third was not due until February 1612, if, indeed, it would ever be collected. "The conclusion," Caesar wrote, "is that before midsomer next there must bee provided 366,290 libri."[24]

In order to reach this goal, all of the crown's present resources would have to be carefully conserved, meaning that the king would have to abate his expenses. It is likely that James was approached to solicit his agreement to a plan for reserving certain large parts of his revenue for public purposes, while setting aside a smaller sum for his "liberality." Such a scheme would limit his freedom to dispose of the revenue as he wished, but he might be impressed by the gravity of the crisis he faced, and, if he could live within his extraparliamentary means, the inconvenience of summoning another Parliament might be postponed. A memorandum had been drawn up in 1607 listing "those thinges which are so naturally and peculiarly to be converted to the sole mayntenaunce of his Majestys own estate, as they cannot be reserved for his liberality without extreme prejudice."[25] Foremost among these items were the lands in fee farm and fee simple that were in the crown's possession—essentially a restatement of Salisbury's entail of royal lands created in July 1604.[26] The crown, moreover, could not grant away the customs, impositions, licenses to export, prohibited goods, monopolies, fines, and assarts because they constituted the basis of crown finance, the fisc, and the government was determined to prevent its being alienated.

Important though a policy of abatement would be, there was common agreement in government that the king's liberality had to be provided for; thus, casual revenues were reserved to the crown for that purpose. Within certain limits, the king was free to dispose of goods and lands of those who were attainted of treason or whose lands were escheated to him for murder or felony. The king also could do anything he liked with "any new inventions of gain not repugnant to the law nor burthensome to the subject." When a new list of grantable and ungrantable suits was made in 1608, it incorporated the memorandum of 1607, including the old debts, the royal third, and the moiety. There was, however, an absolute ban on all other grants unless "they bee proiects whereof profit may grow to the king and shalbe first referred by the Masters of Requests to the 3 Lords Chief Justices and Chief Baron and by them recommended to the Privy Council as fit and convenient to bee granted." All of this was undertaken until "it shall please God to rid [the king] of our debt and that hee equalled his revenue to his charge."[27]

By the time that Salisbury returned to London, Caesar was ready to start to work improving the revenue. Their first task was to appoint a number of administrators and commissioners who would uncover and enforce such revenue-producing ventures as the collection of debts owing to the crown, both before and after 30 Elizabeth; the collection of noblemen's and bishops' debts; the enforcement of fees paid for the right to sell unstretched cloth; and the collection of several bonds. Other appointees were to initiate inquiries regarding the sale of wood from royal forests, breaches of building restrictions, and the value of uncovered recusants' lands and goods. During the next year, the returns from these inquiries reached Caesar and are preserved throughout his Exchequer papers.

From the autumn of 1608 until the end of 1609, Salisbury and Caesar struggled with the nearly insoluble problems of royal finance, but by the end of the period, it was becoming increasingly apparent to them that the only satisfactory answer was to recommend another Parliament to the king. As hard as they had worked, they had been unable to produce increases in the receipt sufficient to retire the debt, to pay current expenses, and to satisfy the crown's re-

quirements. In short, they needed the proceeds of the expected subsidy. Yet for nearly fifteen months, the crown had benefitted from
the various extraparliamentary projects and programs with which
they had been experimenting.

In June 1608 Salisbury and Caesar were commissioned to lease
the royal lands at increased rates. Although this was not an unusual
commission, Salisbury attacked it with characteristic vigor in an
effort to transform the crown from a passive landlord to an active
magnate extracting maximum value from the royal estates. This policy was economically and politically sound. Few Members of Parliament could condemn the crown for making its own lands pay a
reasonable return, and the Commons, with their large complement
of successful landlords, had been insisting that the king should live
of his own. The commission authorized the lease of mills, manors,
messuages, granges, hereditaments, and tenements for twenty-one
years or three lives at or above the accustomed rent with the customary entry fines.[28]

In his analysis of Salisbury's administration of the treasury, F. C.
Dietz points to his reliance on the increase in land revenue to bridge
the gap between receipt and issue. Salisbury first tried to raise the entry fines, then raised the rents themselves, relying throughout on new
surveys. Wherever possible, copyhold tenants were to acknowledge
that their entry fines were uncertain so "that the crown might have a
constantly mounting revenue from that source." And when the fine
was certain, copyholders were to be "persuaded to buy their freedom
at from twenty to fifty years' purchase."[29] His techniques were hardly
subtle, and, in the case of selling mills, his approach to the prospective purchasers was blunt. Caesar was ordered to carry out a survey
of the mills to establish their value, because, Salisbury wrote, "You
knowe, Sir, we have a purpose to make money of some [of them]." The
present tenants were to be offered the mills, which were decaying, in
fee farm. They were to be told that the offer was being made to spare
the crown additional expense; repairs had to be carried out either by
the new owners or by contractors who would undertake the work. If
the tenants would not agree to buy the mills in their present state of
disrepair, then more drastic action was to be taken. The Chancellor
was to direct the Auditors, "at their audit, to give notice to the tenantes
of the kings lands that they shall buy their mills in fee farme, if they
will offer roundly. Otherwise [the Auditors] may lett them know that

the king must pass [the mills] away to others rather then to beare the burden of reparation."[30] Salisbury had hoped to raise the prices by pitting the incumbent tenants against the prospective contractors.

New or increased revenue was also sought in the careful exploitation of administrative procedures. The enforcement of proclamations, for instance, resulted in increased extraparliamentary revenue. Because it was always a problem to find sufficient jurors to serve in the counties and Westminster, proclamations were issued requiring all fit men to appear for jury service. Those who would not serve were to be fined and the proceeds sent to the Exchequer. For Caesar, the proclamation of jurors was a device for raising revenue. On 21 August 1607 he wrote that

the still increasing disbursements and the overpressing wantes doe enforce me at this present instantly to pray for your Lordships remembrance of some speedie proceading in the business of the jorors. Time runneth on most swiftly and extremities foreseen are better prevented then bourne when they fall. My Lord Chanceler expecteth the proclamation; my Lord Tresorer inveyeth at the stay, my selfe humblie desire your spedie remembrance thereof.[31]

The commission had been issued by 5 October.[32] Caesar's estimate of the value of the proclamation was measured in terms of the fiscal ends that it would serve.

Commissions made up of six "principall gentlemen" were to be established in each shire to make compositions in lieu of jury service and to verify the sheriff's writs of dotage excusing prospective jurymen by reason of advanced age or infirmity from service and from liability to the penalties imposed by the proclamation. Severe penalties would be imposed if the commissioners found that the sheriff had issued false writs. The same was true in the case of shrieval corruption in the selection of jurymen, the ultimate threat being the prospect of an appearance before Star Chamber. When the compositions were being arranged, the commissioners were required to keep in mind a schedule of acceptable amounts: either £20, 20 marks, or 20 nobles, depending on the social station of the compounder. The provision for enforcement went so far as to require a special clerk in the Exchequer to strike tallies for jury fines.[33] The Exchequer appears to have expected a large return of jury fines and had planned carefully to account for them.

The sheriffs were the most important administrative connection between the central government and the county community, but a variety of structural problems made them, at the same time, the weakest link. As unpaid tax and debt collectors they were forced to bear the responsibility for the county's financial obligation as a personal liability, and it is little wonder that many were corrupt. Because of their importance to the receipt, dishonest sheriffs presented a serious national problem. They were, for instance, the officers traditionally employed in the collection of crown debts estreated (copied onto the court rolls for collection) into Exchequer from other courts, and they appeared determined to make what profit they could out of their unpopular position. Each year the sheriff was issued summonses in Hilary Term and Easter Term that were sealed with the green wax of the clerk in the Pipe Office, who was charged with issuing the writs and collecting the returns. The sheriff was required either to collect the debt or to submit his reason for not doing so to the Exchequer. If the reason was not accepted, the liability for the debt remained with the sheriff. But these officers served for only one year, and at the end of their service they passed the accumulated obligations to their successors whenever they could.

Sheriffs had, over the years, developed a variety of corrupt practices to draw off money for themselves. A debtor would be told that he could give the sheriff a sum equal to a fraction of the face value of the debt in return for a fraudulent acquittance (i.e., a written receipt stating that the debt had been paid), and the sheriff would see to it that the entire debt was canceled. Alternatively, the sheriff would collect the debt, issue an acquittance, and then report to the Exchequer that it was unenforceable because there had been insufficient property or goods to seize in satisfaction of the obligation. This latter practice, known as nichiling (from the Latin *nihil*, "nothing"), had been designed for a legitimate reason: it was, in a sense, an early form of bankruptcy; however, by the turn of the seventeenth century, it was more often than not abused. Some sheriffs were alleged to have returned nothing to Exchequer, having ignored the Green Wax summonses and writs completely and having developed techniques to avoid liability.

There was a Clerk of the Nichils, an office lying in the Chancellor's gift, and it was his task, according to the King's Remembrancer, Sir Henry Fanshawe, to gather the nichiled returns and arrange them under the headings of the various courts from which they had been estreated. The Clerk would then summon the sheriffs to justify the nichils or pay the debt themselves. It would appear from the account that follows that the system did not work as smoothly as Fanshawe's description would suggest.[34]

Because nichiled debts and other shrieval abuses were costing the crown much needed revenue, it is not surprising that in 1607 a project was under consideration in the Exchequer for discovering false nichils, enforcing an honest levy of felons' goods, and correcting abuses in county administration. By 1608 Sir Stephen Proctor, who was making a career of farming the fruits of justice and the flowers of the prerogative, had managed to gain omnibus authority to correct these abuses.[35] In effect, he was setting up as a superintendent of sheriffs, and he was widely resented for it. By 1610 Proctor found himself facing an angry Parliament bent on impeachment. He complained that he had been unable to conduct his commission properly because of a recent general pardon that had put many debtors beyond his authority and excused the erring sheriffs.[36]

Proctor also turned his attention to a profitable racket among the common informers. It appeared that they were using the threat of an information as a weapon for blackmail. What they could not extract from the victim by extortion they obtained by working out collusive arrangements with sheriffs and other local officials. In June 1608 Proctor received authority from Salisbury to prosecute unscrupulous informers by English Bill (an equity bill) in the Exchequer Court. He was likewise authorized to use the English Bill against sheriffs who nichiled illegally and collectors and receivers who were suspected of fraud.[37]

Informers had been a problem in Elizabeth's reign as well as James's. Holdsworth indicates that they stirred up litigation only to compound for a sum of money; the threat to sue was an easy form of extortion. "A '*turbidum genus*' of informers arose whom Coke classes with 'the monopolist, the concealer, and the dispencer with publick and profitable penal lawes' as the four varieties of 'viperous vermin which endeavoured to have eaten out the sides of church and commonwealth.'"[38] There was legislation on the books to restrict informers, but they persisted in their behavior. Proctor suggested the establishment of a Clerk of Compositions in the Exchequer to deal with the informers. The position would have two purposes: "The one to prevent and correct the abuses in common informers which are infinite. The other to helpe the King to come to some reckoninge of profitt upon populer informaccons which will not be felt if the people may be eased of that powlinge [sic] and vexaccon which by the foresaid abuses they doe endure." Proctor insisted that there would be no new fees or charges associated with the clerkship, although this seems most unlikely. In general, he wanted to create a position in which all compositions and informations would have to pass through his hands. All informers would be required to provide certificates of their names and addresses and of their good behavior so that malicious informers could be either discouraged or discovered and prosecuted. If double informations were laid against the same party, the Clerk would attempt to discover whether there had been collusion and have one of the informations withdrawn.[39]

James was delighted with Proctor's proposals, and we find that the projects for nichils and informers were receiving favorable consideration in Exchequer even though an official as important as Fanshawe was decidedly opposed to them. He was not even sure that some of Proctor's schemes were legal.[40] As we have noted, Proctor became so unpopular that he was one of two royal servants against whom Parliament moved impeachment proceedings in the 1610 session.

Perhaps the most controversial of all the new revenue schemes was Salisbury's reintroduction of impositions on a scale more far-reaching than had ever been known before. Bate's Case in 1606 had confirmed the legality of impositions notwithstanding their manifest unpopularity. By 1608, the Irish War was growing incrementally more costly, and drastic measures were required. Large sums of money had to be raised quickly, and borrowing was not the answer. Thus, on 11 June, Caesar reported that

the Lord Treasurer attended by the Chanceler and Barons of the Exchequeur went to the Custome House and there in the assembly of the chiefe merchants of England assembled from all principall portes of the land, did make an excellent speech to prove that impositions might lawfully be imposed by Sovereine Kinges and Princes on all merchandises issuing out or coming in to theire portes, and that no King or Prince living or dead doth or ever did deserve better of the continuance of that liberty and priviledge then our Soverain King James who in the excellent vertues naturall, morall, and politicall surmounteth all other Kings living or dead, that his present necessities occasioned for the use of the publick, especially for Ireland, contrary to his owne will and the admirable swetenes of his owne naturall inclination have occasioned him to use this lawfull and just meanes of profit. Which speech hee had no sooner knit up with a particuler repetition of imposition now seeming burdensome, and ordered by his Majesty for the ease of his subjects to be lightened, as likewise most things of necessary important use to the poore to bee exempted from any imposition. Then every man after some little contradiction, consented to this generall imposition noue establisshed, which will prove the most gainfull to the King and his posterity as anyone daies worke done by any Lord Treasurer since the time of King Edward the 3.[41]

Dietz has observed that this massive imposition, which exempted little more than foodstuffs and ships stores, was the catalyst that drew together the opposition to the crown's financial program in 1610.[42] In his speech to the merchants, Salisbury departed from the traditional idea that the king must live of his own. That day in the Customs House, Salisbury enunciated the modern policy that the king must be supported by the nation if he was to provide for its welfare and safety; the idea of "support" would figure prominently in the Great Contract proposed by Salisbury to Parliament in 1610. The Great Contract was the grandest of a succession of bold attempts to reshape the fundamental premises on which public finance was based.

The cases we have discussed illustrate Salisbury's and Caesar's labors in the Exchequer until the close of 1609. Their projects and programs were legion, their concentration intense. They made remarkable progress in paying the debt and raising new revenue. But rising prices, the Irish War, and the king's spending outstripped their ability to meet rising expenses and to realize Salisbury's ambitious goal of retiring all crown indebtedness. There was no option but to advise the king to summon Parliament in anticipation of extracting additional revenue at the lowest political cost to the crown.

VII

A Sacred Offer Not to Be Refused

IN THE PARLIAMENTARY SESSIONS of 1610, Caesar wore several hats: he was a Member of Parliament, a Privy Councillor, and the Chancellor of the Exchequer, but of even greater importance, he was Salisbury's principal assistant. As such, he was an important but secondary participant in the debates on the Great Contract who worked at the center of national politics, not as a leader and shaper but as a dutiful follower and technical expert. When he rose to speak as Chancellor of the Exchequer, he addressed fiscal issues such as the amount of ready money needed to conduct the king's government, and he appeared to stand on fairly firm ground. But on other occasions, when he ventured into general political debate, he seemed, perhaps, to be in deeper water than he may have thought.

When we consider the Great Contract and Caesar's place in its story, we must spend more time with the Contract itself than his role would appear to merit. Yet he was the crown's senior spokesman in the Lower House, and, because of a document he prepared during the summer recess that was critical of the Contract, historians have assumed that he was instrumental in its eventual failure. We shall, therefore, assess Caesar's place in the Parliament and determine what role, if any, he played in the Contract's defeat.[1] Our examination of the Contract begins with our recalling the last parliamentary session and the intervening administration of the new Lord Treasurer.

Although Lord Treasurer Dorset had been candid with Parliament in 1606 about the crown's indebtedness, he had introduced no fiscal program to meet the king's needs. The Members voted subsidies and fifteenths, but there were no substantial changes either in the king's spending or in the nature and extent of the revenue.[2] A variety of sensitive subjects were raised in 1606, not the least being James's proposed union of England and Scotland, but the king had discovered that debates in Parliament provided the opportunity for the Members to raise issues that he found inappropriate, indeed, distasteful. His response was brusque: "I am your king; I am pleased to govern you and shall answer for your errors; I am a man of flesh and blood and have my passions and affections as other men. I pray you, do not far move me to do that which my power may tempt me."[3] By the end of the 1606 session, the Members had been stalled and their grievances remained unanswered. By 1610 they were ready to renew their struggle to discuss elements of the prerogative that previously had been closed to them. It would have been inconceivable to the newly assembled Members of Parliament, however, that Salisbury and his proposal to repair the deficit would throw open the door for them to discuss the arcane mysteries of the prerogative. The parliamentary sessions of 1610 promised to be unusual.

As we have seen, since becoming Lord Treasurer, Salisbury had tried to solve the problem of the growing deficit through unconventional techniques. The new Book of Rates, the Great Farm of the Custom, and the extension of impositions had been Salisbury's opening moves in the extension of prerogative taxation, but they did not address the question of apportioning the responsibility for public expenditures between crown and people. It has been argued that, of all aspects of government, the early Stuart system of public finance "remained the most evidently medieval both in its mechanisms and outlook." When there were debates on the supply, the Members employed "a framework of conventions governing the terms upon which taxes were demanded, granted, and spent, which by long and enduring practice had become central to their constitutional relationship with the crown."[4]

According to ancient practice, a tacit reciprocity obtained between the subjects' responsibility to provide the necessary revenue to assure fiscal resources sufficient to the crown's requirements and the crown's responsibility to conserve their value. Through the agency of Parliament, therefore, the subjects were entitled to a legitimate concern about the crown's management of its treasure, but they were not entitled to dictate to the crown how it would be employed. In the light of this relationship, the king ordinarily "had no claim on his subjects' wealth to maintain the dignity of the crown," but they were obliged to assist in the preservation of the state "in times of exceptional need."[5] Should crown and Parliament fail to agree on the support necessary to meet this need, the king possessed residual sovereign authority to tax by prerogative fiat, although, in doing so, the balance of mixed government was compromised. Medieval Parliaments and medieval kings had carefully avoided reaching such a pass.[6]

These arrangements remained viable until the start of the seventeenth century. War, the one exigency that would justify the award of exceptional revenue to the crown, became such a pressing issue toward the end of Elizabeth's reign that she resorted to Parliament for taxes with incrementally greater frequency while using extraparliamentary sources to pay for the other costs of government and to maintain her dignity. But circumstances changed in 1603 because James was avowedly irenic. He declared peace upon his accession and bent every effort to maintain it. With Spain now an ally, with Scotland and England under the same rule, and with efforts underway to settle Ireland peacefully (although with limited success), the need for extraordinary parliamentary taxation appeared to be greatly diminished, yet the crown continued to ask for taxes that were without "any constitutional basis" and that would assuredly "encounter resistance from a body freshly alerted to its rights, history, and political role." It was against this background that the debates in 1606 had been argued, and the background remained the same in 1610. The Members, in their efforts to settle on and justify their response to the king's demands, turned with increasing frequency to "the principles and practices of the past."[7] From Salisbury's vantage point, this was conceptually and practically inadequate. He believed that it might, perhaps, be possible to restructure English public finance if the Members could be persuaded to abandon their traditional understanding of the correct relationship between king and Parliament. This was the challenge of the Great Contract.

The two houses were convened on 9 February 1610. Prayers were recited and speeches were made as the Fourth Session of the First Parliament of James I settled down to work. Barred by his peerage from addressing the Commons directly, Salisbury had to await a conference of both Houses on 15 February to make his case to the representatives of the Lower House. His speech was a model of reason and good will. He told the conference committee why the session had been summoned and why their meeting was necessary. The Lords and Commons were as one in the body politic, he said, giving their advice to "the king (being the politic head) [who] can receive no other good from the body of this parliament, severed in itself, that the natural head can receive comfort when there is interruption of the passages between the head and the heart, whereof the best issue can be no other than the effects of a dead palsy which taketh away motion first and life after."[8]

Parliament had been summoned for two important reasons: to witness Prince Henry created Prince of Wales and earl of Chester and to procure supply for the king's necessities. Salisbury stressed the good fortune that had been visited on former princes of Wales who had been created in the presence of a Parliament, and then he turned to a detailed exposition of the crown's financial requirements. The Members were not being asked to respond in a vacuum to James's needs; indeed, Salisbury provided a criterion for their use as they determined the appropriate level of supply. They were to ask themselves whether the king's "ordinary receipt be sufficient to bear his ordinary issues, leaving always a portion to answer extraordinaries, which are so certain in proof as all men must provide for, though they know them not beforehand." A great prince, like a private man, must provide for contingencies based on a "fourth part of his ordinary." No prince "can be safe and happy that is not able to offend his enemy upon just cause, to defend himself upon sudden injury, or assist his friend in causes of oppression and violence."[9]

With this criterion in mind, Salisbury had prepared the Members to hear the details of the king's necessities. He told them that James had received in subsidies, since coming to England, a total of £820,000, but that the revenue had not been of any immediate use to him because it was already committed. Subsidies voted during the late queen's reign had yielded about £350,000 since 1603, and this had been applied to her debts. The subsidies that had been voted in 1606 and the aid for knighting Prince Henry had been used by the crown to reduce the standing debt by an additional £67,000. More than £400,000 had been paid into the Treasury as result of the sale of mills, and of parsonages and chantries in fee farm. Copyholds, fines for defective titles, and the revenues from the sale of woods had contributed another £100,000, thus keeping the money from "being drunk up by the stewards," as had been the practice. "There hath also been raised, by calling in of just debts and arrearages which should have been paid in former years, all due since 30° of the Queen, together with some other effects of abridging loose accompts and liberal expense in inferior ministers, well near the sum of two hundred thousand pounds."[10]

Turning next to a justification of the king's expenses, Salisbury concentrated on the dignity and estate that James's subjects expected him to maintain. Had the nation expected the king to come down from Scotland like a private gentleman? Was his noble queen to have no more to keep her estate than a countess? Were ambassadors from abroad to outshine the monarch to whom they were accredited while he could not afford to dispatch embassies of his own? Each rhetorical, goading enquiry was answered with a resounding "no," for certainly the Members would have rejected any other answer. In summary, the Lord Treasurer said "that for the 820,000 libri, which his Majesty hath received, he hath spent in the military charges and those of magnificence 1,400,000 libri."[11]

The final phase of Salisbury's address was devoted to an explanation of the two motions the king and Council found suitable for Parliament to consider. One was to grant "some such supply as may make this state both safe and happy"; the second was to confer among themselves to entertain "any reasonable request for the public good" that the king might make. He told the Members that there could be no more suitable response to a gracious monarch who extended his favor to his subjects and granted them their requests than "to give some good supply of money" in the form of subsidies and fifteenths. Though the subjects might sacrifice, it did not appear that James, at this early stage in the Fourth Session, was prepared to surrender anything. According to Salisbury, the king's purpose was straightforward enough: "He desires not anything that may make you fear any change of liberties, pressing of new laws, to satisfy fury or private passions, every man may dwell in safety under his own olive in this King's days."[12] His majesty did, of course, enjoy the power to lay impositions upon trade, a power recently upheld in Bate's Case, but he had no liberty to harm commerce. He had the power to assume the wardships of the minor heirs of his deceased tenants-in-chief, but he had no authority to destroy their inheritance. Within these constraints, James was free to make concessions and to favor just petitions. In short, he was willing to relieve the Members' grievances. The Lords, for their part, were unsurpassed in their readiness to "concur . . . in consultation . . . or join . . . in humble requests, for a further retribution" in those cases where the Commons would deal openly with them and would show suitable respect to the crown and restraint in debate.[13]

At this point, Salisbury had broken no new ground. The Contract had yet to be proposed. He would have had the Commons believe that a cooperative king and House of Lords were awaiting the opportunity to work with a respectful and "modest" Lower House. The extent of the crown's indebtedness had been exposed, and a carefully phrased invitation had been extended to present grievances to the king.

Attorney General Hobart, Mr. Solicitor Bacon, and Sir Edwin Sandys reported the Lord Treasurer's address to the House of Commons on Sunday, 17 February 1610.[14] Committees were formed to prepare responses to the Lords, and on 20 February Caesar had his first opportunity to address the king's case. Because he was a member of Privy Council and a senior minister, his speeches and observations had to be taken as reflections of government policy. Even on those occasions when he spoke for the House in conference meetings, he approached his task as Salisbury's principal lieutenant. Speaking as Mr. Chancellor, he told his colleagues in a Commons committee that the king's "wants were such as there was expected 200,000 libri by year in increase of revenue for himself and his children and 600,000 libri besides to redeem his debts and wants." Caesar had addressed them "in angry manner," reporting the king's displeasure with their delays occasioned by committee meetings to consider grievances before voting supply. He also displayed his own frustration when he reported that the daily rate of expense amounted to £1,400, excluding interest on the debt; it should have been clear that the crown could ill afford any further delays in Commons. For their part, the Members in their committees wanted to consult further with the Lords before making any commitments.[15]

When the representatives of the two Houses met in conference on 24 February, Caesar spoke for the Commons, but, at the same time, he was privy to the strategies of Salisbury and, perhaps, of the Lords and the king. The conference meeting was the next step in presenting the Contract, and it bore the appearances of careful stage management between the Lord Treasurer and the Chancellor of the Exchequer. That morning, Salisbury had told the Lords what the king expected of Parliament before he would consider retribution; the afternoon conference gave him the opportunity to advise the Commons through their representatives.

Caesar rose to open the meeting with a question on the part of his fellow Members: "We desire to know of your Lordships what quantity in our contribution do you expect; for ourselves, though our willingness is very great to do the King service, yet the demand so great that without an exceeding noble retribution, we cannot satisfy, which retribution we do likewise desire to know of your Lordships, what shall be given us."[16] The Lord Treasurer's reply was sharp and angry; he was not used to repeating himself before men of such great judgment as the assembled Members. He had already told them why their revenues were needed: if the king was to defend the realm against the continual threat of invasion by papists from overseas and meet his other obligations, he would need £600,000 in supply and another £200,000 in "support," a new category of tax in the form of an annual grant unrelated to subsidies and fifteenths.[17] Salisbury repeated the necessity for these revenues: "The demand, therefore, is for supply 6 hundred thousand pounds, for revenue 2 hundred thousand pounds, that we of his council may not be driven to stand as we have of late with our caps in our hands to the usurers."[18] Even though the Jacobean peace should have meant the end of extraordinary expenses for defense, Salisbury cited the specter of invasion to justify the taxes he had demanded of them.

Caesar answered the Lord Treasurer's statement with a reminder to all of the Lords present that, according to tradition, the subsidy had never before been raised so early in the session and that, when it had been moved, it had originated in the Commons. There then followed a dramatic (but hardly spontaneous) exchange between Caesar and Salisbury:

MY LORD TREASURER. The demand so transcendent, so rare, yet so necessary to be had as we expect some propositions from you in what kind you will offer. If our demands be too great, offer what you will and then we will shew you our reasons without prevarication.

MR. CHANCELLOR. Your Lordships dealeth most nobly with us that you leave us unto our offers, but we have no commission to deal with your Lordships until we have reported unto the House.[19]

Between them, Caesar and Salisbury had managed a lovely finesse. They had no reason to have expected the Members to initiate a tax measure on the scale of £800,000 or to create an entirely new category of taxation called "support." However, by taking the initiative, Salisbury had first put a price tag on the king's requirements, and Caesar had followed with a challenge to the propriety of the Lords' proposal. This left the door open for Salisbury to bow to the Commons' privilege after having first set the price, his purpose all along. Finally, they had managed to introduce the novel concept of "support," which became a central element in the subsequent debates in the Lower House. Caesar had also advised the Lords that the Commons delegation could do no more than transmit messages; it had no power to negotiate. Salisbury could no longer manage Commons directly, and the restrictions on the Members attending conference further attenuated his influence. Yet, having arranged the opening gambit as they did, he and Caesar presented the crown's case, showed suitable sensitivity to the privileges of the Commons, and suggested the possibility of a fuller debate than Commons had expected, but they stood firm on the priority of contribution over retribution.[20]

Sir Henry Montagu, the Recorder of London, rose to ask specific permission for the House to debate the prerogative and those "tenures in which wardships and other points of tenure are contained."[21] The principles of the Great Contract were embedded in Salisbury's reply. Although the king would not sell the right of purveyance, he would, of his grace, consider that purveyance "be taken away and a market at the court gate [be established] as after the manner of France."[22] James would also limit his active campaign to recover debts and uncover concealed leases. Such limitations would have secured future generations from harassment and deprived common informers of an important part of their livelihoods. In addition, he agreed to compound en masse for debts dating from before 30 Elizabeth and to abolish "misrecitals and misnamings" of manors, a practice that led to expensive litigation for the landholder in question. Insofar as the Court of Wards was concerned, Salisbury could see no serious problem with the status quo and, thus, could not imagine why any changes were needed. However, he did allow that the Wards returned too little to the king while attracting popular hostility. Thus, he offered to honor a motion requiring him to administer sworn audits to protect the wards' inheritances. Salisbury closed his comments with a thought for the Members to ponder. If they enjoyed having the opportunity to debate various points of the prerogative and to rid themselves of some of their tenurial obligations, they had only to act. But if they wanted to abuse this limited invitation by debating the prerogative as such, or if they wished to lower the bargaining price, the king could manage without them. He "will but sell 1500 libri a year of his old rent [which] will make him a hundred thousand pounds and so in like proportions, more or less."[23]

The Commons had decided, by 26 March, on terms that they would report to the House of Lords. On behalf of his fellow Members, Mr. Recorder Montagu said that the feudal tenures were to be wiped away except for aids that were to be fixed at £125,000 each for the king's eldest son when he was knighted and his eldest son and daughter when they were married. In return for these concessions, the House of Commons was prepared to vote £100,000 per annum in supply. No mention was made of the means to levy the supply or of a system to assure compliance by the contracting parties.[24]

During the first months of the session, Caesar had not figured prominently in the debate. He had spoken out during conference and committee meetings, but it was Sir Francis Bacon who spoke longest and most passionately for the king's position. On the opposite side, Sir Edwin Sandys and his colleagues strove to reach a settlement that would extract the most from James at the least sacrifice to themselves and their constituents. While the House was not yet stridently opposed to James, they were not inclined to support his excessive spending. Sandys had hardly to twist arms to gain support.

Although there were Members who debated the Contract without any intention of securing a perfected bargain with the crown, there were also those Members who were opposed to the Contract in principle because they found bargaining for the regality distasteful. In the Lords, a collateral line of opposition developed among peers who feared that an attack on the prerogative was only a step away from an attack on their own privileges. Yet most of the Members and many Lords appeared to welcome this opportunity to engage in a general debate on the prerogative, a hitherto forbidden subject.

While the committees were engaged in discussing the Contract, the remainder of the House expanded its incursion into the king's privileges on other fronts. Dr. John Cowell's newly published law dictionary, *The Interpreter*, was roundly condemned for its naively inflated praise of the prerogative. At the same time, efforts were underway to impeach two crown officers, and a morass of ecclesiastical grievances provided a forcing bed for further opposition.[25] To their knowledge, there had never been a Parliament that had been allowed such latitude in debate, such freedom to penetrate the sanctum of the regality. The Members in opposition were determined not to lose this opportunity to anatomize and criticize the prerogative. The debate continued with unrelenting vigor on several fronts at once; Easter recess was all the more welcome because it gave everyone time to consider the decisions that had to be made. Rumors flew: some Members thought that James would hold out for £300,000, while the Venetian ambassador reported that the Lords were planning to refuse payment of their share if the Contract were approved.[26]

The pace quickened after the recess. On 20 April, Salisbury advised a conference meeting that James was willing to have them discuss the incidents of feudal tenure but not the tenures themselves, a compromise wrung from the king by the Lord Treasurer to keep the discussions alive. Even though the tenurial incidents were open to discussion, Salisbury reminded the conference meeting that "the king is as well lord over the land as person in respect of the seignory though he have not the lands in his hands." There were Members who wanted assurances that the king would not restore the incidents in the future. Salisbury answered them rhetorically: If the incidents were of the prerogative, could an Act of Parliament touch them? In reply he said that "all homage you will take but fealty, the particular tenures may be taken away though the general remain. I leave it unto you whether the king may not bind himself by an act of parliament, I know not what an act of parliament may not do." The Members were invited to frame their measures as they would, and if they did so *salvo jure*, the Lords would join them with a will. Otherwise, the Upper House would be rocklike in their resistance to the Commons.[27]

At issue in the debate over tenures was the fundamental distinction between the king as lord, with specifically inhering tenurial rights, and the king as sovereign, to whom every Englishman owed allegiance without regard for property relations. While the enforcement of tenurial rights might be surrendered in certain instances, there could be no compromises with allegiance. As Hobart told the House the following day, the king would reserve to himself knight's service in chief and grand serjeanty; the rest might be discussed. The king would not transfer these tenures to new manors, and the House, "without jealousy, without suspicion, without needless fears," should conclude their discussion. Hobart encouraged his colleagues "to proceed to our security, which best pleased the King when it is most safe for us."[28]

The first "firm ground" was reached in the negotiations when the two Houses returned to conference on 26 April. The Commons had dutifully preserved "the points of honor" regarding tenures, framing their conditions in terms of the incidents alone. Salisbury thanked them for their consideration before turning to their offer of £100,000. They had asked "whether [it] will be accepted or no." He had advised that the king would remain "in an inevitable necessity" if £200,000 in support and £600,000 in supply were not voted. The king, who was in Newmarket, had told Salisbury that if the "points of honor" were preserved, he could announce the king's "pleasure for points of profit." In the light of his requirements, the £100,000 offer was utterly inadequate. Furthermore, the Lord Treasurer noted that the Commons were treating tenures and wardships separately, a departure he neither accepted nor approved.[29] While it was "his Majesty's further pleasure to contract for all in gross," the Commons stood firm in dividing the question into separate issues.[30]

Caesar tried to explain the Commons' intransigence and the belief held by a large body of the Members that the king was asking for more than Parliament could make the subjects pay. The king had greatly honored them by his willingness to negotiate, but they were "not able to give any more without giving discontentment unto the subjects, which we know would be much displeasing unto his Majesty."[31] But Caesar's words triggered an angry reply from Salisbury. He knew that the Commons' delegation had been expressly refused the right to negotiate, or even to debate in conference, and held that the meetings really were not conferences but mere assemblies to hear prepared addresses from the Lower House.[32]

Angered, the Lord Treasurer admonished the Members to remember that the commonality about which they were "followers, servants, and kinsmen" were bound to obey those laws enacted by Parliament. "Your consultations are but schools," he told them, "and you cannot cooperate without us." Professor Foster has queried this curious reference to "schools," but it appears to refer to the exercise quality of schoolboy debate. By analogy, without the necessary cooperation of the Lords, the Commons debates were mere exercises; without their agreement, no manner of disputation in the Commons could bear fruit. Salisbury reminded the Members that "never parliament dealt more lovingly with a lower House than we have done with you." Since negotiations had begun, alienations, purveyance, debts, and wardships had been offered, but without satisfaction. "The King may for his *esse* make more than you offer him for it. What tempest hath carried you that you take the demand so great; though we asked 200,000 libri yet did we not say we would not take less."[33] His best efforts notwithstanding, the Lord Treasurer was failing to manage the Commons with techniques learned from his father's long experience in the Elizabethan Parliaments. He was surprised, if not shocked, to find that the Commons would not acquiesce to the demand for £200,000, and nowhere did he express his awareness of his own failure more clearly than in his angry address to the conference: "did we not say we would not take less."

Four days later, the growing tension of the debate was obscured by the news reaching London from France of the assassination of Henry IV. The enormity of the regicide broke over the House like thunder. Supporters and opponents of the Contract were as one in their fear for their own king's safety. Salisbury, never one to let an opportunity slip by, tried to clinch the Contract by riding on the crest of this ephemeral unity. He ended his announcement of the news of the assassination with a comparison of the "opulent and valiant" late king of France and the "indigence" of the king of England. Although no one knew the reason for Henry's assassination, it was clear that the kingdom of France was, nonetheless, well provided and secure. England's coffers could also be full if Parliament willed it, but, Salisbury added, "To speak to you of the King's necessity, you will say to that end was the calling to you of this meeting, which I protest I never meant; but by how much we see things are as they are, by so much the more need we to have money to be employed and not to seek for upon any occasion." In short, whatsoever the "occasion," if Parliament provided an adequate annual revenue, England would always be prepared for any eventuality.[34] Yet, for all of his eloquence, Salisbury received not revenue but a spate of demands for the persecution of Catholics. The Contract had moved no further.

James's patience was exhausted as he awaited successful results from the Commons. On 11 May he ordered the Speaker to forbid any further debate about his prerogative right to levy impositions. The House and their committees struggled for several days with the best approach to take with their angered monarch. When there was still no answer more than a week later, James sent another message implying that, without their cooperation, he would dissolve Parliament. A tactful and submissive reply followed. By 21 May Caesar told his colleagues that the king was pleased and that he wished to address them that afternoon.[35]

The king's address to Parliament, not the first of the session, was, perhaps, the most pointed. The prince of Wales was to be created on Whitsun following, yet after more than fourteen weeks, the aid had not been voted and the subsidy and supply were stalled. James wanted the Members to know that, although he suffered their protracted debates from a desire to cooperate with them, he could carry on alone. Should he wish to be a tyrant, they could not stop him. These tactless assertions were further aggravated when he stated that "good kings are helped by Parliament, not for power but for convenience, that the work may seem more glorious." He closed with a reiteration of his request for the support and supply that he believed he had the right to expect.[36] Along with a number of his parliamentary colleagues, Caesar carried their answer to James's address in the form of a petition. They met with the king and Council on 24 May and were assured that James had no desire to prevent them from continuing their extensive debates on a wide variety of topics touching on the prerogative, especially the legality of the impositions.[37]

From the earliest weeks of the session, the Commons had charged a committee on grievances with determining what concessions they would require in return for their financial support. The committee had met nearly continuously, and, for greater efficiency, they had divided into a number of subcommittees responsible for particular issues such as penal statutes, impositions, and wardships. In the meantime, in reaction to the king's attempts to interfere with the Commons through his orders to the Speaker, the Members transferred their debates either to grand sessions of the committee on grievances (i.e., sessions open to all Members) or to the Committee of the Whole House in order to get the Speaker, Sir Edward Phelips, out of the chair. Once the Speaker was set aside, there was no limit to the scope of the debate short of the king's dissolving Parliament.

The committees and subcommittees were the setting for the memorable debates in the Fourth Session. Leading opponents of the crown's fiscal policy, such as Sandys and Whitelock, were the most frequently heard, but lesser Members contributed their share, as in the instance of Sir John Savile's refusal to take any part in their proceedings because he found the idea of bargaining away the liberties of the subjects repugnant. He could well imagine the king's instituting new causes of great grievance in order to sell relief to a future Parliament.[38] Interesting though it was, committee debate was not yielding answers to pressing questions. The end of term was drawing near, and nothing had yet been accomplished save for unprecedented bickering and disputation.

Salisbury, his patience worn, his health frail, his reputation at stake, met with representatives of both Houses on 11 June, demanding a subsidy then and there. He reminded them that the king had offered to give up even more of his prerogative when, for instance, he had allowed the impositions to become a part of the Contract. Surely a satisfactory answer could be made to the royal offer, both for the sake of internal political harmony and for England's security. Recalling the recent assassination in Paris, the Lord Treasurer chided them for allowing England to "lie in a lethargy," but his pleas were of no immediate consequence, for, on 19 June, the Commons asked for additional concessions and for a statement of the lowest sum that James would accept. A week later, the king's answer was given to the Lords; the Lower House was advised the following day. James would accept £140,000 per annum plus £80,000 to compensate for the loss of certain prerogative revenues, for a total of £220,000.[39]

During the month of June, parliamentary activity became more intense. As we have seen, Salisbury and the king were growing increasingly more impatient, and, as summer approached, the Members were anxious to go home to the country. Caesar had become more active, carrying messages to the House, speaking for the Commons in conference meetings, moving his brethren to accept the king's good faith and, at the least, to vote a subsidy. It is likely that, during the hectic June meetings, he had begun to formulate his own view of the Contract, its advantages and disadvantages.[40] As June drew to a close, a large-scale debate on the impositions eclipsed all other business. For more than a week, the question of the king's rights to levy impositions without parliamentary assent was anatomized and scrutinized. No record remains of Caesar's taking a vocal part in this momentous debate, but he was among the delegation from the Commons that delivered their demands on impositions to the king on 7 July.[41]

James and several of his Councillors received in state the Chancellor of the Exchequer and twenty other Members. They bore with them two enormous petitions representing the results of their labors since February. Bacon, the spokesman for the group, stepped forward to read their contents to the assembly. One of the petitions dealt with ecclesiastical grievances and does not concern us here, but the other, listing temporal grievances, is of significance. They were set out under eight titles: proclamations prejudicial to the subjects' rights; the removal of the four English border counties from the jurisdiction of the Council of Wales; undue temporal extensions of the authority of ecclesiastical commissions; the employment of prohibitions against such protective writs as *habeas corpus*; impositions on merchandise and sea-coals without parliamentary approval; the sealing of the new draperies; the taxing of alehouses; and, finally, the "monopolies of license of wines upon advantages of obsolete and impossible laws." The Commons wanted the king to give his answer quickly so that they might reach a settlement satisfactory to all.[42]

The king answered the petitions three days later at the new Banqueting Hall in Whitehall. One ambassador, who reported the meeting to his government, indicated that James "received them with ill looks and had little to say that was not caustic and glib."[43] Of "the two scrolls of grievances . . . the one [was] big enough to hang a little room," he said, "the other not so short as contrary to my expectation." The grievances, James continued, could be divided into two parts: those touching honor and those touching profit. As for the first, there could be no bargain made, but regarding the second, which principally concerned impositions, he promised "that none shall be laid but by parliament." Nonetheless, he told them, "I scorn that you stay to give me an answer to the point of supplying my present wants, which was the errand for which I called you together at this time."[44]

Following the king's comments, the Lord Treasurer rose to rebut the conclusions of the recent great debate on the impositions. Both radical Members and merchant Members had, to their satisfaction, virtually destroyed the legality of the impositions. They had concluded that parliamentary assent was necessary, not because of the king's grace but because of the inherent illegality of impositions made by prerogative fiat. Salisbury refused to accept this position, although there was little he could do about it save to lecture the Commons' delegation.[45] The king, once more, spoke to the assembly, announcing his intention to satisfy their grievances, relieve the impositions on sea-coals, and set aside the wine monopoly. He would also honor their plea for the stricter enforcement of the recusancy statutes. The sealing fees for the new draperies remained under consideration, but that was no reason for further delay. "Have regard unto the errand for which you were called, I mean about my supply and support."[46]

One subsidy and one fifteenth were voted when the Commons met the next day, but the House was in turmoil. The king's speech had been offensive enough, but Salisbury had added injury to the insult. The evening before, he had lobbied eight Members in Hyde Park. "When knowledge of it was had in the House, [the lobbied Members] were all suspected as plotters of some newe design. And the great matter of the Contract was in danger, by this jealousy, to have sped the worst which most did seek to advance."[47] The Commons were angered by Salisbury's interference because they were suspect of any moves the government might make, but they were equally irate that the privilege of the House had been violated by the Members who had met him in the park. It was contrary to the rules of the House for any Member to discuss their business with a non-Member. According to the French ambassador, the combination of the king's address and Salisbury's alleged offense brought the House close to rebellion. It fell to Caesar to restore order. Although Professor Foster has acknowledged the difficulty of knowing to what the ambassador was referring or what action Caesar took to calm the House, it is clear that there was an uproar.[48]

The controversial question of voting support, the essence of the bargain, was considered next. On 13 July the committee that had dealt with support recommended to the Commons that they make an offer of £180,000 in return for the abating of the tenurial incidents and of purveyance.[49] Representatives of both Houses met four days later to hear that the king would not reduce his demand below £200,000. That was his final price: he had yielded all that he could, and it remained with the Commons to act appropriately.[50]

James's insistence on an irreducible sum of £200,000 was certainly the product of frustration, and of his not wishing to appear to be giving away too much to an insatiable Parliament. He had been willing to accept £220,000, but £180,000 was inadequate. Relying on traditional accounting techniques, James had no precise basis on which to make such a projection of future needs. Yet he had announced to a conference of both Houses that he had a method. Mr. Recorder Montagu told the Commons that James had based his calculation on a number of converging (or coincidental) factors: "The conference of the lords with him was at Theobalds between 9 and 11. The number of the apostles when Judas was taken away was 11. The ports or gates of knowledge were numbered by the philosophers to be 9. The commandments of God made ten. The portion He took for tithes was the tenth part. His Majesty thought that the best number, therefore set up his rest upon ten score thousand pound." Hearing these words, Caesar rose to declare, "This is a divine ten, a sacred offer, let not our posterity curse us that we have refused it."[51] His reaction was surely rhetorical, perhaps sarcastic; but his words echoed a prevailing belief that certain numbers possessed inherent mystical qualities, especially when they were employed to bring temporal affairs into agreement with cosmic harmony. When Caesar styled the offer a "divine ten," he recognized the "mystical" possibilities in the king's calculation.[52]

Following "some other short speeches," the question of the £200,000 was put to the House: the ayes prevailed. Sir Roger Aston, Groom of the Chamber, reported the vote to James and later wrote to a friend that "for this great sum concluded, his Majesty departs with the wards and tenures, and discharges all purveyance or compositions and [is] only to be served with ready money, which I think will be a cause that his Majesty shall be constrained to lessen his house and to reform the abuses that are in it." All that remained was for "the manner and way . . . to levy this great sum yearly" to be determined. Over the summer recess, "the commissioners of the Lower House [would] return to their countries" and there decide on how best to assess the "support."[53] When the Commons' delegation departed their House to confer with the Lords as the session was ending, Caesar joyfully enjoined his colleagues: "Let us now go forward cheerfully in joint consultation, the Lords as much interested as we."[54]

Thus, after more than six months of parliamentary labor, the Members were close to an agreement, but it was not as yet concluded. Sir George More, three days before dissolution, proposed to the House of Commons that there be a writing containing the agreed terms. The resulting document epitomized the Contract and foreshadowed the problem with assessment that lay ahead. The Members were to carry a copy of the agreement home to their constituencies, and they were to return in the autumn with the means of assessment settled.[55]

Salisbury did not try to force a perfected Contract before the recess.

Although he would have welcomed the revenue it would produce, the chances of upsetting the agreement by precipitous action were simply too great. The Contract was almost made, yet the little that was left to accomplish would undo all that had come before. The summer months would make all the difference to the decisions that would be taken after the Members reconvened in October.

As soon as the summer recess began, Salisbury left Westminster to join the king on progress. Caesar, meanwhile, returned to the Exchequer. His desk was full: a war in Ireland had to be financed, a number of construction and repair projects were underway, and difficulties were mounting regarding foreign bills of exchange. Furthermore, there were myriad short-term cash requirements to be met. The summer would provide a reprieve from Parliament and a chance to catch up on his work. There were many routine duties for him to attend to, and he wrote occasionally to Salisbury reporting his progress in Exchequer. By 9 August, the backlog of business was under control.[56]

The Chancellor of the Exchequer and Sir Henry Fanshawe, the Remembrancer of the Exchequer, met on 10 August to discuss matters ranging from the searching out of old High Commission fines and the reforming of several domestic abuses in Exchequer to an enquiry into the Barons' procedure for taking oaths.[57] Salisbury wrote from his residence at Burghley on 13 August that Lord Wotton should be dispatched immediately to France because news had arrived that the Regent of France had sworn allegiance to the Holy League. A meeting between the Chancellor and the Treasurer was set for the following Saturday, 18 August, at Kensington. The king sent a buck to Lady Caesar to grace her table; a stag would have been sent had the distance to London not been so great.[58] Against this background of serene high-summer well-being, with the storm clouds of parliament remote on the distant horizon, Caesar was quietly laboring to complete a draft of an important document reflecting his own assessment of the Great Contract. He entitled his brief, "A Debate with Question and Answer, whether the Contract between the King and the Two Houses of Parliament be profitable or no."[59] In it he addressed both profitability and politics in the form of an imagined dialogue: we shall examine each in turn.

Regarding profit, Caesar held that the Contract was not going to benefit the king in a manner sufficient to his needs. The £200,000 he would gain was, in fact, poor compensation for his losses. The annual value of his wardships, tenurial incidents, purveyance, penal statutes, and so forth was £115,000, which left an increase of £85,000. The Chancellor argued that this amount could be raised from the same sources without alienating them from the crown or irritating the subjects with a new tax.[60] He supported his argument with an elaborate plan to prove that the king could live comfortably on his own "without the said contract, or further helpe of Parliament at this tyme."[61]

Caesar's plan worked well enough on paper, but it was predicated on a problematic policy of abatement: all loopholes that permitted waste and fraud had to be closed. If, as he estimated, the annual financial shortfall was £198,000, the £200,000 in support would cover the deficit; but there were other and better ways to accomplish the same end. Caesar believed that £85,000 could be raised by improving the collection of revenue from the wards, the alienations, and other sources. An additional £84,000 was available from the better management of the king's lands. A reduction of £19,900 in categories of expenditure ranging from the Irish War to prisons and works would bring the Treasury to within £10,000 of the £198,000 target. The last £10,000 could be achieved if James would abate his personal spending by that amount each year.[62] Still, however, there remained £600,000 in supply, rejected by Parliament but a necessity nonetheless.

The supply had been calculated on the basis of three components: £300,000 for the king's debts before the 1610 session began, £150,000 for the expenses of state, and £150,000 "for a stock to remaine readie for anie future perill."[63] In his argument Caesar dropped the "stock" and advanced the idea that the king "must be pleased to forbeare some part of [the] provision" of ordnance, thus reducing his costs by £51,300, "because the Commons are so sure of their safety, as that they refuse to inlarge themselves to the provision of things necessarie for the mayntenance of the name of England." In other words, if the Commons would not pay their share of the common defense, why should the king extend himself any further in their behalf? Taken together, these two "savings" reduced the grand total of the king's requirements to less than £400,000. The remainder could be raised by the sale of long-term leases of crown property and the rigid enforcement of fines for depopulation, by reclaiming lands from the sea and by escheated estates. Although this scheme would call on James to alienate £22,000 of his present revenue, Caesar was confident that the king could abate at least that much in personal spending and naval expenses.[64]

The analysis of the profitability of the Contract was grounded in the threadbare premise that James could be induced to abate his expenses to make up for the deficit. Salisbury, and Dorset before him, had tried to make James understand the importance of such a policy, but the king had not been willing to cooperate. Perhaps Caesar believed that the extremity of the moment might make James change his mind, but, in the absence of more conclusive evidence, we are left with an unconvincing hypothetical analysis of profitability predicated on a policy of restraint that had been rejected time and again. However unconvincing this first part of Caesar's brief may have been, in the second part he made a more convincing argument that dealt with political and economic issues.

The Chancellor approached the political questions from the point of view that the king would not harm his subjects if he lived entirely of his own. After all, he had recently agreed to limit his use of impositions, taxing only articles of trade considered lawful and tolerable. Regarding the king's lands and prerogative revenues, Caesar argued that the increases generated by a thorough and comprehensive administration of the crown's resources would not harm the subjects but would, instead, direct into the Exchequer profits rightfully belonging to the king: "The generalitie of the Commons shall receive an exceeding great contentment to see their monies, which heretofore were the objects of private men's desires, to be employed to the king's proper use and benefit." The laws would be enforced severely against all offenders for the comfort of the subject and the increase of the revenue.[65]

Throughout the remainder of his discussion of the Contract, Caesar displayed his obvious irritation that the Commons had been obdurate for so long. The king had an obligation to protect his people and they an obligation to provide for the king, but the representatives of the people had failed to uphold their part of the arrangement. This alone was sufficient reason to abandon the proposed Contract. At the heart of his comments was Caesar's unshakable commitment to the reciprocal responsibilities between king and subject. As G. L. Harriss has noted, "One of the best analyses of the respective responsibilities of the king and parliament was made by Sir Julius Caesar. While he acknowledged as fundamental law Fortescue's dictum that 'as the king

oweth the people defence and justice so the people are to furnishe all
the king's necessities,' Caesar maintained that the reduction of the ordinary deficit must remain the king's responsibility; as for the extraordinary deficit, he drew a distinction between those 'wants for necessary defense in times of war, or for necessity, conveniency or Honour
of the King or Kingdom in time of peace' which pertained to the wisdom of parliament to supply, and those extraordinary 'wantes in expenses of pleasure or bountie' which should be left to the king's discretion."[66]

The Chancellor was also troubled by the specter of inflation. If the
king were to sell his traditional rights for a fixed sum, as in the case
of the purveyance, where would he turn to find the money to purchase
supplies in the open market (or at the palace gate) as prices grew
higher? Summarizing his worries, Caesar wrote that "the King shal-
bee a great looser by this contract, which cannot presently proportion
a quantityve certaine to future uncertaine quantities."[67] Yet Caesar's
greatest misgiving about the Contract was entirely political: it would
bring dishonor to the king. "There is nothing more disagreeable to the
honor of a King, then to sell the ancyent prerogatives of his Crowne
for anie monie; but in this contract he doeth so; *ergo*, dishonorable."[68]

After exposing its advantages and disadvantages, Caesar asked rhetorically why the king had agreed to the Contract. Necessity was the
only answer he could advance in the face of its manifest drawbacks.
The king's requirements had to be met, and Parliament was not
cooperating. Under the circumstances, and for the good of the king
and kingdom, the Contract made the best of a bad situation. Casting
his thoughts ahead to the unresolved problem of levying "support,"
Caesar advised Parliament to accept the contract if they wished to benefit from its provisions. Although the king would be the loser, he had
agreed to these terms; the burden of acceptance now lay with the community. Because of the Contract, the king would have to reduce the
size and scale of his household, thus forfeiting the honor due the
crown. It was the constitution, however, that lay in the greatest danger.

Severe and perilous alterations in the constituted relationship between king and Parliament were, in Caesar's opinion, awaiting the
conclusion of the Contract. He reported that, "in the judgment of the
greatest lawyers in this kingdom, this contract will make a strange and
deepe alteracion in the fundamentall lawes of this estate, which is a
greater mischeif and trencheth further then maie be forsene in tyme,

or endured when it cometh."[69] This fear of change reflected the instinctive conservatism of the lawyers, but Caesar exhibited another fear that revealed a keen, yet sophisticated, analysis of current politics. The public debate on the prerogative, forbidden to the Members of earlier Parliaments, had occupied the first part of the year, and it would resume when the Members assembled in the autumn. The debate had corroded the crown's sacred majesty and mysterious singularity; it was, in short, "a readie passage to a democracy which is the deadliest enemy of a monarchy."[70]

As we shall see, Salisbury probably read the document; otherwise, there is no evidence that anyone else saw it. There is no mention of it in the State Papers or in Salisbury's manuscripts. Furthermore, we have no indication that Caesar's analysis played any part in the eventual collapse of the Contract. Clearly, though, Caesar's brief was the measured assessment of a conservative senior bureaucrat to the radical changes under consideration, and an index of his great frustration.

During the summer recess, many Members solicited the opinions of their constituents about the proposed Contract. There was no uniformity of opinion. The idea of ridding themselves of crown agents, purveyors, and informers was appealing, but the commonality (if such a generalization can be used) were not entirely sure that the king could be trusted. Parliamentary leaders who opposed the crown and wanted more from the Contract appear to have used the canvass of their constituents to sow even more doubts about James and his fiscal policies. The king's reply to the grievances against proclamations was so conditional as to suggest that no changes were going to be made, compounding further the problem of mistrust. Thus, the summer recess had not led to the perfection of the Contract; the bargain was still unsettled and open to further amendment.[71]

On 25 October, a week after Parliament had resumed its work, Salisbury berated the representatives of the Commons at a conference meeting. They (and their House) had left for the summer without having finished their work (although with Salisbury's approval at the time), and since their return, they were bent on extracting further concessions while giving nothing and occasioning further delays. If the conclusion of the Contract were postponed any longer, the king would dismiss them and let the bargain go. Once lost, the Contract would never again be presented. "You sit still and do nothing, we proceed.

Where shall we meet? This contract is like the fruit which cometh from the mother, who is delivered after a long labor, and 'twas not possible *in puncto temporis* to have done more than was done in the end of the parliament to be the finishing of this contract."[72]

The delays in Parliament were extremely expensive: the crown's debt increased, the subsidy was inadequate, and the support was not yet assured. On 31 October, Caesar brought a message to the House from the king: "His estate lay a-bleeding, so his honor lay a-bleeding: for to require help of his people and be denied twice [were] a disgrace both to him and his people." The king and Parliament had agreed on the support at £200,000, but the supply was not sufficient at one subsidy and one fifteenth.[73] Both categories of revenue had to be made right, or there could be no agreement. Parliamentary meanness was at loggerheads with the king's refusal to limit further his power of imposition and to foreswear his use of proclamations in place of parliamentary legislation. Caesar tried to introduce an element of practical common sense to the impasse: "Wants reduce to support and supply. We must have both together, for if we relieve the one and leave the debts he [the king] is undone; if we pay the debts and not relieve his supply, the rest must again increase. . . . Let us proceed to know whether we will or no."[74]

The Speaker was ordered to break the deadlock on 7 November. After reporting the king's will, Phelips told the Members that James had never intended to go forward with support alone. In the absence of adequate supply, no bargain was possible. "He appeals both to your reasons and memories . . . for so it cannot be thought the sense of a sovereign monarch to dispossess himself of so great power and royalty and means of reward, except to preserve that honor and strength which ariseth to a king by a settled estate in treasure and revenue."[75] Phelips was confident that the House would understand that the king now required £500,000 in supply, a sum far below his necessities.[76] In a flash, the careful bargaining of the past ten months was set aside. No modest demand was ventured as a bargaining point; instead, an enormous demand was made by the king, with no room left for further discussion. James, at the end of his patience, had thrown down the gauntlet to the Members. If Parliament accepted the new demand, the Contract was on; if they rejected it, so be it. The Commons was in turmoil. A week later, the Speaker brought another message from James, informing the Members that, because of their reluctance to accept the new demand, there would be no further bargaining. The Contract was null and void.[77] Although specific grievances still could be discussed, there was to be no further talk of the proposal that might have revolutionized Stuart finance. Three weeks of bitter recriminations in the Lower House ended with James proroguing Parliament until 9 February 1611 when the Members gathered once again to learn that Parliament was dissolved.[78]

More than twenty-five years ago, Joel Hurstfield wrote: "Sir Julius Caesar, not the most intelligent of the king's ministers, advised him against accepting the Great Contract, for it would cause 'a ready passage to a democracy, which is the deadliest enemy to a monarchy.'"[79] Hurstfield regarded Salisbury as a significant reformer and the Contract as one of the great "might-have-beens" of English history; thus, it was in the political maneuvers during the summer that he located the responsibility for its failure. "Courtier-critics" of the scheme had "convinced the impressionable James that his early doubts were justified." He would not gain as much as he would lose, and the bargain "would betray an important and ancient part of the prerogative to an upstart Commons."[80] These "courtier-critics," however they are defined, were defending their stake in the hierarchy by defending the prerogative whose fruits they enjoyed. Yet the most likely courtier to attack the Contract, Northampton, worked diligently under Salisbury's leadership for its acceptance. Indeed, after having played an important role in introducing the Contract to the House of Lords, he sat on some forty-eight committees and managed the remainder of the Lords' legislative business that did not bear on the bargain.[81]

But the real villain, by Hurstfield's lights, was Caesar. By implication, his assessment of the Contract had influenced the king, thus undercutting Salisbury; to make matters worse, he had given foolish advice. If the Contract had been concluded, Parliament might well have become redundant. The "support" was to have been a permanent provision that would not require further legislation. Therefore, when Caesar argued that the Contract would be "a readie passage to democracy," it appeared that he had gotten things backwards. But such an interpretation depends on a modern understanding of democracy. Parliamentary democracy, as it is used today, had no meaning in the seventeenth century. The closest that one might come to such a term was in the description of the three parts of Parliament: the monarchical, the aristocratic, and the democratic. Caesar, however, was addressing his comments to the likely results of opening the prerogative to popular or democratic discussion in the House and to the dishonor that the king would bring on himself if he traded away the flowers of the prerogative.

Caesar was hardly alone in his fears of "democracy." Lord Chancellor Ellesmere prepared a long memorandum entitled "Special Observaciones touching all the sessions of the past parlement aᵒ 1 Regis, etc.," in which he discussed the importance of the three parliamentary estates' taking care not to usurp one another's peculiar privileges. If the monarch were to "strain too high," it would "tend to tyrannie." If the Lords were to "presume too much and challenge over great power and authoritye, it wyll aspire to aristocracy." Should the Commons "be suffered to usurpe and incroache too farre upon the regalitye, it wyll not cease (if it not be stayed in tyme) untill it breake out into democracy." Ellesmere said that he had no reason to fear the first two, but he was worried about the third: "The popular state ever since the beginning of his Majesties gracious and sweete government hath growne bygge and audacious. And in every session of Parlement swelled more and more. And if wayes be stylle gyven unto yt (as of late hath bene) it is to be doubted what the ende wyll be."⁸² His private misgivings notwithstanding, the Lord Chancellor gave his public support to the Contract.

So, too, did Northampton. Keeping his reservations to himself, he wrote an undated set of notes and observations that were critical of the Contract, especially the alienation of wardships. In arguments similar to Caesar's and Ellesmere's, he expressed his discomfort, yet he was not a public critic, and there is no evidence of his private scheming.⁸³ Spedding tells us that Bacon (never a friend to Salisbury regardless of their kinship) also appears to have kept his own counsel during the Parliament as to his opinions of the Contract; there is no evidence to the contrary.⁸⁴ Indeed, as we have noted, Bacon was a principal spokesman in the king's behalf. After Salisbury's death, however, Bacon was more than a little forthcoming with his objections. In 1612 he wrote to James a scathing critique of the late Lord Treasurer, who had essayed proposals "which carrieth not a symmetry with your majesty and greatness." But the danger now had passed.

He is gone from whom those courses did wholly flow. To have your wants and necessities in particulars as it were hanged up in two tablets before the eyes of your lords and commons, to be talked of for four months together; To have all your courses to help yourself in revenue or profit put into printed books, which were wont to be held *arcana imperii*: To have such worms of aldermen to lend for ten in the hundred upon good assurance, and with [entreaty?] as if it should save the bark of your fortune: To contract still where mought he had the readiest payment, and not the best bargain: To stir a number of projects for your profit, and then to blast them, and leave your Majesty nothing but the scandal of them: To pretend even carriage between your Majesty's rights and the ease of the people, and to satisfy neither: These courses and others the like I hope are gone with the deviser of them; which have turned your Majesty to inestimable prejudice.[85]

As intemperate as these lines were, they were modest by comparison to the paragraph following, which he struck out. It ended with the words "and let me not live if I thought not of the taking away of that man."[86] A year later, Bacon wrote an advice to James in which he berated the Contract once again: "It was *animalis sapientia*, and almost contrary to the very frame of a monarchy, and those original obligations which it is God's will should intercede between King and people."[87] Thus, it seems that Caesar's comments were neither unique nor bizarre; a number of ranking courtiers and officials were displeased with the Contract, but we lack evidence of their trying to undermine it at the time. Yet Hurstfield was not alone in making more of Caesar's brief than it deserved.

A. G. R. Smith studied the contract more recently.[88] Once again, Caesar was accorded an important place in the account. Smith suggested that Caesar's document may have been shown the king. In his analysis of the brief, he tells us that Caesar was "out to argue a case and [that] his statistics cannot be accepted at their face value; he inflated both the deficit in 1610 and the actual cost to the Crown of surrendering the revenues from wardship and purveyance." At the same time, Smith credits Caesar with "some shrewd points regarding inflation and future supply." Yet, in leaving the subject, Smith returns once more, with circumspection, to the possibility that Caesar influenced the king: "Whatever precise effect Caesar's argument had on James, it was certainly the latter who gave . . . the final blow to the Contract."[89] Smith correctly associates the fate of the Contract with Salisbury's political fortunes. He had "become so closely identified with [the Contract] that his reputation . . . was inseparably linked to its success or failure."[90] By the end of the session, "Salisbury lost the confidence of both king and Parliament. The collapse of the Great Contract, in which so much of his credit was bound up, was a blow from which his prestige never recovered."[91]

A more favorable assessment of Caesar's brief was provided by Menna Prestwich, but she, too, held to the theory that it was addressed to the king.[92] Unlike Hurstfield, Prestwich was not impressed with Salisbury's career in the Treasury. As a conspicuous spender of note, would Salisbury have understood abatement as anything more than political rhetoric? She was equally critical of his capabilities as a parliamentary manager because he lacked both skill and tact. As for the failure of the Contract, Prestwich concentrates on Caesar's brief, which she considered a serious and important analysis of the proposal. She made much of Caesar's observation about administrative reform and the abatement of spending. Her most telling point concerns the problem of corruption and waste: Salisbury, for all of his careful presentation of the bargain, failed to limit them before introducing the Contract. Caesar, however, displayed his sensitivity to this omission when he observed that there would be no appreciable cooperation with the Members as long as they distrusted the Court and the courtiers. She also found the Chancellor squarely on target when he pointed to the inflationary consequences of tying the king to a fixed income. Finally, Prestwich, too, believed that Caesar convinced the king to abandon the Contract negotiations, the courtiers and the Commons having already abandoned the enterprise. Against this background, we must venture answers to the questions of who saw the document and with what result.

There is a strong possibility that Salisbury was shown the document by Caesar, perhaps immediately after he had finished writing it. The Lord Treasurer had instructed Caesar to meet with him at Kensington in August: his letter was dated 13 August 1610, and it set their appointment for the following Saturday, 18 August. Since Caesar would have had to leave his office on Friday or early on Saturday to await Salisbury at Kensington, 17 August would have been his last working day before their meeting, and the date "17 August 1610" was inscribed by Caesar in the upper left-hand corner of his rough copy of the brief. This may be a coincidence with no significance, but it is possible that on that Saturday Caesar presented to his master the distillation of his informed opinion. F. C. Dietz has pointed out that the government (i.e., James, Salisbury, and their advisors), following the July recess, "began to repent of its too generous concessions."[93] The first item in his analysis of the government's reaction is Caesar's brief. It clearly represented Caesar's opinion, but there is not the evidence to justify incorporating it into government policy. However, in Dietz's common-sense words, we cannot forget that "Caesar was pretty close to the lord treasurer, and Caesar's view that the surrender of purveyance, the Court of Wards, and impositions was too much to give for an uncertain £200,000 a year probably represented the treasurer's view also."[94] Certainly Caesar's past behavior would indicate that he was not likely to contradict his principal patron and master in the fiscal establishment or criticize fundamental policy, save in strictest privacy and under instruction.

Of course, James may have seen Caesar's opinion, but no firm case can be made on the basis of extant evidence. There is always the unlikely possibility that both James and Salisbury had so thoroughly rejected the proposed Contract that they were seeking both a rationale for ending it and an assessment of how the crown's finance would fare without a completed bargain. But if this was the case, why did the king wait so long to make his last impossible demand? And if Caesar's arguments moved the king, why did none of his words find their way into the king's public statements? The most that we can say is that Caesar entertained grave doubts about the Contract and wrote them down. The fact that they were written as a dialogue rather than in a more sparse memorandum form suggests that Caesar may have intended them to be read by others, but we cannot make much of this point. There is good reason to believe that Salisbury may have read the document; there is no reason to believe that James did. And, above all, there is nothing in Caesar's past behavior or in the circumstances of the moment to suggest that he circumvented the Lord Treasurer, taking his brief directly to the king.

The final assessment of Caesar's role in the Parliament of 1610 came from Salisbury's actions. In January 1611, just before the king dissolved Parliament, some important gifts were made. According to Spedding,

The Speaker of the last House of Commons, who had always been in confidential correspondence with Salisbury and done his best to help the King's business through on some critical occasions, had been rewarded with the Mastership of the Rolls; and Sir Julius Caesar, another earnest and admiring ally, had received a grant of the reversion of the office.[95]

The reversion assured Caesar that he would finally occupy the place for which he had strived for decades. If, as Hurstfield believed, Caesar had undermined Salisbury's proposed Contract, the gift of the reversion was hardly the response one would expect the Lord Treasurer to make to the man who had just ruined his political career.

VIII

Cares and Miseries

PARLIAMENT HAD FAILED, as had Salisbury's political career. The problems that had driven the government to summon the session in early 1610 remained unresolved; indeed, they were further aggravated by the end of the session. In 1611 Salisbury's health failed him, leaving Caesar with the principal responsibility for setting matters right. The political climate in Westminster was badly roiled by the past parliamentary year, and in the country the commonalty was not disposed to be forthcoming in the king's behalf. After Salisbury died in 1612, a difficult situation became nigh impossible. Since 1603 the factional alliance of Cecils and Howards had held lesser factions within its orbit; with Robert Cecil dead their universe wobbled eccentrically as factions split Council and Court. A Treasury Commission was set in place to do the Lord Treasurer's work, more a sop to faction than a new approach to public finance. Then, in 1614, against the better judgment of most political leaders, a new Parliament was summoned that was to be an unqualified disaster.

Caesar, by the summer of 1614, was anxious to leave the Exchequer for the safer haven of Chancery. The three years from the end of the Great Contract debates until Caesar's departure for the Mastership of the Rolls were years of indecision and turmoil. Policy was dangerously adrift.

The deficit remaining in the receipt only worsened after years of political aggravation; it remained Salisbury's and Caesar's task to find the means to make ends meet. One course of action was to abate the king's expenses, a course dependent on the cooperation of a monarch who had never shown any interest in such a policy. A second course was to establish schemes to extract additional profits from the king's prerogative rights. James preferred the second. Dietz has referred to the period 1610–20 as the "era of the projects," in recognition of the king's preferred course.[1] Various means were attempted to farm bits of the prerogative throughout the decade. It was only the ascendancy of Cranfield in 1620 that ushered in attempted reform rather than tinkering. In January 1611 and again in October, Caesar drew up great summations of the problems of receipt and issue, along with suggested remedies. The October statement allows us to reconstruct the program that would prevail in the Exchequer until Cranfield's ministry began.[2]

The statement, entitled "The Kinges wants and the remedy," was written in Caesar's hand. Its basic premise, which was hardly innovative, held that "the growing ordinary want is to bee stopt and remedied, either by improvement of the present revenue or addition of newe, or by abating of yearely issues."[3] The first priority for the better ordering of the ordinary receipt, Caesar wrote, was improvement by abatement with "due respect of honour." This was "the safest and most durable means of stopping the growing ordinary wantes." There then followed eleven major categories of expense and a suggested sum for each that would represent a suitable reduction. The officers of the several departments concerned with spending were to examine their records to find ways and means to reach their targeted levels of reduction. If the program were successful, a yearly savings of £7,000 would be realized, but, in the light of an estimated £100,000 deficit, this saving hardly began to remedy the problem.[4]

The second proposal, the one that was adopted, concerned the improvement of the king's revenue, "with due regard that the subiect bee not oppressed." Caesar proposed to effect the increase at no further cost to the subjects by assuring that all payments made to the crown's receivers "shall run to the right center of the kinges cofers." A goal of £43,000 was set for the Great Customs, the Receivers General, the sheriffs, the Court of Wards, the Hanaper, and respite of homage. Collection costs and corruption were to be reduced, thus providing the additional revenues without additional cost to the kingdom. Had this proposal been workable, it would have halved the deficit, but it was doomed to failure from the start. The balance of £50,000 in the inequality was to be made up by discovering new, yet lawful, means to add hitherto untapped revenue to the receipt. On this point there were no concrete proposals, merely pious hopes.[5]

Turning from the ordinary to the extraordinary side of the balance sheet, Caesar estimated that, on average, the issues were about £100,000 per annum. The figure was inexact "bycause it swelleth greater or groweth lesse, as newe ocasions have been offered." Thus, "it wilbee impossible to bound it within certeine limits, neither is it possible to make certeine provisions for unbounded expenses."[6] This element of uncertainty had been as good a reason as any to abandon the Great Contract and its promise of a fixed revenue. The need for supplying the extraordinary expenses of wartime was so obvious that Caesar merely acknowledged it before moving on to the next issue. Insofar as peacetime extraordinaries were concerned, they grew out of "necessitie, conveniency, honour, pleasure [and] bountie." About the first two items, Caesar said, "I humbly leave the consideration and provision thereof to the greate wisdom of the Parliament, to whom it apperteineth."[7] As for the rest of the "inequality" or deficit, a program would have to be devised to reduce expenses wherever possible. But he insisted that there could be no reasonable objection to those kingly expenses that were coincident with the very nature of a sovereign prince.[8] Caesar had frankly to admit that he had absolutely no idea how to pay the £500,000 debt that shadowed them constantly, but he was certain that there was nothing to be gained from selling land or compounding for the debts already owed to the king. Borrowing to pay the debt was equally self-defeating, and "taking up of midsomer rentes to pay Christmas debtes breedes nothing els but continuance of care and dishonour and increaseth the wantes more and more as wofull experience hath already taught us."[9]

Caesar's program was no more a solution than the Great Contract had been. There was still no answer to the problem of growing deficits that had plagued Lord Treasurers and Chancellors of the Exchequer intermittently since Henry VIII had begun to squander his father's carefully hoarded surplus. It had not yet become an established principle that the national debt was truly national and, thus, the responsibility of Parliament.[10] Wanting revenue and wanting a plan, the only recourse available was Caesar's conservative approach: no alienation of capital resources, a reduction in the king's expenses, and a thorough exploitation of all extraparliamentary possibilities. This was to be the crown's revenue policy for a decade. It could not possibly succeed.

Not only was the government without a plan for a new approach to the financial crisis, but it was also burdened with residual hostility and distrust left over from the parliamentary session of 1610. The debates had raised expectations of change that were never realized, and the government had made representations that proved illusory. Neither the crown nor the Councillors could be trusted, in the minds of many Englishmen. A case in point arose in Hertfordshire. The Commission of the Peace reported to Salisbury in April 1611 that there had been a meeting with the principal yeomen and freeholders of the county about a proposed composition for the purveyance. While the idea of a composition was attractive to them, they feared the crown would continue to harass them for in-kind provisions after they had paid their money. "Their plain meaning being for the composition to be yielded [it is] to bee free of all charge whatsoever rising by any taking or purveyance."[11] Salisbury reported this exchange to the king, whose response, according to Sir Thomas Lake, was to "wish ill to the last Lower House who had been the cause to take all respect of the king and his Council out of the peoples minds."[12]

In the west the Council in the Marches of Wales encountered their own problems, also the aftermath of the recent Parliament. The want of revenue in Westminster had caused instructions to be sent to the Receivers of North and South Wales requiring them to surrender to the Prince of Wales, for his maintenance, all of the money that they had collected. Being stripped of ready cash, the Receivers were unable to contribute their accustomed share to the diet and fees of the Assize judges in their jurisdiction. The obligation had been met by Lord Eure and Sir Richard Lewkenor, who sought reimbursement. The Council in the Marches was further beset with judicial and political challenges to its authority that were costly in time and money. The debate over the Western Shires in Parliament had further exacerbated a long-standing problem.[13]

Popular disaffection from the crown and resistance to additional taxation accounted for the earl of Kent's strategy for collecting the privy seal loan of 1611 in Bedfordshire. He told Salisbury that he had parceled out the sum due from his county among 77 privy seals—a very large number, perhaps "too many for so small a sum of money lent in total." But had he "not made choice of [so many] persons to be set at these easy rates, [he] could not well have performed the service to bring the total to so much as [he had] signified unto your Honor."[14] The division of the privy seals into many small parts was contrary to the wishes of the king. James had advised Sir Thomas Lake that he wished the privy seals to be delivered to a very small number of wealthy persons who could lend large amounts. He did not wish to have a large number of privy seals addressed to small subscribers.[15] But when the returns came in several months later, Chamberlain noted that the response was exceptionally favorable, "specially by the meaner sort."[16]

The privy seal loan was the most ambitious of the government's extraparliamentary forays in the subjects' purses. Ratings were made in every county and borough, local officers were apprised of the upcoming loan, and in Westminster the administrative machinery was set in motion to blanket the kingdom with privy seals attesting to the king's indebtedness to reluctant creditors. A privy seal clerk, Edward Reynolds, was seconded from other duties to devote his full attention to filling in the blank spaces in letters that had been prepared in advance by lesser clerks.[17] We know from the strategy used in Bedfordshire that the political nation was not disposed to subscribe the loan save in very small sums. Salisbury, too, had disliked the loan when it was first discussed, but he finally came to accept its necessity. When the proclamation announcing the loan and the text of the privy seal were delivered to the Lord Treasurer from the king, the clerk noted that "the proclamation was very welcome unto [the king] and he told me the beginning and the process of the resolution for it betwixt him and your Lordship. He said you were cold in it at first and he was glad to find an earnestness in you for it now. Rejoycing that he had won you to his opinion."[18] A certain heavy-handedness accompanied the solicitation of the loan. In the case of the merchant strangers of London, the privy seals were delivered to them as they were leaving their church. The privy seals were thrust upon them in broad daylight, "a course . . . not so well taken to be done in view and sight of all the world, which might have been better performed by delivering them to every man personally at home."[19] In the end, more than 9,700 privy seals were dispatched. The technique of rating in small portions was used in Westminster as well as in the many counties. More privy seals were issued to the personnel of Common Pleas (261) than to Hertfordshire

(258) or Nottinghamshire (254).[20] The results of this policy were gratifying: "The privye seales are dispersed all over and the money dayly payed in is beyond expectation."[21]

In the midst of the government's effort to raise revenue, Salisbury's health was failing quickly. The Lord Treasurer's constitution, never robust, had been unable to withstand the strain of the long 1610 session. He worked with Caesar throughout 1611 to paper over the cracks in the financial structure, but to no apparent avail.[22] At the same time, he had tried to save his political reputation. James, however, was turning with greater frequency to his Scottish retainers, especially Carr, and to the Howards, especially the earl of Northampton, for advice and counsel. Frequently away from London to take the curative waters in Bath or to rest in the country, Salisbury relied on Lord Carew to see to his secretarial responsibilities, and on Caesar to attend to the daily functions of the Lord Treasurer's office. We can establish with some certainty when it was that Caesar effectively assumed the Lord Treasurer's duties: beginning 7 December 1611, *et sic hebdomatisibus sequentibus* until 28 September 1614, he received certificates from each of the officers of the Receipt attesting to the money resting in the Teller's hands. Because he was serving as England's ad hoc principal financial officer, these data were essential to him.[23]

Even with weekly reports and the resources of the Exchequer at his disposal, Caesar's view of the financial landscape was imperfect. Always dependent on junior officers for details, he was at their mercy for the data that he needed to do his work, but there were frequent discrepancies. When, on one occasion, Caesar was making notes about the debt of the Netherlands, he observed that the repayment schedule, prepared by Exchequer officers, would provide £40,000 per annum, amounting to £200,000 from September 1611 through March 1616. Yet the treaty of 1608, on which these figures were to be based, called for repayment at the rate of £60,000 per annum, yielding a total of £300,000. "Quaerie: what is become of that [£]100,000."[24] This could well have been the motto on the Chancellor's seal.

After Salisbury left for Bath in April 1612, James delivered a warrant to Caesar authorizing him to act as treasurer during the "sickness and indisposition of our right trustie and welbeloved cosen and Counsellor . . . our now Lord Treasurer of England." It appears that Caesar had been serving in his master's place for more than a year without proper authority and that the Tellers of the Receipt had complained that they were unable to honor the payments made by Caesar's warrants lest they should be held responsible. The king gave retroactive authority to the Chancellor of the Exchequer, and the matter was settled.[25]

Caesar carried on Salisbury's responsibilities in the Exchequer with no resistance from the swarm of courtiers who sought to replace Salisbury in his several offices. The same was not the case when Lord Carew stood in as locum tenens in the Secretary's office. Sir Thomas Lake was particularly upset by Carew's apparent preferment. Lake, the Second Secretary, disliked the arrangement because he was busily positioning himself to capture the Principal Secretaryship for himself upon Salisbury's death. More than once, Salisbury's recovery from his bouts of illness had frustrated someone's plans for advancement: "My Lordships recovery is like to nip these forward hopes in their first spring."[26] In April, as we have noted, the king installed Caesar in the acting treasurership, and in May, when Salisbury once again departed for Bath, the Venetian ambassador observed that Caesar and Rochester (formerly Carr) were among those standing in his place during his absence. A side comment, to the effect that Caesar's father had been a Venetian subject, reflected the potential importance of the Chancellor in the eyes of an astute foreign observer.[27] Later that month, while returning from Bath, the Lord Treasurer died at Marlborough.

Chamberlain wrote that Salisbury had been racing back to London when he died, his haste occasioned by his desire to "countermine his underminers and (as he termed it) to cast dust in their eyes." So eroded had his position become after 1610 that he was losing friends and supporters. His death was a deliverance for him because "he would never have been himself again in power and credit."[28] The Howards had been closing on him since the failure of the Contract; death spared him further humiliation and brought the Howards the dominance they long had sought. Nonetheless, the relationship between Howard and Salisbury had not been uniformly hostile. Although they were never intimate, Northampton had worked with (and under) Salisbury since he became Lord Treasurer. L. L. Peck convincingly indicates that this was not part of any scheme of Northampton's to undermine Salisbury's hegemony; in a letter to Sir Thomas Edmondes, written before the devastating failure of the Contract, Northampton spoke of working with Salisbury on their common cause of clearing debts and reducing expenses. Styling himself an assistant to the Lord Treasurer in their enterprise, Northampton insisted that he was "both the weakest and worst."[29] However, they were competitive, and by 1612, with Salisbury dead, Northampton was free to pursue a monopoly of patronage and higher place without regard for his late colleague. He was enjoying early success because it appeared that the Treasury had fallen to the Howards when Northampton and Suffolk were named to the usual interim commission along with Caesar and several lesser officers. But rumors circulated suggesting that there would be no new Lord Treasurer, since the place was to remain in commission indefinitely.[30]

The rumor became more believable when the Treasury Commission was sealed on 16 June. Six Commissioners were empowered to exercise the Lord Treasurer's functions, including Henry Howard, earl of Northampton; Thomas Howard, earl of Suffolk; Edward Lord Wotton; and Sir Julius Caesar, who was of the quorum. Anything done by him, with any one or two of the others, had the force of the entire commission.[31] According to Chamberlain's gossip, Northampton was not anxious to accept the Treasurership until some time had passed: "He is willing the state of the revenew and treasure and debts shold be thoroughly looked into before he medle withal, and then he is to be accountable only for the time forward that he enters upon yt."[32] But the fact remained that "Northampton was Lord Treasurer in all but name."[33]

Following Salisbury's death, and the subsequent decision to employ a Treasury Commission, Caesar became "the greatest official authority in matters of the Exchequer."[34] With his new responsibilities, there came the perception of higher status. Chamberlain advised Carleton, who was pursuing a debt owed him by the crown, "to write now to Mr. Chancellor for he may stand you in good stead."[35] Later in the summer, his report of a visit to Caesar sounded more like a visit to a great lord than to a high-ranking functionary. First, Caesar had received him at his new country house in Hertfordshire, recently purchased from Sir Leonard Hide. Then there was a brief reciprocal visit to Ware Park, Chamberlain's home, on Caesar's way back to London. Confidences were exchanged, and the Chancellor's demeanor led Chamberlain to feel that he "could not but take it as a token of extraordinary favor and trust."[36] But Caesar was not fated to enjoy a season of relaxation in the aura of his new prominence. He and his fellow commissioners were set immediately to work to find solutions to the revenue problem in the midst of complex political tensions.

Although Caesar was the recognized financial expert, the difficulties that the Commissioners were trying to overcome were essentially political, and in that arena Caesar was on less sure footing because he had been for so long a dependent of his patrons, whose political judgment he had followed. But after 1612 he had to be more discerning. He had long been associated with the Cecilian faction, and his personal sentiments were clearly Protestant. He had been for thirty years a client of Charles Howard, earl of Nottingham, but Nottingham and Northampton were distinctly hostile to one another regardless of their kinship. With Caesar's goals in the Chancery, Ellesmere was a likely courtier with whom to associate, and Bacon was a friend. For so long as Salisbury was alive, Caesar played his cards evenhandedly, maintaining good relationships secure in the protection of the Lord Treasurer's patronage. But in the wake of Salisbury's death, he had to be exceptionally careful to find the high ground as the waters of factional strife rose around him.[37]

The months following Salisbury's death found Northampton with new power but also new responsibilities. Salisbury had so completely dominated politics and the treasury that the Commissioners and Councillors were initially at a loss to pick up where he had left off. James pressured them to produce results, although he was unwilling to spend much of his own time on the problems of policy and economy. While Northampton consolidated his control and learned what he had to do, he deflected criticism by blaming Salisbury "for the inefficiency and deficiency of the Council, because he had usurped its functions." He was equally critical of Salisbury's handling of the complex affairs of Ireland. Yet when he had become more accomplished at his business, Northampton became less critical.[38]

In the meantime, Caesar maintained his silence. Following his long association with Salisbury and Burghley, he probably found the personal, post mortem attacks on the late Lord Treasurer distasteful, but he was in no position to object. "Outrageous speeches" were legion, accusations of every kind were made, and it became fairly certain that, had Salisbury lived but a little longer, he would have been subject to censure in Parliament. In addition, just before his death, Salisbury had told the king that he was £100,000 the poorer for having been Lord Treasurer.[39] This self-serving carping did not square with the great wealth he was said to have amassed. As charges were laid against Salisbury, and as the state of his finances was anatomized by gossips and political enemies, Caesar hid behind the shield of his professional expertise and did not become involved, but the charges against Salisbury did not go unanswered.

Sir Walter Cope, another longtime Cecilian satellite and an executor of Salisbury's will, felt obliged to write an "Apology for the earl of Salisbury, Lord High Treasurer," in which he attempted to right the record. Caesar was particularly interested in Cope's "Apology" because it was linked to his own career as Chancellor of the Exchequer. His heavily underscored copy bears witness to careful scrutiny by a reader who was interested in more than his late master's memory. Cope touched on the principal attempts to improve the revenue (better employment of royal lands, improvements in woods and forests, the Customs Farm, the alum farm, and wardships), and he was also attentive to charges that Salisbury had been a pluralist, holding too many places of profit at one time. Cope explained that circumstances rather than greed had caused Salisbury to hold simultaneous offices but that at his death he had been in the midst of divestiture. He had already farmed the wardships, and he was in the course of securing the king's consent to relinquish the Secretaryship. Cope ended the "Apology" with an account of Salisbury's deathbed statement: "Ease and pleasure quake to heare of death, but, my life ful of cares and miseries desires to be dissolved."[40] The burden of "cares and miseries" no longer rested on one man, "the little great man" of recent memory; it lay instead on the shoulders of Privy Council and the newly appointed Treasury Commissioners.

The Commissioners, guided principally by Caesar's scheme for abating expenses and increasing revenue, were not likely to succeed because they were facing a daunting task of fiscal planning. Under the best of circumstances, complex planning is difficult and demanding work. A common will and a shared sense of direction are necessary qualities if the planning process is to be successful, but in the years following Salisbury's death, neither of these qualities obtained. Conrad Russell has characterized the years 1612–18 as "years of political drift," but his assessment requires qualification.[41] To be sure, James's determination to be his own secretary, orchestrating the political program himself, was a serious problem, as was the realignment of factions after Salisbury's death. But, as L. L. Peck has demonstrated, there was significant continuity in policy and practice between Salisbury and

Northampton. Northampton's use of patronage to advance loyal and competent clients in government service was a continuation of his predecessor's practice. The Jacobean patronage system depended on this marriage of merit and loyalty.[42] There was also the question of divisive factions: did a war party counter a peace party, did a Spanish faction face a Protestant opposition? Although there were surely distinct factional leaders, their factions were loose associations of common interest rather than committed partisans. Although Northampton received a Spanish pension and was himself Catholic, we cannot assume that his followers were a Spanish pro-peace faction.[43] In short, there was "drift," if not turmoil, but it was not so much the product of self-serving factions as it was the consequence of the transition from more than fifty years of Cecilian dominance. A new body of actors on the political stage were trying to figure out what to do about a variety of serious intractable problems. Their leadership was less skilled than Salisbury had been, and they were new at the business of state. This, then, was the cause of the "drift."

The intractable problem that Caesar and his colleagues faced can be simply stated. During Salisbury's Treasurership, the annual expenses averaged £600,000. The annual income, however, was but £500,000. As we have seen, one solution to the resulting deficit had been the large-scale leasing and selling of crown lands.[44] Other solutions depended on convincing the king that he should reduce his own expenses, on developing or improving extraparliamentary revenues, or on summoning a Parliament. It was clear to the Commissioners that they really had only two options: they could recommend another Parliament, or they could renew efforts to increase extraparliamentary revenue while trying to abate expenses. This was essentially the plan that Caesar had presented in 1611. Opposing another Parliament were the Howards, led by Northampton; their unlikely ally, Rochester; and the Chancellor of the Exchequer.

As the author of the brief against the Great Contract, Caesar was ill-disposed to invite divisive debate once again. Furthermore, he believed implacably that the king possessed all of the powers that he needed to set the finances right. James's judicious use of the prerogative could end the problems they all were facing. For his part, James was not prepared to return to the bull pit of the House of Commons for the money he needed.[45] Left with improving revenue or convincing the king to reduce his own expenses, the principal officers of state chose the former option. They plunged into the business of planning with a will. It was a far easier course than trying to convince James to repair his ways.

The Commissioners began their work by viewing the state of the revenue, investigating new sources of money, and preparing rules to govern future practice in the offices of receipt and issue. Chamberlain wrote in August that a commission was "out till the end of the month" to a subcommittee of Exchequer officers, including Caesar, "to devise projects and meanes for monie." He further observed that "the world thinckes it a strange choise [the membership of the subcommittee] seeing that most of them are noted not for husbanding and well governing theyre owne estate: God kepe them from base courses, yet the speache goes that they harpe most upon debasing of monie."[46] The debasing of the bullion content of the circulating coinage was the seventeenth-century counterpart to the modern practice of printing excess paper money. The inflationary consequences of this easiest and most dangerous of budget-balancing devices were as apparent to observers at the time as they are to the modern reader.

When the subcommittee reported back to the Treasury Commissioners, they presented four means to augment the revenue, but none was especially imaginative. New projects abounded, and the report suggested recourse to a variety of old techniques. "Concealments and disherisons of the kings right" were to be discovered, and the "revealed casualties of tenure" were to be improved. An analytical list of possible ventures followed, citing several discrete categories such as "tenures," the profits of the Mint, and the preferred weight of silver coins.[47] But, even though the subcommittee had reported, no action could be taken because the king was away from London. His absence since mid-July had meant that "no matter of great moment has chanced here."[48] There were plans to be made, but there was no clear leadership to get them started.

Throughout the remainder of 1612 and into the first quarter of 1613, the Commissioners and their subcommittees labored to construct a policy that would lead to satisfactory results. In the meantime, Council turned their attention to various plans for the abatement of crown expenses. Northampton provided the leadership, and Caesar and Bacon were among the most active members.[49] Finally, in March, they produced a comprehensive plan for the improvement of the king's revenue. It was prefaced by a detailed account of developments in the Exchequer since the previous June, shortly after Salisbury's death. The annual deficit had been £160,000, while the debt had stood at nearly £500,000. Efforts had been made to reduce the growing indebtedness, but whereas the rate of increase had been slowed, the debt itself was not appreciably lower. Several alternatives were explored, and Council joined with the Treasury Commissioners to effect results. Prince Henry himself had taken an active hand in the early stages of the deliberations and perhaps would have continued had he not died. Subcommittees worked through the summer and into the autumn, reporting finally on a tentative plan of action. Northampton, with the consent of the Commissioners and in their presence, had advised the king viva voce of their recommendations. They followed their oral presentation with an exhaustive memorandum that laid out the projected abatements and improvements line by line.[50]

The Commissioners claimed that they had, since Salisbury's death, "abated and improved respectively to the kinges profit" the sum of £37,776. They projected an annual reduction in the king's expenditures of about £59,000, but these were highly conditional savings, depending as they did on such phrases as "if the king will" or "if ready money may be found hereafter." The improvements were projected at a yearly rate of nearly £85,000, but there was no indication of how, for instance, the revenues of the Court of Wards would increase by £20,000. The ordinary expenses and receipts promised to be profitable, but the extraordinaries promised even greater advantages to the crown. The largest single improvement was to derive from the sale of baronetcies, £66,666, while the collection of the loan to the Dutch, the sale of woods, lands, and mills, and the forced loans were among the items valued from £40,000 to £60,000. In sum, the extraordinaries were expected to produce more than £300,000 by December 1613. The figure was not as exaggerated as it might appear. More than £200,000 was already in hand, leaving less than £100,000 to be collected.[51] Although the Commissioners' plan represented unprecedented amounts of background work, enjoyed a political consensus, and even had the king's probable support, it lead to nothing. The categories of savings or increases were the same that had been discussed at least as early as 1603; the numbers, too, were uncomfortably familiar. Northampton's purpose had been more likely to audit Salisbury's accounts than to realize substantial financial changes. A sure mark of the failure of the

Commissioners to achieve anything of significance was the necessity, in 1614, of summoning another Parliament.

There had been talk of a new Parliament almost from the moment that the old one was dissolved in February 1611.[52] The decision to proceed with a Parliament in 1614 was grounded in financial necessity rather than sound political intelligence. Indeed, the decision was taken in desperation following months of contradictory advice. Sir Henry Neville, for instance, was convinced that a Parliament would be a notable success if only the king would make a few concessions. Neville actively solicited support for a Parliament from every quarter, but with little to show for his effort. Neville's outspoken association with the opponents of the Great Contract made his task all the more difficult. He was simply not trusted, and he was blind to the deep political division between James I and the House of Commons. Sir Francis Bacon was equally anxious to summon a Parliament, but he and Neville approached the problem differently. Whereas Neville advised making concessions to the Commons, Bacon recommended indirection as a preferable policy: "The ostensible reason for summoning Parliament should not be the king's financial needs." He believed that a more productive course would be characterized by a careful courtship of the Commons over the lives of several sessions. Satisfactory results would take time.[53] In the interim, however, the king should try to influence the outcome of the parliamentary elections. The Howards, for their part, opposed a Parliament, as did Caesar but for entirely different reasons. There was much conflicting advice, but the delays in summoning Parliament were caused by the absence of a firm hand directing the king's affairs after Salisbury's death. The Principal Secretary's place remained vacant as James tried to be his own secretary, with disastrous results.

The vacancy in the Secretary's place was filled just before the opening of the 1614 Parliament. Sir Ralph Winwood was named to the Secretaryship, doubtless with assistance from Rochester, who owned the office but had never filled it. Sir Thomas Lake, another contender for the place, was sworn to Council but without any particular office. Winwood was an implacable foe of the Howards, and his appointment was evidence of their failing fortunes. Had he been Secretary during the discussions leading up to the summoning of Parliament, he would have been likely to have worked against the session. Yet even Northampton, the most prominent Howard, had agreed to a session at the last minute. He was reluctant to provide his opposition a parliamentary arena, but the inability of the Privy Council and the Treasury Commissioners under his leadership to remedy the falling revenue made a Parliament a necessity. In analyzing the factions in Council during the debates about summoning Parliament, T. L. Moir tentatively places Caesar in the Protestant, anti-Howard group.[54] This analysis is, however, unconvincing. While there is no doubt that Caesar was a Protestant, he was too dependent on the goodwill of the Howards to confront them publicly. Furthermore, Caesar had been no friend of Parliament in 1610 when the Howards were Salisbury's ally; in 1614 he had no reason to change this position.

Election writs were issued in late 1614. Northampton used his extensive connections to influence a number of elections, and the king was not reluctant to apply pressure to secure seats for his Privy Councillors who needed assistance. Caesar and Lake stood for election at Uxbridge, and it was a colorful affair. Chamberlain reported that "there was a great concourse at Uxbridge for the choosing of Sir Jul[ius] Caesar and Sir Tho[mas] Lake knights for Middlesex." Sir Walter Cope had been prepared to contest the election, but he withdrew his name at the last minute. Sir Francis Darcy also stood down, but not without letting the electors know why. He "had a man there who getting up upon a table told the assemblie that his master meant to have stoode, but was forbidden by the King, whereupon he desired all his well willers to geve theyre voiyces to Master Chauncellor, and for the secind place to do as God should put in theyre mindes." Darcy's messenger was arrested for making these comments, and Darcy himself would soon be questioned.[55] Caesar apparently was acceptable to the opponents of the courtiers, but Lake was not.

It is difficult to accept Moir's analysis of the political behavior of the Councillors who were Members in 1614 because it leans too heavily on rigid partisan identification. He assumes that Councillors were bound by a discipline characteristic of modern parliamentary practice. Caesar, among others, was described as a disloyal member of the official group in Parliament. When Sir Ralph Winwood, the new Principal Secretary, introduced a proposal for supply, "even the leading officials," including Caesar, failed to give it "the support they owed to official measures."[56]

On closer examination, it appears that their failure to support Winwood may have been the most loyal position for the official Members to take. Winwood had never before sat in Parliament, and his appointment had been made virtually on the eve of the 1614 session. He was also unbending in his honesty and straightforwardness, characteristics that conduce to a difficult personality for a political operative. His inability to deal with compromise made his leadership a nullity.[57] In a modern Parliament, subject to the discipline of the government whip, the success of the legislative program becomes an end in itself. This was not the case in the seventeenth century. In 1614 the Councillors' principal obligation was to serve the king's interests. Had they been able to do so and support Winwood at the same time, well and good, but Winwood's conduct in Parliament was jeopardizing "official measures." He had upset traditional procedure by introducing a motion for supply before the session was a week old, and the Members made clear how much they resented this premature demand for revenue. Caesar knew where his duty lay: he kept the session on course even at the expense of Winwood's motion. Since redress would have to accompany supply, he moved to commit the supply bill and, at the same time, to establish a subcommittee to consider bills of grace. He would not disclose the details of the debt to the whole House, a practice favored by both Salisbury and Dorset in their times, but he did offer to give that information to Members privately.[58] Though a Lord Treasurer might be boldly frank in his disclosures to the House, the Chancellor of the Exchequer, even when he was the principal financial member of the Treasury Commission, could not exercise the same candor.

Before and after the Easter recess, the session made uncertain progress. In Commons there clearly was great tension, much of it the heritage of 1610, much the product of attempted manipulations of the present Parliament. The Members reacted angrily to the efforts of a number of courtiers, led by Bacon, to "pack" the House in the king's interest, but virtually ignored schemes to deliver the House's vote in return for political patronage, known as "undertaking" (the essence of modern parliamentary practice). The source of the greatest tension, however, was the attempt to return to impositions. This policy ruined any chance of success in 1614.[59] When Richard Neile, Bishop of Lincoln, rose to address the House of Lords in favor of the prerogative powers of the crown to levy impositions, he unwittingly touched off the reaction that would lose the session for the king. Perhaps a simple defense of the prerogative would have been tolerable, but Neile stepped over the line when he forcefully denied the right of Parliament even to discuss the matter. In the ensuing turmoil, full attention was devoted to defending or condemning the Bishop. The question of supply was sidelined in an avalanche of explanations, qualifications, apologies, and recriminations.[60] Finally, James ordered the Commons to prepare revenue bills and any other legislation that they believed necessary. They were to grant supply by 9 June or the king would dissolve Parliament forthwith. The ultimatum gave the Members less than a week to conform, but conformity was the furthest thing from their minds.[61] In short, the House of Commons were angry and quite out of control, yet they had been out of control since the early days of the session for want of effective leadership.

Parliament was disbanded, and, within hours of the dissolution, warrants were in hand to arrest the more recalcitrant Members and bring them before Council. Some were imprisoned, others released from custody following the terror of an inquisition before the Privy Councillors. But praise as well as condemnation followed the dissolution. The rewards took the form of several serjeancies awarded to loyal Members. By Moir's account, the penalties and disgraces resulting from the postsessional arrests led to the death of the grieving Master of the Rolls, Sir Edward Phelips, whose son Robert and close associate John Hoskins suffered for their opposition.[62] Chamberlain reported that "the Master of the Rolles that was in great favor with the King hath lost his conceit about this busines, for there be many presumptions that his hand was in yt, his sonne being so busie and factious in the house, and Hoskins one of his chiefe consorts and minions so far engaged, besides divers untoward speaches of his owne, and a notorious envie that any thing should succeed better under another speaker then himself."[63]

Phelip's death was of particular importance to Caesar, who owned the reversion to the Rolls. Of equally great significance in terms of Caesar's future was Northampton's death only a week after the dissolution. Following on the heels of a failed Parliament, the loss of Northampton underscored for James the need to name a Lord Treasurer and disband the Treasury Commission. Although Caesar had doubtless been ready to be free of the Exchequer and the intractable problems of royal finance once the session turned sour, major changes in personnel were required before he could leave his post under favorable conditions. Northampton's death cleared the way in the Treasury for a clean sweep. A new Lord Treasurer would want his own man as Chancellor. Phelip's death vacated the Mastership of the Rolls, and Caesar owned the reversion. He could now exit the Exchequer gracefully.

The interval between 1610 and 1614 had demonstrated that the time was not yet right for thoroughgoing financial reform or for the government of the Treasury by commission. Unlike the Restoration Treasury Commissions, with their complements of expert members, the first Commission was a political expediency calculated to accommodate faction rather than to reform the crown's finances. The second Commission, appointed two years later following the disgrace of the new Lord Treasurer, Suffolk, was better supplied with experienced personnel, but it too was transitory, terminating with the appointment of Lionel Cranfield as Lord Treasurer in 1621. But in 1614 a new political landscape was discernible. Thomas Howard, earl of Suffolk, received the White Staff, but, although he was a Howard and had the dignities of Lord Treasurer, he could not approach the political abilities of his deceased cousin, Northampton. By July, the new Lord Treasurer was confidently issuing orders to Caesar, but in mid-August he was uncomfortably aware of the scale of the task before him. "Do as I do," he wrote, and "thinke of all the wayes that may afforde us any healpe. God, I hope, will give us leave to effect something."[64] Six weeks later, with the Mastership of the Rolls vacant, Caesar left the Exchequer for Chancery. The king's finances were no longer his responsibility; God had afforded him a way out of an office he no longer wished to occupy.

IX

A Doating Time

IN A LETTER to Sir Isaac Wake, John Chamberlain wrote of the remarkable week in 1614 in which "we have four new officers (with the Lord Treasurer) at Westminster that sit in principal places in the Exchequer, Chancery, and the Court of Wards." Of the Chancery, he reported,

> Sir Julius Caesar is setled in the Mastership of the Rolles, but hath fower judges appointed to assist and sit with him by turnes, which is some diminution to a man of so much confidence in his owne sufficiencie, beside the losse of place and precedence he had by his former offices, which points yf he had well ruminated before yt is thought he wold not have been so hastie to exchange.[1]

Aside from questioning Caesar's motives, Chamberlain could not understand why Sir Fulke Greville, the new Chancellor of the Exchequer, a man of advanced age and great wealth, would have left semiretirement for a thankless position at the center of public finance. His rationale for Greville's behavior could as well have explained Caesar's: "Every body hath a doating time, and ambition is blinde."[2] Furthermore, in Caesar's case, the Mastership of the Rolls was an escape from the turmoil of the Exchequer and the achievement of the capstone of his remarkably successful professional career.[3]

Caesar's appointment to the Mastership, unlike his earlier appointment to the Exchequer, did not come as a surprise to him because he had owned the first reversion in the Rolls since early in 1612. According to a draft commission that he prepared, the late queen had intended that Caesar be the Master of the Rolls during her reign. Her death had frustrated this plan, and James had granted the reversion to Edward Bruce, Lord Kinloss. Bruce, in turn, had conveyed his interest to Sir Edward Phelips, the Speaker in 1610, at Salisbury's behest. Thus, Caesar had to await the late Speaker's death before he could exchange his reversion for possession of the Mastership.[4] Now, in 1614, the prize he had sought for so long was to be his.

Caesar's reason for wanting to move to the Rolls was consonant with his earlier career choices. He had always centered his attention on the development and the well-being of his family. His marriages had provided wealth, connections, and children. His careful attention to the will of his patrons, Salisbury especially, had positioned him to capture the Mastership of the Rolls with its attendant advantages. Now, with the office his own, he was ready to increase his fortune and advance his sons. Earlier in the same year, his son Charles had been returned to Parliament in the constituency of the late Thomas Howard, Lord Bindon, which suggests that Caesar's connections were still useful to him.

Apart from contributing to his family's well-being, the exchange of the Exchequer for the Rolls presented three distinct advantages: the first was financial, the second professional, and the third a matter of prestige. In financial terms, the profits of the Mastership were promising. In 1609 the Rolls had produced £2,110 5s. 10d. for the Master.[5] Upon entering office, Caesar predicted that his first year's profits would be £2,350, but twenty years later, looking back at this calculation, he wrote, "Thus the proverb is verified, hee that accomptes without his hoaste, must accompte againe; this exceadeth truth by much for I found it but 2200 libri or there abouts in my 1st yere, and since abated by litle and litle, so that this last yere it amounted to but 1600 libri or thereabout and no more, 1631." Caesar had grossly overestimated the profits of the office in Elizabeth's reign. They had, in fact, ranged from £100 to £1,500 per annum.[6] While these were not insubstantial profits, they were smaller than Caesar had imagined.

Professionally, Caesar had finally reached the pinnacle of a civilian's career. A member of Doctors' Commons could aspire to no higher judicial place than that of the senior Master in Chancery: the Master of the Rolls. If there was a discernible pattern of advancement that had remained constant throughout his career, it was Caesar's pursuit of ever higher place in the Court of Chancery. The Mastership of the Rolls, drawing on both his civilian and his common-law experience, was the prize he had finally captured.

The prestige associated with the Rolls turned out to be more elusive than Caesar had imagined. Shortly after he became Master of the Rolls, Caesar found that the Chancellor of the Exchequer was being accorded precedence over him at the Council Board, and in Privy Council he had to sit below him. From his earlier experience as Chancellor of the Exchequer, Caesar had enjoyed priority, but this had changed with Greville's appointment. Caesar, of course, claimed precedence for himself and turned to the archives to support his position. In due course, he had a sheaf of memoranda attesting to past practice. The office of the Master of the Rolls was senior to that of the Chancellor of the Exchequer. Although Caesar believed that his researches presented a conclusive case, the Chancellor continued to be accorded greater honor in Council.[7] Yet in other manifestations of Court hierarchy the Master of the Rolls occupied a favored position between the two Lords Chief Justice. As a minister he was below most of the Privy Councillors, but as a judge he was superior to the Lord Chief Justice of the Common Pleas and just beneath King's Bench.

The prestige of the Mastership was most apparent in his dispensing of patronage. The extensive professional staff in the Chancery was largely in the gift of the Master of the Rolls. Their places were highly valued, and the Master had the advantage of being in close contact with his appointees in a centralized agency. In theory, his Chancery clients were responsive to his direction, but the great financial value of their offices eroded discipline. Caesar spent a disproportionate amount of his time guarding the value of his patronage from the onslaughts of his clients. They, in turn, to protect their interests, used every scheme they could to assert greater autonomy and more control over the disposition of their offices.

Although he had spent more than twenty-five years as an Ordinary Master in Chancery and was familiar with the duties and responsibilities of the Master of the Rolls, Caesar carefully assembled a collection of documents pertaining to his new office and his duties. He found that the Master of the Rolls was an ideal office for a senior law officer who was not anxious to overburden himself at the apex of his career. With reasonable care, he could enjoy the fruits of office without excessive labor. At fifty-six Caesar had entered into a semiretirement that paid reasonably well. A reading of both Caesar's collection and modern scholarship provides a useful historical context in which to view the conflict between the Master of the Rolls and the constituent subgroups in Chancery. Managing this conflict was an important part of his work.

During the reign of Henry II, in the thirteenth century, one of the Clerks of Chancery had been designated "Keeper of the Rolls."[8] Initially this was an administrative and archival position, but by the early fifteenth century, the Keeper (or Master) of the Rolls had advanced in a parallel judicial capacity to the extent that he was commissioned locum tenens when the Lord Chancellor was absent in France. However, it soon became apparent that the Lord Chancellor needed assistance even when he was in London, and from the reign of Henry VIII on, the Master of the Rolls was considered his principal deputy. Whenever the Lord Chancellor's place was vacant, the Master of the Rolls was of the quorum in the interim commission. The Master's judicial functions had matured to such a degree by the seventeenth century that when Caesar was sworn in 1614, he was also commissioned for life to hear and determine all causes in Chancery, whether the Lord Chancellor was present or not. Caesar was the first incumbent to be awarded such a commission, a distinction clearly at odds with Chamberlain's interpretation of the assignment of four judges to assist him. Although he implied that Caesar was not competent to handle the affairs of the court by himself, it is clear that he was thought sufficiently competent to be awarded a unique commission for life to act as judge in Chancery. Yet the fact that the Master of the Rolls required a separate commission to act as judge points to a fundamental lack of definition in the office. The Master was commonly thought to be the assistant Lord Chancellor, but, still, he required specific authority beyond his letters patent if he were to serve as judge.

The Master of the Rolls was the senior Ordinary Master in Chancery. It was reported in Fleta that in the late thirteenth century there had been a body of Chancery clerks who heard and examined petitions and gave remedies. These quasi-judicial clerks were the forebears of the Masters in Chancery. As the business of the Court of Chancery expanded, the clerks grew in number until they reached twelve. Over time, the Masters in Chancery became less important to the court's administrative functions, but their senior member, the Master of the

Rolls, became decidedly more important. The Masters in Chancery were charged with issuing writs of grace such as *supplicavit* and *certiorari*; they served occasionally as secretaries to the monarch; and they attended on Parliament (ranking below the Serjeants at Law), on Privy Council, and on the Lord Chancellor. Less heavily worked than the other subgroups of Chancery officers, the Masters were not permitted to develop a large, subordinate clerical establishment; by the end of the sixteenth century, each Master was limited to a maximum of three assistants. The Masters had become, primarily, professional legal advisors to the Lord Chancellor and the Master of the Rolls, a status confirmed in Sir Francis Bacon's Orders in Chancery. Because their legal expertise extended to both common and civil law, they could sit as judges on both the law and the equity sides of Chancery. And the Masters were also known for the breadth of their learning: "They were scholars of more than one kind of law, practitioners in more than one institution, and they had an interest and experience which wedded them to the international humanist tradition of their times."[9]

The Master of the Rolls, in the meantime, had become the "chief of staff" in Chancery. The Lord Chancellor's political duties did not permit him to spend much time in Chancery; thus, routine supervision was left to his principal assistant. Thomas Cromwell, as much as anyone, had demonstrated the potential of the Mastership of the Rolls for controlling the apparatus of Chancery. This control was, in part, the result of his extensive patronage powers and, in part, the logical consequence of the exercise of authority in a bureaucracy. There were many subordinates who "wrote in [the Master's] name and whom he appointed and controlled."[10] In his gift lay the Six Clerks, the three Clerks of the Petty Bag, two Examiners, an usher, and seven Clerks of the Rolls Chapel. The Master of the Rolls also appointed a chaplain, a gardener, a porter, a doorkeeper, and three secretaries.[11] Throughout the vast Chancery establishment, the Lord Chancellor appointed only the Cursitors and the Masters in Chancery. The king appointed the Master of the Rolls and the Register. Even in those instances where he did not make the appointments, Caesar was responsible for their supervision.

The principal officers of the Chancery plus their deputies and secretaries numbered in the hundreds, and Caesar benefited financially from most of them. He was compensated for his patronage and received a share of fees. The value of this patronage can best be expressed in comparative terms. The Lord Chancellor's patronage of the Masters in Chancery had netted Bacon as much as £50 each for eight appointments by 1621. Edward Bruce, during his tenure as Master of the Rolls, had received £13,500 from three Six Clerks' places and one Clerkship of the Petty Bag. Another £3,100 had been received for reversions to three other Six Clerkships, two Clerkships of the Petty Bag, and one Examiner's place.[12] Not only was there more patronage for the Master of the Rolls than for the Chancellor; it was far more valuable. It is interesting to note that Caesar never tried to develop a patronage network at large; his reward from official patronage was lucrative (and at no time more so than in Chancery), and it took less time to cultivate.

After 1623, in addition to his judicial and administrative functions, the Master of the Rolls joined regularly with the Lord Chancellor in the regulation of court practice. He assisted the Lord Chancellors when they prepared Orders in Chancery, the rules governing procedure and behavior in the court; but his efforts were not recognized fully until 1635, when Lord Keeper Coventry and Caesar jointly issued new and exhaustive Orders. Another mark of the Master of the Rolls's elevated status was evidenced in the pro forma approval of his decrees accorded by the Lord Chancellor, who applied the seal without question. This reflected a compromise: the Master of the Rolls recognized the Chancellor's superior authority by submitting his decrees to him; the Chancellor recognized the Master of the Rolls's superior knowledge of the details of the individual cases and the law by sealing them as received. As Holdsworth put it, by the 1620's the Master of the Rolls "comes in fact to be the general deputy to the Lord Chancellor."[13]

Shortly after being sworn, Caesar began to identify the incidents of his office that were neither judicial nor administrative. He learned that the Master of the Rolls was the Keeper of the House of Converts in Chancery Lane, a property located almost exactly on the site of the present Public Record Office. This ancient establishment had been the sanctuary to which Jewish converts to Christianity had repaired for instruction and examination prior to their being baptized. Its endowment, as in the case of many ancient foundations, was principally in the form of real property. Some were in London; many more were to be found scattered throughout England. There was an appurtenant garden and orchard. The Keeper of the House of Converts was entitled to the rents from these several sources. By the seventeenth century, however, the establishment had long since ceased to fulfill its original function, its chapel having become the storage place for the rolls of Chancery: the Rolls Chapel.[14]

The Master of the Rolls was also the Master (or the president) of Queen Elizabeth's College in Greenwich.[15] William Lambarde had founded "The College for the Poor of Queen Elizabeth" after receiving letters patent from the queen in 1574. The College originally housed twenty poor men and their wives. Lambarde had written the foundation ordinances and statutes and provided the bequest. Ralph Rookesby, a Master of Requests, had bequeathed £100 to the endowment. Shortly after becoming Master of the Rolls, Caesar was in the thick of a dispute between the inmates and the "upperwardens" of the College over the administration of funds held for the poor.[16] Caesar's prior experience as Master of St. Katharine's Hospital was a helpful introduction to the affairs of Queen Elizabeth's College.

Regardless of the incidents of office, Caesar was principally occupied at the heart of the Court of Chancery and its administration. An exceptionally large agency, Chancery's component parts were located throughout the metropolis from Westminster Palace to the Tower. At Westminster the Lord Chancellor sat as judge; at York House in Charing Cross he resided and also heard pleas. About a thousand yards further east, in Chancery Lane, were the Rolls Chapel and the halls of the Six Clerks and the Cursitors. Further still to the east, in Great Knight Rider Street, was Doctors' Commons, the society of the Doctors of Laws to which the civilian Masters in Chancery belonged, and in the Tower lay a great deposit of the ancient records used in Chancery business. While the nominal judicial center of the Chancery lay in Westminster, the effective administrative headquarters, and a major judicial venue, was located in Chancery Lane. At the end of the sixteenth century, Chancery cases were routinely heard in the Rolls Chapel by the Master of the Rolls. "By 1616, the Rolls was open three times a week for hearings and motions," but there were some litigants who objected to their cases being heard there and not in Chancery. Their objections counted for little, since the proceedings in the Rolls Chapel were as formal and binding as those heard at Westminster.[17] It is not surprising that the Master of the Rolls, located physically at the center of the world of Chancery, was its most important operational officer.

A close examination of the activities in Chancery Lane reveals the characteristic structure of the Chancery establishment. A large and complex staff was organized by function into distinct subgroups that identified with their several senior members and were self-per-petuating, often along family lines. A similar organization could be found in the Exchequer, but there was an important difference. Un-like Exchequer, the dominant organizational structure among the three largest subgroups in Chancery was the corporation.

The Six Clerks, one of these subgroups, had been staffed by clergy until the sixteenth century. In the fifteenth century they had estab-lished their own hall, Harflew Inn, later known as the Six Clerks' Office. Located opposite the Rolls Chapel, the hall belonged to the Six Clerks in fee simple as a result of their having been incorporated for the express purpose of owning property. The second subgroup, the Cursitors, received their letters patent of incorporation in 1573. The twenty-four Cursitors and their twenty-four assistants constructed a large and elegant hall further along Chancery Lane, near Lincoln's Inn. The Chancery Masters, the third important subgroup, did not in-corporate themselves within Chancery because the greatest number of them already belonged to Doctors' Commons. Each of these sub-groups persisted in asserting its own privileges and rights, to the detri-ment of the others and of Chancery. The competition among them and their individual members had a direct impact on the flow of busi-ness in Chancery. As a practical matter, the documents of the Chan-cery, the papers on which all judicial activity was grounded, were to be found scattered about Harflew Inn, Cursitors' Hall, Doctors' Com-mons, the Rolls Chapel, and York House, depending on the particu-lars of a given case. At the center of these little chanceries, the Mas-ter of the Rolls presided in the Rolls Chapel. If coordination among the several parts was to be achieved, he, rather than the Lord Chan-cellor, could provide it.

During his tenure as Master of the Rolls, Caesar served two Lord Chancellors and two Lord Keepers. Ellesmere, who was on the Wool-sack when Caesar came to office, was followed by Bacon two years later. After Bacon's disgrace in 1621, Dr. John Williams became Lord Keeper, but upon the accession of Charles I he was deprived of office. The Attorney General, Thomas Coventry, succeeded Williams and held the post until his death in 1639. Of Caesar's relationship with

Ellesmere little evidence remains save for formal directives and inquiries. Bacon, on the other hand, presents a different picture.

Francis Bacon had been made Lord Keeper in 1616 when Ellesmere surrendered the seal because of old age. In 1617, when Ellesmere died, Bacon was created viscount St. Albans and was commissioned Lord Chancellor. Caesar and Bacon were linked by friendship and marriage. Their friendship went back several years, but the marriage bond was sealed by Caesar's marriage to Bacon's niece in 1615. In May 1614 Lady Alice Caesar died and was buried beneath the communion table at the parish church of St. Helen's, Bishopsgate. The ministers and wardens noted in the parish register that she had been buried "about midnight."[18] The new Lady Caesar, Anne Hungate, was the sister to Lady Killigrew and daughter to Bacon's sister.[19]

A measure of the easy relationship betwen Caesar, Bacon, and the senior judicial officers with whom they associated is to be found in their Whitsun week festivities in 1617, when the countess of Arundel spread a great feast at Highgate for Bacon, Caesar, the two Lords Chief Justice, and several others. As Chamberlain reported, "Yt was after the Italian manner with fowre courses and fowre table clothes, the one under the other, and when the first course and table cloth were taken away, the Master of the Rolls, thincking all had ben don, saide grace as his manner is when no Divines are present, and was afterwardes well laught at for his labor."[20] Although Bacon occasionally seemed to be insensitive to the interests of the Master of the Rolls, Caesar still did him good service. Together they conducted the affairs of the court and consulted on new orders governing conduct in Chancery. Caesar was careful to take down the content of Bacon's speeches, as in the case of the Lord Chancellor's address to the judges prior to their departure on Summer Circuit in 1618.[21] Following Bacon's disgrace on charges of bribery, Caesar was among those appointed to treat with his creditors and preserve his honor.[22] Bacon died of exposure following a snowstorm four years later. Some accounts have him dying in Caesar's arms, but Spedding makes no mention of it.[23]

After Bacon returned the seal to James, Caesar was of the quorum in a commission to exercise the judicial and authenticating powers of the Chancellor until a new appointment could be made. From 1 May until 10 July, Caesar and the other commissioners acted for the Chancellor. Then Dr. Williams, formerly the secretary to the late Lord Chancellor Ellesmere, was made Lord Keeper. The following October he was consecrated Bishop of Lincoln.[24] Following Williams's appointment, Caesar stepped out of the limelight; both his age and his other compelling interests kept him from the public view in Chancery after 1622. Although he still heard cases and was very active in the administration of Chancery, we do not find Caesar any longer in a public position of leadership or advocacy. In fact, the only time he comes to the fore again in Chancery was in 1635, a year before his death. He and Lord Keeper Coventry had been working on a new set of Orders in Chancery. Although we cannot be certain of Caesar's precise contribution to the Orders, we do know that they were issued jointly in both Coventry's and Caesar's names.[25] The Orders were noteworthy for their clarity; unwarranted "innovations" were excised, and the discipline of Chancery was brought firmly within the strict control of the Lord Keeper and Master of the Rolls.

If any one issue occupied Caesar's attention or characterized his tenure as Master of the Rolls, it was his attempt to assert control over the rival subgroups in Chancery. Their struggles among themselves and with him frustrated the effective functioning of their common enterprise. A survey of the three major subgroups of Chancery officials and a closer examination of one of them, the Six Clerks, and of Caesar's relations with them holds a mirror to his career in the Rolls.

The Six Clerks' considerable judicial and administrative duties had, over time, caused them to assemble a staff of their own assistants. Initially, each Six Clerk had appointed one underclerk, but by the 1590's each had appointed ten or more. This larger body of assistants, known by some as the Sixty Clerks, represented a number of serious difficulties: they were too numerous to be supervised properly, and their training was, at best, haphazard. But in 1574 a large number of underclerks left Chancery when the Six Clerks and the Clerks of the Petty Bag managed to incorporate as the Clerks of the Enrollments, thus depriving the underclerks of many of their traditional duties. They believed that their superiors were closing doors to their advancement and to the augmentation of their incomes. They were probably absolutely right. For the next twenty years the court was left understaffed, and nothing was done to address the underclerks' complaints until 1596 when Sir Thomas Egerton, then the Master of the Rolls, turned his attention to the problem and produced a workable solution in his Orders in Chancery.

It was clear to Egerton that the underclerks desired status and security, both of which the Six Clerks had withheld, and that the Master of the Rolls had to find a way to discipline these important subordinates and their staffs. Both of these concerns were reflected in his Orders. Each Six Clerk would be permitted to employ a maximum of six underclerks, five of whom had to be recognized as accomplished in the Chancery hand. The Master of the Rolls would, thereafter, swear all of the underclerks himself, thus being able to determine whether each was qualified before administering the oath. The underclerks (or sworn clerks) were permitted to employ their own assistants (waiting clerks) but were required to limit them to writing documents and no more. At the request of the Six Clerks, Egerton allowed some modification of these Orders: each sworn clerk was allowed to train one assistant accomplished in all of the functions of his superior, not just writing, and a clerk could not be employed in more than one office at a time, nor could a former clerk be reemployed by another Six Clerk without the consent of his previous employer.[26]

Egerton's Orders made each Six Clerk responsible to the Master of the Rolls, each sworn clerk to a Six Clerk and the Master of the Rolls, and each waiting clerk to his direct employer. But as soon as the orders were published, the limitations on the numbers of underclerks were waived, and by the 1620's there were about forty employees of every type in each Six Clerk's office.[27] The cohorts of sworn and waiting clerks produced great profits for their masters even though they themselves could not charge a fee. The official fee was paid directly to the Six Clerks and the Master of the Rolls. The underclerks charged an unofficial fee (a form of gratuity, in fact), which was their only source of income. Jones tells us that by the 1630's they were remitting from 30s. to 50s. to their respective Six Clerks for each case that was readied for hearing. Among them, the Six Clerks were thought to receive £1,050 each year from the labors of their underclerks.[28] Caesar, in turn, received 6s. 8d. for each decree, dismission, and exemplification passing the Great Seal and a like amount for shrieval patents, commissions *dedimus potestatem*, and Exchequer oaths.[29] Although there is no tally to verify Caesar's profits, it stands to reason that the thousands of documents passing the Great Seal yielded many hundreds of pounds in fee revenue each year.

In the years between Elizabeth's reign and the 1630's the Six Clerks had become wealthy, independent men of means whose offices in

Chancery were valuable fee-simple properties. Whereas the Elizabethan Six Clerks "went on foot and waited humbly on the Master of the Rolls . . . those of the 1630's seem to have gone by coach or some other form of carriage when they went to work."[30] The Master of the Rolls, naturally, was conscious of the exceptional value associated with an appointment as a Six Clerk, but so was the king. During Caesar's incumbency, Charles I moved to annex their appointment to the crown; Caesar regarded the king's efforts as unwelcome encroachments on his personal property and as unwarranted innovations in Chancery practice. One was as bad as the other.

In most cases, the problems associated with the Six Clerks were the result of their attempts to expand their own profits by encroaching on the privileges and profits of other Chancery officers. Early in his career in the Rolls, Caesar was drawn into the turmoil attendant on their expansionist enterprises. Questions had arisen over which officer in Chancery had the exclusive right to make enrollments. A careful reading of the Six Clerks' patent of 16 Elizabeth showed that they had limited enrollment authority respecting indentures of bargains, sales, and recognizances. One of the Six Clerks, known as the Riding Clerk, was authorized to enroll patents, gifts, commissions, and the like, but his authority did not extend to all of the Six Clerks. The Riding Clerk, who was in constant attendance on the king when he traveled beyond the suburbs of London, had originally been rotated among the Six Clerks on an annual basis, but in the late sixteenth century the rotation had stopped when one of the Clerks volunteered to take the task during his tenure. Unlike his colleagues, the Riding Clerk kept the rolls in the Chapel and did not carry them "to the Alehowses as now they usually are."[31] This reference to the careless dispersal of court documents among the Six Clerks reflects their perception of their relationship to Chancery. They were private entrepreneurs who "mined" the Rolls Chapel for the documents needed for the conduct of their business without regard for the convenience of other officials who had to use them or for the integrity of Chancery records.

The Six Clerks were more concerned with their own self-interest than with the smooth operation of the court of Chancery, and this was reflected in their inattention to technical detail. In many instances, they acted in the name of the Master of the Rolls, but without his authority and without remitting his share of the fees. They were not

empowered on their own authority to pass such documents as commissions to examine witnesses and writs of *habeas corpus* or *corpus
cum causa*, and yet they did. The Six Clerks "write to the Greate Seale
not as patentees under his Majesty but as clerks to the Master of the
Rolls; where for seeinge they cannot passe any writtes as officers in
their owne names, it is greate reason the Master of the offyce shold be
answered by some fees by his clerkes as other Masters . . . in other
Courts in England are." If the Six Clerks did not want to pay, the Master of the Rolls would have to "appointe [an] offycer to discharge the
busyness that will be accomptable unto him for all such thinges as
passe in his name, and this cannot be denyed by any whatsoever, for
all Clerkes or deputyes of offyces must of necessity be answerable for
every busyness they passe in their Masters name."[32] In the margin next
to these words Caesar drew heavy lines of emphasis; this was the nub.
The Six Clerks, on the one hand, probed for inconsistencies and lacu-
nae that might give them an opening to increase their authority and
raise their revenues. They sought a course around the Master of the
Rolls that would permit them greater independence and less interference. Their answer to their problem would lead eventually to direct
crown control of their offices, a control that would be more institutional and less intrusive than that exercised by a proprietary Master.
Caesar, on the other hand, regarded the Six Clerks as unruly subordinates who had to be brought to heel. He regarded their attempts to
circumvent his rightful authority as nothing less than poaching on his
perquisites.

Caesar used a variety of techniques to monitor their behavior and
to remind the Six Clerks that it was he who was in charge. On one occasion, he required them to identify their underclerks (the sworn
clerks) by name. The officers replied with lists indicating that there
were, on average, fifteen underclerks working for each Six Clerk.[33]
The information was not particularly important in itself, but their
having to provide it reminded the Six Clerks of their subordinate status. As for the number of underclerks, Caesar was not especially displeased; but he was clearly unhappy to discover, at about the same
time, that there were several Chancery functions, such as making
licenses for wine imports and all commissions for charitable uses, that
had been parceled out to individual projectors with an accompanying
loss of revenue.[34] Had the Chancery staff been able to recover all of
their traditional functions and fees, there might have been sufficient

revenue to prevent internal warfare among the subgroups and with the Master of the Rolls.

By 1618 Caesar had to intervene in what he called a "poore project, or rather idle and malicious by the 6 Clerkes." They were attempting, and not for the first time, to encroach on the privileges of the Examiners in Chancery.[35] Actually, there was more to the Six Clerks' plan: having been incorporated by act of Parliament in 31 Henry VIII for the express purpose of purchasing the premises of Harflew Inn, they now wished to receive letters patent of general incorporation. As a corporate body they would be able to exercise rights to all aspects of their offices without the intervention of any superior officer, particularly the Master of the Rolls. Furthermore, they might subsume the duties of the Examiners in their letters patent if they could persuade the king that there were advantages to such an arrangement. At James's request, Buckingham referred the Six Clerks' petition to Bacon and Caesar, who were to consult with the Attorney General and Solicitor before writing an opinion.[36] The Examiners responded quickly when they learned that the decision hung on Caesar's and Bacon's opinion. They begged a stay of the letters patent until their own rights and privileges could be examined.[37] There had been an informal, de facto division of responsibility according to which the Examiners received, preserved, and published (when ordered) all examinations taken within the court. The Six Clerks assumed the same responsibility for examinations taken by commission beyond the suburbs of London, but in their petition they asserted an absolute right to receive and preserve all documents, including all examinations wherever they were taken. They also claimed the lucrative right to make copies of documents as needed.[38] The Clerks of the Petty Bag, who would likewise lose by the Six Clerks' petition, weighed in with their own objections. As in the case of the Six Clerks, the Clerks of the Petty Bag were clients of the Master of the Rolls. They had traditionally received and filed declarations of privilege, attachments of privilege, and writs of *habeas corpus* and *corpus cum causa*. If the Six Clerks won, they would no longer profit from these duties.[39]

In order to frame a reply to the Six Clerks, Caesar compared the circumstances surrounding their petition with those surrounding the incorporation of the Cursitors of the Chancery in the 1570's. The Cursitors had received letters patent at the request of the Lord Chancellor, in whose gift their places lay. In the case of the Six Clerks, their petition was "against the will of the Master of the Rolls in whose gift they are and have been for 200 years past at least." Furthermore, they wished for themselves things already "at the will and dispose [sic] of the Master of the Rolles, whose clerks and servants they are." The Cursitors had already accomplished about the same thing that the Six Clerks desired, but with the consent of their master. The critical issue was a matter not of comparison but of Caesar's assertion of an absolute freehold interest in the Six Clerks' places. Their petition, and any letters patent that might follow from it, "tendeth to the prejudice and [is] a disseisin of a private freeholder, to wit the Master of the Rolls, in his profits and ancient rights of his office, whereof he hath the freehold under the Great Seale of England during his life and hath the disposition of those 6 Clerkships at his pleasure."[40]

If the Master of the Rolls believed that he owned a freehold interest, the Six Clerks were equally convinced that they owned freeholds as well. Caesar had made a list of all Six Clerks since their initial incorporation in 1545. It was clear from the data that a pattern of individual appointments that had obtained from 1545 had begun, in the 1570's, to give way to familial succession to office. Of the thirty-three names on the list, several were repeated, indicating the possibility of familial interest in these offices. However, a second list, with the same names arranged in two columns, showed the name of each Six Clerk vacating a place and the name of his immediate successor. Beginning in 1578, we find the first father-son (or uncle-nephew) succession. This happened twice again in 43 Elizabeth, when two places changed hands within the same families, and once more in 4 James.[41] The last of these kindred successions had been within the Evelyn family. George Evelyn had followed his father in 1607, and in 1636 George's son, Arthur, would become a Six Clerk. When George had died in 1634, the first reversion to his place had belonged to Robert Caesar, Sir Julius's son. He had taken up the reversion immediately, but his untimely death left the second reversioner, Arthur, free to become the first third-generation Six Clerk.[42] Whatever rhetorical devices may have been used by the contestants in the Six Clerks' enterprise, the issue was, at root, a matter of freehold property and the revenues of office. This applied as well to an Evelyn as to a Caesar.

The Six Clerks' petition for letters patent was examined by common lawyers, by civilians, and by Robert Henley, an officer in the Rolls whose duty it was to advise Caesar of the impact of the petition on his own interests. Henley advised that there seemed to be nothing in their request that was necessarily prejudicial, "yet, as from all novelties and inventions so from this, many mischiefs and inconveniences may arise which no man may foresee."[43] The common lawyers held that the Examiners had the sole right to the custody of all examinations, wherever they were taken. Furthermore, the old division of custody between the Examiners and the Six Clerks was to end, and the Examiners were to be restored their customary privileges. There were two bases for this opinion. First, the Examiners were the only officers in Chancery sworn to keep safe and secret all examinations. Second, the Six Clerks were constantly removing documents from the Rolls Chapel without taking care to return them. Caesar noted that the Six Clerks had never been authorized to keep examinations or any other records and that it had only been since their earlier incorporation, in 1545, when they owned premises outside the precincts of the Rolls House, that they had made unauthorized changes in procedure.[44] The civilians, too, were convinced that the Examiners should be the sole custodians of the examinations. Drawing on their experience in ecclesiastical and civil-law courts, they noted that an attorney could not properly keep the sworn testimony taken in a trial in which he had an interest. Since the Six Clerks were attorneys representing active litigants, it was a clear conflict for them to have custody of the original examinations and the exclusive right to make copies.[45] Finally, after studying these opinions, Caesar framed his own response.

Both the Six Clerks and the Examiners lay in the gift of the Master of the Rolls, and there was no advantage for Caesar in overthrowing the one for the other. The Six Clerks, however, had many sources of profit, whereas the Examiners were limited to the making and keeping of examinations. Because the practice in the courts of Wards, Exchequer, Requests, and the Duchy did not permit attorneys to keep original examinations, there was no reason for Chancery to make an exception. Using a somewhat opaque aphorism, Caesar summed up his decision to deny the petition: "Hee that will remove stones which have layed quiet for 100 yeres must endure the curse of the people."[46]

Within a few weeks, Caesar had to deal with a new petition from the Six Clerks in which they asked the king to establish among them an office for the writing of all sheriffs' and escheators' patents. James would receive an annual sum of money from the proposed office, but that was not the most important benefit. The petitioners contended that the king's prerogative was the sole authority in the granting of preferment; by creating the position that they suggested, he would "alsoe settle and confirm an office in [himself] for [the] gratification of well deserved servants." Their petition revealed more about the Six Clerks than they might have intended. Clearly, they had no express authority to write the patents they were presently writing and on which their petition was predicated. Rather than attempt to cover up what they had done, the Six Clerks admitted to having usurped the authority several years before to protect the prerogative. Now they brashly asked for the king's confirmation. And, to underscore the benefits that the king would enjoy if he granted their petition, they reminded him that "the ancient fees which have beene and are paid to the Master of the Rolles for these several letters patents amounts to the somme of [£]28 or neare thereaboutes."[47] Caesar was able to frustrate the Six Clerks this time, but he had to be vigilant lest they find another way around him.

Although it may seem that Caesar's only relationship with the Six Clerks was hostile, he did, in fact, defend them against attempts by others outside of Chancery to diminish their rightful interests. There was, for instance, the case of the duke of Buckingham's petition in behalf of his servant, Sir Endimion Porter, and a Mr. Darlington, a servant to the Prince of Wales, who wanted to be given an office in Chancery for the filing of bills and answers. Toward the end of Elizabeth's reign there had been such an office, but it had been mired in controversy. In the 1590's Sir John Parker had been awarded the newly created Keepership of Pleadings. The office promised to have some significance because the Six Clerks made it very difficult to assemble a complete file in any given case, since each one received bills and pleadings in his own chambers. The new Keeper of Pleadings was to be a central receiving officer for the bills and pleadings in all cases; in theory, this was a vast improvement. The Six Clerks, of course, complained bitterly, leading Egerton to take action as soon as he became Master of the Rolls. Although he could not void the queen's patent, he did find a useful loophole: the Master of the Rolls had to swear the Keeper of Pleadings, and Egerton was always able to find a reason not to do it.[48] Now, more than twenty years later, Buckingham was trying to resurrect the office for Darlington and Porter. No doubt recalling Egerton's ploy, Buckingham solicited Caesar's support. He told him that the office had never "yielded any profit to you nor any of your predecessors, nor hath any dependence upon your place, [but] for the better establishing of it" he sought Caesar's agreement. It "in no wise [is] prejudicial to you."[49]

By August, Buckingham sought Caesar's favorable opinion in the suit.[50] The Six Clerks were afforded an opportunity to reply to the proposal during a hearing in October. Caesar presented their case with conviction: "Whatsoever hath bene promiscuous and generall amongst many offices, that the king may setle in one officer, but whereas the things are setled in a certain, that was never in the kinges disposition to any other, to the prejudice of that officer."

As for the precedent set by Parker's having received letters patent, Caesar noted that Parker had enjoyed his office for three terms in the absence of a Master of the Rolls and that he had collected only a 12d. gratuity from each litigant; being unsworn, he could not compel a fee.[51] Caesar's notes, written in early November, analyzed the problem from both sides. The Six Clerks' strongest point was that Parker had never been sworn or allowed to occupy the office. The petitioners' strongest point was that Parker's office was not in the gift of the Master of the Rolls "as a remitter but as a new graunte unto him by reason of the kings [sic] letters patents dated 9 April 6 Elizabeth." Caesar was as free to exercise his discretion as had been Egerton before him, but he asked a commission of the common-law judges for a legal opinion to support his findings. They had heard Parker's petition in 1604 and had found that the keeping of bills, pleadings, and other records is "peculyar only to the said Master of the Rolles and to no other." If further orders were necessary for the preservation of these records, the Master of the Rolls should make them, not Sir John Parker.[52] Caesar warned the petitioners that they should take no comfort from Parker's patent; the old course was still the best, and the interest of the Six Clerks had to be preserved.

A year later, in 1621, the disaster that all who worked in the Chancery must most have feared was finally realized. Chamberlain's account is brief but vivid.

On Thursday about three or fowre a clocke in the morninge a great fire brake out in the sixe clerkes office in Chauncerie-lane, that burnt downe that howse and fowre more, besides others quite pulled downe, and that which was Sir Mathew Caries scaped narrowly, but yet is in a manner quite defaced and torn to pieces: the fire was so vehement that yt caught hold of the Rolles on the other side of the street, but by great labour and daunger it was quenched, for which service Sir Julius Caesar gave twentie pound among them that best deserved yt. There is a great store of monie said to be lost, besides other things of value, but the losse of rolles, recordes, and writings is irreparable.[53]

The records that had been taken away from the Rolls to the Six Clerks' premises by their small army of underclerks were destroyed in the fire. They were irreparable, to be sure, but they were also irreplaceable; their loss would cost numerous litigants untold amounts of time and money. Lady Anne Caesar conveyed Caesar's reaction to the fire in a letter to Lionel Cranfield: "I umbly besech you to pardon my husband for what passed from him to your servant yesterday, he was not him self being almost totally desstracted by that feaerful and viuolent accedent of fier, and his goods being carried away not knowing wheather nor by who."[54] A few weeks later, when Caesar was writing about the advantages of the Rolls Chapel over the Tower as the deposit for Chancery records, he emphasized the fire-resistant lime and stone masonry.[55] The fire in Chancery Lane muted the question of moving the records elsewhere, and the Six Clerks maintained a very low profile for several years thereafter. We next hear from them in the 1630's when they renewed their petition for letters patent of incorporation. Although Charles I would grant their request in 1635, they were forced to reckon with Caesar's rights and perquisites at every turn. That he was a formidable adversary becomes apparent when we consider Caesar's remarkable tenacity in the face of strong pressures to vacate his place.

When, for example, Sir Francis Bacon was sworn to Privy Council in 1616, he wanted to be Lord Chancellor, but he had to await Egerton's death. In the meantime, Bacon's allies, principally Buckingham (then Villiers), were trying to gain other advancement for him. They reckoned that Caesar could be removed from the Mastership of the Rolls and given back his place in the Exchequer, thus making it possible to install Bacon in the Rolls Chapel. But everything was contingent on Caesar's agreement: "yf [he could] be won to yt by faire means or fowle."[56] Ultimately, Caesar did not agree, and Bacon was subsequently sworn Lord Keeper. Along with efforts to dislodge him from office, he had to cope with frequent speculation in reversions to his Mastership. In one case, Buckingham, acting in the king's name, had promised Sir Henry Wotton a reversion to the Rolls.[57] Hindsight tells us how long Wotton would have had to wait for possession of Caesar's place, but contemporaries saw the reversion as a rich reward that would soon be in hand.

In 1621 Caesar was sixty-three years old and in indifferent health. A rumor was current that his age and "weakenes" would lead shortly to his being retired from the Rolls with a peerage. Had a vacancy occurred, there would have been intense competition. Sir Thomas Chamberlain, Sir Randall Carew, Sir John Walter, and Walter Pye were on one short list of prospective candidates. Referring to them, John Chamberlain advised, *capiat qui capere potest.*[58] Caesar refused to consider being removed from office, even for a barony. "The Master of the Rolls kepes his station and hath no mind to remove, and the king says he shall not be forced." Chamberlain, who rarely lavished praise, went on to write, "I commend his confidence in that he thincks himself as sufficient for the place as any man in the kingdom."[59] By autumn there was more pressure on Caesar to vacate the Rolls. "Sir Julius Caesar was moved to give over his place as Master of the Rolls, but will not stir. I fear he will be made to leave it."[60] Sir Robert Heath, the Solicitor, who was greatly favored by Buckingham, was also interested in the Mastership of the Rolls, but by October Caesar had mounted a spirited resistance. In danger of being dismissed in favor of Heath, he was said to have told the king that "he might as well take his land or his life, as his office (which he had under the Greate Seale of England) unless he were convicted of corruption or injustice."[61] A few months later, Buckingham attempted unsuccessfully to arrange an exchange of offices between Sir Lionel Cranfield, the Master of the Wards, and Caesar.[62] Although he had retained his office, the pressures did not abate.

When Sir Henry Wotton returned to England from his Venetian embassy, he owned a second reversion in the Mastership of the Rolls and another reversion to a clerkship. But of even greater value was the high favor in which he was held by Prince Charles and Buckingham.[63] Several years earlier, in 1614, while posted to the Hague, he had learned that the then Master of the Rolls, Sir Edward Phelips, had died. Caesar, who owned the first reversion, had claimed possession of the Mastership along with all vacant clerkships during his lifetime. Being overseas at the time, Wotton had been unable to challenge Caesar's claims, but when he did return, he petitioned the king that "Sir Julius Caesar may be drawn by your Supreme Authority to confirm unto me my reversion to the second clerkship whereof I have a patent under your great seal."[64] By 1620 the stakes were higher because he had been awarded the first reversion to the

Mastership of the Rolls. Wotton now had a valuable property to protect.[65]

In the meantime, Buckingham had been trying to remove Caesar in favor of Heath, who had become Attorney General. Failing in that effort, he tried to secure Wotton's reversion for his client. Wotton claimed that the duke had been offered £5,000 for the reversion to the Mastership of the Rolls following Caesar's death and that he wanted to seal the reversion to Heath. At Buckingham's request, Wotton conveyed the reversion to the duke in return for a promise of compensation of equivalent value. As for Wotton's reversion to one-half of a Six Clerk's place, he determined that it was worth the value of the Provostship of Eton and then proceeded to use it to buy out the claim of a rival for that office.[66] While the exchange appeared a fair one, Caesar held all the good cards, thus controlling the game. Late in the year, Wotton was begging Buckingham to speed up the settlement with Caesar because everything hinged on his willingness to comply. In the end, Wotton received the Provostship, but Heath did not receive the reversion.

Four years later, one John Dinely was in pursuit of preferment in Chancery. He asked Charles I to confirm a grant of vacant Six Clerkship upon Caesar's death. He told the king that the confirmation could be made "without any prejudice to the said Mastership of the Rolls because I desire [the Six Clerk's place] not till the vacancie [of the Mastership] when as the whole power shall remain solely in his Majesty."[67] Later in the same year, a memorandum was drawn noting that James I and Charles I each had granted one-half the benefit of a Six Clerk's place to Sir William Beecher, a Clerk of the Council, and one-half to Sir Henry Hungate, Caesar's stepson. Both awards were contingent on the death of the present Master of the Rolls.[68]

As successful as Caesar had been in preserving his interests, there were clear signs of erosion. The Master of the Rolls owned the patronage associated with the Six Clerks, yet it became necessary for him to seek higher patronage in order to hold on to that which was his anyway. Patronage had become so complicated by multiple reversions, fractional interests, and active royal intervention that Caesar found that it was prudent to give £1,000 to Buckingham in payment for a Six Clerkship should one fall vacant during his lifetime. The transaction had been undertaken to provide a Six Clerk's place for Lady Caesar's son, Sir Henry Hungate. Following the duke's assassination, the commissioners of his estate, the earl of Rutland and the viscount Strange, were asked by Edward Nicholas, a secretary to the Admiralty, to return the money from the estate to Lady Caesar. Nicholas was trying to remove obstacles to preferment of his own. Hungate had apparently made promises to him, and Nicholas could only ask the commissioners to intervene for him.[69] In the end, Nicholas received a first reversion to an Examinership and Hungate was awarded the benefit of one-half of a Six Clerk's place.[70] Caesar had gained the result he wanted, but at some cost; he clearly did not have a free hand.

Caesar did manage to secure a Six Clerkship for his son Robert.[71] Another son, Charles, was awarded the second reversion to the Mastership of the Rolls following Sir Dudley Digges. Robert, with a Six Clerk's place in hand, later refused an offer from the king to turn in his grant for a new one. He perhaps suspected that he would not get it back again, for there were important changes afoot. Adverting to Robert Caesar's refusal, Secretary Windebank noted that "an act of state" was to be made of his failure to cooperate and another concerning the rights of the Six Clerks "as they are now settled."[72] Windebank's meaning had been made clear as early as February 1635 when a proposal had been tabled in Council "to compound with the Six Clerks for their offices."[73] The king was finally taking the gift of the Six Clerkships entirely into his own prerogative. A Six Clerk's place was currently valued at about £6,000, and the proceeds were divided among several officers and the king. This was simply too valuable a source of revenue to be left in private hands.[74] Although Caesar may not have been pleased to see the Six Clerkships about to pass from the patronage of the Master of the Rolls, his own interests had been secured. His intransigence had held off this day for twenty years, and even for the king to "annex [the Clerkships] in perpetuity to the Crown" had to await the demise of the Master of the Rolls and the honoring of the grant that Caesar had made to his son Robert. It was probably for this reason that Robert had not wished to jeopardize his grant when the king offered him a new one. On the same day, by letters patent, Charles created a corporation of the Six Clerks and settled their fees "with the allowance of the Lord Keeper, the Master of the Rolls, the Attorney General and Privy Council." Even at this late date, and after months of consultation, there was some lingering doubt about taking over the Six Clerks. Provision was made for making corrections in the letters patent should any defects be discovered.

The revisor was to be Caesar or Sir Dudley Digges, the Master of the Rolls in reversion.[75] Regardless of appearances, the difficulties with the Six Clerks were not settled. Only the interlude of the Civil War muted their quarrels, and when the monarchy was restored in 1660, so was the patronage of the Master of the Rolls. Their victory had been temporary.

Throughout the twenty years of their competitive relationship, it was clear that neither Caesar nor the Clerks had any wish to become bureaucrats in the sense of losing their proprietary interests in their places; each had distinctly different understandings of the concept of office-as-property. Caesar unequivocally asserted the rights of freehold tenure in his own office and its incidents. The Six Clerks, for their part, were determined to secure titles to their own offices, but they reckoned that their interests would be better served if they were directly dependent on the crown rather than the Master of the Rolls, and that if they were to take the form of a corporation, their estates would be secure from the intervention of their traditional superior. Though this movement toward reliance on the king for their appointments and their corporate status appears to be a step in the direction of bureaucratization, that was not their intent. They were, instead, conducting themselves in the tradition of independent guildsmen owing corporate allegiance to the crown. Caesar's response to this and other attempts to reduce the patronage of his office was the response of a "feudal" minister defending his tenurial rights. With due allowance for anachronistic usage, "feudal" is apt in this context. Caesar had received a property of value from the king, the incidents of the Rolls, and he returned service to the king while expecting royal protection of his interests. This was a compelling position. Both James and Charles had honored Caesar's rights even against such a powerful courtier as Buckingham, who was trying to undermine them.

Although dealing with the Six Clerks occupied much of Caesar's time, it was not the only personal problem that he faced. On every side were individuals attempting to interfere with the incumbent officers of the Chancery. An endless number of proposals and projects were presented to him calling for the consolidation of existing offices in a new one, or for the addition of extra officers to the staff of the Chancery. Caesar was frequently in opposition because the project in question would dilute fees and, thus, jeopardize the well-being of the incumbent officers. On one occasion, a patent was proposed for the benefit of Sir Robert Lloyd, granting him a monopoly on the copying of wills and indentures. As the sole copier, Lloyd would deprive existing clerks of their fees. Caesar objected for that reason and because the proposal was deficient in law and policy. Nonetheless, the Attorney General found the idea attractive and did all that he could to promote Lloyd's interests. He went so far as to argue that serious reforms would derive from this new appointment because Lloyd and his clerks would be sworn officers, their fees would be lower than those currently charged, and their fees would be fixed according to a schedule. Furthermore, the new officer, in the course of protecting his monopoly, would prevent usurping clerks from assessing their own fees.[76] In the end, Caesar prevailed.

Shortly thereafter, Caesar again defended the status quo when a proposal was advanced to add a third Examiner in Chancery. He objected because there were already two incumbents with freehold interests in their places. A third would have cost the Examiners one-third of their present revenue. Furthermore, there was a technical problem of some importance to Caesar. The Master of the Rolls was technically the Examiner in Chancery; the officers bearing the title "examiner" were his deputies. Thus, he argued, he had promised the next vacant Examinership to Sir Patrick Murray and his heirs, and he could not very well push Murray aside in favor of a newly created "vacancy." In more general terms, Caesar held that there should be no expansion of places pursuant to the king's orders of 18 July 1620 forbidding the creation of new or supernumeral offices in Chancery, the law courts, and Exchequer.[77]

Along with the problem of the creation of redundant offices, the level of fees in the courts was a significant political issue. Layers of clerks, attorneys, lawyers, masters, and judges generated massive fees that were a ruinous burden on the litigants. From time to time, commissions were seated to quiet popular complaints and to determine whether the king was getting his share. When suggestions were made that the fees should be increased, the more responsible law officers remembered that there was strong public sentiment that they already were too high. Indeed, in the Parliament of 1621, James had promised the Commons that fees would be reduced in every court sitting "in Westminster Hall." In long notes to himself, Caesar rehearsed the king's commitment to reduce fees in the face of contrary pressure from incumbents and projectors of administrative "innovations."[78] The

abuse of the power to set fees led eventually to the seating of a commission to examine "exacted fees" and "innovated offices" since 11
Elizabeth. They reported in 1630, telling of the exactions of the three
Prothonotaries of the Common Pleas, the Six Clerks of the Chancery,
and the Clerk of the Hanaper.[79] Not surprisingly, their investigations
revealed a long history of overcharging and abuse. The problem was
serious, and there were no easy answers in sight. It was certainly not
to be settled in Caesar's lifetime.

During his tenure as Master of the Rolls, extending over more than
two decades, Caesar displayed remarkable tenacity in defense of his
interests. His pride was at stake, but so was the most valuable property in his possession: the office and its patronage.

X

〰〰〰〰〰〰〰〰〰〰〰〰〰〰〰〰〰〰〰〰〰〰〰〰〰

Proper Days for Every Business

EVER SINCE he had first been sworn to Privy Council in 1607, Caesar had spent increasingly greater portions of his time either at the Council Board or with commissioners appointed as subcommittees of Council. At first he had been a source of expert advice on admiralty matters and the laws of foreign commerce. Then, after Salisbury's death, he became the ranking financial consultant among the Councillors. When, finally, he moved to the relatively less demanding Mastership of the Rolls, Caesar's seniority and wide-ranging experience caused him to be appointed to an extensive variety of commissions even though he was not always an active member. In the following pages we shall examine in some detail his work as a Privy Councillor from 1614 until 1636. At first he was a busy, keenly observant, if allegedly overworked, senior Councillor. We last see him, more than twenty years later and well into his seventies, detecting in the Caroline regime elements of the Elizabethan style of government he had known as a younger man.

Privy Council membership required his attendance at several meetings a week throughout the year; at the same time, he was the minister responsible for the daily operation of Chancery. Aside from meetings of the full Council, there were numerous ad hoc committees to discuss discrete issues. Furthermore, the parliamentary sessions of 1614 and 1621 required much advance preparation, and attendance in Parliament was another call on Caesar's time. In reviewing the variety of commissions and committees on which he served, it becomes apparent that the crown was drawing on his particular expertise in law and foreign relations. Yet the most time-consuming of all of his responsibilities outside of Chancery was his continued association with public finance through membership in the second Treasury Commission. The demands of his many functions became too burdensome for Caesar during the 1621 Parliament, causing Secretary Calvert to write to him "that it is his Majesties pleasure you fayle not to be in the lower howse tomorrow morning being Monday and to so contynue everyday as long as this house sitts notwithstanding yor terme busynesse, which may well give way to his Majesties service in the Parliament, rather than be a hindrance to your attendance there." Calvert was a trifle embarrassed by the tone of the letter. He told Caesar that he was sending the order "in the very formal wordes as I have received it."[1]

The Treasury was in commission again in 1619 following the charges of peculation, embezzlement, and fraud that had been brought against Lord Treasurer Suffolk, his wife, and Sir John Bingley, the Remembrancer of the Exchequer. As serious as these allegations were, it appeared that Suffolk might be able to persuade the king to dismiss them. In April 1618 James placed the effective management of the Treasury in the care of a committee of Privy Council, but he did not yet remove Suffolk.[2] By July, the evidence was mounting, along with political pressure from Buckingham, who wanted Suffolk to be deprived. He had his way when the Lord Treasurer was dismissed and replaced by the Treasury Commission, of which Caesar was a member.[3]

Although his work on the new commission was demanding, Caesar did not appear to play the central role he had on the first commission. Buckingham was a masterful organizer, working his will in the commission through the expertise of Sir Lionel Cranfield. Between them they attempted substantive changes in the conduct of public finance. The Chancellor of the Exchequer, Fulke Greville, provided the day-to-day contact with the mechanisms of receipt and issue as Caesar had done when he was Chancellor. Although he was long removed from office in the Exchequer, Caesar was useful to the Commission because, as Chancellor, he had attempted to turn the king toward a policy of retrenchment. The new Treasury Commission was considering a similar policy in 1619. Caesar would spend a great deal of his time on Treasury business during the second Commission, but he was more a marginal than a pivotal member. At the same time, there was much other Privy Council business to occupy the attention of the Master of the Rolls.

Throughout Caesar's muniments there are papers concerning Council business. An especially useful collection of his holographic notes from Councils held between 1619 and 1622 displays in some detail the business of government and of Caesar's particular involvement. These notes were taken in meetings held for the most part during summer months, suggesting that the Master of the Rolls spent more of the long vacation in or near London than did many of his colleagues. These were not law-term months, and he had more time to spend away from the Rolls Chapel on Council affairs. The first of these notes was written in July 1619 as James was preparing to depart London on progress. Meeting with Privy Council, the king heard reports of current business: the Suffolk trial, the state of bullion exports, proposals for the minting of coins of baser alloy, and the sentence to be handed down against Secretary Lake.[4] A week later, James met with the Treasury Commission to issue orders for the period that he would be away. Of the more than thirty items covered in the instructions, most dealt with particulars. The prosecution had begun in Star Chamber of a number of Dutch merchants who had illegally carried gold out of England. The Treasury Commission and Privy Council were instructed to cooperate with one another in prosecuting the merchants, and Council was directed to brief the Commissioners on the current status of the case. The prosecution was apparently making only cautious progress, prompting Caesar to write at the foot of his notes of the instructions: *qui nil dubitat, nihil intelligit.*[5]

In September, at another Council, the king and Buckingham spent the entire meeting delivering an exposition on foreign policy positions regarding the Palatinate.[6] Under similar circumstances in January, again on the eve of a progress, the king instructed his Councillors. Finance, coinage, and bullion were added to the agenda, but there were serious changes in the air. Reversions to office were to be stayed, no new offices in the law courts were to be created, and no new projects were to be entertained. Along with financial and procedural concerns, another matter of a very different nature was recorded: "Provision to bee taken for preventing of weomens wearing of mens apparell: ruffles hanging down, short wastes, pointes, girdles, short haire, broade hates, stillettoes, long scharves, bootes and spurres, breeches, etc.

Abomination." There then followed citations to Deuteronomy 22:5 and
1 Corinthians 11:4–17.[7]

Council appeared to be coming to closure by April on a number of
issues that they had been considering for several months. The Dutch
cause had been concluded; all that remained was to assess the fines.
Former Lord Treasurer Suffolk's lands were forfeit, but a reluctant king
was busily seeking a penalty that would not ruin his friend. Although
new projects were no longer welcome, Council pursued the older ones
with gusto.[8] When they turned to "Causes of Decay of Trade Among
English Merchants," Dutch duties on English dressed and dyed cloth
and the German exchange were held principally responsible. The suggested remedies were quite straightforward: only unfinished cloth was
to be exported in order to take advantage of lower import duties, and
its price was to be kept artificially low to undercut the Dutch in their
own market by the "cheape selling of our cloth." The German exchange was to be avoided wherever possible.[9]

When James departed London later in July, Caesar headed his
notes: "To wind up the clok for this great vacancy." The current issues
included the location of the Merchant Adventurers' staple, Irish business, Scottish coinage, tobacco, wine, slanderous speeches, and the repair of St. Paul's. The memorandum provides a particularly interesting view of the detailed organization of Council business. They had
decided to make the best use of their time by appointing "proper days
for every business" and by putting them "to dispatch." They further
resolved "that meetings be always certain and upon certain days unless extraordinary business demanded extraordinary days." Implementation of this new efficiency began immediately: in the margin, next
to the items of business, were such notations as "on Friday 21 July in
the morning," "on Thursday 20 July in the afternoon," or "Saturday
morning."[10]

By autumn, the dominant issues were finance and the Palatinate.
James briefed the Council on the status of the Elector Frederick and
Princess Elizabeth, explaining his reasons for exercising great caution
in his response to their danger. Beneath his expressions of high policy, cool diplomacy, and paternal concern lay James's fear that moving too quickly would jeopardize the peace with Spain and be
ruinously costly. The Council advised him that this was a defensive
war and, thus, an expense chargeable to the nation. But the question
remained, how should the nation be assessed?[11]

Privy seals, contributions, or a Parliament: these were the options, and, Caesar noted, it was "resolved by the whole Council Table that a Parliament is the best." It was further resolved that, prior to calling a Parliament, personal contributions should be collected from Councillors, judges, "and such great persons." There followed a list of 28 names; 11 were rated from £1,000 to £200, Caesar being among the £200 contributors.[12] The contribution was notably successful among the Chancery officers. By mid-October, a total of £2,851 13s. 4d. had been collected from 62 officials of the court.[13]

In June 1621 Parliament was in session and the Council's leading item of business was the list of complaints advanced by the Members. Among the heads of these complaints was "abuses of the courts of justice." The particulars included extortionate fees in the courts and the presence of "multitudes of attorneys." Lawyers' fees were thought excessive, but the principal grievance concerned clever, obstructionist motions to frustrate litigants wishing to bring a suit to an end.[14] In December Caesar noted that James was bitter because Parliament had not followed his instructions in several important matters. King and Council joined in a formal resolution to dissolve a Parliament that had yielded as much as they reasonably could expect and was becoming more trouble that it was worth.[15]

Throughout these several meetings, it becomes apparent that, except for the war in the Palatinate, the same issues continued to occupy Council, and that the members of Council were expected to be more than passive sounding boards for the king. The Councillors attempted, as best they could, to study and solve problems and to govern in deed. Council was, in short, returning to the style of a working and governing board less riven with faction than when the Howards held sway. Although Buckingham would become the central figure in Council in the early years of the Caroline reign, he was not an overbearing force in the Jacobean Council.

While domestic issues and conflict on the Continent took up most of Council's time, there was a keen awareness of the problems of North American colonization. Chartered companies were responsible for the daily operation of the colonial settlements, but the resolution of conflicts usually ended up before Council. As we shall see, the problems in Virginia were of especial concern for Caesar because his brother-in-law was a leading adventurer in the Virginia Company and a fiercely independent and troublesome member of the community. Although Caesar did not use his considerable influence to develop an extensive patronage network, he did work hard in the interest of his family and kin. An excellent example of this behavior is revealed in his efforts in behalf of his first wife's brother, Captain John Martin, one of the founders of the colony at Jamestown.

The settlement of Virginia in the early seventeenth century was beset by nigh-insuperable difficulties.[16] The Virginia Company dispatched three ships in December 1606 to take up the settlement rights surrendered to the crown by Sir Walter Raleigh, whose colony at Roanoke Island had failed in 1587. By April 1607 the *Susan Constant*, the *Godspeed*, and the *Discovery* lay in the Chesapeake Bay, having lost 40 of the original 144 mariners and adventurers who had left England. For the next eighteen years the tiny colony held on to the fragile base at Jamestown and nearby plantations along the James River until a bankrupt Virginia Company was superseded by the crown. Malaria, a nearly total massacre by Indians, and ceaseless internal struggles among the settlers characterized these early years, and always near the center of affairs was Captain John Martin. He was one of the original adventurers named to the first Council of the settlement, and many years later it was noted that he was the last surviving resident in Virginia of the original party. We know that Caesar was much involved in Martin's affairs at a critical moment late in the Virginian's turbulent career; there may have been other occasions of which we have no record.

A brawling, aggressive adventurer, Martin appears to have been a law unto himself. He had been involved at a very early date in plotting to depose Edward Wingfield, the first President of the Council in Virginia. Martin was himself named president in 1609, but a contemporary account reports that he, "knowing his own insufficiencie, and the companies scorne, and conceit of his unworthinesse, within 3 houres, resigned [the presidency] againe to Captaine Smith." Apparently, Martin's unworthiness had to do with his reputation as a careless soldier who wasted his resources and with his treatment of the Indians, which was taken to be irresponsible.[17]

Martin traded on his father's reputation. A member of the Goldsmith's Company, an alderman, and a recent Lord Mayor, Sir Richard Martin was a valuable connection for John even though he recently had been embarrassed by bankruptcy. Martin sent a barrel of fool's gold back to England, hoping to convince his father, several wealthy backers, and the king to continue to supply his requirements in anticipation of the wealth that the "gold" promised. Sir Walter Cope wrote to Salisbury of the incident: "It apeared at sight so suspycyous, that we were not satysfyed untill we hadd made fowre Tryalls by the best experyenced abowte the cytye. In the ende all turned to vapore, and Martyne hath cosyned the pore Captaine [Christopher Newport], the Kinge and the State, and meant as I heare to have drawen hys owne father to have made over unto him somm supplyes, which otherwyse he dowted never to procure."[18] His involvement (along with his father and Caesar) in the Mineral and Battery Company probably accounts for Lord Delaware's decision to put John Martin in charge of the Battery Works in Virginia in 1610.[19]

Along with more than 100 followers, Martin quickly established himself at Martin Brandon south of the James River. On the occasions that he returned to England, he brought settlers back with him to work his holdings. Martin's rights and privileges under his several patents, together with the remote location of Martin Brandon, made him a nearly free agent. Indeed, more than a decade later, in 1619, when the Virginia Company authorized government by elected delegates, John Martin's burgesses were refused seats in the first Virginia Assembly because of a clause in his patent for Martin Brandon giving him and his heirs exclusive government over the people of his settlement save in times of common defense against domestic or foreign enemies. The patent stipulated that Martin was "to enjoye his landes in as lardge and ample manner . . . as any lord of any mannours in England dothe holde his grounde." Such a peculiar jurisdiction was found repugnant under the new charter, and the burgesses elected from Martin Brandon were told that they could not sit until Martin surrendered his old patent and accepted a new one that omitted the offending clause.[20] Martin refused to submit, claiming to be educated in the law and to be seised of rights that were fair compensation for early services to the Company and the colony. Martin, the only member of the original Council still living in Virginia, no doubt owed his survival to his tenacious independence.[21] The government of the colony by the Virginia Company was on its last legs by the early 1620's: the Company was bankrupt, the complaints against it were legion, and, following the Indian massacre of 1622, the devastated plantations had to be reestablished. Martin had been fortunate to be in England when the disaster occurred. He employed all of his political connections to preserve his unique patent and to deprive the Company of its powers.

In a long brief that he sent to Caesar and other notables, he drafted the first proposal for the shiring of Virginia along lines generally similar to those in England. He reckoned this would duplicate most of the self-sufficient characteristics of the English county. As Martin saw it, his privileges were not remarkable by domestic English standards; therefore, the best way to preserve them would be to create a domestic English polity in Virginia. At the same time, he produced a fascinating idea that was never taken up in a formal manner but that indicated just how much the Virginia plantations were regarded as the westernmost counties of England. He wrote of the desirability of attracting a sufficient number of men with "good estates" to establish plantations in Virginia "with their persons and goods and to cause the planters in Virginia to plant estates in England." This was not the blueprint for a dependent colony but for an integrated community of English gentry whose wealth would flow both to and from England.[22] Attached to the same document was a proposal for bringing "the Indians into subiection without makinge an utter exterpation of them." Martin's reasons for not wishing to exterminate the Indians were grounded in two critical points: the Scriptures would not permit it, and there were too many practical reasons for preserving a submissive native population.[23]

The question of how to deal with the turmoil in the Virginia Colony led, in 1624, to the crown's naming a commission "for settling a government in Virginea." Made up of numerous Councillors (including Caesar), aldermen, and merchants, the commission was charged with determining how to make the transition from the private interests of the company to the "public" interests of a crown colony. Judging from his marginal notes, Caesar was alert to Martin's interests and protected them as best he could. He noted that "no former iust interestes [were] to bee taken away from former adventurers," even though their former charters had been "made voyde by lawe." The passage against which Caesar had noted that preexisting interests would be protected contained an important proviso: they would be protected "so farr forth as their present interests shall not preiudice the publique plantations."[24] This left a wide loophole for the government to defeat the terms of Martin's patent when the time was right.

Caesar was deeply involved in developing the terms of the new colonial government of Virginia. At the same time, both the commission on which he sat and Privy Council provided for Martin's interests. The court of the Company wrote a commendatory letter in his behalf to the Governor and Council in Virginia, and Privy Council endorsed his claims and supported his litigation in Virginia against a previous governor. But Martin was not satisfied. As late as 1627, he was writing to Caesar asking for further assistance in preserving the terms of his old patent. His plantation at Martin Brandon had been relatively undamaged during the massacre in 1622, and his trade with England grew after the colony began to plant tobacco more extensively. Yet Martin held tenaciously to his notion that his settlement was virtually a sovereign peculiar. On the other hand, from the time of the exclusion of Martin's burgesses from the first Assembly, most Virginians believed that his privileges had no place in the colony. "The publique plantations," thus, were prejudiced by Martin's patent, and he was forced to accept a new grant preserving his property interests but not his colonial "lordship." For more than twenty years Martin had managed to survive in the Virginia wilderness; not the least of his assets had been a helpful and influential brother-in-law back home.

At the end of March 1625, James I died at Theobalds. His last illness had lingered; his death relieved both his mortal pains and his subjects, who were ready for a new monarch.[25] Initially, Charles I turned his attention to the formalities of succession and to the arrangements for his father's funeral. Once those were behind him, his duty was to marry Henrietta Maria, and his passion was to restore decorum and ritual to his court. The effective governor of the kingdom was not its king, however, but the duke of Buckingham. As a recent study has demonstrated, "in the three years after James's death . . . Buckingham in many ways ruled England, making the period from Charles's accession to Buckingham's assassination a whole."[26]

Sir Henry Goring, writing to Carlisle and Holland to announce the news of James I's death in 1625, told of the new king's early intention to restore formal dignity at Court.[27] A few weeks later, Chamberlain advised Carleton that the king had come to Whitehall accompanying his father's corpse and that he remained there to continue the settlement of his household as he brought it back "to the auncient forme." All of the late king's servants of every rank were ordered to attend on the body in Denmark House, but they feared obeying the order, "that by their absence they might be dispossest of their places and lodgings." Excess personnel were pared from the establishment as the new king remade the Court in a smaller and more dignified form. Fewer servants, less waste, and more dignity: these characterized Charles's apparent goals. "The King shows himself every way very gracious and affable, but the court is being kept more strait and privat than in the former time."[28]

Later in April, Tobie Matthew wrote to Carleton with more news of Court, the first item being the fact that "the king is well, active, resolute, and a friend of state and order in his Court."[29] Following years of a clumsy and splintered Privy Council under James I, Charles and Buckingham were determined to establish a small Council that would be responsive to their demands. "There is talk of a select or Cabinet Council," Chamberlain reported to Carleton, "whereto none are admitted but the Duke of Buckingham, the Lords Treasurer and Chamberlain, Lord Brooke and Lord Conway."[30] Both Matthew's and Chamberlain's comments contained unspoken comparisons with the conduct of the previous reign that was found unsuitable by the new king. References to "ancient forms" and to the king's "being a friend of state and order" suggest that the model on which Charles based his changes was not his father's court. No mention of other examples of dignity, propriety, and efficiency were made, but the reduced Council and Charles's style of government were redolent of Elizabethan practice.

As early as 31 March, Charles began to introduce decorum to the Court, replacing his father's relative casualness. Privy Council was ordered to control the access of the poor and ill as well as of the courtiers, who seemed to know no restraint in terms of approaching the royal person. But these were mere stopgaps pending the completion of investigations and inquiries by committees empowered by the new king as he and Buckingham took control of his government.[31] At the heart of the changes that he would introduce lay Charles's propensity to see things "in ceremonial, or symbolic, terms." He was devoted to ritual in all that he did, and he was convinced that his changes were hardly innovative. They were, instead, the restoration of an Elizabethan order that had been abandoned during his father's reign. But the fundamental weakness that lay embedded in these notions was that ritual, decorum, and the reports of investigative committees were sufficient in themselves. The king had little appreciation of the daily politics and management involved in the translation of these theories into the reality of effective government.[32]

During the summer of 1625, Charles's coronation Parliament met, first in plague-ridden London, then in Oxford, and finally in London once more. The session was the first test, and first failure, of Caroline policy. Rather than wait to prepare for Parliament, and thus assure a larger number of sympathetic Members, Charles insisted on a session right away to raise money to fight his war with Spain. Sufficient money was refused, and the crown lost control of the debate through a lack of careful planning. Without carefully briefed Councillors to guide the discussions in the House of Commons, the debate soon turned from war finance to Catholicism. In the end, a small subsidy and an annual grant of tonnage and poundage were voted, and when criticism of Buckingham was broached, Charles preferred sending Parliament away to abiding their comments.[33] Soon thereafter, a forced loan was collected to fund the Cádiz expedition. A study in ineptitude from start to finish, the expedition returned in a shambles in November.

It was the Spanish war and Lord Keeper Williams's reaction to it that caused Charles and Buckingham to remove Williams from office, although Laud's hatred of Bishop Williams was no small factor in the decision. Actually, there had been a number of occasions when Williams had protested one policy or another, each making him less popular. When he finally carried his strenuous objections to the war with Spain into Parliament, he crossed the line into opposition.[34] That would have been serious enough since he was Lord Keeper, but his greatest sin was to have crossed Buckingham, whose creature he had been. On 25 October Sir John Suckling served the Lord Keeper with a warrant ordering him to surrender the Great Seal that was to be bestowed on Sir Thomas Coventry, the Attorney General. Writing to Buckingham, Suckling held that the deprivation of the Lord Keeper was "a due disgrace to one who has been unthankful and unfaithful to his Grace and may the like misfortune befall all such as tread in his [Williams's] hateful path, and presume to lift their heel against their maker."[35] A week later, Caesar presented the king with a long memorandum entitled "Concerninge the Private Counsell of the most high and mighty kinge of Greate Britaine, France, Scotland and Ireland." The document was probably the result of one of Charles's many investigations, and it presented timely advice and counsel in the wake of Williams's dismissal. Caesar wrote that all monarchs possess the discretionary power to appoint their own Councillors even though, by tradition, a new king held over the majority of his predecessor's appointees. The general rule, however, was that "every good king hath alwayes used at his entrance in his kingdome, to select out of his greate bodie some fewe servants (more or fewer at his owne pleasure) to be Privie Counsellors unto him in a body of a setled private Counsell, to be as watchmen for the preservaccon of his royal person and issue" in every respect, and to this end they are specially sworn. There followed a detailed account of the Council's procedures and practices. The members were responsible for keeping safely a record of their acts and correspondence. A small number of Councillors were to meet daily to receive letters, reports, and intelligence. As examples of the reports that they might receive, Caesar noted "the weekly states of the marketts, and provisions, or wantes of the countreys." One of the Secretaries of State was always to be present at every meeting of the Councillors, "standinge att the upper ende of the table" to brief the Council on business and to solicit their opinions one by one. Lords who did not have lodgings at Court or who were "ordinary greate officers of the howsehold" did not usually attend Council unless they were specifically summoned. But, if they were called to Council they were obliged to attend or to "send a sufficient excuse of theire not appearance."[36]

This report and a similar document submitted by Secretary Coke were emblematic of the changes that Charles was making in government.[37] Caesar appeared to welcome and appreciate the Caroline style, even though Buckingham had caused Council to cease functioning "as a body for the full discussion of business and as adviser to the crown."[38] Actually, since Caesar was more concerned with the nurturing of his own fortune and the advancement of his family than with governmental affairs, Buckingham's policy may have suited him perfectly.

As a Privy Councillor, Caesar later analyzed the results of the 1626 Parliament in documents prepared for the king's use when plans were laid to levy a forced loan. His conclusions were to be expected: Parliament in 1624 had "persuaded and put the King into this war" with Spain; thus, in 1626, they continued to be obligated to assist in paying for the war. A grant of four subsidies and three fifteenths, yielding £320,000, would have met their obligation, but since they would not cooperate, a loan was essential. He advised that great care be taken in choosing the commissioners to collect the loan and that "this beginning is fit to bee first taken here in London, Westminster and places adjacent [among] Counsellors, Noblemen, and Judges."[39] A year later, he prepared a long memorandum in Latin covering four large pages in which he explained in detail the crown's right to levy fines and penalties against its subjects. These four closely written pages of careful research appear to have been associated with the crown's prosecution of the Five Knights' case.[40] Even Caesar's commonplace book was a source of data as he prepared briefs on taxes, benevolences, and contributions.[41] Likewise, he caused a document to be prepared from Chancery records in the Tower enumerating the "meanes by which kings have formerly used to rayse moneys." The source of the information was a number of patents dating from 1, 2, and 3 Edward I.[42] The document appeared to have been addressed to Council as they prepared to find additional alternatives to parliamentary finance.

In the aftermath of the 1628 Parliament, Charles washed his hands of the encumbrance of troublesome Members. He turned to his advisors, political and legal, to prepare the way for those years known as the "Personal Rule"; the primary motive was efficiency. Parliament, with its agenda of grievances and provincial interests, was clearly inefficient standing squarely in the path of a well-ordered government. Caesar was greatly impressed by the administrative and stylistic changes that followed.

The "Personal Rule" was of a piece with the king's efforts at his accession to correct the failings of the Court he had inherited and to introduce efficiencies. While others may have thought of these changes as innovations, Charles thought of them as the restoration of Elizabethan practices. Although there were some apparent similarities between the Caroline and the Elizabethan senses of presence and style, there were striking differences as well. Elizabeth, for instance, had maintained an uncanny feeling for the sensibilities of her subjects; Charles would lose touch with the sentiments of the political nation. His advisors pressed relentlessly for a policy of rationalizing and centralizing the king's authority regardless of the consequences. It is difficult to imagine Cecil, Walsingham, or Dorset becoming as disastrously detached from political reality as Laud and Wentworth would become. But at the beginning of the "Personal Rule," the experiment in government without Parliament seemed attuned to the requirements of the counties and their governors. Stability and continuity were highly prized, and the policy of "Thorough" that informed government by Council seemed, initially, to provide them.

Caesar's reactions to these important changes are found in oblique evidence. Fortunately, he was an inveterate collector and annotator. In his personal copy of *The Ancient State*, bound with interleaved blank sheets, he added page after page of additional notes, stopping only when he became too involved in other affairs and when the Requests was no longer in danger. More than twenty years later, in 1623, Caesar returned to *The Ancient State* to enter on the remaining blank pages a curious Jacobean order about the conduct of Council. It forbade the wearing of spurs at Court, allowed no one to approach the royal person unbidden, and required greater dignity and decorum.[43]

Although this order had no apparent connection with Caesar's defense of the Court of Requests, it did relate to his conviction that the center of a well-ordered commonwealth was a well-ordered Court and Council. According to this way of thinking, grounded as it was in the ethos of the civil law, the monarch and courtiers were highly privileged, but, at the same time, they bore a heavy responsibility; indeed, the crown's exceptional powers imposed limitations that others did not have to heed. In the Court of Elizabeth, where he had first learned the practical arts of government, Caesar had adopted an ideal type that remained with him. But the Jacobean Court had fallen short of its Elizabethan predecessor. There had been attempts to bring order, but they were of little consequence. The Court was in such a condition at the death of James that the new king, as we have seen, moved immediately to restore ancient practices.

Caesar wrote in his copy of *The Ancient State* once more, and for the last time, in 1630. The king had issued a set of orders regulating the conduct of business before Council, and the old judge indicated with margin lines the points that held the greatest interest for him. Council was to meet regularly, it was to dispatch its business quickly, and, of greatest importance, the members of Council were no longer to proceed to their meetings by way of back halls and secret passages unless there were an emergency. Instead, they were to make a seemly procession through the Court, a symbol of the power, dignity, and majesty of their company.[44] It appeared that the fractioned and disordered Council of the Jacobean period had finally been reformed. The essential unity displayed by the Councillors in procession through the Court was, in symbolic terms, diametrically opposed to rumors of shadowy Councillors moving alone or in clusters along back passages to conduct the secret business of state and faction. Although the Elizabethan Council had been divided by faction, in retrospect it symbolized unity. Thus, the Caroline reforms may have been perceived by an old hand such as Caesar to be reminiscent of the government he had known as a young man.

The "Personal Rule" was an extension on a national scale of the same desire to achieve dignity and efficiency that had put the Council's house in order. When Charles and his advisors had decided to govern without Parliament, they developed a systematic, "thorough" reordering of governmental responsibility from the Commission of the Peace to the Council. The *Book of Orders*, published in 1631, reflected this new style of government. After more than a century of unplanned, piecemeal accumulation of judicial and administrative tasks at the county level, the river of proclamations, orders, and statutes flowing from the center to the provinces had become unenforceable. The Justices of the Peace were limited by medieval statutes to a few meeting (or Quarter Session) days a year. They were further limited by restrictions on what they could do in the name of the whole commission outside of the Sessions. To make matters worse, the local governors were inadequately supervised. The *Book of Orders* was issued in response to this accumulation of administrative misery. Such books were not unusual; consolidated statements of rules and procedure, they are encountered in law courts and administrative agencies. But the *Book* of 1631 was remarkable for the scope of its concerns. It was directed at nothing less than the reorganization of English local administration. The *Book of Orders* originated with the ideas of Sir Edward Cecil, viscount Wimbledon, who sent the king a proposal in 1630 that was passed on to Secretary Carleton, who, in turn, brought it to the attention of the earl of Manchester. Perhaps in response to the fears of his brother Councillors over the social consequences of the disastrous harvest the country was experiencing, Manchester proposed the *Book of Orders* for adoption.[45]

At the center of the *Book of Orders* lay the enforcement of the Poor Law. Topic by topic, the whole range of legislation that had been the responsibility of the Justices of the Peace was systematically codified. Responsibility for enforcement was now vested in a three-tiered hierarchy. The Justices of the Peace, at the lowest level, were primarily responsible, aided and supervised by the Assize Judges for the circuit.

At the top, there was to be a subcommittee of Councillors who, together with the Assize Judges, would maintain vigilance and pressure. In the counties the reaction to this new scheme was almost enthusiastic. With its emphasis on the enforcement of the quintessentially Elizabethan Poor Law and the accompanying increase in the effectiveness of government by Council, the *Book of Orders* signified an attempt to restore a quality of governance not seen in England for more than thirty years.[46]

Caesar was among the Councillors who approved the *Book of Orders*, and he was of the commission for its enforcement. Along with the Lord Keeper and the Chancellor of the Exchequer, and several other Councillors, Caesar was a member of a subcommittee responsible for Hampshire, Dorset, Wiltshire, Somerset, Devon, and Cornwall. They were to join with Lord Chief Justice Richardson, Baron Denham, and the Assize judges for the Western Circuit in supervising enforcement in that region.[47] While there is no reason to think that Caesar, at more than seventy years old, was vigorously involved in the supervision of the several Commissions of the Peace in the west, it is apparent from his copy of the *Book of Orders* that he was enthusiastic about this exercise in governance by Council.

Throughout his personal copy of the *Book of Orders*, Caesar marked important passages in the margins and copied citations to Elizabethan statutes. Finally, following the commission, the orders, and a section of directions, Caesar wrote the following phrase, in Greek, in a firm round hand at the foot of the last printed page in the book: "PASA PANTOTA MONO TO THEO DOXA, AMEN. 14 JANUARY 1631" (All glory everywhere to God alone, amen).[48] This doxology, a curious statement at the end of a book of temporal regulations, was a heartfelt hymn of praise from an old servant of the crown and kingdom for their deliverance from the disorder of the previous thirty years. The new order, for which he was so thankful, was, in appearance if not in substance, reminiscent of a bygone Elizabethan era. When Caesar died, in 1636, the Caroline edifice was weakening; fortunately, he did not live long enough to witness its collapse.

XI

Enrolled in Heaven

SIR EDWARD COKE, who was six years older than Caesar, died in 1634. The occasion moved Caesar to write a brief autobiographical memorial listing chronologically the high points in his own long life.[1] The last entry was 3 September 1634, the day that Coke died. Having reached great age at a time when longevity was exceptional, Caesar was understandably moved by the death of a friend, colleague, and occasional adversary who was over eighty. Thus, we find an old man nearing the end of his own life recapitulating its principal events. He covered the years from 1558 through 1615 in some detail, recalling births, deaths, and marriages within his large family along with the notable milestones in his long career. But the years following 1615 were swept away in four entries. Having reached the pinnacle in Chancery and having married for what was surely the last time, Caesar appears to have been satisfied with his lot. He had stopped climbing the ladder of privilege and place. His family had prospered, although there had been tragedies; his marriages were advantageous, and his properties grew in number. In short, Caesar was a model of success at Court, at law, and in the country.

Just after James had come to the throne, Caesar had secured from the queen consort, Anne of Denmark, a new grant of the Mastership of the Royal Hospital of St. Katharine by Tower Hill. But, always cautious, he had then gone to the king for a second, confirming grant. Although the Hospital was traditionally in the gift of the queen (consort or regnant), he was taking no chances on the newcomers' giving the grant to someone else.[2] This exercise in caution cost Caesar £661, which he tried to raise from the tenants within the liberty of the Hospital. In the same year, 1603, he named his brother Thomas to the Surveyorship of the Hospital for life. Caesar was a careful administrator who instituted much needed reform within the precincts and also greatly enhanced the rental value of Hospital lands throughout England. Furthermore, he was a generous benefactor to the paupers for whom the Hospital was responsible. His lasting gift to St. Katharine's was an octagonal pulpit, kept to this day by the successor foundation, bearing on each of its faces views of a riverside city looking very much like London.[3]

From the time that Caesar had become the Chancellor of the Exchequer and continuing into his tenure as Master of the Rolls, he encountered the costly expectations attendant on high ministerial office. Fortunately, during those same years his wealth grew materially. Examples of these expectations may be seen in his New Year's gifts and in his public benefactions. The account books of Belvoir Castle show that from 1609 until 1613, Caesar was giving to the earls of Rutland at the New Year gifts of silver-gilt standing cups with covers. Their average cost was about £19, and they were only exceeded in value by the gifts of Egerton, Northampton, and Suffolk.[4] At the same time, Caesar was on the earls' lists of those to whom New Year's gifts were regularly given.[5] In 1613 Caesar, the public benefactor, was joined by his wife, Alice, in laying the foundation stone of his chapel in the Strand. She witnessed its consecration a few days before her death in 1614.[6] There is no remaining record of this building; in fact, Caesar's reference in his memoir is the only evidence we have. It may have been associated with the Temple or with a parish church.[7] Considering that it took only eight months to complete, the chapel was probably not large and may have been an annex to an existing structure. Regardless of its location and dimension, it is interesting to consider why Caesar built it. He may have wished to make a pious offering of a place of worship; he may also have wished to emulate Cecil's tradition of building in the Strand. The fact that he was able to build a chapel is a significant indicator of his wealth and aspirations in the early Stuart milieu of conspicuous spending and courtly posturing.

Caesar's private life during the years of his highest public standing is quite obscure, but this is not surprising when we recall that his life was principally oriented toward his family. We do know from his property portfolio that he attended to his estate. He probably became a bit

more intimately involved with county society, particularly in Hertfordshire, Lincolnshire, and Norfolk, after he acquired properties there,
but his lifelong inclination to spend most of his time in London must
have limited his time in the country. Furthermore, as we shall see
below, Caesar was faced with tragic losses in his family: three children,
a wife, and a brother died. On the other hand, he did marry again,
for the third and last time.

It is not surprising to find that the few remnants of Caesar's social
life point to his colleagues in the central government and the church.
For instance, in 1617, when James was in Scotland, the principal members of Council took their turns hosting their colleagues as they went
"afeasting." "Beginning with the bishop of London the 24th of last
moneth, they were on Tewsday bountifully entertained by the Master
of the Rolles, and are to be the 8th of this present with the archbishop
of Caunterburie, and so forward as yt falles out."[8] On another occasion, Caesar and Lady Anne were planning to visit Lord Zouche, but
their plans were set aside. Zouche wrote to Caesar telling him how
much he would have enjoyed their visit but that had they seen one another, there would have been no letter from Caesar "stuffed with much
religious matter." We might assume that their visit would have been as
morally enlightening as the letter. Zouche ended his letter with a
prayer that characterized much of Caesar's later life: "Lett me intreate
you so to be ruled as that you forgett not to make your lyfe comfortable whylest you live to the comfort of your frends and the good of
gods children. It is commanded by the word."[9]

Throughout his adult life, Caesar had a penchant for antiquarian
learning that was generally directed to law and government, but in the
1620's he returned to an interest in religion that he had manifested as
a young man. He copied the three traditional Christian creeds into
Italian and wrote the Ten Commandments in Greek.[10] He made extensive holographic notes on the names and dates of the Church Fathers and their writings.[11] From one of the clerks in the Chancery establishment, he received a set of notes on the spiritual nature of man.[12]
Along with his legal and religious materials, Caesar also maintained
a library of works in Italian translation. An inventory listed forty-two
titles, ranging from religious works to collections on architecture,
agriculture, and geometry.[13]

The one notable occasion when public duties imposed themselves
on Caesar's private life occurred in 1629 when Council decided to re-

strain the earl of Bedford. Caesar was commanded to keep Bedford "for that short time with you in your howse." A clerk of Council would deliver him to Caesar, who was to assure that he would be unable to communicate with anyone or to receive letters without the express consent of Council.[14] Bedford, Robert Cotton, Oliver St. John, and the earl of Clare were kept in custody because the king and Council were convinced that they had circulated a seditious tract.[15] The pamphlet, advocating the imposition of absolute monarch to discipline a contentious Parliament, had been copied by Cotton from a writing sent to the earl of Somerset by Sir Robert Dudley in 1614.[16] After Bedford had spent a week in custody, Caesar wrote to Secretary Coke that the earl wanted answers to questions he had posed to the Secretary when they last met. Failing answers, "without your assente, hee will speake to some other frend. The Lord Jesus blesse you in all your affaires." On the same sheet Coke advised Caesar that Bedford need not worry about his papers being searched without his solicitor or another attorney present. In fact, Coke was confident that there would be no search at all, and Bedford was advised that he was free to address Caesar or Coke if and when he wished.[17] Coke's prediction was quite accurate: although Charles tried to make political profit with Parliament by arresting the alleged tyrants, the whole affair soon fizzled and the crown backed away.

Caesar remained fairly healthy for his age. His correspondence contained references to his having been ill from time to time, but the chronic problem that tortured him was "the stone." One attack in particular, in the spring of 1620, was sufficiently severe for him to remember it many years later when he prepared his autobiographical memoir.[18] Like many of his contemporaries, Caesar collected and exchanged recipes for cures for specific ailments. Treatments for the stone were well-represented, along with other concoctions for toothaches, the plague, consumption, "ill breath," and two particularly interesting cures for the "wind collick" sent to him by James Ley, formerly Lord Chief Justice of King's Bench and then, as the earl of Marlborough, the Lord Treasurer. Concern for flatulence in high places presents an engaging picture of the governors of the Caroline kingdom.[19]

Apart from his personal life, Caesar continued to serve as the principal among his surviving siblings. Of Caesar's two surviving brothers, Henry made his career in the church, while Thomas, staying close to Julius, made his career at law. Their sister, Anne Peck, required Caesar's assistance up to the year of her death. Once he had returned to England to enjoy Walsingham's patronage, Henry Caesar had moved into the church hierarchy with remarkable ease.[20] By 1614, he was created Dean of Ely for life.[21] The following year he turned to his brother Julius for legal assistance regarding a contested property in Cambridgeshire claimed by the Dean and Chapter.[22] Henry continued to derive an income from a canonry in Westminster Abbey that he finally resigned in 1625.[23] When he died in 1636, the same year as Julius, he was buried beneath the choir of Ely Cathedral with a suitable monument to his memory. Throughout his later years he was a good friend and doting uncle to his nephew Charles.

Thomas Caesar had died in 1610, shortly after having become Puisne Baron of the Exchequer, but his widow, Susan, remained resident in Leyton Grange in Essex.[24] Susan and her sister, Mary, Sir Thomas Lake's wife, inherited the estate from their father subject to an annuity to their mother. Over the next several years, through clever manipulation of interests, Susan came to enjoy an incrementally reduced interest in the estate that was to have been her principal support.

Caesar's sister, Anne Peck, had been widowed for a number of years when she wrote a most pathetic letter to Caesar in 1629 begging him not to be angry and to please help her, for she was "much greeved and trowbled in my mind." She had given her bond for a debt incurred by one of her sons "which is nowe with the Lorde." The debt had been for £20, but Anne had talked the creditor, one Mistress Downes, into settling for £8. "Sweete brother, now helpe me, and I vowe to god I will never troble you to pay any dette for me, so longe as I leve agayne." At the foot of the letter Caesar noted that he paid the debt and canceled the bond in the presence of another of Anne's sons, John Peck, whom he ordered to deliver it to her.[25] A few months later, in the following January, Anne died and was buried under the "greate stone under the Communion Table, *where there is no vault.*"[26]

A year after the death of Lady Alice, Caesar married again. His bride was the granddaughter of Sir Nicholas Bacon, and Sir Francis Bacon's niece. Indeed, it was Francis Bacon who gave her in marriage in the Rolls Chapel on 19 April 1615.[27] Born Anne Woodhouse, she first married a Hogan, then a Hungate, and finally Sir Julius Caesar.

Until her third marriage, she was firmly rooted in Norfolk, and, even after she joined Caesar in London, she maintained houses and connections in East Anglia.

Lady Anne brought to their marriage the wealth she had inherited from her first two husbands. In itself, this was unremarkable; fortunes passed along through second and third marriages quite commonly. But Lady Anne's wealth becomes noteworthy because, allegedly, she defrauded the heirs to her first husband's estate shortly before her son's death. Eventually, "The Lady Caesar's Case" was decided in her favor because, at law, her behavior was technically correct.[28] She had been married to Henry Hogan of Norfolk, who had settled a large jointure on her composed of all of his lands in Norfolk and some in other counties for the term of her life without impeachment of waste. At his death, in 1592, Hogan's only heir was his son, Robert, a baby of "the age of 36 weekes and 4 daies." The residual legatees were his nieces, Anne and Elizabeth, who were also coheirs to the estate of Hogan's father. Robert became a ward of the crown, but Anne managed to obtain his guardianship for herself. Taken together, her jointure and the guardianship gave her sole control over her late husband's entire estate.

After some time had elapsed, Anne Hogan remarried, becoming Anne Hungate. She continued to reside at East Bradenham in Norfolk and was responsible for her son's well-being. In his late teens Robert established a residence of his own nearby. In his twentieth year he became consumptive, and it appeared unlikely that he would live long enough to attain majority. His mother moved quickly, for she "coveted to gayne the inheritance of the said manors and landes to her selfe from [his] right heires," the cousins who enjoyed a residual interest in his estate.[29]

The complex plan that Anne employed to secure title to all of the land bore the marks of careful planning with the advice of counsel. One of her kinsmen was the Feodary of the County, the local official responsible for the supervision of the crown's wards; his advice alone would have been invaluable. The scheme began with Lady Anne's visiting her ailing son, who was "much decaied both in body and mynde through the extremity of sicknes, and in the tyme of such his greate weakenes, as that his principall nourishment was by milke from a womens [sic] breast 2 monethes before he died." She had arranged to have a rumor reach him that her jointure was defective and would be challenged by his cousins. In order to protect his mother, Robert agreed to execute a fine under which he promised to pay her ten shillings by 1 September next coming, in person, at her residence in East Bradenham. If the fine were paid on time, the fee would be converted to use for Anne's life with the inheritance to Robert and his heirs, but if the fine were not paid on time, the fee would be converted to the use of Anne and her heirs. The fine was dated 1 June 1612.

A *dedimus potestatem* was sued in the Court of Wards on 10 June, the commission being charged with taking cognizance of the fine. The commissioners were local people, friends of Anne, including the Feodary of the County. Robert should have been examined as to his age, but he was not. It would appear that there had been collusion among them, although it was never proved.

Robert Hogan died a few weeks later on 3 July 1612, but Anne kept the fine secret until 1 September when she claimed the entire use for herself in default of payment. By maintaining secrecy, she had prevented Robert's heirs from paying the ten shillings for him. As the purchaser of the estate in default of an obligation, Anne did not have to honor any of the debts or benefactions that inhered in the estate when Robert was alive.

For the next several years, the heirs to the estate pursued Anne through a number of courts. In the meantime, her husband, Hungate, had died, and in 1615 she married Sir Julius Caesar. This match could only assist her as she defended herself in the maze of central courts. According to an earlier petition in the Court of Wards, Caesar had become involved in the case when he, "in the right of the said Anne, his wyfe," entered into possession of the manors and lands, thus depriving the heirs to Robert Hogan. As was the case when the second Lady Caesar, Alice Dent, brought her valuable guardianship with her into marriage, Caesar was actively engaged in defending his wife's interests. In the first instance, clever dealing by Alice Dent's late husband had opened the way to her wealth by frustrating the inheritance of cousins. In the present instance, Lady Anne had done her own scheming.

Because Robert had been under twenty-one when he levied the fine, the claimants held that the transaction was void. They further claimed that Lady Caesar had fraudulently altered dates on key documents. Her counsel in a later action in Common Pleas, Serjeant Heneage Finch, the Recorder of London, summarized the long history of the litigation when he said, "This land in quest[ion] hath walked long in Westm[inster] Hall. My Lady Caesar hath ben questioned for it crimi-

nally in the Starre Chamber, there dismissed and freed by sentence—
M[ichaelmas] 12 Jac[obus]. She was after questioned in the Chancery
and the bill dismissed. And lately in Parliament and the bill throwne
out of the house. Now they end where they should have began, for we
are now here before your Lordships in the proper and natural court for
the final determining and setling of the rights of inheritance."[30] For
more than fifteen years the litigation continued in court after court,
with Lady Caesar prevailing in the end. The combination of Sir
Francis Bacon, her uncle and the Lord Chancellor during part of the
legal battle, and Sir Julius Caesar, her husband and the Master of the
Rolls, surely contributed significantly to the successful outcome of
"The Lady Caesar's Case."

Caesar's first two wives had borne his eight children: one daughter
and five sons lived to adulthood; two sons died in infancy. Later, in
1608, two of his adult children died. Dorcas, his only daughter and his
first wife's namesake, died at her home in Surrey of dropsy, being at
the time "23 years and 6 months old, and childless."[31] As sad as was
the natural death of Dorcas, it paled beside the murder of his namesake (nicknamed July) and eldest surviving son earlier in the year.
Both infant and spousal mortality were common, and the deaths of
two infant sons and two wives had occasioned timely mourning; but
the death of a twenty-year-old son at the hands of another young man
produced a different and longer-lasting grief that was compounded by
the death of his daughter.

The earliest evidence of young July is a Latin letter to his father
from Oxford in 1602. Full of filial affection and accompanied by a
verse of his own device, the letter was the unremarkable product of an
adolescent trying to please or placate a stern parent.[32] The elder Caesar packed him off to the Inner Temple in 1604, sending with him a
seven-part remembrance to the officers of the Inn. They were to enforce a Spartan intellectual and religious regimen as well as Caesar's
strict rules governing July's pocket money. In addition, July was to
foreswear prostitutes, gambling, and "all resorting . . . to the Fenscole
[fencing school]."[33] The young man never finished his studies at the
Inner Temple, for his father sent him off to the Continent a year later
to further his education and learn proper manners. It is likely that a
carousing son with the same name would have been an embarrassment to a careerist making the transition from judge to courtier.

In January 1606, July was in Paris with an attendant seeking chambers where their "English diet might be provided." The young man was said to be keeping good company with friendly Englishmen living in Paris. His attendant noted that July was not frequenting "the haunt of weomen," not because of his strong moral fiber nor in consideration of admonitions to stay away from whores, but simply because, being "a stranger in there [sic] language hee is also a stranger to them." July prayed regularly, read daily in Greek and French, and was quite put off by the sight of Catholic priests and their beads. Caesar was apparently concerned about the influence of the Catholic church on his son, but he was put at ease by the knowledge that the sight of popish practices bred contempt in July rather than a "desire to emulate them." After serving up a good report of July's behavior, his companion added that "beinge properly given to action hee is altogether unapt for contemplation." Caesar underscored these words and noted them in the margin.[34] Sir George Carew, the English ambassador in Paris, reported similarly a week or two later, adding that he was counseling with July whenever problems arose. "I will have a care upon him," Carew wrote, "and if I shall understand any thinge which shall geve me cause to doubt, I wil first deale with him my selfe, to reforme it, and after informe you ife need shall require."[35] His being "properly given to action" led July to depart for the Netherlands by the summer. Writing to Caesar in August, he told him that he had joined Sir Horace Vere's company of soldiers. It was probably helpful that Vere was related by marriage. July asked his father to continue his allowance of £10 per month until the following spring because he had a petition before the cabinet of the States for a commission to organize a company with himself as captain.[36] Nothing more remains about this venture, but if it did succeed it was only short-lived. By 1607, July was in Padua, a student in his grandfather's university.

Apart from his university studies, July attended the "Fenscole" forbidden by his father when he was in London. At the school, in January 1608, he suffered what was called "an unlucky accident." To make matters worse, the accident looked very much like homicide, and the church in Padua refused to bury July because, by their reckoning, he was a "Calvinist." Sir Henry Wotton, the English ambassador to Venice, objected so strongly that the Podesta of Padua, a city under Venetian rule, ordered a public funeral over the objections of the ecclesiastical authorities. In the meantime, however, the man who had killed July had taken sanctuary in the church. Further inquiry revealed that the situation was hardly as clear-cut as it first had appeared. July had contributed to the fracas and shared in the responsibility.[37] Because the English ambassador was so persistent, the Venetian authorities ordered the Podesta to expedite the case and to inform them if he required additional powers.[38]

The subsequent investigation confirmed that July had been responsible for much of what happened when he was killed. During a fencing bout with one Thomio Brochetta of Padua, July had been slightly injured in the hand. Brochetta had refused to apologize for the wound, and July, in turn, had threatened to kill him. A little later, when Brochetta was leaving the fencing school, he was met in the street by young Caesar, who fired a pistol at him and missed. The Paduan, in turn, drew his sword and mortally wounded his opponent. The Podesta ended his report to the Venetian Cabinet with the conclusion that this was "an unfortunate case, brought about by the deceased, as is clear from the enquiry." Wotton was undeterred by these findings. He insisted on a full-scale homicide prosecution that would lead to Brochetta's being ordered to surrender to prison.[39] In addition to Wotton's influence in Venice, the Podesta had also to face angry delegations of English students in Padua who insisted that Brochetta had murdered July Caesar outright. They further charged that a local church had secretly disposed of July's body without burial. The Podesta insisted that everything that could be done had been done; no further action was possible unless the students could prove their charges.[40]

When Brochetta finally surrendered himself to the town authorities, he advised the prosecutor that he wished to defend himself *per patrem*, his right to be tried under Paduan law by a jury of his fellow Paduans rather than by Venetian law. The practical importance of Brochetta's request was that the trial would be held in Padua in the open rather than in Venice in secret, and that local witnesses would carry the day for him. The defendant and his allies were popular local men who would not be likely to be found guilty in their own city.[41] Wotton objected strenuously to the *per patrem* proceedings and submitted a petition to the Doge asking that the Podesta be authorized to proceed in secret to examine both Brochetta and the witnesses to July's death.[42]

Caesar learned of July's death from several sources, including the

Venetian ambassador, Zorzi Giustiniani, who paid an official visit on behalf of the Doge and Senate. He had expressed Venice's condolences, but in such a way as to suggest that the young Caesar's own vitality and high spirits had contributed to his death. Caesar answered that he had sent his son to Padua to learn at the university and to improve his manners. Far from being angry, the bereaved father expressed his gratitude and devotion to the Doge; Wotton conveyed the same sentiment a month later in an audience in Venice. In his report to his principals, Giustiniani mentioned that Caesar was a Venetian subject by virtue of his father's birth who had "managed so well" that he had achieved high rank in the crown's service. This datum was surely considered in the calculus for future action.[43]

The Doge, for his part, had installed a new Podesta in Padua whose investigations probably got as close as was possible to what actually happened. July had defeated Brochetta in the contest but had been challenged to another. In the course of the second bout, Brochetta had broken the rules of fencing by drawing blood. He had wounded July on the left hand; July, in reply, had hurled a dagger that had missed its mark. The fencing master had stepped in at this point to bar young Caesar from the school. Fortunately, an English doctor had been able to stop July's extensive bleeding. The following morning, July had returned to the fencing master's house armed with a pistol to await Brochetta. When they finally met, a shot was fired — accidentally, according to some witnesses — and the Englishman slipped on the ice; Brochetta drew his sword at that moment and killed him. The Podesta, in reporting these findings to Venice, noted that the prosecutor was allowing the *per patrem* defense, although every effort was being made to proceed otherwise to satisfy the English.[44]

The Doge was clearly tiring of the whole affair. By the time that Wotton's secretary came before the Venetian cabinet, he was expressing the Ambassador's gratitude for their having revoked the *per patrem*; the culprits were on trial, according to Venetian law, before the Podesta. He was advised that the Doge had intervened to please Wotton and the English. There was little more the English could hope to achieve by applying pressure to the Venetians.[45] Throughout the investigation of July's death and the trial of the accused, the Podesta had seemed more interested in preserving the peace in Padua than in sorting out the circumstances surrounding the brawl. Fortunately for Caesar, his old friend, Sir Henry Wotton, was an ambassador with a reputation for relentless pursuit of justice in behalf of Englishmen who were robbed or murdered, and the Venetians did capitulate to his demands.[46] But, as important as his intervention was, equally important was the fact that Caesar was accounted a Venetian subject with high rank in the service of an ally that Venice wished to please.

The end of the incident was reported to Caesar a year later. Wotton wrote that an Englishman in Padua, one George Rooke of Kent, had retained the services of an Italian informer, who had been sentenced to banishment for a term of years. The informer watched Brochetta until he ventured "beyond the boundes limited in his sentence: in which case hee was condemnable to the Galies." The informer had been asking Wotton for money but was stalled while Rooke gathered up some necessary legal papers relating to the case for Wotton to dispatch to Caesar. He had wanted to send along at the same time, "for your especiall comfort, a Greeke Testament wherein your sonne before his meales was wont everyday to reade two chapters, as I am since informed, which giveth me this assurance that though his end was fatal and sodayne yet he had always good thoughtes aboute him even in the midst of some imperfections rather of his age than of his nature." Unfortunately, the Inquisitor would not surrender the book to him. Wotton had "urged [him] so farr bothe by privat and publique meanes as that he hath been forced to denie the havinge of it."[47]

Young Julius Caesar had been caught up in a series of circumstances illustrative of the problems of early seventeenth-century English travelers. He met the hostility of local folk toward foreigners, his body was refused a decent burial for religious reasons, and, even after his death, the Inquisition was investigating his possession of a Greek Testament. In Italy two vain and stubborn young men had clashed, with fatal consequences, in a university city. July Caesar was killed; it could as easily have been Brochetta.

Although his two eldest children were dead, Caesar still had a large family of boys who were closely allied with their father as they pursued their own careers. As the years passed, he could well reflect on having escaped the fate of his friend, Sir Thomas Mildmay, who had been slandered and abused by a son on whom he had settled a sizable portion of land. Writing to Caesar, he had wished that "if you be a father of chyldren as I ame, I praye God give them grace to use you with the reverent respecte and dewtie that belongeth to a father, and that shall theye be comforte."[48] The first of the remaining sons was

Charles; he was followed by John, Thomas, and Robert. Providing for his sons was the central focus of Caesar's career agenda.

Charles Caesar, the next oldest son after July, followed a career pattern similar to his father's. Born in 1589, he matriculated in Magdalen College, Oxford, in 1602 and proceeded to B.A. in 1606 as a member of All Souls College and then to M.A. and B.C.L. in 1608. James I had intervened on his behalf in 1605 when he was seeking a fellowship in All Souls, but he did not become a fellow until 1607. Like his father, Charles studied law in Paris; in 1612 he was awarded his Doctor of Civil Law at Oxford. His father's standing in the Inner Temple led to his being granted a special admission in 1610. He was also associated with Doctors' Commons in 1613 and accorded full admission in 1623.[49] On 6 October 1613 he was knighted in the Gallery at Westminster in the presence of Privy Council, and a fortnight later he married a bride worth £5,000.[50] She was Anne Vanlore, daughter of the wealthy Dutch merchant Sir Peter Vanlore. Through this marriage Charles came to be closely associated with the Sackville family, his brother-in-law being Sir Thomas Glemham.[51] Had Caesar and Lady Alice had their way, Charles would have married his stepsister, Elizabeth Dent. Not only did she have wealth from her own father's estate, but she was also the recent widow of Sir Francis Vere, with a life interest in his estate. A month before Charles's wedding to his first wife, Anne Vanlore, his parents were working hard to keep other suitors away from Elizabeth for his sake.[52]

A well-connected young man, Charles appears to have been an agreeable person who was welcomed by older members of the legal and ecclesiastical establishment. On one occasion, he and his uncle, Dean Henry Caesar, were at the Bishop of Winchester's table for dinner when the Bishop raised a cup to toast the "courteous" Sir Charles, saying, "*Vivat Carolus Caesar et non moritat.*"[53] Two years later, in 1620, Justice Davies, having completed the Western Circuit with Charles in his entourage, wrote to Caesar reporting his esteem for the young man. "His discretion and sweetness of manners hath caused everyman to take care of his entertainment everywhere, which did deminish my care, but did encrease my love towards him."[54] When he was on the Continent, Charles enjoyed Wotton's confidence. The ambassador entrusted a confidential packet to him concerning papal spies rather than send it through ordinary diplomatic channels.[55] Later in the same year, Wotton sent home, by way of Charles, a model of "that engine which will cleanse our river of the softer matter."[56] Like those of his father before him, Charles's connections also reached into the City. Following the death of Anne Vanlore, herself the daughter of a merchant stranger, Charles married Jane Barkham in 1626. Her father, Sir Edward Barkham, had been Lord Mayor in 1622.[57]

A civilian like his father, Charles was employed principally in the ecclesiastical and admiralty courts and in Chancery. Admitted a Master in Chancery in 1615, he also served on admiralty and piracy commissions in London and Middlesex. His career was clearly directed toward the ecclesiastical courts, as was indicated by his frequent inclusion in High Commission from 1620 forward. In 1627, when Archbishop Abbott was excluded for his criticism of Charles I's government, Charles was named to the commission exercising the archiepiscopal jurisdiction. In the commission it was noted that the lawyers who were included along with the bishops were noted for their being learned in ecclesiastical law. According to the commission, Charles was already the Judge of the Court of Audience and the Master of Faculties for life.[58] Here he remained until three years following his father's death, when he became Master of the Rolls himself at a reputed cost of £15,000. In addition to holding judicial offices and serving on commissions, Charles was a Member of Parliament once, sitting in 1614 for Weymouth and Melcombe Regis, Dorset, the former seat of the late Thomas Howard, viscount Bindon.[59]

Early in his adult life, Charles began to accumulate lands and manors. Following its purchase by his father, Bennington Manor, Broadwater Hundred, Hertfordshire, was conveyed to him in 1614 by Frances, countess of Clanricarde.[60] Bennington Place, as the house that Charles built was known, remained the seat of the Caesar family into the early eighteenth century when, after a half century of declining financial and political fortune, the family suffered ruin.[61] From Anne Vanlore, Charles gained an interest in her father's manor of Speen (also known as Speenhamland), Faircross Hundred, Berkshire.[62] His uncle, Henry Caesar, who had no children, provided for Charles in his will: Toseland Manor, Huntingtonshire, was purchased by Henry in 1624 and was settled on Charles later that year along with the manor of Butlers in the same county. He came into possession in 1636 when Henry died.[63] Spurred on perhaps by the estate awaiting him at his uncle's death, Charles assembled his own portfolio of property in Huntingtonshire. He purchased both Rippington Manor Farm and the manor of Great Gransden, to which it belonged in 1631. A few years later, after coming into possession of Toseland, he began carefully to assemble the remainder of the manors in Toseland Hundred. When he died in 1642, he had united Butlers with Yelling Greys, thus restoring the integrity of an ancient manor.

John, Robert, and Thomas were Caesar's "second" family, being the sons of Lady Alice and nearly a decade younger than the youngest of Dorcas Caesar's children. John was born in 1592 and Thomas in 1600, both at St. Katharine's. Robert was born in 1602.[64] In 1613 John was sent from Eton up to Magdalen College, Oxford.[65] We next encounter John in 1617 on a visit to Scotland with James I. On 29 June of that year he was knighted in Edinburgh, where he "took his oath of knighthood in the kinges presence, with all other Honorable Ceremonies according to the Custome of Scotland."[66] Caesar settled property on John as early as 1612, although he did not come into possession of Hyde Hall, Hertfordshire, until the first year of the reign of Charles I.[67] In Caesar's will John is identified as resident of "Hidehall, Herts."[68] The manor of Reed, Odsey Hundred, Hertfordshire, was also settled on John at an early date, but, again, possession was not realized until 1 Charles I. It appears that John maintained property interests along with the family of his stepmother, for in 1668 he and an Anne Hungate sold Reed to a William Newland.[69] The remainder of Odsey Hundred, Caesar's concentration of wealth in Hertfordshire, was granted to John Caesar in 1633. The grant was probably conditional, however, since Odsey Hundred appeared in Caesar's *Inquisition Post Mortem*.[70]

Thomas Caesar and his younger brother Robert were at Oxford at the same time. Following his characteristic practice, Caesar drafted detailed instructions for their behavior away from home and had them delivered to their attendant, John Luggar. Thomas remained at university longer than Robert, and, three years later, another set of orders was prepared.[71] In the following year, with Thomas removed to Cambridge, a remembrance was prepared by someone who had been watching him (perhaps Luggar) in anticipation of Caesar's writing to the warden of his new college. Thomas was to keep to his prayers, disputations, and exercises; to have no money in his purse, as it was the source of trouble; to be denied the extension of credit when purchasing beer and wine; and to take care that he wore only appropriate clothing. A more serious issue concerned the whereabouts of a ring:

he was to be examined as to "what is become of his seale gold ring with his armes engraven thereon geven by H. Dods." Finally, the warden was to be advised, "yf Mr. Thomas may have his will he often will ride abroade unto the bordering gent[ry]. He is with all acquainted and will carrie thether unruly company to the great trouble of the same gent[ry], and will not returne againe at his appointed tymes." The warden was, therefore, charged with restraining Thomas's liberty and with taking a weekly account of his studies.[72]

Several years later, his behavior apparently mended, Thomas was pursuing an advanced academic career. When he proceeded to his doctorate in Cambridge University, John Collins, the Provost of Kings College and a Regius Professor, wrote to the elder Caesar in the spring of 1632 advising him of Thomas's outstanding intellectual qualities. Collins indicated that he would be pleased to accede to such patrons as Henry and Julius Caesar by according a high place in the College to Thomas: "I see not but Mr. Dr. Caesar, your honors sons deserts of schollership, and his Universitie of Oxford, which ought to be deare to us, may challendge all and more then is done by men hitherto." A few days later, one Frances Hughes informed Caesar that the doctorate had been awarded with extraordinary honors and that Collins would shortly name Thomas the "Senior Doctor," the highest honor that he could bestow.[73]

We encountered Robert Caesar, the youngest of Caesar's children, in an earlier discussion of the Six Clerks in Chancery.[74] His training prepared him for service in the Chancery hierarchy. His tenants of the demesne lands of Barwick in Elmet, Yorkshire, forced him to appear before Council because, having surrendered their lands to him before Charles I's accession so that Robert could gain a new lease, the tenants had yet to receive their estates back again. In the meantime, Robert had sold the leases to a Mr. Goodrick. The result was that Robert was scolded for his maltreatment of the tenants, and Goodrick was ordered to pay them the amount of their losses with interest "after six in the hundreth."[75]

Upon his death, Caesar owned an extensive portfolio of property throughout the southeast. The *Inquisition Post Mortem*, taken at Hatfield, Hertfordshire, revealed that he held estates in that county as well as in Lincolnshire, Kent, and Middlesex.[76] In addition, his will noted three houses, one in Hackney, Middlesex, another in Tremnall,

Essex, and a third in Bradenham, Norfolk.[77] Although we lack estate records—a regrettable gap in Caesar's otherwise voluminous muniments—we can understand why. Charles Caesar inherited the bulk of his father's estate, while other brothers enjoyed estates in specific parcels. Over successive generations, the several estate records were separated from Caesar's political and personal papers. Nonetheless, we can identify most of Caesar's holdings and determine how some of them came into his possession.

In Lincolnshire Caesar enjoyed possession of the Manors of Linwood, Bullington House, East (or Market) Raysen, and Muston Chantry in the Manors of Leake and Leverton. In Kent he was seised of the Manor of East Green, and in Middlesex he possessed a house on the corner of Humberton Street, Hackney. Hertfordshire, however, was where the most extensive of his holdings were located: the Hundred of Edwinstrey and Odsey, the Manor of Challers and Chamberlain, and the Manor of Sanson, both manors being in Reed Parish. Of all of these estates, only Odsey reveals the traces of Caesar's ownership in the surviving records. An indenture of sale in 1613 between William Whittmore and James Werdon, one party, and Caesar, the other, together with a fine and an attested receipt from John Caesar a half century later, attest to the long tenure of Caesars in the manor.[78]

To appreciate the scale of Caesar's accomplishment, we must examine carefully how he amassed the fortune that he possessed when he died. If we look for a moment at the Hospital of St. Katharine, we can see how his own estates became commingled with the wealth of the institution that he represented. He collected the rents of his tenants, within and without the precincts of the Hospital, but he enjoyed the use of this revenue until such time as he had to pay it out to the poor of St. Katharine's. When his brother Sir Thomas Caesar wrote to him on one occasion about the state of Quarly Woods, Hampshire, it was clear that he was treating the woods as Caesar's own property. This was all the more questionable when we realize that the manor of Quarly belonged to St. Katharine's.[79]

Apart from Caesar's large interests in Hertfordshire, Lincolnshire was the other basis of his landed wealth. As early as 1604, he was awarded a reversionary interest in the manor of Linwood, Lincolnshire, and in 1605 the entire manor was his.[80] A letter from Thomas Caesar the year before suggests that Caesar may already have had an interest in the Lincolnshire manors of Boston and Southickham, but his possession of Linwood marked his great entrance into the Lincoln-shire county community. Shortly after receiving the grant to Linwood, Caesar found himself with the problems of an absentee landlord. Sir Nicholas Saunderson, the sheriff, wrote to Caesar asking him to re-tain one William Calverley as manorial bailiff.[81] Earlier that year, San-derson had been busy finding a suitable property for Caesar to pur-chase: the house he had wanted initially was thought to be too expen-sive. Sanderson had told him at the time to hurry up and make a purchase because there were many in Lincolnshire who wanted Cae-sar to join in their number.[82]

While most of Caesar's wealth was revealed in the *Inquisition Post Mortem*, it appears that some lands in Staffordshire were missed, by inadvertence, ignorance (the inquisition was taken in Hertfordshire), or collusion. The manors of Blurton, Trentham, Hanchurch, and Clayton, Staffordshire, were not included in the inquisition even though they had been devised to Caesar for a term of 99 years if Julius, Charles, or Dorcas "shall live so longe."[83] Although July and Dorcas were dead, Charles was very much alive when his father died.

Not all of Caesar's wealth was in a form that he could bequeath to his heirs. For instance, the house at East Bradenham, Norfolk, be-longed not to Caesar but to Lady Anne. It obviously was not his to de-vise, although he enjoyed its use during his married life. Likewise, he owned ecclesiastical livings such as the advowson of Nutfield Church, Reigate Hundred, Surrey. He had received a grant from Henry Bruton and Walter Cole, and in 1626 he had presented it as he saw fit.[84] Throughout his long career, Caesar had seemed intent on grabbing what he could. Yet on closer inspection he proved to be a prudent pro-vider whose principal interest was in caring for his family and perpetu-ating his line. His concern for the well-being of his sons was a partic-ularly notable motif that colored the latter part of his life. He patiently amassed the money necessary to provide secure futures for the next generation of English Caesars.

The three houses noted in Caesar's will contained books and per-sonal effects that he left specifically to his sons Charles, John, and Robert.[85] To Charles in particular he bequeathed his "written booke in folio called Polyanthea Caesario . . . and my Enchiridion written by my owne hand in 16° and the one moyety of all my written bookes being at the tyme of my death either in my study att Hackney, or in my twoe great presses att the Rolles or in my studie there and likewise

my written booke of the Tenn Commandements, the Lordes Prayer
and the Three Creedes in Six Languages, with divers Psalmes of St.
David in Latten and *verba verbi incarnati* in Greeke written all with
my owne hand in 16°."

To John, Caesar left "all of my bookes being either in the cupboard
or in anie part of my Chaple of my house at Hackney to remaine to
that Howse during the continuance of that House and Chapel in my
name, or myne heir forever." Robert, the Six Clerk, received the most
appropriate bequests of all. To him "I bequeath my written book
called the Register of the Chauncery, my last Book of Informacions
both written and in 4ᵀᴼ . . . and the other moyety of the said written
bookes being in my study att Hackney or in my study at the Roules,
or in either of my two presses att the Rolles standing in a chamber
commonly called the Intero Chamber, or elsewhere being at the tyme
of my death." The remainder of his valuables, wherever they might be
found, were to be conveyed to Lady Anne for her use.

Shortly before his death, Caesar had made a more substantial provision for Lady Anne. When they had married, Caesar's estate was
fully committed to his children. There was no property left for him to
create a jointure, nor did Lady Anne have a dower interest in Caesar's
lands. Thus, he placed £2,000 in trust with her kinsmen Sir Edward
Bacon of Redgrave, Suffolk, and Sir Roger Townsend of East Rayn-
ham, Norfolk. They were to be true and faithful custodians of the
money, and on the direction of Lady Anne or her assigns they were to
pay it over immediately.[86]

A later seventeenth-century account of Caesar's life adverted to his
prodigious bounty, given in such abundance "that he might seem to
be Almoner-general to the Nation."[87] Indeed, Caesar had a reputation
for great generosity, although I have never seen direct evidence to support it. Nonetheless, it would not have been uncharacteristic of him
to give away great sums of money to aid the poor. His will alone suggests the extent of his benefactions. It was not uncommon to make bequests to the poor, but Caesar managed to omit no one. To the three
Brothers and three Sisters of the Hospital of St. Katharine he left £3
each. To the ten poor Beadeswomen or Almswomen of St. Katharine's
he left 40s., and to the very poorest denizens of the precincts of St.
Katharine he left £10, to be distributed by the Overseers of the Poor.
Caesar left further bequests for the sick of the Hospitals of St. Bartholomew and St. Thomas; for the inhabitants of the two Counters

of the City of London; for the prisoners of the Fleet, Newgate, Ludgate, King's Bench, Marshalsea, White Lion, and the Gatehouse of Westminster; and for the inmates of Bedlam: £5 to each institution.[88] In addition, a year or two before his death, Caesar made a gift of plate to Great Gransden Church, Toseland Hundred, Huntingtonshire.[89]

Caesar died on 18 April 1636; a notation in Justice Hutton's diary recorded the event.[90] The following day, he was buried next to the altar in Great St. Helen's, Bishopsgate, according to his wishes. He was surrounded on every side by the tombs of his mother, siblings, children, and friends.[91] Prior to his death, Caesar had installed his funeral monument in the church. Fashioned like a table, the monument was made of black marble. Lying atop the table was a parchment-colored stone carved to look like a deed or obligation. The words carved in Latin on the "document" spoke of the deceased's engagement to pay his debt of mortality to nature whenever God would be pleased to summon him. The parchment was fashioned with a pendant seal whose ribbons had been cut, signifying that the debt had been paid. Across the bottom of the tabletop, in a separate cartouche, were inscribed the words *Irrotulatur Caelo*, the fine conceit of a contented man.[92]

XII

‎𝔒𝔄

Epilogue

ADVANCING AGE is frequently the parent of candid restrospection, whereas the death of contemporaries focuses the mind on one's own mortality. By the time that William Herbert, earl of Pembroke, died in 1630, Caesar was over seventy, and the "most excellent sermon" preached at the earl's funeral caused him to note a particularly trenchant passage: "The bodie of man is nought els but a bellowes full of winde, a bag full of dung, a bottle full of smoke."[1] Four years later, when Coke died, an even older Caesar cast his mind back over his own career as he prepared a curriculum vitae devoted to the high points in his long life.[2] Births, marriages, deaths, and the acquisition of office filled the pages. This was hardly surprising, but it is noteworthy that he included very little else about himself and his life and times. Sensing his own mortality in Coke's death, he reflected his life's priorities in his choice of important moments.

Caesar's father had died when he was still quite young, and, as the eldest surviving child, he had been parent to his siblings; as father to his own children and stepchildren, he had arranged their marriages, assisted their careers, and grieved their deaths. And as a lawyer, judge, minister, and minor courtier he made his place and amassed a fortune that he invested in country properties, which he gave to his children. Yet Caesar never aspired to a great country seat nor to an imposing urban edifice. In short, his career was ambitious but realistic. It was in the service of his family, and his family was the center of his life. He brushed the skirts of greatness daily but did not try to achieve a greatness that was beyond his reach. Although this was doubtless not a unique career pattern, it is the only one of its kind that can be documented so thoroughly.

It would be a marvelous stroke of good fortune to discover some writing of Caesar's from early in his career indicating the goals he wished to reach and his view of the world he occupied. Without such a document, we have to look at his behavior to uncover the clues to his early plans. But we can also refer to his commonplace book for the maxims and aphorisms that formed his early mentality and continued to attract his attention during his mature years. It is here that we find, in an early entry, an apt epitome of his behavior throughout his career: "It is better for a man continually to keape himself cheefe in his own place, though it be inferiour, then to leave the same to make himself second to a greater."[3] Throughout his life, Caesar habitually sought preferment in those offices wherein he was effectively in charge. Though Judge of the Admiralty or Master of the Rolls might have been less important places than Chancellor of the Exchequer, they offered the great advantage of being relatively independent of their superiors. In the Exchequer, the Chancellor was tied to the Lord Treasurer, succeeding as he succeeded, failing as he failed.

Caesar's behavior provides a number of indications of his priorities. We know that he was actively engaged in the lives of his surviving siblings; we also know that he never married a maiden, always a widow with resources. We know that he knew the value of managing a property portfolio: he was Master of St. Katharine's Hospital, and he had asked Walsingham to petition the queen for the headship of any one of a number of educational and charitable corporations with widespread real estate holdings. We also know that he was particularly single-minded in his pursuit of higher place in the Chancery establishment. And, of especial interest, we know that he invested heavily in his family's future by giving handsomely to the Inner Temple and receiving, in turn, the right of appointment to a number of chambers in Caesar's Building. As individual data, these mean less than they do in aggregate. They suggest that he was devoted to his family, that he was certain where he and they would have the best opportunities to prosper, and that he was gaining experience in sound investment practices.

When his sons reached the age to leave home for Inns or university, Caesar provided exacting and demanding guides for their moral and scholarly discipline. When they were ready to embark on their careers, he assisted them through his own patronage. His daughter and step daughters married well in unions that benefitted the family as much as the women.

If Caesar's career goals were to advance his family, the test of his success must be the balance sheet at the end of his life. His eldest surviving son, Charles, himself a senior civil lawyer, was well established both in the ecclesiastical courts and in Chancery. Within a very few years he would occupy the Rolls Chapel as his father had done. His next son, Robert, was also an officer of Chancery and would be a Six Clerk. John, the youngest, with his doctorate behind him, was a scholar. Each son had been provided an estate and appeared to have been prospering when Sir Julius died. Judging by these results, it would seem that Caesar had been remarkably successful.

As a young man, Caesar had written in his commonplace book: "Those things bee most worthily termed the best matter of honour, which die with the partie, and yet make his line through honorable remembrance, though hee have no successour but the common weale, which is generally surest, bycause private succession in blood is oftime some blemish." Next to this passage taken from Richard Mulcaster, Caesar later drew a firm line in the margin.[4] It is an interesting passage when we consider that Caesar allegedly declined a barony in order to remain Master of the Rolls. Had he accepted it, his son Charles would have inherited a title but no Chancery preferment. By keeping the Master's place, Charles and Robert were able to advance in Chancery. In the calculation that apparently underlay Caesar's decisions we have an epitome of his priorities and values. Caesar seemed to place greater value on the worth and the prospects of the office in hand than on the honor of a peerage.

From the earliest days of his career (indeed, from the circle of godparents surrounding him at baptism), Caesar depended on the good offices of others for advancement. He was client, in succession, to the major patrons of his time. From Burghley to Salisbury to the Howards and Buckingham, Caesar was assisted in his climb to high office; his children, in turn, were served by their father's connections. But a curious pattern in this patronage bears explanation. In the Elizabethan years, especially, Caesar was Burghley's client, but he was also patronized by Nottingham, Walsingham, and, sometimes, Essex. We have anatomized the ways that he used simultaneous patronage, always being careful not to offend or dishonor them by playing them off against one another. This is a pattern that merits further examination in future studies, for it adds depth to an otherwise two-dimensional picture of patron-client relationships.

While Caesar was Chancellor of the Exchequer, Dorset and Salisbury were his benefactors, and he surely courted Northampton after the Lord Treasurer's death. But at this stage in his life there is a marked absence of the rich evidence we find in the earlier part of his career. Actually, the last significant advantage that a patron provided him was the office of Master of the Rolls in reversion, and that was done by Salisbury in 1611. After Caesar became Master of the Rolls, it is nearly impossible to analyze his patrons' activities in his behalf. To be sure, he married into Bacon's family, and we know that Buckingham was of assistance to him on occassion, but Buckingham also tried to get Caesar out of the Rolls in favor of someone else. Given the political realities of early Stuart England, it is inconceivable that he could survive without patronal assistance.

Two answers to the question of his patrons in later life suggest themselves. In the first place, his correspondence indicates that he was on good terms with a host of influential courtiers. For instance, Buckingham, viscount Brackley, and Lord Charles Herbert each wrote to thank him for small favors, good advice, and "his swete nature."[5] In each of the cases, he was doing something for a patron, and this is important. It would seem that he was continuing to use multiple patrons, doubtless with the same caution he had exercised as a younger man, but that he positioned himself so that he would not have to make requests. This is the second answer to our question. If he was able to hang on tenaciously to his place in the Rolls with no ambitions beyond serving his children's interests, if he maintained either a facile deceptiveness or a strict neutrality in the contests among factions, and if he was available to be of assistance to all, then perhaps he could remain on the sidelines of the patronal arena. Because we are accustomed to Stuart courtiers and officeholders in ceaseless pursuit of advantage, we have to readjust our sights when we encounter one whose ambition seemed to be no more than to be left alone with what he had. But we must not forget that his property interest in the Master of the Rolls' office protected him as much as did any patron. Caesar's career is not an important new source of illumination regarding the patterns of patronage, about which there is already a rich literature, but it does

show us one officeholder who managed to escape the pattern to prosper on his own.

Having examined Caesar as client, we turn to his role as patron.
Until he entered Exchequer, there was no patronage for him to exercise. In the Admiralty all appointments were in the Lord Admiral's gift.
The little patronage that might have been associated with the Court
of Requests would have been in the gift of the Lord Privy Seal or the
crown. Exchequer certainly opened possibilities, but Caesar kept no
record of his use of his own patronage. There were clerkships and col-
lectorships both in London and in the counties, and Caesar had access to the presentation of some of them. But, since he kept no record
and there is no mention made in his correspondence, it is likely that
the Lord Treasurer or the king controlled most of these offices. The
one documented instance of patronage, or, at least, influence, that he
exercised in Exchequer concerned the appointment of Thomas Caesar, his brother, Puisne Baron of the Exchequer Court. The office was
not in his gift, but his stepdaughter Mary Dent was married to Sir
Henry Savile, whose late brother, Sir John Savile, had been a Baron
until his death in 1607. Furthermore, as Chancellor, Caesar had influence with Salisbury and, through him, with the king.

The picture changed when Caesar became Master of the Rolls. As
we have seen, he had more Chancery places in his gift than did the
king and the Lord Chancellor combined. The value was great: in
1624 the office and its reversion were said to have been the subject of
a £10,000 offer. And fifteen years later, when Sir Charles Caesar
purchased the Rolls, the price had risen to £15,000 without the
reversion.[6] While a part of the calculation of value was based on fee
revenue, a larger part was based on the value of the offices in the
Master's gift. Once again, it would have been useful to find a list or
account of Caesar's, but he was no longer as thorough as he had
been as a young judge, when he kept journals of the work he did in
the Admiralty and of the fees owed him. The only patronage that we
know that he exercised benefited his sons. Thus, we must conclude
that, in his later career, Caesar was limited in his activities as patron
to the official patronage belonging to the Master of the Rolls. This
yielded revenue, but, unlike the personal patronage of most courtiers, it did not advance his standing in the world. His efforts were
concentrated on preserving what he had and on using it to increase

his fortune and advance his family. Even when we read of gratitude of the authorities at Cambridge for his support and assistance, his efforts in the university's behalf had been expended to assist one of his sons.

As a young man, Caesar was decidedly religious. He kept his commonplace book in John Foxe's *Pandectae Locorum Communium*, and many of his entries were from the German-Swiss reformers and Calvin. He had grown up with the community of puritans of a Calvinist nature who were associated with the Lok family. He translated a commentary of Beza, he valued his first wife for her religious qualities, and he was clearly biased in sympathy with the Protestant conventiclers brought before him in the Bishop of London's commissary court. In his early twenties he read and marked Stephen Gosson's *A Schole of Abuse*; the passage on theatrical plays is illustrative: "Plaies are the inventions of the Devill; the offerings of idolatry; the pomps of Worldlings; the blossomes of Vanitie; the roote of Apostacy; the foode of iniquity, riot, and adultery. Detest them."[7] Caesar subscribed to the idea that a godly education was the key to the reformed spirit, and we see this reflected in his instructions to his sons when they were away from home. They included admonitions to pray regularly, to read scripture daily, to learn by the good example of their superiors, and to conduct themselves with moral probity. In short, Caesar was a puritan Anglican: he was clearly Protestant, in sympathy with many of the tenets of the Puritan sectaries, but always within the fold of the Church of England. He was religious in a way that was more than conventional but less than excessive, and he viewed his world with a nigh-Calvinist fatalism. God's will would be done, and it was beyond the power of man to do anything about it. Thus, it was not surprising to find him writing a doxology at the end of his copy of the *Book of Orders* when he believed that God's will was made manifest. In like manner, his prayer that the pharaoh James would send a wise Joseph to set the crown's finances right was less a plea to the king than to God, for God alone could find the solution to their problems, in this case in the form of the earl of Salisbury.[8]

Toward the end of his life, Caesar made a number of entries in the margin of his commonplace book that reflect on his religious interests as he grew older. In 1623 he noted that he had read William Crompton's comparison of the writings of Augustine with those of both papists and Protestants, along with John Walker's *Spectrum pro Papistis et Puritanis.*[9] He had read and noted Lord Mansfield's "Contemplatio mortis et immortalitatis," and in the following year he noted a sermon preached by Dr. Wren, the Master of Peterhouse, entitled "De obedentia deo et principibus" and Samuel Rowland's *De Mundi Vanitate.*[10] And one of his last entries dealt with a tract published at Cambridge in 1635 in which the author held that the pope was not the antichrist and that the antichrist had not yet come.[11]

The same fatalism that characterized his religious outlook was reflected in Caesar's approach to secular problem solving. He did not imagine that he would develop new answers to the questions that he faced, but he rarely shrank from trying to institute changes or make estimates of the future based on his recourse to authority—in this instance, antiquarian research. It was remediation rather than innovation that he held to be the most important. One commonplaced entry, made in his youth, was perhaps a source of this attitude: "In reforming thinges of common practise, the cleering of the olde, which is abused, and not the breeding of the new, which is untried, is the natural amendment."[12] As for the value of the published authorities, Caesar would have agreed with the spirit of a letter written to him in 1629 by Sir Simonds D'Ewes, who said that the observations he was making were grounded in "some strange if not miraculous prophesies or predictions (choose which title you please) out of our moore ancient and modern writers."[13] Caesar shared a similar penchant for mining the writings of authorities to determine appropriate courses of action. Whether he was dealing with his notions of the proper relationship between the Lord Admiral and the Judge of the Admiralty or with an analysis of the undertreasurer's commission, Caesar's authority was the ancient record. In his defense of the Court of Requests, Caesar gathered together an opaque collection of precedents pointing to the identity of the court and Privy Council; he adduced his own precedents to overcome the countervailing precedents advanced by his common-law critics.[14] In each of these instances, the answers to the questions at hand lay hidden; it was Caesar's task to bring them to light.

When we consider that, from the early 1580's until 1636, Caesar was never far from the center of power, it is notable that he was not particularly interested in political theory, except when the resolution of an issue directly affected his own career and theoretical arguments might help him. We know that he read works of philosophy and politics in addition to religion and literature, but Caesar tended to focus on answering the question at hand rather than on political implication and speculation. But a significant exception arose in the summer of 1610 when he wrote his critique of the Great Contract.[15] Here he did expand on the political consequences of the proposal before Parliament, and with notable perception, but he broke no new ground.

Although not a theorist, Caesar entertained deeply held political convictions characterized by a conventional commitment to good order and the rule of a strong monarchy. He made an early notation in his commonplace book that "it behoveth a prince to know to whom hee commiteth authority, least the sword of justice, appointed to chasten the lewde, wound the good: and where good subjects are wronged, evill officers receive the benefit and theire soveraigne beare the blame."[16] When the queen's prerogative powers were vested in experienced professionals, such as judges, they were protected from abuse by competing courtiers, and when the monarch was clearly above the political arena, her majesty was enhanced. But if she permitted her prerogative to be exercised capriciously, she invited political trouble. Arguing the merits of a limited prerogative, Caesar sounded like a Huguenot constitutionalist, which was not surprising since he had studied law in France in the decade following the St. Bartholomew's Day Massacre. Much later in his life, when Caesar expressed his delight with Charles I's restoration of formal order at Court, he was responding to his nearly instinctive commitment to good order that he associated with constitutional limitations on the unrestricted prerogative.

Before we leave this assessment of Caesar's political ideas, we must note that he was possessed of a peculiar ideology to which he was passionately devoted. He was determined that the civil lawyers should and would survive in England. When he had been in the admiralty he had tried to persuade Charles Howard that the Lord Admiral was crucial to the survival of the community of English civilians; he was their protector and guardian because it was only in his court that they could find employment in significant numbers. Nearly fifty years later, only three years before his death, Caesar was still active in the same cause. At his behest, Privy Council drafted an order in the king's name in behalf of the Doctors of Civil and Canon Law. The order held that the kingdom needed to provide reasonable comfort and encouragement to the civil lawyers, and to that end, "his majesty, according to the intentions of his father of ever blessed memory, and to the end that the same may take effect hath resolved hereafter, he will have all places that shall become vacant of Maisters of Requests to his majesty and lykewise eight of the eleven places of the Maisters of the Chancerie shalbe supplied with one of theise professors of civill and canon lawes onely."[17] This order was Caesar's last contribution to the legal system — and its attendant political values — that he had served with distinction for a lifetime.

In the Introduction, I referred to the problems presented by the terms "bureaucrat" and "bureaucracy" in the early seventeenth century.[18] A little more needs to be said on the subject. At each step in Caesar's progression to higher office, he depended absolutely on the favor of a patron who had the office in his own gift or whose influence with the crown would secure it. Technically, the crown bestowed each office on him (the judge of the Admiralty Court being the exception), but the crown depended on courtiers and senior ministers to advise on appointments as much as they depended on the crown to make them. On the basis of Caesar's career, a base too small to permit generalization, we can see that the crown had little or no personal acquaintance with the recipient of place. It is doubtful that James had any particular sense of Caesar as finance minister, but the assurances of Dorset and Salisbury were sufficient to merit the appointment. Therefore, it appears that intermediate patronal intervention was as important as the formal crown appointment. In such an environment, Caesar was as much concerned with serving his patron as he was with serving the crown. Fortunately, their interests usually coincided.

Because his early career was spent on the bench, where a different relationship obtained, it is only in Caesar's later years, when he was Chancellor of the Exchequer and then Master of the Rolls, that bureaucratic behavior was apparent. While he was associated with Salisbury, Caesar shared in the control of policy and administration, although he always served as the Lord Treasurer's man. But when he was Master of the Rolls, Caesar was less bound to the Lord Chancellor. He was central to the policy and administration of Chancery, and his tenure was secure as a consequence of his fee-simple ownership of the place. If he was not yet a fully developed bureaucrat in modern terms, he was more than a crown servant.

We turn, for the last time, to Caesar's commonplace book, to an entry made in his youth that might be said to epitomize his sense of the correct function of civil government and, by logical extension, of the judges and ministers who served in it. He placed a mark in the margin next to the entry as if to remind himself of its contents or to signify his approval. "Antigonus, a king in Asia, seeing the insolency of his sonne toward his subjects, saide unto him: doest thou not knowe, my sonne, that our kingdome is no other than a noble service."[19] For the most part, the career of Sir Julius Caesar was a mirror of this timeless and worthy sentiment.

Reference Matter

Notes

Complete authors' names, dates, and publication data are given in the Works Cited, pp. 298–304.

INTRODUCTION

1. See Aylmer, *King's Servants,* especially pp. 453–69.

CHAPTER I

1. Margery has been identified both as the daughter of George Perient, a gentleman of Hertfordshire, and as the daughter of Martin Perient, Treasurer of Ireland. There is no reference to Caesar's maternal origins in his vast collection of papers, yet he did spend much time documenting his paternal origins, even to the extent of establishing probable ancestral connections in the court of Charlemagne. He reinforced his Italian origins later in his life when he sent his son and namesake to study in Padua at his father's university.

2. See Chapter 4, pp. 95–96.

3. Worshipful Company of Goldsmiths, Apprentice Register, 1: 36; Hakluyt, p. 45.

4. Public Record Office (henceforth PRO), SP 12/239/62.

5. W. Foster, pp. 9 and 6. My thanks to Dr. David Fischer for these references to the elusive William Caesar.

6. Madge, p. 191.

7. British Library (henceforth BL), Add. MS. 12504, fo. 243 (5 Feb. 1566).

8. BL, Lansd. MS. 3, fo. 149 (24 June 1557).

9. BL, Add. MS. 12497, fos., 191–92 (13 Sept. 1563).

10. BL, Add. MS. 11406, fo. 106 (5 July 1569).

11. Collinson, "Role of Women."

12. BL, Add. MS. 38170, fos. 3v–16.

13. Ibid., fos. 4 and 3v.

14. Arber, 2: 412.

15. Beze, pp. 39f.

16. BL, Lansd. MS. 157, fo. 240 (11 Sept. 1588).

17. The two largest properties held by Caesar's father were the house in Great St. Helen's and the House in Tottenham where Caesar was born. Of the first we know that the IPM taken in 1575 indicated that Caesar's mother enjoyed the occupancy of the messuage and took the profits therefrom. The property was valued at £2 13s. 4d. per annum (PRO, CHAN IPM, 17 Elizabeth 75). The house in Tottenham was under lease in 17 Elizabeth to Henry Lord Compton and to Richard Martin, later his father-in-law (BL, Add. MS. 12497, fo. 205).

18. See Hurstfield, *Queen's Wards*, especially pp. 255–56.

19. The university register indicates that Caesar matriculated and entered under the same date: 10 January 1575. J. Foster, p. 229.

20. See BL, Add. MS. 12507, fos. 42–45, 87, 276–303.

21. BL, Add. MS. 6038, fos. 1–iv.

22. Levack, pp. 16–30. Levack's work is an excellent (and the most up-to-date) study of the organization and function of the Doctors' Commons.

23. BL, Add. MS. 11406, fo. 150 (18 Dec. 1579).

24. Ibid., fo. 150v.

25. BL, Add. MS. 4160, fos. 18v–23. This was an autobiographical memorial written by Caesar in 1634, just after the death of Coke.

26. BL, Lansd. MS. 157, fo. 212v (23 Jan. 1585).

27. Ibid., fo. 65 (17 Oct. 1588).

28. BL, Add. MS. 4160, fo. 18v (9 Oct. 1581).

29. Caesar himself made the same error in his autobiographical memorandum. See above, n. 26.

30. The one valuable study of St. Katharine is Jamison, *Royal Hospital*.

31. BL, Lansd. MS. 157, fo. 184 (12 Apr. 1585).

32. Although we have no valuation for Dorcas's wealth, it is useful to note that in 1582 Caesar required a bond from his sister's new husband, Nicholas Wright, requiring him to provide Caesar £100 free of debt for Margaret's use. If this was considered sufficient income for his sister if she became a widow, then perhaps it was near the amount he received when, the following year, he married a widow himself. BL, Add. MS. 11406, fo. 178 (15 Jan. 1582), and see Chapter 4, p. 96.

33. Carlton, *Court*, p. 37.

34. BL, Add. MS. 12503, fo. 243v.

35. Ibid., fo. 222 (31 Dec. 1582).

36. Ibid., fo. 235 (28 Jan. 1583).

37. Ibid., fo. 239 (16 May 1583).

38. City of London, Guildhall Library, Rep. 20, fo. 436b.

39. Ibid., fo. 432b.

40. BL, Add. MS. 12503, fo. 233 (16 June 1583).

41. Ibid., fo. 243v.   42. Ibid., fo. 240 (5 Oct. 1583).

43. Ibid., fo. 254 (? Dec. 1583).   44. Ibid., fo. 255 (? Dec. 1583).

45. BL, Lansd. MS. 157, fo. 167 (18 Mar. 1585).

46. BL, Add. MS. 11406, fo. 315 (31 Mar. 1582). For more about Henry Caesar, see Chapter 4, pp. 96–98.

47. BL, Lansd. MS. 157, fo. 186 (18 May 1584).

48. BL, Add. MS. 12503, fo. 248 (18 Apr. 1584).

49. BL, Lansd. MS. 157, fo. 165 (22 July 1583).

50. PRO, HCA 3/19/77v.

51. PRO, HCA 3/19/78.

52. BL, Lansd. MS. 157, fo. 212 (23 Jan. 1585).

53. PRO, SP 180/14. See also PRO, Patent Rolls, 27 Elizabeth, pt. 10, m. 23; SP 237/66 concerning the commission to Caesar and Dale. And see Marsden, 2, p. xii, and BL, Lansd. MS. 145, fos. 28f (for the common-law viewpoint).

54. *Coram venerabilibus viris Domino Valentius Dale legem doctore supplicum libellorum magister, et Julio Caesar legum doctore alme Curie Cancellarie, principalibus, et commissarriis generalibus dicte Curie.* PRO, HCA 3/19/145v (4 Feb. 1585).

55. *Proviso quia tu Julius Caesar officium predictum nuper exercuisti auctoritate ultimi Admirallie nostri et magnos labores in eo exercendo sumpsiti volumut quod tu habeas et retineas tibi in proprios tuos usus duas partes proficuorum dicto officio pertinentium in tres partes dividendorum.* PRO, Patent Rolls, 27 Elizabeth, pt. 10, m. 23. (30 Jan. 1585).

56. Ibid., 27 Elizabeth, pt. 10 (5 July 1585).

57. See Kenny, *Elizabeth's Admiral.*

58. BL, Add. MS. 15208, fo. 8 (15 Apr. 1585).

59. BL, Lansd. MS. 157, fo. 370 (18 Sept. 1585).

60. BL, Add. MS. 11406, fo. 100v (6 Oct. 1592).

61. Shakespeare, *The Merchant of Venice,* III, iii.

62. BL, Add. MS. 15208, fo. 20 (2 Aug. 1585); Lansd. MS. 133, fo. 17 (7 and 8 Aug. 1585).

63. See Dietz, p. 56.

64. BL, Add. MS. 15208, fo. 37 (23 Sept. 1586).

65. Ibid., fo. 45 (28 Sept. 1586).   66. Ibid., fo. 67v (28 Sept. 1586).

67. Ibid., fo. 68 (28 Sept. 1586).   68. Ibid., fo. 51 (28 Sept. 1587).

69. Ibid., fo. 73 (26 Aug. 1587).

70. BL, Add. MS. 12505, fo. 296 (14 Oct. 1589).

71. For examples of Caesar's problems with collecting his share, see BL, Add. MS. 11406, fos. 165–74; Add. MS. 12497, fo. 203.

72. BL, Add. MS. 11406, fo. 166 (6 June 1602).
73. Ibid., fo. 168 (18 June 1602).
74. BL, Add. MS. 15208, fo. 370 (6 May 1595).
75. BL, Lansd. MS. 133, fo. 21v–26.
76. BL, Add. MS. 11406, fo. 290 (8 Nov. 1595), and see below, Chapter 4, pp. 99–109 and *passim*.
77. PRO, Index 6800, fo. 615v (30 Oct. 1596).

CHAPTER II

1. For a full discussion of this process, see Richardson, *Tudor Chamber Administration*, and Elton, *Tudor Revolution*.
2. BL, Add. MS. 12505, fo. 269.
3. Ibid., fo. 269v.
4. Ibid.
5. For a full discussion of the circuit and its relationship to local government, see L. M. Hill, "Admiralty Circuit."
6. BL, Add. MS. 12505, fo. 270v.
7. The diplomatic history of the period is well developed in Wernham, *Before the Armada*, and Crowson, *Tudor Foreign Policy*.
8. There is some disagreement about the extent of Spanish control over the Holy League. I am persuaded by the position developed by Jensen, *Diplomacy and Dogmaticism*, which comports with the archival evidence I have examined.
9. Letters of marque were not used, since Elizabeth did not acknowledge a formal state of war between England and Spain and did not wish to do so by commissioning private vessels in her service. A ship sailing under a letter of reprisal was, technically, serving the interests of the master or owners.
10. See Andrews, *Elizabethan Privateering* and *English Privateering Voyages*, in which there is the best conspectus for the layman of the procedure used in the High Court of Admiralty, as well as of the problem of privateering.
11. See BL, Lansd. MS. 151, fos. 207–16, for a calendar of Caesar's "Bookes of Forren Treatises with England done by William Bagwell." There are also several volumes devoted to the causes of French, Danish, Dutch, and, of course, Spanish litigants. Their contents exemplify the cosmopolitan jurisdiction of the court, and they would provide abundant material for a much-needed analysis of the diplomatic functions of the High Court of Admiralty during the privateering war.
12. See Jensen, *Diplomacy and Dogmatism*.
13. Malynes, *Consuetudo*, p. 87.
14. Holdsworth, 5: 79f.
15. The act dates from 1390.
16. 15 Richard II, cap. 3 (1391).

17. See, for instance, 32 Henry VIII, cap. 4, regarding freight and cargo damage claims; 43 Elizabeth I, cap. 12, later in the century, would vest jurisdiction for the trial of insurance claims in the admiralty court. In both cases, parliamentary authority vested the additional powers in the High Court of Admiralty.

18. Holdsworth, 5: 140. See also Blatcher, *Court*, for a longer discussion of the venue fiction.

19. Holdsworth, 5: 143.

20. 25 Henry VIII, cap. 19.

21. BL, Add. MS. 12505, fo. 197 (12 May 1575).

22. Ibid.

23. On the *corpus cum causa*, see Jones, p. 500.

24. PRO, HCA 3/542.

25. Holdsworth, 1: 202.

26. 167 *English Reports* 550 (Burrell 232; 8 July 1584).

27. BL, Lansd. MS. 157, fo. 175 (20 Nov. 1584).

28. Ibid., fo. 171 (22 Nov. 1584).

29. Ibid., fo. 405 (22 Aug. 1590).

30. Ibid., fo. 258 (22 Aug. 1590).

31. 74 *English Reports* 99 (1 Leonard, 107) Easter Term 30 Elizabeth in King's Bench.

32. *Calendar of State Papers, Foreign: 1588* (July–Dec.), p. 378 (14 Dec. 1588).

33. *Acts of Privy Council: 1588*, p. 314 (30 Dec. 1588).

34. Regarding Holliday's conduct concerning the claims of several Bretons, whose ships he spoiled on an earlier occasion, see ibid., *1589–90* pp. 252, 384f; *1591*, p. 5.

35. Ibid., *1597*, pp. 31f (10 Apr. 1597).

36. Ibid., p. 197 (14 June 1597).

37. Ibid., p. 217 (29 June 1597).

38. Ogilvie, p. 124.

39. BL, Add. MS. 29439, fo. 179. This volume contains Francis Clerke, "Ius Gentium," bound in manuscript with his "Praxis in Curiis Ecclesiasticis et Admiralitis."

40. BL, Add. MS. 145, fo. 24. See also Warnicke, especially p. 132.

41. BL, Add. MS. 29439, fo. 179.

42. BL, Lansd. MS. 145, fo. 24v.

43. Ibid.

44. BL, Lansd. MS. 129, fo. 80 (endorsed 26 Feb. 1592).

45. Ibid.

46. Ibid., fos. 80v f. Compare Caesar's words with the nearly identical passage in Clerke's "Ius Gentium," BL, Add. MS. 29439, fo. 179.

47. BL, Lansd. MS. 129, fo. 81v.   48. Ibid., fo. 82.
49. BL, Add. MS. 36111, fo. 41.   50. Coke, p. 135.
51. BL, Lansd. MS. 129, fo. 82 (from *Liber* 2, "de origine juris," sect.
"eodem tempore").
52. BL, Lansd. MS. 129, fo. 82v. See also Oxford University, Bodleian
Library, North MS. a.1, fo. 85 and BL, Add. MS. 12505, fos. 278f.
53. See n. 52 for sources.
54. *Acts of Privy Council: 1599–1600*, p. 44.

CHAPTER III

1. BL, Lansd. MS. 157, fo. 34 (20 Oct. 1584).
2. BL, Add. MS. 12503, fo. 248 (18 Apr. 1584).
3. BL, Add. MS. 4160, fo. 19 (21 June 1584).
4. The distinction between "extraordinary" and "ordinary" Masters is similar to the distinction made in American universities between the professorial
ranks and the (often extensive) range of other teaching positions: adjunct
professor, instructor, lecturer, and so forth. The "ordinary" Masters and the
professorial ranks are the traditional, and presumably "normal," complement
of personnel. The "extraordinary" Masters and the other faculty positions are
often the result of newer circumstances that necessitate expanding the capa-
bility and the function of the traditional personnel without expanding their
numbers and, thus, diluting their influence.
5. Jones, pp. 117–19.
6. Ibid., pp. 103–6, 110–11.
7. Levack, p. 62.
8. BL, Add. MS. 12503, fo. 260 (28 Apr. 1587).
9. BL, Add. MS. 4160, fo. 19 (9 Oct. 1588).
10. BL, Lansd. MS. 157, fos. 22 (29 Oct. 1589), 226 (2 Feb. 1588).
11. BL, Add. MS. 12504, fos. 211 (15 May 1589), 213 (20 Dec. 1590).
12. Ibid., fos. 223–41.
13. BL, Lansd. MS. 157, fo. 22 (29 Dec. 1587).
14. BL, Lansd. MS. 53, fo. 134 (3 Dec. 1587).
15. See Neale, "Elizabethan Political Scene," and MacCaffrey, "Place and
Patronage." For a discussion of patronage and corruption, see Hurstfield,
"Political Corruption."
16. I am indebted to Dr. Michael Weiss for his data and analysis of late-
fifteenth-century indentured relationships developed in his "Loyalty My Lie."
These exclusive relationships may have continued in remote parts of the kingdom in the late sixteenth century, but Caesar's pursuit of advancement at the
center clearly was not dependent on a single patron.
17. MacCaffrey, p. 110.
18. BL, Lansd. MS. 157, fo. 226 (2 Feb. 1588).

19. Ibid., fos. 85f (16 Mar. 1589).
20. D. Thomas, pp. 68–69.
21. BL, Lansd. MS. 157, fos. 85f (16 Mar. 1588).
22. Ibid.   23. Ibid., fo. 228 (21 Apr. 1588).
24. Ibid., fo. 83 (19 Apr. 1588).   25. Ibid., fo. 24 (21 Apr. 1588).
26. Ibid., fo. 329 (20 Apr. 1588).   27. Ibid., fo. 228 (21 Apr. 1588).
28. Ibid., fo. 81 (7 June 1588).
29. Ibid., fo. 238 (25 Aug. 1588 — Caesar to Howard).
30. Ibid., fo. 22 (29 Dec. 1588); Lansd. MS. 157, fo. 75 (24 Sept. 1588).
31. BL, Lansd. MS. 157, fo. 56 (5 July 1589).
32. Ibid., fo. 26 (16 Dec. 1589).
33. Ibid., fo. 29 (29 Apr. 1588).
34. Ibid., fo. 18 (25 May 1588).
35. Historical Manuscript Commission, *Hatfield*, 6: 215.
36. *Acts of Privy Council: 1590–91*, p. 207; BL, Add. MS. 11406, fos. 92, 94. The oath is to be found in BL, Add. MS. 11406, fo. 187, and elsewhere in Caesar's papers.
37. Levack, p. 61.
38. Ibid., pp. 61, 266f, 260; Allsebrook, "Court of Requests."
39. The information that follows is taken from Allsebrook, pp. 37–58.
40. Allsebrook, "Court of Requests."
41. Leadam, *Select Cases*.
42. Holdsworth, 1: 412–16; Coke, *Fourth Institutes*.
43. Elton, *Tudor Constitution*, pp. 184–95, and for particular consideration of the origins of the court in the context of the origins of the Privy Council, see Elton, "Early-Tudor Council." Also see Elton, *Tudor Revolution*, p. 317.
44. Ogilvie, *King's Government*.
45. Published in two parts as *The Ancient State . . . of the Court of Requests*, London, 1597, and as *Actes, Orders, and Decrees Remaining among the Records of the Court of Requests*. The attributed date for the second part is 1592, but it is likely that it was published with the first part in 1597. Although the two parts belong to the same work, they are occasionally found separately.
46. L. M. Hill, ed., *Ancient State*.
47. See ibid., pp. ix–xxi, for a fuller treatment of the conflict between the Court of Requests and the common lawyers. See also L. M. Hill, "Public Career," ch. 6. The following abbreviated account is taken from these sources.
48. See above, Chapter 2, p. 43.
49. Elton, "Early-Tudor Council," and see L. M. Hill, ed., *Ancient State*, pp. xxxviii–xl.
50. L. M. Hill, ed., *Ancient State*, p. 117.
51. Ibid., pp. 248–52, and see BL, Lansd. MS. 125, fos. 33v–35r, 40v–42v, 167v–168r.

52. Jones, p. 21.
53. BL, Lansd. MS. 161, fo. 27.
54. See Levack, pp. 84–85, 98–102.
55. Ibid.
56. BL, Lansd. MS. 161, fo. 131 (no date).
57. BL, Lansd. MSS. 129 and 133.
58. PRO, HCA 3/19, 22, 23, 25, 26.
59. PRO, HCA 24/52, 53, 61, 62, 70, 71.
60. Levack, *Civil Lawyers*, s.v. Crompton, Trevor, Dun, and Martin.
61. PRO, REQ 1/47.

CHAPTER IV

1. The following biographical data are from Caesar's memorial of his own life, BL, Add. MS. 4160, fos. 18–23.

2. See Stone, *Family*, p. 409, on the "practice of substitution, of giving a new-born son the name of one who had recently died." Howard was reluctant to be the godfather to the second Charles Caesar, feeling that it would be bad luck for the godfather of a dead brother to repeat his office. BL, Add. MS. 15208, fo. 177 (29 Jan. 1590).

3. BL, Add. MS. 11406, fo. 342 (note made 24 July 1598).

4. BL, Lansd. MS. 157, fo. 368v (26 June 1595).

5. BL, Lansd. MS. 161, fos. 135–36 (Dec. 1595 or Jan. 1596), and BL, Add. MS. 12497, fos. 299–301v (will dated 15 Apr. 1595, codicil date 15 May 1595).

6. BL, Add. MS. 12497, fo. 421 (15 Jan. 1596).

7. Ibid., fos. 297–297v.

8. Ibid., fos. 295–295v, 318–319v.

9. Ibid., fos. 299–301v (15 May 1595).

10. Ibid., fo. 423, and Hurstfield, *Queen's Wards*, pp. 81–82. Hurstfield was careful to point out that Caesar's expenses are not to be taken as exceptional but simply well-documented.

11. BL, Add. MS. 12497, fo. 227 (1 Feb. 1597), and see also fos. 295–295v.

12. BL, Add. MS. 11406, fo. 189 (29 July 1597).

13. BL, Lansd. MS. 157, fo. 144 (1 Feb. 1588).

14. BL, Add. MS. 12497, fos. 413–413v (13 Dec. 1599).

15. Ibid., fos. 417 (8 July 1604), 419 (4 Sept. 1606).

16. *Calendar of State Papers, Domestic: 1598–1601*, p. 96 (17 Sept. 1578).

17. Hotson, *Entertainment*. These are Hotson's observations, and they are congruent with the subject in a very general way. Hotson, however, revealed his unfamiliarity with the styles of importunity of the sixteenth century and of the mentality of contemporary careerists when he referred to Caesar as a "shameless beggar" because of the tone of his speech to the queen.

18. BL, Sloane MS. 4160, fo. 20.

19. Hotson indicates that "Poet, Painter, and Musician" was similar to a work attributed to Lyly that had been performed at Burghley's Theobalds Entertainment in 1591.

20. Hotson, pp. 29–30.   21. Ibid., p. 27.

22. BL, Sloane MS. 4160, fo. 20.   23. Ibid.

24. BL, Add. MS. 12497, fo. 329 (17 June 1587). The original mortgage was dated 3 February 1579.

25. Ibid., fo. 327 (27 Dec. 1588).

26. Ibid., fo. 320.

27. *Acts of Privy Council: 1597*, 29 (10 Apr. 1597).

28. For Zacharius's letters see *Calendar of State Papers, Domestic: 1598–1601*, pp. 130–31.

29. *Acts of Privy Council: 1598–99*, pp. 421–22 (31 Dec. 1598).

30. *Dictionary of National Biography*, s.v. Lok, M.

31. Armytage, 1: 106 (13 Jan. 1582); 1: 112 (4 Oct. 1582).

32. Ibid., p. 147.

33. Rowse, p. 336. Rowse incorrectly identifies Henry as Julius Caesar's nephew. See Hicks, p. 216.

34. Rowse, pp. 335–36.

35. See Chapter 1, p. 14.

36. *Calendar of State Papers, Foreign: 1589–90*, pp. 239 and 302.

37. BL, Lansd. MS. 157, fo. 42 (22 Jan. 1590).

38. BL, Add. MS. 11406, fo. 317 (23 Jan. 1590).

39. Ibid., fo. 307 (20 July 1591).

40. *Acts of Privy Council: 1591–92*, p. 174 (7 Jan. 1592), and BL, Add. MS. 11406, fo. 321 (7 Jan. 1592).

41. BL, Add. MS. 11406, fo. 142 (16 July 1592).

42. Ibid., fo. 144 (15 July 1593).

43. Ibid., fo. 140 (16 July 1593).

44. PRO, Index 6800, fo. 552 (Oct. 1595).

45. BL, Add. MS. 12506, fo. 387 (9 Nov. 1600).

46. My thanks to the History of Parliament Trust for permitting me to inspect their biographical entry for Thomas Caesar. I have taken the following data from that biographical entry except where otherwise noted.

47. Armytage, p. 175 (4 Jan. 1589).

48. See source in n. 46.

49. Ibid.

50. See for example BL, Add. MS. 11406, fo. 224 (8 Nov. 1599).

51. Inderwick and Roberts, p. 407 (6 July 1595).

52. BL, Add. MS. 12503, fo. 269 (17 Feb. 1597).

53. BL, Add. MS. 12504, fo. 127 (17 Feb. 1604).

54. Ibid., fos. 125 (4 July 1605), 123 (27 Oct. 1610).

55. BL, Add. MS. 11406, fo. 290 (8 Nov. 1595). According to Stone's calculations, in 1602 the mean gross income for the 58 members of the peerage was £3,360 and the mean net income was £2,930. Stone, *Crisis*, p. 762 (appx. ix). These sums would suggest that Howard's estimate was not an exaggeration.

56. BL, Lansd. MS. 157, fo. 63 (1 Jan. 1589).

57. BL, Add. MS. 11406, fo. 295 (27 Dec. 1596).

58. See Chapter 1, p. 12.

59. *Masters of the Bench*, (1883), p. 17; Inderwick and Roberts, p. 372.

60. Inderwick and Roberts, p. 372 (7 Feb. 1591).

61. Ibid., p. 376 (10 Oct. 1591).

62. Ibid., pp. 378 and *passim*, 409–16; *Masters of the Bench* (1901), p. 17.

63. Inderwick and Roberts, pp. 411–12 (8 Feb. 1596).

64. BL, Add. MS. 157, fos. 395–96; fos. 401–4 (4 Mar. 1585).

65. Donald, p. 73.

66. Ibid., pp. 72, 75, 189f. See also BL, Add. MS. 12503, fo. 146, concerning Caesar's and Beale's prosecutions. Caesar and Martin were sworn 22 January 1594, BL, Add. MS. 12503, fos. 154, 155.

67. Donald, 72.

68. See Raab, *Enterprise and Empire*. Raab's data reveal the extent of Caesar's overseas mercantile investments.

69. BL, Lansd. MS. 157, fo. 73 (25 Sept. 1588).

70. Ibid., fo. 67 (5 Oct. 1588).   71. Ibid., fo. 48 (20 Feb. 1588).

72. Ibid., fo. 52 (7 Mar. 1589).   73. Ibid., fo. 50 (1 July 1589).

74. BL, Add. MS. 11406, fos. 205 (28 Apr. 1587), 213 (10 Apr. 1587).

75. Ibid., fo. 211 (28 Nov. 1587).

76. Ibid., fo. 396 (31 Dec. 1587); *Acts of Privy Council: 1587–88*, pp. 316 (30 Dec. 1587) and 331 (7 Jan. 1588), a further arrest order to settle the claims of several fishermen against Leveson.

77. *Calendar of State Papers, Domestic: 1581–90*, p. 465 (21 Feb. 1588).

78. BL, Add. MS. 11406, fo. 391 (11 Feb. 1590).

79. *Acts of Privy Council: 1590*, p. 310 (9 July 1590).

80. BL, Add. MS. 11406, fo. 389 (27 Feb. 1591).

81. *Calendar of State Papers, Domestic: 1591–94*, p. 128.

82. Ibid., *1581–90*, p. 670 (8 June 1590), and various orders in BL, Add. MS. 11406, fos. 389, 391–96 (1590).

83. *Calendar of State Papers, Domestic: 1581–90*, pp. 702 (6 Dec. 1590), and 670 (8 June 1590).

84. BL, Add. MS. 11406, fos. 214–14v (9 Dec. 1591).

85. See ibid., fo. 207 (17 Apr. 1592), for one of the many promises.

86. Regarding the other ships see *Acts of Privy Council: 1592–93*, p. 89 (29 Feb. 1593).

87. BL, Add. MS. 11406, fo. 218 (Apr. 1594).

88. BL, Add. MS. 12504, fos. 136 (1–8), 137 (9–16) (31 July 1595).
89. Ibid., fo. 139 (1–8) (4 Oct. 1597).
90. BL, Add. MS. 11406, fo. 393 (Trinity Term, 1598).
91. *Calendar of State Papers, Domestic: 1597–1601*, p. 36 (25 Mar. 1598).
92. See, for example, BL, Add. MS. 11406, fo. 339 (15 Aug. 1599).
93. *Calendar of State Papers, Domestic: 1598–1601*, p. 130 (8 Dec. 1598).
94. Ibid., pp. 400–402.
95. Ibid., pp. 406–7 (3 March 1600).
96. Ibid., *1601–3*, p. 134 (28 Dec. 1601).
97. Ibid., p. 259 (4 Nov. 1602).
98. BL, Add. MS. 11406, fo. 389 (Oct. 1590).
99. My thanks to the History of Parliament Trust for permitting me to read their biographical entry for Caesar. I have taken this information from their material.
100. D'Ewes, p. 570a.
101. Ibid., p. 582, enacted as 39 Elizabeth, cap. 18, sects. 7 and 35.
102. Ibid., p. 680a, enacted as 43 Elizabeth, cap. 12.
103. Ibid., p. 477a, enacted as 35 Elizabeth, cap. 2; also pp. 578a, 579.
104. Ibid., pp. 622b, 641b.   105. Ibid., p. 649b.
106. Ibid., p. 667b.   107. Ibid., p. 685b.
108. Ibid., p. 474a, enacted as 35 Elizabeth, cap. 13.
109. Ibid., p. 478a.
110. Ibid., p. 481a.
111. BL, Add. MS. 4160, fos. 18–23.

CHAPTER V

1. Beckinsale, p. 185.   2. Ibid., pp. 177–79.
3. Ibid., pp. 183–84.   4. Ibid., p. 185
5. *Calendar of State Papers, Domestic: 1598–1601*, p. 80.
6. PRO, SP 12/268/18 (7 Aug. 1598).
7. PRO, SP 12/268/78 (20 Oct. 1598).
8. PRO, SP 12/268/111 (19 Nov. 1598).
9. PRO, SP 12/269/6 (8 Dec. 1598).
10. *Calendar of State Papers, Domestic: 1598–1601*, p. 194 (15 May 1599); PRO, SP 12/270/127 (21 May 1599).
11. Historical Manuscript Commission, *De L'Isle* 2: 413.
12. Dietz, pp. 67 and *passim*; Beckinsale, p. 239.
13. PRO, SP 12/269/6 (8 Dec. 1598).
14. See Ashton, "Deficit Finance," p. 25.
15. The following discussion is adapted from several sources, including Willson's classic biography, *James VI and I*, the less scholarly work of D. Mathew, *James I*, and the more recent works: J. N. Brown, "Scottish

Politics, 1567–1625," in Smith., ed., *Reign of James VI and I*; and Houston, *James I*.

16. R. C. Munden, "James I and 'the growth of mutual distrust': King, Commons, and Reform, 1603–1604," in Sharpe, ed., *Faction and Parliament*, p. 54.

17. Houston, p. 9.

18. Ibid.

19. See Willson, *Privy Councillors*, pp. 205–46. Although Willson's argument has been dominant, Houston warns that there is more to the story: the end of sympathetic relationships between councillors and MPs, the replacement of a generation of competent councillors by second-rate successors, and the loss of Privy Council's political exclusiveness as its numbers were more than doubled. Houston, pp. 34–35.

20. BL, Add. MS. 12497, fos. 189f (3 July 1606).

21. Kansas University, Kenneth Spencer Research Library, MS. Q 12: 16, fo. 341 (20 Feb. 1607).

22. BL, Lansd. MS. 183, fo. 94.

23. The following discussion of the Exchequer and of the Chancellor's functions has been freely adapted from Tout, *Medieval Administrative History*; Elton, *Tudor Revolution*; H.M.S.O., *Public Record Office*; and Richardson, *Court of Augmentations*. A modern study of the organization and practices of the Exchequer is much needed. Aside from the works cited above and F. C. Dietz's studies of English public finance, there are only occasional observations and descriptions in a number of monographs, articles, and biographies. The receipt and audit, the planning and maintenance of crown revenue remain terra incognita with occasional borders of illumination. The extensive collection of papers and notes that Caesar gathered to instruct himself, especially BL, Lansd. MS. 168, is perhaps a sketch map of the interior parts.

24. For a more detailed discussion of the administrative problems presented by the persistence of traditional behavior and private interests in the Exchequer of Receipt, see Elton, "Elizabethan Exchequer," pp. 219 and *passim*.

25. See, for instance, Elton, "Elizabethan Exchequer," pp. 213–18.

26. BL, Lansd. MS. 168, fo. 177.

27. Ibid., fo. 265.

28. Ibid., fo. 316 (17 July 1606). The pension was actually apportioned for service in two offices. As Undertreasurer, Caesar would receive £176 6s. 8d.; as Chancellor, he would receive £26 13s. 4d. These customary sums reflect the relative importance of the two offices at an earlier date when the stipends were first set.

29. Ibid., fo. 177 (26 July 1606). The last item referred to rooms occupied by the Auditor of the Receipt, Vincent Skinner.

30. Ibid., fos. 239 (18 July 1606); 233(16 July 1606); 324 (7 July 1606); 240–44v (18 July 1606), a list of Clerk's writs; 228 (16 July 1606); 350(18 July 1606).

31. Ibid., fo. 177 (26 July 1606).

32. For instance, Historical Manuscript Commission, *Hatfield* 10: 153 (21 May 1600), 9: 347 (6 Sept. 1600).

33. Stone, *Crisis*, pp. 159, 760 (appx. iii, b).

34. Handover, p. 190; Coakley, p. 74.

35. Historical Manuscript Commission, *Hatfield* 11: 324–25 (7 Aug. 1601).

36. *Calendar of State Papers, Domestic: 1601–1603*, p. 299 (9 Mar. 1603).

37. Harriss, p. 81.

38. BL, Add. MS. 34324, fo. 39.   39. Ibid.

40. Ibid., fo. 30.   41. Ibid., fo. 41.

42. Ibid., fo. 171 (13 Mar. 1607).

43. BL, Add. MS. 36767, fo. 109 (9 June 1607).

44. Ibid., fo. 109v (9 June 1607).

45. Kansas University, Kenneth Spencer Research Library, MS. Q 12:16, fos. 341–42 (20 Feb. 1607).

46. BL, Add. MS. 36767, fo. 97v (31 May 1607).

47. Ibid., fos. 97–97v.

48. Ibid., fo. 90 (26 May 1607).

49. Ibid., fo. 100 (31 May 1607).

50. Ibid., fos. 102–3v, 105 (8 and 9 June 1607).

51. Dietz, p. 120.

52. BL, Lansd. MS. 166, fos. 125–26 (30 Oct. 1606).

53. Ibid., fo. 125r.

54. BL, Lansd. MS. 151, fo. 73 (12 Oct. 1607).

55. BL, Add. MS. 11402, fo. 138v. "This day the Earle of Dorrsett, being Lord Treasurer, departed out of this world as he satt in Councill with the rest of the Lords about 3 or 4 of the clocke in the afternoone."

56. BL, Lansd. MS. 164, fo. 419 (23 Sept. 1606).

CHAPTER VI

1. BL, Add. MS. 9045, fos. 2–2v (22 Apr. 1608). See also PRO, SP 38/9 (23 Apr. 1608).

2. BL, Lansd. MS. 164, fos. 389–89v (24 Apr. 1608), 391 (28 Apr. 1608).

3. BL, Lansd. MS. 168, fo. 297.

4. Ibid.

5. The journal is found in BL, Lansd. MS. 168, fos. 296–307v. It has been published in L. M. Hill, "Caesar's Journal." Citations will be to the printed text.

6. Spedding, 4: 151.

7. L. M. Hill, "Caesar's Journal," p. 325.

8. Ibid., p. 329.   9. Ibid., p. 327.

10. Ibid., p. 319.   11. Ibid., p. 320.

12. Dietz, p. 122.

13. BL, Add. MS. 36767, fo. 194 (1 Aug. 1608).

14. Ibid., fo. 198 (6 Aug. 1608).

15. PRO, SP 14/35/53 (12 Aug. 1608).

16. PRO, SP 14/35/204 (21 Aug. 1608).

17. McClure, 1: 258–59 (7 July 1608).

18. BL, Lansd. MS. 164, fo. 427 (14 Sept. 1608).

19. Hatfield MS, 128, fo. 104 (5 Mar. 1610).

20. BL, Lansd. MS. 168, fos. 298 (cf. 20 and 21 May 1608), 302 (cf. 7 July 1608).

21. Ibid., fo. 69 (21 Sept. 1608), Doc. "B."

22. Ibid., fos. 76–77v (22 Sept. 1608), Doc. "L."

23. Dietz, p. 121.

24. BL, Lansd. MS. 151, fo. 83 (22 Sept. 1608), Doc. "N."

25. Ibid., fo. 73 (12 Oct. 1607).

26. Dietz, p. 106.

27. BL, Lansd. MS. 151, fo. 74 (22 Sept. 1608), Doc. "I."

28. PRO, SP 14/34/26 (June 1608).

29. Dietz, pp. 117–18.

30. BL, Add. MS. 36767, fo. 196 (1 Aug. 1608).

31. Hatfield MS. 122, fo. 29.

32. I am grateful to Fr. Frank Larkin for providing this date and for discussing with me the use and significance of proclamations.

33. Northumberland MS. 9, fos. 1–1v (8 Feb. 1608).

34. PRO, E 369/131/46 (manuscript copy of Fanshawe's "Practice in the Exchequer").

35. BL, Lansd. MS. 167, fos. 113–13v (21 Dec. 1607).

36. Ibid., fos. 90–90v (30 Aug. 1607).

37. BL, Lansd. MS. 166, fo. 117 (28 June 1608).

38. Holdsworth, 4: 356, quoting Coke, *Third Institute*, p. 194.

39. BL, Lansd. MS. 167, fos. 149–50 (6 Feb. 1608).

40. Regarding the king's approval, BL, Add. MS. 36767, fos. 204–4v (21 Aug. 1608); regarding favorable consideration, BL, Lansd. MS. 168, fo. 41 (14 July 1609); regarding Fanshawe's disapproval, BL, Lansd. MS. 167, fos. 144–48.

41. L. M. Hill, "Caesar's Journal," p. 319.

42. Dietz, p. 125.

CHAPTER VII

1. Notestein, *House of Commons*; Gardiner, *Parliamentary Debate*; E. R. Foster, *Proceedings in Parliament.*

2. See above, pp. 128–30.
3. Notestein, p. 250.
4. Harriss, p. 75.
5. Ibid., p. 76.
6. Ibid.
7. Ibid., p. 81.
8. E. R. Foster, 2: 10–11.
9. Ibid., 2: 15.
10. Ibid., 2: 18–19.
11. Ibid., 2: 21–23.
12. Ibid., 2: 24.
13. Ibid., 2: 26–27.
14. Ibid., 2: 356–57.
15. Ibid., 2: 358–59.
16. Ibid., 1: 13–14.

17. Ibid., 1: 14. "Support" differed substantially from "supply," the conventional form of parliamentary taxation. Supply was levied in the form of "subsidies" and "fifteenths." The subsidy was assessed on personal land holdings at a traditional rate of 4s. per pound sterling of value and on goods at the rate of 2s. 8d. The individual holder of personal or real property was the unit of taxation. The fifteenth, on the other hand, was assessed in gross on the borough corporations, and it was their business to apportion the burden among the residents. While subsidies were rated according to a traditional formula, the returns would vary according to the value of the lands and goods taxed. The fifteenths bore no relation to actual value; they were assessed according to a traditional sum levied on the burghal corporation. But now, in 1610, an entirely new form of tax, the "support," was introduced to Parliament. It bore some resemblance to the fifteenth, being a sum levied in gross, but on every county and borough in the kingdom. This was the striking novelty of the Great Contract.

18. E. R. Foster, 1: 14.
19. Ibid.
20. Ibid., 1: 14–15.
21. Ibid., 1: 15.

22. Ibid. See Woodworth, "Purveyance," and Aylmer, "Last Years," for a discussion of the complex purveyance problem.

23. E. R. Foster, 1: 15–16. The "misrecitals or misnamings" of manors refers to the practice of intentionally making an error in conveying a manor, only to bring the issue back to court to collect the fees and fines that would accompany setting the matter right.

24. E. R. Foster, 1: 53–54.
25. Ibid., 2: 32 and *passim.*
26. Ibid., 2: 68.
27. Ibid., 1: 66.
28. Ibid., 2: 69–70.

29. Ibid., 1: 70. Wardships had been proposed as a separate issue earlier, but they had been temporarily set aside pending a discussion of their suitability for debate. Montagu had included them in his statement of the elements of the bargain. See above, p. 158.

30. E. R. Foster, 2: 75.   31. Ibid., 1: 80.
32. Ibid.   33. Ibid.
34. Ibid., 1: 84.   35. Notestein, pp. 310–21.
36. E. R. Foster, 2: 100–107.   37. Ibid., 2: 114–17.
38. Gardiner, *Parliamentary Debate*, pp. 46–48.
39. E. R. Foster, 1: 117, 2: 169; Gardiner, *Parliamentary Debate*, p. 121.
40. Notestein, pp. 327–47.   41. See ibid., pp. 361–85.
42. E. R. Foster, 2: 253–71.   43. Notestein, p. 386.
44. E. R. Foster, 2: 273.   45. Ibid., 1: 130–33.
46. Ibid., 1: 133–34.   47. Ibid., 2: 274.
48. Ibid., 2: 276.   49. Ibid., 2: 277.
50. Ibid., 2: 283.   51. Ibid., 2: 284.
52. See K. Thomas, *Religion*. Writing of this period, Thomas has noted the reemergence of numerological calculations in the seventeenth century at the junction between the intellectual and the mystical.
53. E. R. Foster, 2: 285–86.
54. Ibid., 2: 286.
55. Ibid., 2: 289–90. For a detailed discussion of the intricacies presented by the levy, see 2: 290, n. 3.
56. Hatfield, MS. 96, fo. 13 (9 Aug. 1610).
57. BL, Lansd. MS. 168, fos. 209–9v (10 Aug. 1610).
58. BL, Add. MS. 36767, fo. 284 (13 Aug. 1610).
59. BL, Lansd. MS. 151, fos. 32ff (rough draft) and 125ff. See also Gardiner, *Parliamentary Debate*, appx. D, pp. 163–79. The text as cited below is taken from Gardiner.
60. Gardiner, *Parliamentary Debate*, p. 164.
61. Ibid., p. 168.   62. Ibid.
63. Ibid., p. 165.   64. Ibid., pp. 169–70.
65. Ibid., pp. 170–72.
66. Harriss, p. 84, citing Gardiner, *Parliamentary Debate*, p. 173.
67. Gardiner, p. 174.   68. Ibid., p. 175.
69. Ibid., p. 176.   70. Ibid., p. 177.
71. Notestein, pp. 393–97. There is little evidence of the efforts of the Members during the summer, but Notestein makes a credible case for the emergence of a definable parliamentary opinion.
72. E. R. Foster, 2: 300.   73. Notestein, p. 401.
74. Ibid., p. 405.   75. E. R. Foster, 2: 314.
76. Ibid., 2: 314–15.   77. Ibid., 2: 327.
78. Ibid., 2: 347.
79. Hurstfield, *Queen's Wards*, p. 323.
80. Ibid., p. 320.
81. Peck, pp. 198–202.

82. Huntington Library, MS. EL 2599, fos. 1–1v, and printed in E. R. Foster, 1: 276–83. My thanks to Professor L. Knafla for first bringing this document to my attention.

83. Peck, pp. 203–4.

84. Spedding, 4: 238.

85. Ibid., 4: 313 (18 Sept. 1612).

86. Ibid., n. 2.

87. Ibid., 4: 371 (1613).

88. A. G. R. Smith, "Contract," pp. 111–27.

89. Ibid., p. 123.

90. Ibid., p. 120.

91. Ibid., p. 125.

92. Prestwich, pp. 33–45.

93. Dietz, p. 137.

94. Ibid., p. 141.

95. Spedding, 4: 240.

CHAPTER VIII

1. Dietz, pp. 144–81.

2. BL, Lansd. MS. 165, fos. 148–49 (16 Jan. 1611), fos. 138–39 (12 Oct. 1611).

3. Ibid., fo. 138.

4. Ibid.

5. Ibid., fo. 138v.

6. Ibid.

7. Ibid., fos. 138v–39.

8. Ibid., fo. 139.

9. Ibid.

10. For a careful exposition of this complex subject see Harriss, "Medieval Doctrines."

11. PRO, SP 14/63/1 (1 Apr. 1611).

12. PRO, SP 14/63/29 (12 Apr. 1611).

13. PRO, SP 14/63/46 (24 Apr. 1611).

14. PRO, SP 14/67/38 (19 Nov. 1611).

15. PRO, SP 14/66/69 (13 Oct. 1611).

16. PRO, SP 14/68/35 (29 Jan. 1612).

17. PRO, SP 14/66/101 (30 Oct. 1611); *Calendar of State Papers, Domestic: 1611–1618*, p. 103 (28 Dec. 1611).

18. PRO, SP 14/67/43 (22 Nov. 1611).

19. PRO, SP 14/67/104 (18 Dec. 1611).

20. PRO, SP 14/68/19 (19 Jan. 1612).

21. PRO, SP 14/68/35 (29 Jan. 1612).

22. Hurstfield, *Queen's Wards*, p. 324.

23. BL, Lansd. MS. 164, fos. 3–380v.

24. BL, Add. MS. 14027, fo. 170. In a note at the end of the memorandum, Caesar observed that "the treaties of Flandria and Hollandia [containing the repayment terms] are put together and layed on the chest under the windoe in the Tresory."

25. BL, Add. MS. 15235, fo. 43 (27 Apr. 1612).

26. PRO, SP 14/68/67 (16 Feb. 1612).

27. *Calendar of State Papers, Venetian: 1610–1613*, p. 356 (21 May 1612).
28. PRO, SP 14/69/57 (27 May 1612).
29. Peck, p. 80.
30. *Calendar of State Papers, Venetian: 1610–13,* p. 376 (14 June 1612).
31. BL, Add. MS. 15235, fos. 53–56 (16 June 1612). On 21 June the commissioners received their first privy seal.
32. McClure, 1: 358 (17 June 1612).
33. Peck, p. 95.
34. Spedding, 4: 283.
35. McClure, 1: 358 (17 June 1612).
36. PRO, SP 14/69/71 (17 June 1612), SP 14/70/67 (11 Sept. 1612).
37. As Peck has indicated, the fluid factional constellations characterizing Jacobean political life were especially fragile at times of crisis such as "Salisbury's death or Somerset's fall and Buckingham's rise." Peck, p. 26.
38. Ibid., p. 87.
39. PRO, SP 14/69/75 (25 June 1612).
40. BL, Lansd. MS. 151, fos. 112–23v (endorsed 1 July 1612).
41. Russell, *Crisis of Parliaments*, p. 281.
42. Peck, p. 36.
43. Ibid., p. 77.
44. PRO, SP 14/71/50 (Nov. 1612), and see Chapter 6, pp. 144–45.
45. See Spedding, 4: 283.
46. PRO, SP 14/70/38 (11 Aug. 1612). Regarding proposed debasement schemes, see also SP 14/70/39, 40, 42 (Aug. 1612), SP 14/72/139 (May 1613), and SP 14/74/23 (4 July 1613). By July 1613 the question had been laid aside for the time being.
47. BL, Cotton MS. Cleopatra F. V., fos. 82f, as cited in Spedding, 4: 314–27 (11 Aug. 1612).
48. PRO, SP 14/70/83 (Sept. 1612).
49. Spedding, 4: 283; Peck, pp. 98f.
50. BL, Lansd. MS. 165, fos. 223–24v.
51. Ibid., fos. 224v–26.
52. Moir, pp. 10 and *passim*. A marked hiatus in Caesar's papers account for there being virtually no documents relating to this session.
53. Ibid., p. 19.
54. Ibid., p. 25.
55. McClure, 1: 517–18 (17 Mar. 1613).
56. Moir, p. 92.
57. Ibid., pp. 76–77.
58. Ibid., p. 92.
59. Roberts and Duncan, pp. 481 and *passim*.
60. Moir, pp. 117 and *passim*.

61. Ibid., pp. 136f.
62. Ibid., p. 148.
63. McClure, 1: 540–41 (30 June 1614).
64. BL, Add. MS. 36767, fo. 262 (17 Aug. 1614).

CHAPTER IX

1. McClure, 1: 556 (12 Oct. 1614).
2. Ibid.
3. Deprived of office since 1603 because Salisbury did not like him, Fulke Greville was free to pursue place again after the Lord Treasurer died. He turned to both Northampton and Carr for assistance. He had not been able to win the Secretary's place that Winwood secured. When Caesar vacated the place of Chancellor of the Exchequer, Fulke Greville pursued it with a will, using strong Howard support and Somerset's acquiescence. He was sworn 1 October 1614. See Rebholz, p. 233.
4. BL, Lansd. MS. 163, fo. 359 (1614).
5. Ibid., fo. 100 (30 Mar. 1611).
6. Ibid., fo. 336 (20 Sept. 1614).
7. Ibid., fos. 288–319 (1614).
8. For the following discussion I have drawn freely on Maxwell-Lyte, *Historical Notes*; Holdsworth, *History*; and Jones, *Elizabethan Court*. In addition, the documents in Caesar's papers have been helpful.
9. Jones, p. 117. See also Pocock, *Ancient Constitution*, for a trenchant discussion of the provincialism of the common lawyers and the relative sophistication of the continental civil lawyers. The distinction was primarily a result of their very different educational backgrounds and the presuppositions informing their respective legal systems.
10. Jones, p. 51.
11. BL, Lansd. MS. 163, fo. 213 (13 Sept. 1614).
12. Jones, p. 51.
13. Holdsworth, p. 420.
14. Jones, p. 66.
15. BL, Lansd. MS. 162, fos. 11–22.
16. Ibid., fos. 11, 12, 14–19v, 21, 22.
17. Jones, p. 54. See also Warnicke, p. 45 and *passim*.
18. Bannerman, p. 275 (14 May 1614).
19. Maclean, ed., *Letters* (May 1617).
20. McClure, 2: 83.
21. BL, Lansd. MS. 160, fo. 331 (16 June 1618).
22. Spedding, 7: 3984 (14 Nov. 1622).
23. See Spedding, 7: 51. According to one account, "That glorious and melancholy instance of the extent of human wisdom and weakness, the Philos-

opher Bacon, found, after his disgrace, an asylum in the bosoms of his nephew and niece; composed many of his immortal works in an utter retirement in the house of Sir Julius Caesar; became a dependant upon his beneficence for a becoming support; and expired in his arms." Lodge, p. 32. Lodge's version derived from the work of D. Lloyd, who reported that Bacon died in Caesar's arms, but also that "Sir Julius Caesar (as they say) look[ed] upon [Bacon] as a burden of his family" and finally had to remove him from his home. Lloyd also declared that Bacon had not treated Caesar well earlier on, when the Master of the Rolls had served the Lord Chancellor. Lloyd (1665 edition), pp. 606, 705.

24. *Calendar of State Papers, Domestic: 1619–1623*, p. 297 (9 Oct. 1621).
25. PRO, SP 9/12/194 (17 Nov. 1635).
26. Jones, pp. 123–24.
27. See BL, Lansd. MS. 163, fos. 242–51.
28. Jones, pp. 126–29.
29. BL, Lansd. MS. 163, fo. 79.
30. Jones, p. 135.
31. BL, Lansd. MS. 163, fos. 147–48 (8 Dec. 1615).
32. Ibid.
33. Ibid., fos. 242, 244, 246, 249, 251 (Dec. 1616).
34. Ibid., fos. 145–45v (13 Dec. 1616).
35. BL, Lansd. MS. 174, fo. 1 (n.d.).
36. BL, Lansd. MS. 163, fo. 124 (21 Mar. 1618).
37. Ibid.
38. Ibid., fo. 125 (21 Mar. 1618).
39. Ibid., fo. 120 (27 Mar. 1618).
40. Ibid., fo. 106 (2 Apr. 1618).
41. Ibid., fos. 122–22v (26 Mar. 1618).
42. *Calendar of State Papers, Domestic: 1635–36*, p. 270.
43. BL, Lansd. MS. 163, fo. 118 (31 Mar. 1618).
44. BL, Lansd. MS. 174, fos. 108–17 (1618).
45. BL, Lansd. MS. 163, fos. 127–30 (27 Mar. 1618).
46. Ibid., fos. 111–12v (16 Apr. 1618).
47. Ibid., fo. 94 (1 May 1618).
48. Jones, pp. 72–76.
49. BL, Lansd. MS. 174, fo. 45 (19 July 1620).
50. Ibid., fo. 41 (31 Aug. 1620).
51. Ibid., fo. 47 (28 Oct. 1620).
52. BL, Lansd. MS. 163, fo. 141 (28 June 1604).
53. McClure, 2: 416–17 (22 Dec. 1621).
54. Sackville MS. (Old Number) 1093 (10 Dec. 1621).
55. BL, Lansd. MS. 174, fos. 49–50 (19 Jan. 1622).

56. McClure, 2: 10 (22 June 1616).
57. *Calendar of State Papers, Domestic: 1619–1623*, p. 113 (16 Jan. 1620).
58. McClure, 2: 388 (14 July 1621).
59. McClure, 2: 392 (28 July 1621).
60. Historical Manuscript Commission, *De L'Isle and Dudley*, 5: 424–25 (3 Sept. 1621).
61. McClure, 2: 399 (13 Oct. 1621).
62. L. P. Smith, 1: 243n (9 Jan. 1622).
63. Ibid., 1: 69 (c. 1620).
64. Ibid., 2: 86f (1623); Barcroft, p. 125.
65. Reversion dated 16 January 1620, *Calendar of State Papers, Domestic: 1619–1623*, p. 113; L. P. Smith, 1: p. 69; Barcroft, p. 125.
66. L. P. Smith, 1: 200 (1624).
67. PRO, SP 16/132/8 (13 Jan. 1628).
68. PRO, SP 16/114/59 (Aug. 1628).
69. PRO, SP 16/215.
70. *Calendar of State Papers, Domestic: 1631–1633*, p. 215 (1631).
71. Ibid., *1634–35*, p. 95 (21 Mar. 1635).
72. Ibid., p. 12 (6 Apr. 1635).
73. Ibid., p. 513 (14 Feb. 1635).
74. See Aylmer, *King's Servants*, pp. 72ff, 227.
75. *Calendar of State Papers, Domestic: 1635*, p. 251 (5 July 1635).
76. Ibid., *1619–1623*, p. 187 (29 Oct. 1620).
77. BL, Add. MS. 34324, fos. 185–85v (29 June 1622).
78. Ibid., fos. 188–89v (7 Sept. 1620).
79. *Calendar of State Papers, Domestic: 1629–1631*, 301 (11 Apr. 1630).

CHAPTER X

1. BL, Add. MS. 34324, fo. 163 (25 Nov. 1621).
2. *Calendar of State Papers, Domestic: 1611–1618*, p. 534 (14 Apr. 1618).
3. Ibid., p. 560 (30 July 1618).
4. BL, Add. MS. 34324, fo. 105 (9 July 1619).
5. BL, Lansd. MS. 151, fos. 57–58 (18 July 1619).
6. BL, Add. MS. 34324, fos. 107–7v (10 Sept. 1619).
7. Ibid., fos. 109–9v (10 Jan. 1620).
8. Ibid., (4 and 19 Apr. 1620).
9. Ibid., fos. 191–91v (7 July 1620).
10. Ibid., fo. 117 (18 July 1620).
11. Ibid., fos. 119–20v (29 Sept. 1620).
12. Ibid., fo. 120 (30 Sept. 1620).
13. Ibid., fos. 127–28v (14 Oct. 1620).
14. Ibid., fos. 145–45v (21 June 1621).

15. Ibid., fos. 147–48 (30 Dec. 1621).
16. For instance, see Bailyn et al., pp. 30 and *passim.*
17. Tyler, pp. 192–93.
18. Brown, p. 46 (22 Aug. 1607).
19. Neill, p. 43.
20. Tyler, pp. 253–55 (30 July 1619).
21. Brown, pp. 316–17.
22. BL, Add. MS. 12496, fo. 454 (9 Dec. 1622).
23. Ibid., fos. 459f (15 Dec. 1622).
24. Ibid., fos. 464–72 (15 July 1624); cf. fos. 468f.
25. Carlton, *Charles I,* pp. 60ff.
26. Ibid., p. 60.
27. PRO, SP 78 (Uncalendered State Papers, French). My thanks to Professor Russell for bringing this to my attention.
28. McClure, 2: 609 (9 Apr. 1625).
29. *Calendar of State Papers, Domestic: 1625,* p. 10 (17 Apr. 1625).
30. Ibid., p. 12 (23 Apr. 1625).
31. Carlton, *Charles I,* p. 62.
32. Ibid., pp. 62, 78. Carlton presents a significant revision of the analysis of the essential weakness of Caroline monarchy.
33. Ibid., pp. 68–71.
34. Ibid., p. 72.
35. *Calendar of State Papers, Domestic: 1625–1626,* p. 132 (24 Oct. 1625).
36. PRO, SP 16/8/77 (31 Oct. 1625).
37. *Calendar of State Papers, Domestic: 1625–1626,* p. 38 (Oct. 1631).
38. K. Sharpe, "The Earl of Arundel, His Circle, and the Opposition to the Duke of Buckingham, 1618–1628," in Sharpe, ed., *Faction and Parliament,* p. 227.
39. BL, Add. MS. 34324, fo. 256 (13 Sept. 1626).
40. Ibid., fos. 264–65v (26 July 1627).
41. Ibid., fos. 260–61 (19 Mar. 1627); 262–63v (1 June 1627).
42. Ibid., fos. 269–74v (25 Jan. 1628).
43. See L. M. Hill, ed., *Ancient State,* pp. 248–49.
44. Ibid., pp. 249–52.
45. Carlton, *Charles I,* pp. 180–88; Sharpe, "The Personal Rule of Charles I," in Tomlinson, pp. 60–65.
46. When I first wrote of *The Book of Orders* in an essay entitled "County Government in Caroline England" (in Russell, ed., *Origins*), the debate over provincialism in the early seventeenth century and the Civil War was in its early stages. Were I writing on the subject today, I would, for instance, have to account for Morrill, *Revolt of the Provinces,* and Kishlansky, *Rise of the New Model Army,* as well as such corrective essays as C. Holmes, "The

County Community in Stuart Historiography," *Journal of British History* 19 (Spring 1980), and D. Hirst, "Court, Country, and Politics before 1629," in Sharpe, ed., *Faction and Parliament*. More recently, Fletcher has returned to elements of Morrill's interpretation in "National and Local Awareness in the County Communities," in Tomlinson, ed., *Before the English Civil War*.

47. BL, Add. MS. 12496, fo. 299v.
48. Ibid., fo. 290v.

CHAPTER XI

1. BL, Add. MS. 4160, fos. 18–23.
2. *Calendar of State Papers, Domestic: 1603–1610*, p. 32.
3. Jameson, pp. 82 and *passim*.
4. Historical Manuscript Commission, *Rutland* 4: 463 and *passim*.
5. Ibid., p. 353.
6. BL, Add. MS. 4160, fos. 18–23 (cf. 10 Aug. 1613, and 8 May 1614).
7. The parish church that Caesar attended after he became Master of the Rolls was St. Dunstan's-in-the-West, and he may well have been a part of that congregation earlier on. His third wife owned a pew there and his friend John Donne was the vicar after 1624. Hence the possibility exists that Caesar contributed to one or another improvement or repair that he refers to as "his chapel," although St. Dunstan's was in Fleet Street and not in the Strand. I appreciate Professor Dennis Flynn's observations on this point. See also, Bald, pp. 454 and *passim*.
8. McClure, 2: 68 (5 Apr. 1617).
9. BL, Add. MS. 12496, fo. 163 (20 July 1621).
10. Ibid., fos. 167–68v, 171 (7 Jan. 1628).
11. Ibid., fos. 387–87v, 389–89v (20 Mar. 1626).
12. Ibid., fo. 402 (17 Feb. 1623).
13. BL, Lansd. MS. 161, fos. 47–48.
14. BL, Add. MS. 12496, fo. 151 (5 Nov. 1629).
15. Sharpe, *Sir Robert Cotton*, pp. 143–45.
16. Gardiner, ed., *Fortescue Papers*, n. 1 on pp. 11–12.
17. BL, Add. MS. 12496, fo. 153 (12 Nov. 1629).
18. BL, Add. MS. 4160, fos. 18–23 (cf. 27 Apr. 1620, "Afflicted with a severe fit of the stone in the kidney").
19. BL, Add. MS. 12496, fos. 335, 336 (17 Apr. 1629), 337 (1621), 339–39v (11 Sept. 1629), 341–41v (22 Oct. 1625), 343 (25 May 1624, 9 Dec. 1627), 345–45v (4 Jan. 1622), 347–47v (22 Jan. 1630); BL, Add. MS. 12497, fo. 249.
20. See above, Chapter 4, pp. 96–98.
21. BL, Add. MS. 12504, fo. 135; Grant Book, p. 147 (17 Oct. 1614).
22. BL, Add. MS. 11406, fo. 176 (30 Jan. 1615).

23. Historical Manuscript Commission, *Report IV*, p. 187; Westminster Abbey MSS., press 7, shelf 1, parcel 55 (1625).

24. Regarding Thomas Caesar, see above, Chapter 4, pp. 98–99.

25. BL, Add. MS. 12496, fo. 149 (13 Oct. 1629).

26. Bannerman, p. 286.

27. BL, Add. MS. 4160, fos. 18–23 (cf. 19 Apr. 1615).

28. The following account of the case is drawn from PRO, SP 14/121/16, 17, 19 (May 1621).

29. PRO, SP 14/121/19.

30. My thanks to Professor T. G. Barnes for alerting me to this reference contained in a manuscript of the pleadings in his possession. See also *Cooper v. Edgar*, 124 *English Reports* 87 and *passim*. The litigants in this action were the tenants of the complaining heirs and Lady Anne Caesar, respectively. The Star Chamber case was *Day v. Hungate*, 81 *English Reports* 367–69. The case was defined as "*Bill la pur procurant un enfant a levy un fine.*"

31. BL, Add. MS. 4160, fos. 18–23 (cf. 1 Apr. 1608).

32. BL, Add. MS. 11406, fo. 96 (Oct. 1602).

33. Ibid., fo. 297 (25 Aug. 1604).

34. BL, Add. MS. 12503, fos. 353f (13/21 Jan. 1606).

35. Ibid., fo. 336 (10 Feb. 1606).

36. BL, Add. MS. 11406, fo. 194 (19/29 Aug. 1606).

37. *Calendar of State Papers, Venetian: 1607–1610*, pp. 84–85 (20 Jan. 1608).

38. Ibid., p. 85 (21 Jan. 1608).

39. Ibid., p. 86 (23 Jan. 1608).

40. Ibid., pp. 87–89 (28 Jan. 1608).

41. Ibid., pp. 93 (8 Feb. 1608), 98–99 (24 Feb. 1608).

42. Ibid., p. 99 (24 Feb. 1608).

43. Ibid., pp. 99–100 (24 Feb. 1608), 108 (24 Mar. 1608).

44. Ibid., pp. 112–13 (29 Mar. 1608).

45. Ibid., pp. 116–17 (8 Apr. 1608).

46. L. P. Smith, 1: 68–69.

47. BL, Add. MS. 12504, fos. 259–60 (17 Apr. 1609).

48. BL, Lansd. MS. 161, fo. 182 (19 June 1603).

49. Levack, p. 215.

50. BL, Add. MS. 4160, fos. 18–23 (cf. 10 Dec. 1612, 6 Oct. 1613, 19 Oct. 1613); Add. MS. 12496, fo. 310.

51. *Victoria County History*, Berkshire 4, (1924), p. 101.

52. McClure, 1: 476–77.

53. PRO, SP 14/104/6 (3 Dec. 1618).

54. BL, Add. MS. 12504, fo. 99 (16 Aug. 1620).

55. Wotton, 2: 101 (30 July 1616).

56. Ibid., 2: 105f (11 Oct. 1616).
57. Lodge, p. 49.
58. PRO, SP 16/80/72 (9 Oct. 1627).
59. Levack, p. 216. Lord Bindon died in 1611.
60. *Victoria County History*, Hertfordshire 3, p. 75.
61. Stone and Stone, pp. 158–59, 200.
62. *Victoria County History*, Berkshire 4, p. 101.
63. Ibid., Huntingtonshire 3, pp. 277–78.
64. BL, Add. MS. 4160, fos. 18–23 (cf. 20 Oct. 1592, 17 Mar. 1600, 9 Oct. 1602).
65. Ibid. (cf. 25 Feb. 1613).
66. BL, Add. MS. 12496, fo. 310 (29 June 1617).
67. *Victoria County History*, Hertfordshire 3, p. 274.
68. See below, n. 78.
69. *Victoria County History*, Hertfordshire 3, p. 250. Lady Anne Caesar (Anne Hungate) died the year after Caesar. She was buried in St. Helen's, Bishopsgate, on 30 August 1637. See Bannerman, p. 291.
70. *Victoria County History*, Hertfordshire 3, p. 193; see below, p. 254.
71. BL, Add. MS. 11406, fos. 299 (15 Aug. 1616), 193 (1619).
72. Ibid., fo. 201 (20 Mar. 1620).
73. BL, Add. MS. 34324, fos. 300 (28 May 1632), 302 (6 June 1632). Thomas appears to have died by 1636 because he was not mentioned in his father's will.
74. See above, Chapter 9, pp. 211 and 218.
75. *Calendar of State Papers, Domestic: 1629–1631*, p. 211 (12 Mar. 1630).
76. PRO, CHAN 142/560/159 (4 Aug. 1637).
77. PRO, PCC 34/PILE (27 Feb. 1636) Probate 19 Apr. 1636.
78. Hertfordshire R.O. 10480 (10 Jac.I), 6988 and 6989 (15 Car.II), 10481 (1663).
79. BL, Lansd. MS. 162, fo. 153 (17 Mar. 1598).
80. PRO, Index Warrant Book, p. 27 (13 June 1604); Patent Roll, 2 Jac.I, p. 13 (1605).
81. BL, Add. MS. 12503, fo. 356 (2 Nov. 1605).
82. BL, Add. MS. 12497, fos. 386–86v (7 Aug. 1605).
83. BL, Add. MS. 11406, fos. 301–05.
84. *Victoria County History*, Surrey 3, p. 228.
85. See above, n. 73.
86. University of Chicago Library, MS. 4409 (18 June 1632). My thanks are owed to the late Professor Joel Hurstfield for bringing this document to my attention and for procuring a photocopy for me to study.
87. Lloyd (1670 ed.), p. 934.
88. University of Chicago Library, MS. 4409 (18 June 1632).

89. *Victoria County History*, Huntingtonshire 2, p. 301n.
90. Historical Manuscript Commission, *Report 12*, p. 127 (appx. ix).
91. Bannerman, pp. 255 and *passim*.
92. The text of the inscription on Caesar's tomb reads as follows. In the "indenture" itself: *Omnibus Christi fidelibus ad quos hoc presens / Scriptum pervenerit: Sciatis, me Julium Adelmare alias Caesarem, militem: utriusque Juris Doctorem: Elizabe / thae Reginae supremae Curiae Admiralitatis Judicem, et / unum e magistris libellorum: Jacobo Regia privatis con / siliis, Cancellarium Scaccarii et Sacrorum Sereniorum Magistrum / hac presens Carta mea confirmasse me annuente Divino / numine naturae debitum libenter soluturum quam primum / Deo placuerit. Juruins rei testimonium manum meam / et sigillum opposui. Datum xxvii / februarii anno Domini MDCXXXV [o.s.]."* There then followed a facsimile of his signature. Below and behind the pendant seal, the following entry was made: *per ipsum, tempore mortis suae, Carolo / Regi a privatis Consiliis, nec non Rotulo / rum Magistrum, vere pium. Apprime / literatum pauperibus in poitu Charitatis re/ceptaculum, patriae, filiis et Amicus suis percharis/simum solutum est. Obiit 18 die Aprilis / Anno Domini 1636, Aetatis sue. 79.* At the foot of the slab were inscribed the words: *Irrotulatur Caelo*, and around three of its four borders was incribed: *In cuius memoriam Domina / Anna Caesar viduata haec marmora posuit et secum / hic requiescit.* The tomb still stands in Great St. Helen's, Bishopsgate to the left of the altar. See Lodge, plate 2.

CHAPTER XII

1. BL, Add. MS. 6038, fo. 269v.   2. See above, p. 272, n. 25.
3. BL, Add. MS. 6038, fo. 116.   4. Ibid., fo. 209v.
5. BL, Add. MS. 34324, fo. 294 (29 Apr. 1628), 296 (6 July 1630), 298 (endorsed 21 Apr. 1632).
6. Aylmer, *King's Servants*, p. 222.
7. BL, Add. MS. 6038, fo. 349.
8. My thanks to Professor V. N. Olsen for discussing with me the distinctions between Calvin's theology and the quite fatalist Calvinism of his successor, Beza, and for alerting me to the useful concept of a puritan Anglican.
9. BL, Add. MS. 6038, fo. 482.
10. Ibid., fos. 400v, 403v, 416v.
11. Ibid., fo. 135.
12. Ibid., fo. 573.
13. BL, Harl. MS. 374, fo. 69 (30 Mar. 1629).
14. See L. M. Hill, ed., *Ancient State*.
15. See above, Chapter 7, pp. 167–71.
16. BL, Add. MS. 6038, fo. 495.
17. BL, Add. MS. 34324, fos. 282–82v (13 Dec. 1633).

18. The best analysis of seventeenth-century bureaucracy is Aylmer's *King's Servants*, especially pp. 453–69. He holds that bureaucrat and bureaucracy are terms that are without meaning in the early- to mid-seventeenth century, because the crown was still the source of preferment and deprivation and because the crown's servants were not, as yet, a coherent and self-conscious body of disinterested governors such as are found in the nineteenth century. While I agree with this analysis in its general terms, I am convinced that there is a bureaucratic (or proto-bureaucratic) element in the second tier of crown servants whose offices were secured through intermediates and who owned an effective freehold interest in them that made their deprivation extraordinarily difficult.

19. BL, Add. MS. 6038, fo. 495.

Works Cited

MANUSCRIPTS

British Library, London
  Additional Manuscripts: 145, 4160, 6038, 11402, 11406, 12496, 12497,
    12503, 12504, 12505, 12506, 12507, 14027, 15208, 15235, 29439, 34324,
    36111, 36767, 38170.
  Cotton Manuscripts: Cleopatra F. V.
  Harlean Manuscripts: 374
  Lansdowne Manuscripts: 3, 53, 125, 129, 133, 145, 151, 157, 160, 161,
    162, 163, 164, 165, 166, 167, 168, 174, 183
  Sloane Manuscripts: 4160
City of London, Guildhall Library
  Reportory 20
The Henry E. Huntington Library, San Marino, California
  Ellesmere Manuscripts: 2599
Hertfordshire Record Office
  Manuscripts: 6988, 6989, 10480, 10481
Kansas University, Kenneth Spencer Research Library, Lawrence, Kansas
  Manuscript: Q 12: 16
The Manuscripts of His Grace, the Duke of Northumberland, K. G.,
as preserved in Alnwick Castle, Northumberland
  Northumberland Manuscripts: 9
The Manuscripts of Lord Sackville, as formerly preserved at Knole,
Sevenoaks, Kent
  Sackville MS: (Old Number) 1093
The Manuscripts of the Most Honourable, the Marquis of Salisbury, K. G.,
as preserved in Hatfield House
  Hatfield Manuscripts: 96, 122

Public Record Office, London
  CHAN 142/560
  CHAN IPM, 17 Elizabeth 75
  E 369/131
  HCA 3/19, 22, 23, 25, 26, 542
  HCA 24/52, 53, 61, 62, 70, 71
  INDEX 6800
  INDEX WARRANT BOOK (1604)
  PCC 34/PILE
  PATENT ROLLS, 27 Elizabeth; 2 Jac. I
  REQ 1/47
  SP 9/12
  SP 12/239, 268, 269, 270
  SP 14/34, 63, 66, 67, 68, 69, 70, 71, 72, 74, 104, 121, 215
  SP 16/8, 80, 114, 132, 215
  SP 78
  SP 180
  SP 237
University of Chicago Library
  Manuscripts: 4409
University of Oxford, Bodleian Library
  Manuscripts: North MS. a.1
Worshipful Company of Goldsmiths
  Apprenticeship Register, vol. 1

PRINTED WORKS

Acts of Privy Council: 1580–1604; 1613–27.
Allsebrook, W. B. J. "The Court of Requests in the Reign of Elizabeth." University of London, M.A. thesis, 1936.
Andrews, K. R. *Elizabethan Privateering*. Cambridge, 1964.
———. *English Privateering Voyages to the West Indies, 1588–1595*. Hakluyt Society Publications, 2d series, 111 (1959).
Arber, E., ed. *A Transcript of the Registers of the Company of Stationers of London, 1554–1640*, vol. 2. London, 1876.
Armytage, G. F., ed. *Allegations for Marriage Licences issued by the Bishop of London, 1520 to 1610*, vol. 1. Harleian Society Publications, vol. 25. London, 1887.
Ashton, R. *The Crown and the Money Market 1603–1640*. Oxford, 1960.
———. "Deficit Finance in the Reign of James I," *Economic History Review*, 2d series, 10 (1957): 15–29.
Aylmer, G. E. *The King's Servants, The Civil Service of Charles I*, vol. 1: *1625–1642*. Revised edition. 1974.

————. "The Last Years of Purveyance, 1610–1660." *Economic History Review*, 2d series, 10 (1957): 81–93.

Bailyn, Bernard, et al. *The Great Republic.* Lexington, Mass., 1985.

Bald, R. C. *John Donne: A Life.* London, 1970.

Bannerman, W. B., ed. *The Registers of St. Helen's, Bishopsgate, London.* Harleian Society Publications, Register Section, 4, vol. 31. London, 1904.

Barcroft, J. H. "Carelton and Buckingham: The Quest for Office," in H. S. Reinmuth, Jr. ed. *Early Stuart Studies.* Minneapolis, 1970.

Beckingsale, B. W. *Burghley, Tudor Statesmen, 1520–1598.* London, 1967.

Beze, T. de. *Chrestiennes meditations*, ed. M. Richter. Geneva, 1964.

Blatcher, M. *The Court of King's Bench.* London, 1978.

Brown, A. *The First Republic in America.* New York, 1969.

Calendar of State Papers, Domestic, 1581–1636. London.

Calendar of State Papers, Foreign, 1588–90. London.

Calendar of State Papers, Venetian, 1607–13. London.

Carlton, C. *Charles I, the Personal Monarch.* London, 1984.

————. *The Court of Orphans.* Leicester, 1974.

Coakley, T. M. "Robert Cecil in Power: Elizabethan Politics in Two Reigns," in H. S. Reinmuth, Jr., ed., *Early Stuart Studies.* Minneapolis, 1970.

Coke, E. *The Third Part of the Institutes of the Laws of England* [*The Third Institute*]. London, 1797.

————. *The Fourth Part of the Institutes of the Laws of England* [*The Fourth Institute*]. London, 1669.

Collinson, P. "The Role of Women in the English Reformation Illustrated by the Life and Friendships of Anne Locke," in *Studies in Church History II.* London, 1965.

Crowson, P. S. *Tudor Foreign Policy.* London, 1973.

D'Ewes, S. *The Journal of the House of Commons.* London, 1682.

Dietz, F. C. *English Public Finance*, vol. 2. Reprinted London, 1964.

Donald, M. B. *Elizabethan Monopolies.* London, 1961.

Elton, G. R. "The Elizabethan Exchequer: The War in the Receipt," in S. T. Bindoff et al., eds., *Elizabethan Government and Society: Essays Presented to Sir John Neale.* London, 1961.

————. *The Tudor Constitution.* London, 1962.

————. *The Tudor Revolution in Government.* London, 1953.

————. "Why the History of the Early-Tudor Council Remains Unwritten," in Elton, *Studies in Tudor and Stuart Politics and Government*, vol. 1. London, 1984.

English Reports: 74, 81, 99, 124, 167, 550.

Foster, E. R. *Proceedings in Parliament 1610.* 2 vols. New Haven, 1966.

Foster, J. *Alumni Oxoniensis: The Members of the University of Oxford, 1500–1714*, vol. 1. London, 1891.

Foster, W., ed. *The Travels of John Sanderson in the Levant, 1584–1602.* Hakluyt Society Publication, 2d series, 67 (1931).

Gardiner, S. R. *Parliamentary Debate in 1610.* Camden Society Publications, o.s., 81 (1862).

Gardiner, S. R., ed. *The Fortescue Papers.* Camden Society Publications, n.s., 1 (1871).

Hakluyt, R. *Principal Navigations*, vol. 6. London, 1908.

Handover, P. M. *The Second Cecil.* London, 1959.

Harriss, G. L. "Medieval Doctrines in the Debate on Supply, 1610–1629," in K. Sharpe, ed. *Faction and Parliament.* Oxford, 1978.

Hicks, L. *An Elizabethan Problem.* London, 1964.

Hill, C. *Economic Problems of the Church from Archbishop Whitgift to the Long Parliament.* Oxford, 1968.

Hill, L. M. "The Admiralty Circuit of 1591: Some Comments on the Relations Between Central Government and Local Interests." *Historical Journal,* 14, no. 1 (1971): 3–14.

———. "The Public Career of Sir Julius Caesar, 1584–1614." University of London, Ph.D. diss., 1968.

———. "Sir Julius Caesar's Journal of Salisbury's First Two Months and Twenty Days as Lord Treasurer: 1608," *Bulletin of the Institute of Historical Research,* 4–5 (Nov. 1972).

Hill, L. M., ed. *The Ancient State, Authoritie, and Proceedings of the Court of Requests by Sir Julius Caesar.* Cambridge, 1975.

Historical Manuscripts Commission. *Fourth Report; Twelfth Report,* app. ix; *De L'Isle and Dudley,* vol. 5; *Hatfield,* vols. 6, 9, 10, 11; *Rutland,* vol. 4.

[H. M. S. O.] *Guide to the Contents of the Public Record Office.* 2 vols. London, 1963.

Holdsworth, W. *A History of English Law,* vols. 1, 4, 5, 7th ed, revised. London, 1956.

Hotson, L., ed. *Queen Elizabeth's Entertainment at Mitcham.* New Haven, 1953.

Houston, S. J. *James I.* Harlow, Essex, 1973.

Hurstfield, J. "Political Corruption: The Historian's Problem," in Hurstfield, *Freedom, Corruption and Government in Elizabethan England.* London, 1973.

———. *The Queen's Wards.* London, 1958.

Inderwick, F. A. and R. A. Roberts, eds. *Calendar of Inner Temple Records,* vol. 1. London, 1896.

Jamison, C. *The History of the Royal Hospital of St. Katharine by the Tower of London.* London, 1952.

Jensen, De L. *Diplomacy and Dogmaticism: Bernardino de Mendoza and the French Catholic League.* Cambridge, Mass., 1964.

Jones, W. J. *The Elizabethan Court of Chancery.* London, 1967.

Kenny, R. W. *Elizabeth's Admiral: The Political Career of Charles Howard, Earl of Nottingham, 1536–1624.* Baltimore, 1970.

Kishlansky, M. A. *The Rise of the New Model Army.* London, 1979.

Knafla, L. *Law and Politics in Jacobean England.* Cambridge, 1977.

Leadam, I. S., ed. *Select Cases in the Court of Requests, 1497–1569.* Selden Society Publications, 12 (1898).

Levack, B. *The Civil Lawyers in England, 1603–1641: A Political Study.* London, 1973.

Lloyd, D. *The Statesmen and Favourites of England Since the Reformation.* [*State-Worthies.*] London, 1665 and 1670 editions.

Lodge, E. *The Life of Sir Julius Caesar, Knt.* London, 1827.

Luders, A., et al., eds. *Statutes of the Realm.* 11 vols. London, 1810–28.

MacCaffrey, W. "Place and Patronage in Elizabethan Politics," in S. T. Bindoff, J. Hurstfield, and C. H. Williams, eds., *Elizabethan Government and Society.* London, 1961.

Maclean, J., ed. *Letters from George Lord Carew to Sir Thomas Roe, Ambassador to the Court of the Great Mogul.* Camden Society Publications, 86 (1860).

McClure, N. E. *The Letters of John Chamberlain. American Philosophical Society Memoirs,* 12, pts. i–ii (2 vols., Philadelphia, 1939).

Madge, S. J., ed. *London Inquisitions Post Mortem, 4 to 19 Elizabeth,* vol. 2. London, 1901.

Malynes, G. de. *Consuetudo, vel Lex Mercatoria, or the Ancient Law-Merchant.* London, 1622.

Marsden, R. G. *Select Pleas in the Court of Admiralty.* Selden Society Publications, 11 (1897).

Masters of the Bench of the Honourable Society of the Inner Temple, 1450–1882. London, 1883.

Masters of the Bench of the Honourable Society of the Inner Temple: Supplement 1883–1900: to which is appended a list of the Treasurers: 1501–1901. London, 1901.

Mathew, D. *James I.* London, 1967.

Maxwell-Lyte, H. C. *Historical Notes on the Use of the Great Seal of England.* London, 1926.

Moir, T. L. *The Addled Parliament of 1614.* New York, 1958.

Morrill, J. G. *The Revolt of the Provinces.* London, 1976.

Neale, J. E. "The Elizabethan Political Scene," in Neale, *Essays in Elizabethan History.* New York, 1958.

Neill, E. D. *History of the Virginia Company of London.* New York, 1968.

Notestein, W. *The House of Commons, 1604–1610.* New Haven, 1971.

Ogilvie, C. M. G. *The King's Government and the Common Law: 1471–1641.* Oxford, 1958.

Peck, L. L. *Northampton, Patronage and Policy at the Court of James I.* Hemel Hempsted, Herts., 1982.

Pocock, J. G. A. *The Ancient Constitution and the Feudal Law.* 1957.

Prestwich, M. *Cranfield: Politics and Profits Under the Early Stuarts.* Oxford, 1966.

Raab, T. *Enterprise and Empire.* Cambridge, Mass., 1967.

Rebholz, R. A. *The Life of Fulke Greville, First Lord Brooke.* Oxford, 1971.

Richardson, W. *The Court of Augmentations.* Baton Rouge, La., 1961.

———. *Tudor Chamber Administration.* Baton Rouge, La., 1952.

Roberts, C., and O. Duncan. "The Parliamentary Undertaking of 1614," *English Historical Review,* 368 (July 1978): 481–98.

Rowse, A. *Tudor Cornwall.* London, 1957.

Russell, C. *The Crisis of Parliaments.* London, 1971.

Russell, C., ed. *The Origins of the English Civil War.* London, 1973.

Sharpe, K. *Sir Robert Cotton 1586–1631.* Oxford, 1979.

Sharpe, K., ed. *Faction and Parliament: Essays on Early Stuart History.* Oxford, 1978.

Smith, A. G. R. "Crown, Parliament, and Finance: The Great Contract of 1610," in P. Clark, A. G. R. Smith, N. Tyacke, eds., *The English Commonwealth, 1547–1640: Essays on Politics and Society presented to Joel Hurstfield.* Leicester, 1979.

Smith, A. G. R., ed. *The Reign of James VI and I.* London, 1973.

Smith, L. P. *The Life and Letters of Sir Henry Wotton.* 2 vols. Oxford, 1907.

Spedding, J., et al., eds. *Life and Letters of Francis Bacon,* vols. 4 and 7 of *Works* (14 vols., London, 1857–74).

Stone, L. *The Crisis of the Aristocracy.* London, 1965.

———. *The Family, Sex, and Marriage.* New York, 1977.

Stone, L., and J. Stone. *An Open Elite? England 1540–1800.* London, 1985.

Thomas, D. "Leases in Reversion on the Crown's Lands: 1558–1603." *Economic History Review,* 2d series, 30, no. 1 (Feb. 1977): 67–72.

Thomas, K. *Religion and the Decline of Magic.* London, 1971.

Tomlinson, H., ed. *Before the English Civil War.* London, 1983.

Tout, T. F. *Chapters in Medieval Administrative History.* 6 vols. Manchester, 1920–1937.

Tyler, L. G., ed. *Narratives of Early Virginia, 1606–1625.* New York, 1966.

Victoria County History of England: Berkshire 4; Hertfordshire 3; Huntingtonshire 2, 3; Surrey 3.

Warnicke, R. M. *William Lambarde, Elizabethan Antiquary, 1536–1601.* London, 1973.

Weiss, M. "'Loyalty My Lie': Richard III and Affinity Politics in Northern England." University of California, Irvine, Ph.D. diss., 1977.

Wernham, R. B. *Before the Armada: The Growth of English Foreign Policy, 1485–1588*. London, 1966.

Willson, D. H. *King James VI and I*. London, 1962.

——— . *The Privy Councillors in the House of Commons, 1604–1629*. Minneapolis, 1940.

Woodworth, A. "Purveyance for the Royal Household in the Reign of Queen Elizabeth," *Transactions of the American Philosophical Society*, n.s., 35 (Philadelphia, 1945).

Index